Law in the New Democracy

Law in the New Democracy

PAULA JANE BYRNE
WITH RIGHT OF REPLY BY
FIRST NATIONS/
ABORIGINAL PEOPLE

ANU PRESS

ANU PRESS

Published by ANU Press
The Australian National University
Canberra ACT 2600, Australia
Email: anupress@anu.edu.au

Available to download for free at press.anu.edu.au

ISBN (print): 9781760467135
ISBN (online): 9781760467142

WorldCat (print): 1542884505
WorldCat (online): 1542886396

DOI: 10.22459/LND.2025

Cover design and layout by ANU Press

Cover image: Children's drawing, c.1864. Source: Cliefdon Station Records, State Library of New South Wales, MLMSS 100009.

This book is published under the aegis of the Social Sciences editorial board of ANU Press.

Text copyright © Paula Jane Byrne, 2026
Design and typography copyright © ANU Press, 2026

Contents

List of illustrations	vii
Acknowledgements	ix
Preface	xi
Introduction	1
1. Democracy	23
2. South	43
3. North-West	75
4. West	119
5. South-West	181
6. North	215
7. Getting into Court	245
Conclusion	271
Bibliography	275

List of illustrations

Figures

Figure 2.1: Origin of cases: South Coast	61
Figure 3.1: Origin of cases: North-west	81
Figure 4.1: Origin of cases: Molong	122
Figure 4.2: Origin of cases: Orange	145
Figure 4.3: Origin of cases: Carcoar	175
Figure 5.1: Origin of cases: Yass	183
Figure 6.1: Origin of cases: Grafton	236

Maps

Map 0.1: New South Wales, Victoria and the settled portion of South Australia	xii
Map 2.1: The South Coast and hinterland of New South Wales	44
Map 3.1: The north-west of New South Wales	76
Map 4.1: Western New South Wales	120
Map 5.1: The south-west of New South Wales	181
Map 6.1: Northern New South Wales	217

Tables

Table 7.1: Defence counsel argument examples	254
Table 7.2: Cases for which jury activity reported in the Maitland press, 1843–1869	256
Table 7.3: Professions of jurors from surviving lists	265
Table 7.4: Results of cases	269

Acknowledgements

This book began in 2013 at the University of New England, where I went to work on the Bent family of the eighteenth and early nineteenth centuries, my own family history and the democracy of the Tweed Valley of far northern New South Wales. Reading the criminal case *Wollumun*, I became again interested in how people used criminal law—this time, considering the pencil markings in the margins of documents and what they told of the relationship between magistrates' benches and the metropolis, as Sydney was referred to by contemporaries. I thank David Andrew Roberts, Matthew Allen, Adrian Walsh and Shirley Rickard for facilitating my association with the university and its excellent Dixson Library. I also spent some time at the University of New England Archives, where I received the helpful attention of Phillip Ward and Michael McIlveen. This is essentially a Covid book—written in those long lockdowns of 2020–21. Research for the book was carried out mainly in the NSW State Archives Collection, which is now part of the Museums of History NSW. I thank all the archivists and staff for their work in assisting with this project. I sent early publications to Emily Hanna and was pleased to find how useful they were for archivists. From 2021 to 2024, I was a visiting scholar at the State Library of New South Wales for a separate project based on the Rusden and Scott papers, though Tom Rusden and Richard Ottley found their way into this book. It was at the library that I had the companionship of other scholars, and I thank the Mitchell librarian Richard Neville and Rachel Franks for being so welcoming. All the librarians at the Mitchell have been encouraging and helpful. A great many scholars have read sections of this work, and I am grateful for their criticism and advice. Articles that have appeared include 'Mapping Power: Yass and the Law in the 1850s', in *Law & History*, vol. 9, no. 1 (2022). I thank the Australian and New Zealand Law and History Society for permission to print parts of that work. 'Taking Depositions at Molong: The Operation of Legal Power in 1850s New South Wales' appeared in *Law, Crime and History*, vol. 11, no. 1 (2023), and I thank the editors and readers of that work. Parts of Chapter 7 appeared in 'Jury Trial in Colonial New South Wales 1840–1870: The Maitland Circuit of the Supreme Court' (*Journal of Australian Studies* 44, no. 3, 2020), and I thank the editors and reviewers. Mark Finnane kindly read and responded to all the chapters I sent him, and I am most grateful for his advice. Alecia Simmonds kindly provided advice on one section. For discussions, I thank Jamie Schmidt, Jonathan Richards, Kamilaroi lawyer and scholar Lydia McGrady (on some legal terminology), Bruce Kercher, for encouragement and discussion of case law and Beverley Kingston, whose subtle reading of Australian history has always been inspirational. All my audiences at ANZLHS conferences have been enthusiastic and supportive, particularly in Christchurch, New Zealand, in 2017 and at UNSW in 2024. Timely advice was provided by Glenine Hamlyn. All separate chapters have been read by First Nations/Aboriginal people, and many generously gave their time to think about the idea of right of reply or to give replies to individual chapters. I thank Lou Glover, Serene Fernando, Larry Brandy, Michael Bell, Gulwanyang Moran, Pam Handy, Fiona Prince Martich and Micklo Jarrett. This book was published with the aid of The Francis Forbes Society, and I am most grateful to Geoff Lindsay and Simon Chapple for this assistance. Emily Gallagher and Frank Bongiorno managed the project through its early stages, and I thank the readers of the manuscript. I am grateful to ANU Press and the copyeditor Jan Borrie for her sharp eye and her dedication to her task. This book is dedicated to John Geoffrey Byrne (1914–66).

Preface

In my first book, *Criminal Law and Colonial Subject*, I explored depositions in terms of what they told of ordinary people's understanding of the law in the early nineteenth century. This research answered questions asked in English social history where depositions had not survived. Unfortunately, my method of numbering the records was misinterpreted by legal historians in Australia, who mistakenly referenced the depositions as criminal cases. Numbers used in footnotes only reflected where the depositions were in the bundles of records, and I note that NSW State Archives has undertaken the same approach in its numbering system for the early deposition boxes. Searches for case law using these depositions were fruitless, and my research was never intended for that purpose, as my introduction made clear. *Law in the New Democracy* uses depositions that *did* become criminal cases. The numbering relates to the deposition, the information and the various registers, and there is always a result in court. Yet, cases are not entered here as they would be in formal case law because the depositions are distinct documents in themselves, and they hide letters and secrets that were kept hidden in the courtroom. Pencilled notes from the attorneys-general were never read out in court, misgivings not noted, and the skirmish between magistrate and metropolitan official never discussed. This book centres on that skirmish as it moves geographically through the colony of New South Wales (Map 0.1). Placenames are those given by the clerks of the colony and may not reflect current spellings. Surnames during this period are rendered differently than today; spelling was not consistent.

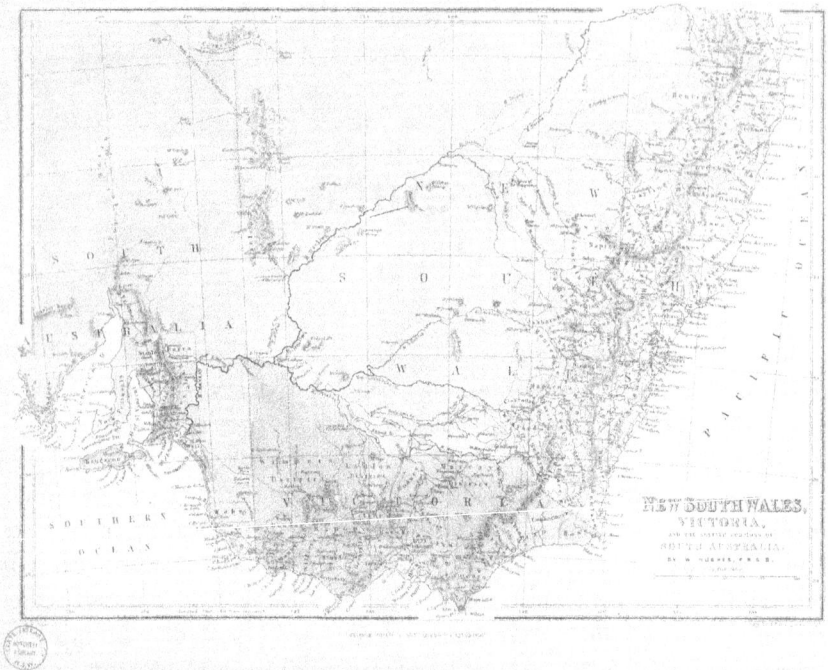

Map 0.1: New South Wales, Victoria and the settled portion of South Australia
Note: Subsequent maps are details of this map.
Source: W. Hughes, London G. Phillip and Son, 1858, State Library of New South Wales, MLZ/M1 806/1858/1.

In the 1980s, non-Aboriginal historians did not write Aboriginal history; it was not our place, and there were enough Aboriginal people writing to have their voices and histories included in our classrooms. Today, non-Aboriginal historians must make our position and our approach clear before we consult Aboriginal people as to the manner in which their history is represented. Non-Aboriginal historians must make space, recognise that space and leave that space be. Each of the chapters in this book has been read by Aboriginal people, and some chapters have travelled widely. These single chapters invited right of reply, and each chapter has a section at the end where comments have been written unless it was decided that no reply was needed. I use the terms First Nations and Aboriginal interchangeably unless I have been requested by an Aboriginal reader not to use the term First Nations.

I first became aware of right of reply in reading Kua Swan's description of the forging of new relationships around archives and the use of archives by non-Aboriginal people. This links to the idea on the part of Aboriginal people that there should be 'nothing about us without us'. My research into law showed that it was impossible to discuss history without looking at the words and actions of Aboriginal people, and I had to think about how I would deal with this. Right of reply distinguishes Aboriginal history from my own white history and allows points to be made in response to my conclusions. Those First Nations/Aboriginal people who have replied to my chapters or who have read them have done so because they strongly believe that Aboriginal people have a right to respond to any references to their people. In doing so, they shift the ground of Australian history.

Introduction

The 1858 Grafton case against Joseph Wilkes contains only a cover sheet and a note. This note reads:

> The papers in this case are in the left-hand cupboard in the clerk's office.[1]

The left-hand cupboard has long evaporated into history and there is no hope of finding the documents. Yet, in my mind's eye, I see the clerk placing the papers in the cupboard, thinking they were safe, that they would be taken back out of the cupboard and put with cases from the Sydney Supreme Court criminal sessions of 1858, where Joseph Wilkes was sentenced to death for murder.[2] The actions of the clerk, his understandings of the meaning of the spatial outlines of his office and his relationship to the papers remind us of the tiny components of activity that are the workings of the law.

A case formally begins with a sheet of foolscap paper and a pen. A clerk is confronted with an act deemed criminal. Accounts will come into the police office to be written out. What a muddle of decision-making goes into this act of writing. There is the language of the witness or the person requesting a warrant, or perhaps making a second deposition when the prisoner is brought into court. These persons bring their own understandings of what law is. For the clerk there is the misheard, the crossing out, writing in the columns, the 'x' as a signature signed at the end of the evidence, witnessed or not witnessed. Scattered across the 'interior' or the 'far interior' were the desks of the clerks of the court, each making his decision about how to approach the blank sheet of paper. We already know from Australian historians that

---

1 *R v Joseph Wilkes* 1858, 1, NSW State Archives Collection [hereinafter SR], 9/6415.
2 List of capital convictions, *Empire*, 11 December 1867. Wilkes' sentence was commuted in the moments before his hanging, and he was sentenced to hard labour for life. *Bell's Life in Sydney and Sporting Reviewer*, [hereinafter *Bell's Life*], 24 April 1858.

their overseers, the magistrates, were diverse in their understandings of how such work should be done. They were incompetent, unlawful, even.[3] Clerk and magistrate had their own understandings of law.

This book sets out to explore exactly what such understandings were in the early democracy of the 1850s, exactly how power operated in the 'interior' of the colony of New South Wales. Power here is used in the sense of the body: constrained, restricted, harmed, comported or resisting according to local custom.[4] Where is your hat? Are they your shoe tracks? How did you get out of the lockup? Where are your witnesses? This power is partly a product of the proscriptive nature of law countenanced by the Crown with its empire-wide emphasis on policing and new kinds of offences, as Lisa Ford has described and Matt Allen has applied to bench records in his study of the policing of alcohol in the colony.[5] It is also a product of cultures that sought to utilise law for different reasons.[6] Power is interlaced with the imaginary—what kind of system of law people or officials imagined themselves in and how they expressed their relationship to it.[7]

Lies, you will say, lies and fantasies make up these criminal depositions— but such lies are the stuff of power. Each collection of sheets of paper completed by the clerk, folded in four and termed a deposition, represented a human body or bodies languishing in the lockup or out on bail. These defendants and witnesses for or against them were the inhabitants of the new democracy, many without the franchise but seeing themselves as political actors, and this included First Nations/Aboriginal people. Rhetoric around the new democracy claimed the legal system to which they were subject

---

3   Hilary Golder, *High and Responsible Office: A History of the New South Wales Magistracy* (Sydney: Sydney University Press, 1991); Mark Finnane, ed., *Policing in Australia: Historical Perspectives* (Sydney: UNSW Press, 1987); John Lowndes, 'The Australian Magistracy from Justices of the Peace to Judges and Beyond', *Australian Law Journal* 74, no. 8 (2000): 509–32; Tim D. Castle, 'The Practical Administration of Justice: The Adaptation of English Law to Colonial Customs and Circumstances', *Journal of Australian Colonial History* 5 (2004): 44–72; Eugene Schofield-Georgeson, *By What Authority? Criminal Law in Colonial New South Wales 1788–1861* (Melbourne: Australian Scholarly Press, 2019).
4   Judith Butler, 'Bodies and Power Revisited', *Radical Philosophy* 114 (2002): 13–19.
5   Lisa Ford, *The King's Peace: Law and Order in the British Empire* (Cambridge, MA: Harvard University Press, 2021); Matthew Allen, 'Policing a Free Society: Drunkenness and Liberty in Colonial New South Wales', *History Australia* 12, no. 2 (2015): 144–65.
6   Lawrence Rosen, *Islam and the Rule of Justice: Image and Reality in Muslim Law and Culture* (Chicago: University of Chicago Press, 2018), 5; Paula Jane Byrne, *Criminal Law and Colonial Subject* (Cambridge: Cambridge University Press, 1993).
7   Russell L. Hanson, *The Democratic Imagination in America* (Princeton: Princeton University Press, 1985), 10.

derived from an oppressive England and there was much discussion if this was necessarily right in the Legislative Council and Legislative Assembly of the period.

Depositions were sent to the attorneys-general in Sydney and they were pencil marked by them, with varying degrees of diligence. Pencil marks, or the absence of them, show the workings of a legal mind. Points may have been underlined, a pointing hand drawn next to crucial evidence and questions were written in the columns. This was an act of interpretation. Sometimes the entire deposition set would be sent back to the magistrates along with a letter of castigation. Communication was had between the criminal Crown solicitor and the attorneys-general: humorous notes or in-house references. The attorney-general in New South Wales during the period under discussion *was* the grand jury of the colony. In an initial reading at his desk, he decided whether a case would proceed to trial. In England, this decision was in the hands of the grand jury—a group of local dignitaries. To replace such a venerable institution was not a task relished by the occupants of the office of attorney-general in New South Wales and frequent complaints were made. The skirmishes between these men, local magistrates and clerks form the substance of the way law worked in the interior.

Defendants, witnesses, jurymen, barristers, clerks and judges poured into the courtrooms to hear the results of such diverse consultations at the 'assizes' or circuit courts when the Supreme Court was on circuit to Goulburn, Bathurst, Maitland, Brisbane and, from 1859, Deniliquin and Armidale. Cases from the south and north coasts were heard in Sydney before the Supreme Court. In newspaper reports, we have evidence of the sheer aggression and outspokenness of jurymen in cases: their requests for the judges to stop talking, their halting of cases, their interpretations of the information before them—sometimes far from law. The work of the barristers of the colony was to charm the jury with elaborate speeches and careful choreography. The assizes and the Supreme Court are not a smooth development from what came before them but a raucous reinterpretation, a new reading of the case. In the juror is the ultimate New South Wales democratic man.

Ethnography and law

Ethnographic approaches to law refuse to be bound by the way law sees itself.[8] That is, the legally accepted method of approaching a case—the facts, the relevance to law, decisions of the attorneys-general, common law, statute law—an approach adopted by legal historians of the criminal law, does not figure. Rather, an ethnographic approach asks 'by whom and under what cultural conditions is "law" constituted'.[9] It is concerned with the 'narratives, rhetoric and images of law that generate structure and shape our systems of knowledge'.[10] Csaba Varga describes ethnography of law as examining 'a customary network, also prevailing in the presence of the state's law, mostly at its periphery, which effectively assures its respect in less formalised ways'.[11] In New South Wales, such 'customary' activity was diverse as inhabitants were First Nations, Irish, American, Chinese, Malay as well as those from England, who brought their own understandings of law. Interpretations were also produced in the colony; a network of understandings prevailed in each region of the interior.

Hilary Golder and Russell Hogg have written that 'law produces cultures around itself'.[12] Such cultures are illustrated well in Jane F. Collier's anthropological work on law in Hteklum, Mexico. She made three observations: that her female presence in the court disrupted the legal

---

8   This is also the postcolonial perspective of Alpana Roy, 'Post-Colonial Theory and Law: A Critical Introduction', *Adelaide Law Review* 29 (2008): 315–37. See also June Starr and Mark Goodale, eds, *Practicing Ethnography in Law: New Dialogues, Enduring Methods* (New York: Springer Nature, 2002); Aditya Pratap Deo, *Kings, Spirits and Memory in Central India: Enchanting the State* (Boca Raton: CRC Press, 2021); Thomas Scheffer, *Adversarial Case Making: An Ethnography of English Crown Court Procedure* (Leiden: Brill, 2010); Ann Griffiths, 'Law as an Enduring Concept: Space, Time and Power', in *The Oxford Handbook of Law and Anthropology*, eds Marie Claire Foblets, Mark Goodale, Maria Sapignole, and Olaf Zenker (Oxford: Oxford University Press, 2022), 300–17; Didier Fassin, 'Boredom', in *Writing the World of Policing: The Difference Ethnography Makes*, ed. Didier Fassin (Chicago: University of Chicago Press, 2017), 269–92.
9   Eve Darian-Smith, *Ethnography and Law* (London: Routledge, 2007), xiii; see also Eve Darian-Smith, 'Ethnographies of Law', in *The Blackwell Companion to Law and Society*, ed. Austin Sarat (Hoboken: Blackwell, 2004), 545–68.
10 Marilyn Strathern, 'Criminal Justice and Cultural Justice: The Limits of Liberalism and the Pragmatics of Difference in the New South Africa', in *Ethnography and Law*, ed. Eve Darian-Smith (London: Routledge, 2007), 397–413; Eric Hirsch, 'Introduction: Working Through Other People's Descriptions', in *Property, Substance and Effect: Anthropological Essays on Persons and Things*, by Marilyn Strathern (London: HAU Books, 2022), ix–xxxiv, at x.
11 Csaba Varga, 'The Theory of Law: Legal Ethnography or the Theoretical Fruits of Inquiries into Folkways', *Sociologia del Diritto* [*Sociology of Law*] 1 (2010): 81–100, at 82.
12 Russell Hogg and Hilary Golder, 'Policing Sydney', in *Policing in Australia: Historical Perspectives*, ed. Mark Finnane (Sydney: UNSW Press, 1987), 59–73.

officials' 'leisure pastime of sexual joking'; cases were rarely heard in the new imposing court but instead in the small back offices where judges could speak to disputants; and when asked to make a list of crimes and punishments, legal officials could not do so, yet they recalled all cases in terms not of the offence, but of relations between disputants.[13] It is at this detailed level that I seek to work—what Lawrence Friedman refers to as the microscopic.[14]

Though she exhibits the same sensitivity to marking and records, I take a different approach to Sally Engle Merry in her analysis of the court records of a small town in Hawai'i. She considered marriage and kinship relations between judges, attorneys and missionaries between 1852 and 1913.[15] There is an obstruction in such an approach. In it, law is essentially seen to service economic and social relationships. This effectively obscures what is interpreted as law by different cultures. The centre of my concern is law, legalities, symbolics and imaginary descriptions. I am enabled to see by such an approach that Aboriginal people used law, that masters and servants operated in different dynamics and that magistrates, though wealthy squatters, were markedly different in their perceptions of the purpose of law. I did not open the first deposition I looked at in expectation of finding different kinds of material and social relationships. Rather, I looked at what the deposition told of law.

Readings by magistrates skittered out of control. They overstepped the bounds of textbook law in attempts to streamline contradictory information; in some places, they developed an obsession with evidence that in turn created a local culture; they sent cases to Sydney that had very little indication of culpability, even to the nineteenth-century mind. Localised 'law' existed in multiple places.

The attorneys-general had their own readings of law. But legal decisions were also culturally influenced. For example, John Hubert Plunkett was attorney-general until 1856 when the position became an elected office. The rhetoric surrounding Plunkett as a champion of Aboriginal people was

---

13 Jane F. Collier, 'Analysing Witchcraft Beliefs', in *Practicing Ethnography in Law: New Dialogues, Enduring Methods*, eds June Starr and Mark Goodale (New York: Springer Nature, 2002), 72–86, at 73.
14 Lawrence M. Friedman, 'A Few Thoughts on Ethnography, History and Law', in *Practicing Ethnography: New Dialogues, Enduring Methods*, eds June Starr and Mark Goodale (New York: Springer Nature, 2002), 185–89, at 186. On the microscopic, see Byrne, *Criminal Law and Colonial Subject*, 6.
15 Sally Engle Merry, 'Ethnography in the Archives', in *Practicing Ethnography in Law: New Dialogues, Enduring Methods*, eds June Starr and Mark Goodale (New York: Springer Nature, 2002), 128–42.

due to his insistence on a second trial in the Myall Creek massacre cases of 1837–38.[16] Yet, he was not an advocate of Aboriginal rights in the early 1850s. As we shall see, he allowed cases to be sent to the Supreme Court with clearly falsified confessions and inadequate evidence that he could see and had underlined. Plunkett and other attorneys-general exhibited a selectivity that would shape how law was understood.

Words give us the cacophony of local readings of law. Examination of speech and silence has long been a concern of ethnographic work. Jeanne Favret Saada has written of the silences and words around witchcraft in 1970s France. She writes of people being 'caught' in a net of suspicion, envy and revenge.[17] Being 'caught' in a web of words—sometimes Gaelic, sometimes pidgin and sometimes cant—is an accurate means of describing the position of defendants in the 1850s. Being 'pulled' or 'screened' into 'court work' is something spoken of. The information by the witness or complainant was sometimes a total fabrication, no-one was assaulted, no-one's horse was stolen, the murderer was quite often someone who got to the courthouse or the constable first to accuse someone else. Plays with truth show how far law had been captured by local populations. A rowdy jury produced the 'criminals' of New South Wales, counted by criminologists who recognise the low rate of 'crime' during the period.[18] The jury must be incorporated into a reading of how law was understood; they were 'the people' so often referred to in the rhetoric of the Legislative Council.

First Nations people

Annalise Riles suggests the idea of 'unwinding' knowledge systems to avoid restrictive analytical categories and assumptions.[19] This is particularly important in examining Aboriginal cases and indeed such an unwinding has been practised for some time by First Nations scholars—those particularly

---

16 Jane Lydon and Lyndall Ryan, 'Introduction', in *Remembering the Myall Creek Massacre*, eds Jane Lydon and Lyndall Ryan (Sydney: NewSouth Publishing, 2018); John Molony, *John Hubert Plunkett in New South Wales 1832–1869* (Canberra: ANU Press, 1973); T.L. Suttor, 'John Hubert Plunkett (1802–1869)', *Australian Dictionary of Biography* (Canberra: National Centre of Biography, The Australian National University, 1967) adb.anu.edu.au/biography/plunkett-john-hubert-2556/text3483.
17 Jeanne Favret-Saada, *Witchcraft in the Bocage* (Cambridge: Cambridge University Press, 1980).
18 John Braithwaite, 'Reducing the Crime Problem: A Not So Dismal Criminology', *Australian and New Zealand Journal of Criminology* 25, no. 1 (1992): 1–10, John Braithwaite, 'Crime in a Convict Republic', *The Modern Law Review* 64, no. 1 (2001): 11–50.
19 Annalise Riles, 'Real Time: Unwinding Technocratic and Anthropological Knowledge', in *Ethnography and Law*, ed. Eve Darian-Smith (London: Routledge, 2007), 169–82, at 170.

tired of the space offered to them in settler historiography. Natchee Blu Barnd identified overlapping Indigenous and colonial geographies and Lisa Brooks stressed continuities in Native space.[20] Indigenous scholars have been critical of settler-colonial studies' view of Indigenous people as 'wallpaper' to critical readings of settler expansion.[21] These and the work of scholars of India, particularly the critical work of Durba Ghosh on what she terms 'many locals' of empire and 'the productive place of exceptions, margins, secrets, and anxieties', assist to create a space from which to view the 'law' of the 1850s in New South Wales.[22]

Jemmy Darcy appears in a criminal deposition in 1856 saying, 'All whitefellow go home and go to bed, there is nothing to do here, one blackfellow's quarrel has nothing to do with English laws.'[23] This is also good advice to non-Aboriginal historians. First Nations history is not built on the same ground as non-Aboriginal history, it does not have the same 'cosmology' or 'centre of gravity', as Aditya Pratap Deo would put it.[24] Aileen Moreton-Robinson refers to Aboriginal history emerging from a different way of being in the world.[25] Often the past is mutable or subject to the requirements of today, particularly in native title disputes. History is living, the present, past and future combine.[26] It is extremely difficult for those of us in the enlightenment tradition of history to comprehend that our help is often not needed. First Nations historians also negotiate this terrain if they seek to publish.[27] This book has sought right of reply to different sections and the results of those consultations appear at the end of the chapters.

---

20   Natchee Blu Barnd, *Native Space: Geographic Strategies to Unsettle Settler Colonialism* (Corvallis: Oregon State University Press, 2017); Lisa Brooks, *The Common Pot: The Recovery of Native Space in the Northeast* (Minneapolis: University of Minnesota Press, 2008).
21   J. Kēhaulani Kauanui, '"A Structure, Not an Event": Settler Colonialism and Enduring Indigeneity', *Lateral* 5, no. 1 (2016); Jane Carey and Ben Silverstein, 'Thinking With and Beyond Settler Colonial Studies', *Post-Colonial Studies* 23, no. 1 (2020): 1–20; Barnd, *Native Space*.
22   Durba Ghosh, 'Another Set of Imperial Turns?', *The American Historical Review* 117, no. 3 (2012): 772–93, at 773.
23   *R v Jemmy Darcy* 1853, 21, SR 9/6386.
24   Pratap Deo, *Kings, Spirits and Memory in Central India*, xviii.
25   Aileen Moreton-Robinson, 'Incommensurable Sovereignties: Indigenous Ontology Matters', in *Routledge Handbook of Critical Indigenous Studies*, eds Brendan Hokowhitu, Aileen Moreton-Robinson, Linda Tuhawi Smith, Chris Andersen, and Steve Larkin (London: Routledge, 2020).
26   Francoise Dussart, *The Politics of Ritual in an Aboriginal Settlement: Kinship, Gender, and the Currency of Knowledge* (Washington, DC: Smithsonian Institution Press, 2000).
27   For example: Shauna Bostock, *Reaching Through Time: Finding My Family's Stories* (Sydney: Allen & Unwin, 2023); Callum Clayton Dixon, *Surviving New England: A History of Aboriginal Resistance and Resilience through the First Forty Years of the Colonial Apocalypse* (Armidale: Newarea Aboriginal Corporation, formerly known as the Anaiwan Language Revival Program, 2019).

The right to discuss or describe the First Nations polity—and I deliberately use the word as singular in terms of long-distant links between groups—belongs to Aboriginal people and I direct readers to their websites so that more knowledge is obtained. This information is dated at the time of research; things might change, groups dissolve or new groups form and websites alter, as is the nature of First Nations politics.

A great deal of what I have found in cases challenges some of the truisms of general histories of Australia. First, there is no loss of authority or loss of law the further one moves away from settlement and the 'frontier' is close to Sydney rather than being at an extreme distance.[28] Frontier has been defined in different ways but I am using its original meaning and its language of 'outrage', 'mischief' and 'savagery' discussed by Henry Reynolds.[29] In language, the frontier is present in the language of Sydney legal officials but not in that of the magistrates of the furthest districts. Second, First Nations people played a considerable role in enforcing law in the north-west of the colony—through providing information and through being trusted above non-Aboriginal people. Third, though this has been recognised by anthropologists and the historian Marie Fels, First Nations people had their own uses for law, for policing, in terms of their own disputes.[30] Fourth, First Nations people did not 'come in' to runs, nor were runs safe spaces for favoured First Nations groups.[31] A most likely group to attack Aboriginal camps in the early hours of the morning were their own employers.[32]

---

28 Lisa Ford and David Andrew Roberts, 'Expansion 1820–1850', in *The Cambridge History of Australia*, eds Alison Bashford and Stuart Macintyre (Cambridge: Cambridge University Press, 2013), 121–48. Ford and Roberts refer to 'legal protection of Aboriginal people on new colonial frontiers … hundreds of miles from the centre of colonial governance' (p. 146). In the same book, Stuart Macintyre and Sean Scalmer write of an 'elongated frontier far from the seat of government': Stuart Macintyre and Sean Scalmer, 'Colonial States and Civil Society, 1860–90', in *The Cambridge History of Australia*, eds Alison Bashford and Stuart Macintyre (Cambridge: Cambridge University Press, 2013), 189–217, at 215.
29 Henry Reynolds, *Frontier: Aborigines, Settlers and Land* (Sydney: Allen & Unwin, 1987). Lynette Russell has used 'frontier' in a different way, in terms of intimate household relationships or what she terms negotiated encounters: Lynette Russell, '"Dirty Domestics and Worse Cooks": Frontiers, Southern Australia, 1800–1850', *Frontiers: A Journal of Women Studies* 28, nos 1–2 (2007): 18–46; see also Jan Chritchett, *A Distant Field of Murder* (Melbourne: Melbourne University Press, 1990).
30 Marie Fels, *Good Men and True* (Melbourne: Melbourne University Press, 1988).
31 Heather Goodall, *Invasion to Embassy: Land in Aboriginal Politics in New South Wales, 1770–1972* (Sydney: Sydney University Press, 1996), 71.
32 Paula Jane Byrne, 'Australian Squatter Space 1850–1860', *Britain and the World* 16, no. 1 (2023): 58–85.

It has long been recognised that Aboriginal people traversed the legal system in a different way to non-Aboriginal people and that there was in fact another 'English law' for First Nations people.[33] In the early 1850s, this could be a good thing for an Aboriginal man wanting to get back to his country. If there was no interpreter, he was discharged and could go home.

Aboriginal women did play a role in the north-west in the important control of information that characterised that region and they were referred to as 'belonging' to squatters. Their names were recorded in cases, but usually well into the case, after being referred to in general terms earlier. The law related to them differently than it did to Aboriginal men. They did not access the realm of sentiment that brought Aboriginal deaths to the court.

White women

Depositions question the idea of the 'interior' as a masculine or male-dominated world, one of gender imbalance.[34] White women were major players in the courts during this period. They were thoroughly imbricated in the business world of the interior as publicans and storekeepers, as managers of money and controllers of household finances. Women drank as much as men; they left their households in the charge of their daughters and went to public houses. They set up their own huts as public houses and had numbers of men sitting and drinking with them. Women were players in the system of law that ordinary people needled to instil in the colony, where law became part of a continuum of dispute. Cases involving sexual assault were always seen as part of this realm of dispute.

---

33 Michael Sturma, *Vice in a Vicious Society: Crime and Convicts in Mid-Nineteenth-Century New South Wales* (Brisbane: University of Queensland Press, 1983); Finnane, *Policing in Australia*.
34 Originally from Russell Ward, *The Australian Legend* (Oxford: Oxford University Press, 1966); critiqued or developed by Graeme Davison and Marc Brodie, *Struggle Country: The Rural Ideal in Twentieth Century Australia* (Melbourne: Monash University Press, 2005); Martin Crotty, *Making the Australian Male: Middle-Class Masculinity 1870–1920* (Melbourne: Melbourne University Press, 2001); Lisa Featherstone, 'Sex and the Australian Legend: Masculinity and the White Man's Body', *Journal of Australian Colonial History* 10, no. 2 (2008): 73–90; Marilyn Lake, 'On Being a White Man in Australia', in *Cultural History in Australia*, eds Hsu Ming Teo and Richard White (Sydney: UNSW Press, 2003); Melissa Bellanta, 'Feminism, Mateship and Brotherhood in 1890s Adelaide', *History Australia* 5, no. 1 (2008): 1–14.

Democracy

Australian historians have written of the exuberance of the early democracy. Frank Bongiorno writes that colonial democracy was 'performed in the streets, the emporium and the hotel, not only in the parliamentary chamber'.[35] John Hirst has described the 'democracy of manners' of the 1850s and 1860s and Bongiorno and Messner have discussed the shift in power begun on the goldfields. Alan Atkinson has considered the importance of print and the press in the dissemination of democratic ideas.[36] This democracy had been hard fought for until 1856 and the establishment of the Legislative Assembly. Democracy introduced new symbolism and new understandings of the public or the people. I use the word democracy in the manner of Sean Wilentz: it is 'a frame of mind', a way of perceiving the self in a changing world.[37] New languages were not orderly in their arrival, logical or genuine, and this disorderliness is to be found in the House and, as Frank Bongiorno has written, it was characterised by bluster and performance.[38] The clear opponent in rhetoric was the Crown. The law, the judges, the attorney-general, the solicitor-general were identified in this rhetoric as its representatives, despite opposition to the Crown by these individuals at various times. The newspapers put on the tables of the public houses in the interior carried this rhetoric throughout New South Wales. Historians might say the stories were imaginatively embroidered, the speeches puff, but this imaginary world was political reality for those who heard the papers read out, who listened to candidates at elections and who may or may not have had the vote. Inclusive language made for people who felt themselves included. Legal officials were not necessarily respected by the press and some of the attitudes we find among magistrates, constables and the lower classes derived from where 'the people' were positioned in relation to the Crown.

---

35 Frank Bongiorno, *Dreamers and Schemers: A Political History of Australia* (Melbourne: La Trobe University Press, 2022), 50.
36 John Hirst, *Freedom on the Fatal Shore: Australia's First Colony* (Melbourne: Black Inc., 2008), 392; John Ferry, *Colonial Armidale* (Brisbane: University of Queensland Press, 1999), 69; Frank Bongiorno and Andrew Messner, 'New England', in *People and Politics in Regional New South Wales, 1856–1950*, ed. Jim Hagan (Sydney: The Federation Press, 2006), 150–89, at 152; Alan Atkinson, *The Europeans in Australia. Volume 2* (Sydney: UNSW Press, 2016).
37 Sean Wilentz, *Chants Democratic: New York City and the Rise of the American Working Class, 1788–1850* (Oxford: Oxford University Press, 1986), 4–6.
38 Bongiorno, *Dreamers and Schemers*, 50.

Democracy was influential in the kind of understandings of law we find ourselves confronted with in the 1850s. Magistrates had their own practices; they resisted the advice of the attorneys-general. The emphasis on 'the people' empowered the juries of the colony; they saw themselves as the top of the hierarchy in the courtroom. Local populations had their own idea of 'justice', which could simply mean assuring their neighbour went to gaol for concocted reasons.

Historians of law

Michael Sturma's *Vice in a Vicious Society* examined criminal records from 1831 to 1861 to consider moral entrepreneurs and offences committed in this period. He was concerned with dominant values and use of the court system. He discovered 'a lack of traditional channels for imposing authority and mediating relations encouraged colonists to resort to the courts', and 'New South Wales was over policed by contemporary standards'.[39] He considered bench books as well as the records of the higher courts. My own study deals with the process from offence to higher court and the decision-makers at every point of that process in the 1850s. Returns of the Supreme Court list only those who were found guilty. But these processes I examine incorporated those who were found not guilty, those who had 'no case' against them and those who went home because no witnesses appeared.

A study of words and writing does not focus on any idea of crime in society. For the late-nineteenth-century studies, Australian historians have concentrated on statistical returns and judgements, examining the scope and range of the law. Historians such as Michael Sturma, Judith Allen and Andy Kaladelfos examined constructions of criminality and crime in the late nineteenth century.[40] Mark Finnane in the 'Prosecution Project' has used newspaper reporting as well as statistics in analysing all cases for New South Wales in the late nineteenth century. Gary Highland explored the paradoxical relationship of criminal law to Aboriginal people in north Queensland, where the law could protect Aboriginal people against violence under specific conditions—those where Aboriginal people were not sole witnesses, were recipients of European patronage and an offence was

---

39 Sturma, *Vice in a Vicious Society*.
40 ibid.; Judith Allen, *Sex and Secrets: Crimes Involving Australian Women Since 1850* (Melbourne: Oxford University Press, 1990); Andy Kaladelfos, 'The Politics of Punishment: Rape and the Death Penalty in Colonial Australia', *History Australia* 9, no. 1 (2012): 155–75.

committed close to white settlement.⁴¹ Alan Pope examined the criminal records of South Australia that concern Aboriginal people and bases his study on the type of offence committed and criminal cases in the courts rather than depositions.⁴²

In exploring influences on law, Alan Lester and Fae Dussart discuss the 'register of humanitarianism' and its undisciplined and erratic foray into the rhetoric and behaviour of imperial individuals involved in administering law.⁴³ While I have found language related to sentiment, I have found none related to the idea of protection in any form. In terms of the relationship between Aboriginal people and the law, Heather Douglas and Mark Finnane in their examination of cases concerning intra-Aboriginal violence show continual legal uncertainty about the status of Aboriginal people as subjects of the Crown well into the twentieth century. They also found Aboriginal people utilised English law for their own purposes.⁴⁴ Libby Connors, though she did not use the term, showed an Aboriginal polity existing in Brisbane, where Europeans were not the focus of Aboriginal existence.⁴⁵ Amanda Nettelbeck has discussed magistrates who were given the status of protectors of Aboriginal people in the 1830s and 1840s. She found they represented 'an increasing misalignment of views about the place of protection policy in the scheme of colonial governance' due to their involvement in violence, legal and extra-legal. Magistrates as protectors had a sometimes conflicted, sometimes compatible role as cultural intermediaries. She also argues that Aboriginal people were adept cultural brokers and that colonial and Aboriginal objectives could intersect in 'sometimes serendipitous ways'.⁴⁶ The 1850s in New South Wales is where Nettelbeck recognises considerable

---

41 Gary Highland, 'A Tangle of Paradoxes: Race, Justice and Criminal Law in North Queensland 1882–1894', in *A Nation of Rogues? Crime, Law and Punishment in Colonial Australia*, eds David Philips and Susanne Davies (Melbourne: Melbourne University Press, 1994), 123–40.
42 Alan Pope, *One Law for All? Aboriginal People and the Criminal Law in Early South Australia* (Canberra: Aboriginal Studies Press, 2011).
43 Alan Lester and Fae Dussart, *Colonization and the Origins of Humanitarian Governance* (Cambridge: Cambridge University Press, 2014).
44 Heather Douglas and Mark Finnane, *Indigenous Crime and Settler Law: White Sovereignty After Empire* (Basingstoke: Palgrave Macmillan, 2012).
45 Libby Connors, *Warrior: A Legendary Leader's Dramatic Life and Violent Death on the Colonial Frontier* (Sydney: Allen & Unwin, 2015). The term 'Aboriginal polity' has begun to be used only recently in Australian history writing and it refers to the political organisation of kinship structures and the links between Aboriginal groups. Tim Rowse, *Indigenous and Other Australians Since 1901* (Sydney: UNSW Press, 2017); Ann McGrath, *Illicit Love: Interracial Sex and Marriage in the United States and Australia* (Lincoln: University of Nebraska Press, 2015).
46 Amanda Nettelbeck, *Indigenous Rights and Colonial Subjecthood: Protection and Reform in the Nineteenth-Century British Empire* (Cambridge: Cambridge University Press, 2019), 110–30.

loosening of the conscience of protection policy—something earlier discussed by Ann Curthoys and Jessie Mitchell, who see it as being a result of the emergence of the debates and concerns of self-government.[47] My own research refers to the language magistrates used but rather than looking at the derivations and inconsistencies of such language, I see what that language led to in terms of the nature of power. My central concern is how law was understood in the dynamic democracy of 1850s New South Wales and this existed wildly outside discourses about law or protection or the punitive raid. This regional study of magistrates' relationship to the centralised offices of the criminal courts in Sydney shows what kind of perspectives of law produced statistics as well as what kind of language was brought into play in its administration, and this is to view the law as it is pieced together by its diligent or incompetent agent. This is a different project to that of Gwenda Morgan and Peter Rushton, who found that local magistrates in the north-east of England had considerable scope for invention and innovation. My perspective incorporates acts that were outside the contemporary ideas of the correct way to construct a case, ideas of evidence and the interpretation of these by the metropolis.[48] As such it draws law into the complex realm of administrative culture where customs and manners jostle each other in everyday life in the making of ledgers and records.[49]

Reading in cases forms the basis of the system of common law and Charlotte Furth sees this as part of the way law develops: one case has the capacity to inform others, it can 'lead to claims of empirical knowledge and point to problem solving interventions in the world'.[50] This book has another way of reading a case than that specified or required by law. I disjoint cases, take them apart and look at the components of legal understanding in local areas. Evidence, then, does not lead to 'a result' but rather forms complex patterns concerning not only evidence and signs of guilt but also ownership and personhood. This book is centred on the process of committal. In its close examination of documents, it has a relationship to the work of Chris Owen on policing in the Kimberley, particularly where he writes that constables

---

47 Ann Curthoys and Jessie Mitchell, *Taking Liberty: Indigenous Rights and Settler Self Government in Colonial Australia, 1830–1890* (Cambridge: Cambridge University Press, 2018).
48 Gwenda Morgan and Peter Rushton, *Rogues, Thieves and the Rule of Law: The Problem of Law Enforcement in North-East England 1718–1800* (London: UCL Press, 1998).
49 For example: Susie S. Porter, *From Angel to Office Worker: Middle Class Identity and Female Consciousness in Mexico, 1890–1950* (Lincoln: University of Nebraska Press, 2018).
50 Charlotte Furth, 'Thinking With Cases', in *Thinking with Cases: Specialist Knowledge in Chinese Cultural History*, eds Charlotte Furth, Judith T. Zeitlin, and Ping-chen Hsiung (Honolulu: University of Hawai'i Press, 2007), 1–30, at 3.

sent muddied and deliberately inaccurate letters to the administration, but these may be deciphered to show actual policing.[51] I have a different scope than policing or control.

Legalities

Despite deposition boxes looking disorderly and ragged, they are surprisingly complete. When cross-checked with newspaper records or registers, most 1850s depositions have survived. Moving across geographical areas shows the position of law in the colony of New South Wales; its footprint in different places was mediated through constables, magistrates and the ordinary population. Pages of criminal depositions were gathered by the clerk of petty sessions in each district. He numbered the pages, attached recognisances, those records of witnesses bound to appear and included a letter of introduction from the magistrate's bench before forwarding the documents to Sydney. Clerks of petty session or clerks of the bench were appointed by the colonial secretary before 1856 and the chief or colonial secretary (or, in today's terms, premier) after that year. Clerks could be transferred or moved by him to different regions. Patrick Murray began as clerk of the peace at Balranald and was later police magistrate on the South Coast. This was a rare transition as police magistrates were usually recruited, like commissioners of Crown land, from the impoverished ranks of bankrupted or unsupported gentlemen. Samuel North and Helenus Scott at Carcoar and Phillip Ditmas at Wellingrove all fitted this description.

Clerks of petty sessions were interested in emoluments and the opportunities available in office. The clerk at Kiama applied to practise as a certified conveyancer in 1859—a request that was refused.[52] Clerks often used three names—Archimedes Byrne Luscombe at Molong, Samuel Charles Valentine North at Carcoar or James Edward Snape at Warialda—and they cut fashionable figures in the towns, adopting a genteel lifestyle. James Snape lived in the courthouse in Warialda. His bedroom had a curtain at the door and he informed a visitor, 'If you go into that room, my bedroom, you will see plenty of books with which you can amuse yourself.'[53]

---

51   Chris Owen, *Every Mother's Son is Guilty: Policing on the Kimberley Frontier* (Perth: UWA Press, 2016), 16.
52   *Illawarra Mercury*, 11 March 1859.
53   Statement of Jeremiah Mullane, 19 December 1853, Warialda Bench Book, State Archives Collection, SR 4/5679 [hereinafter WBB].

INTRODUCTION

Depositions were constructed ideally in terms of the requirements of the common law and later *An Act to adopt and apply certain Acts of Parliament passed for facilitating the performance of the Duties of Justices of the Peace* 1850 (14 Vic., No. 43) and the *Justices Act Amendment Act* 1853 (17 Vic., No. 39), both acts deriving from the Imperial *Jervis Acts* of 1848 (11 and 12 Vic., No. 43).

Depositions were made in the presence of two kinds of magistrates in the 1850s. The justice of the peace (JP) was an honorary appointment, without renumeration, and magistrates were selected from local wealthy persons—at this time, mainly landholders. Police magistrates obtained paid positions. John Lowndes writes of the *Metropolitan Courts Act 1839* in Britain, which 'marked the establishment of a professional stipendiary magistracy; all appointees of the magistracy had to be a barrister'.[54] The appointment of paid or police magistrates in New South Wales began in 1832 though there were earlier single appointments.[55] These men were not barristers. The move to a paid magistracy in England was part of a series of decisions to end corruption in the magistracy. That was not the reasoning in New South Wales. John Lowndes quotes Hilary Golder concerning police magistrates in New South Wales: 'Ministers were free to appoint relatives, friends, political supporters and even political enemies, many of whom were perfectly competent magistrates.'[56] These men were 'barely distinguishable' from the traditional justice of the peace—an honorary and unpaid position existing from 1788 consisting of local wealthy citizens. The first appointments of stipendiary magistrates in New South Wales were not until 1881.[57] Therefore, in the 1850s, while the rights of the accused were protected by the importation of the *Jervis Acts* of 1848, those persons who at the local level would administer those acts were not of the same standard of legal training as in England. Justices of the peace and police magistrates were not barristers, and they were thoroughly entrenched among local elites. While historians argue that police magistrates administered the *Masters and Servants Act* in ways that were fairer than justices of the peace,[58] police magistrates, as we shall see, seem indistinguishable from justices of the peace in their style

---

54 Lowndes, 'The Australian Magistracy', 510.
55 Schofield-Georgeson, *By What Authority?*, 76–77.
56 Lowndes, 'The Australian Magistracy', 513, quoting Golder, *High and Responsible Office*.
57 Lowndes, 'The Australian Magistracy', 515.
58 Schofield-Georgeson, *By What Authority?*, 104–5.

of administration of other criminal cases and they were also likely to sign themselves 'JP' rather than 'PM' on depositions, indicating they thought JPs were of higher status.[59]

The precise process to be followed in the constructing of depositions was set out in *Blackstone's Commentaries* edited in 1849, in Burn's *Justice of the Peace and Parish Officer* (a supplement being published in 1853 following the *Jervis Acts*) in 1835 and in Plunkett's *Australian Magistrate* in 1847.[60] A deposition had to be taken on oath in a judicial proceeding with the prisoner present. Magistrates had to be 'extremely careful in preparing depositions and should make a full statement of all the witnesses say upon the matter in question'. Depositions were not to be varied without the magistrate's signature, indicating that the change came from the witness himself or herself.[61] Burn's *Justice of the Peace* set down the requirements for magistrates and clerks in recording depositions. They should be in the first person, magistrates had to sign the statement of each witness and the depositions must be in the 'very words or near as possible words' of the witness.[62] These practices were derived from earlier acts and the common law and all these texts give information on cases, with Plunkett referring to New South Wales.[63]

This process of setting down depositions was based on prior acts and the common law and in each of the legal texts it is possible to trace the development of the law regarding depositions. *Burn* and *Plunkett* were specifically designed for magistrates and the contents of the volumes

---

59   For example: Samuel North at Carcoar was initially a JP sitting alone in 1850 and, in 1851, is described as police magistrate (PM). He alternates between signing himself 'JP' and 'PM' after that year. Helenus Scott, who was appointed PM after North in 1853, was a former JP at Invermein. He signed himself 'JP'. Robert Massie was a PM and Commissioner of Crown Lands on the Macleay River. Henry Whitty at Molong was formerly Commissioner of Crown Lands on the Maranoa. None of these people were legally trained and all made similar mistakes to JPs and worked alongside them. In 1857, commissioners of Crown lands at Nundle, Liverpool Plains and Uralla were made magistrates of their districts. None was legally trained. *Empire*, 2 September 1857. If one examines the *Government Gazette* for listings of new police magistrates during this period, all are referred to as 'Esq.'. According to the *Goulburn Herald and County of Argyle Advertiser* (15 November 1856), police magistrates came from 'too confined a circle and encompass mainly the wealthy and the locally noted'.

60   James Stewart, *The Rights of Persons being the First Book of Blackstone's Commentaries Incorporating the Alterations down to the Present Time* (London: Spettigue and Farrance, 1849) [hereinafter *Blackstone's Commentaries*]; Joseph Chitty and Thomas Chitty, *Richard Burn's Justice of the Peace and Parish Officer. In Six Volumes* (London: Sweet, Stevens & Sons, and A. Maxwell, 1837); *Sydney Morning Herald*, 23 April 1853; Edwin C. Suttor, *Plunkett's Australian Magistrate: A Guide to the Duties of a Justice of the Peace, with Numerous Forms* (Sydney: W.A. Coleman, 1847) [hereinafter *Plunkett's Australian Magistrate*].

61   Stewart, *Blackstone's Commentaries*, 76.

62   Chitty and Chitty, *Richard Burn's Justice of the Peace and Parish Officer*, 118.

63   *Plunkett's Australian Magistrate*, 90.

are organised alphabetically. In 1848 in England, the *Jervis Acts* codified common law in terms of the duties of magistrates, essentially for their legal protection. They could no longer be subjected to civil actions due to the decisions they made, nor could their mistakes in documentation result in the dismissal of a case. Alex Castles, Tim Castle and Bruce Kercher have written about the sometimes-erratic transferral of law to New South Wales.[64] Eugene Schofield-Georgeson writes of the application of the *Jervis Acts*. The 1850 acts introduced refinements to the process of criminal law at the level of magistrates' hearing of criminal cases. They codified common law fair trial rights. These were the right to silence (s. 18), the voluntariness of confessional evidence including the requirement of a warning against incrimination (s. 18), the right for the accused to cross-examine prosecution witnesses (s. 17), time limits on detention for investigation of eight days (s. 21), bail for all offences except treason (s. 23), documentation by magistrates of all cases of imprisonment and the movement of people using warrants (s. 24), the right to obtain depositions (ss. 3, 27), the right to copies of examination and cross-examination (s. 3) and the right to appeal (s. 12).[65] The 1853 additions concern the right for the defendant to cross-examine witnesses (s. 15), increased powers for paid magistrates, who could act alone where justices of the peace could not (s. 11), appeal to judges (ss. 5, 10) and ensuring attendance by funding the travel of witnesses for the defence (s. 14).[66]

Magistrates had access to legal texts and were sent copies of the relevant acts. Edward Ogilvie, for example, became magistrate in 1847 at Grafton and immediately obtained a copy of *Blackstone*.[67] *Blackstone's Commentaries* was mentioned in the press regularly in the 1850s.[68] The widespread use of Plunkett's *Australian Magistrate* was demonstrated by the *Sydney Morning Herald* in 1859: 'Every time a new batch of justices of the peace were appointed, the booksellers were always besieged for a fresh supply of "Plunkett's Magistrate".' The paper announced a new 'handy … pocket

---

64 Bruce Kercher, *An Unruly Child: A History of Law in Australia* (London: Routledge, 1995); Alex C. Castles, 'The Reception and Status of English Law in Australia', *Adelaide Law Review* 2, no. 1 (1963): 1–31; Castle, 'The Practical Administration of Justice', 47.
65 Schofield-Georgeson, *By What Authority?*, 101.
66 ibid., 105; *An Act to Amend the Justices Act of 1850 in respect of Prohibitions and Amendments and Other Matters* 1853 (17 Vic., No. 39), www.austlii.edu.au/au/legis/nsw/num_act/tjaaao1853n39296.pdf.
67 Charles Tindal to Father, 25 August 1847, Tindal Family Papers, Mitchell Library, State Library of New South Wales [hereinafter ML], A2068.
68 *Sydney Morning Herald*, 23 July 1850, 17 June 1858; *Freeman's Journal*, 6 August 1853; *Goulburn Herald and County of Argyle Advertiser*, [hereinafter *Goulburn Herald*], 11 April 1857; *Empire*, 8 March 1856, 21 August 1856.

edition' that 'consists simply of a reprint of the first Sir John Jervis Acts, together with the colonial statute adopting it, with notes by the editor furnishing additional information on colonial details'.[69] However, even in 1851 at Wellingrove, a prisoner was 'duly cautioned in the manner directed by the Act of Co [struck through] Parliament in such cases' before he gave his defence, indicating there was much discussion of the *Jervis Acts* at the time of their application.[70] The acts had been 'frequently adverted to' in the press of the 1850s.[71] As the *Herald* explained in 1853 about the Act, 'this statute, though in the form of a code does not abrogate all the pre-existing duties of the magistrates but leaves them untouched except where they are interfered with or altered by express enactment'. The major concern in 1853 was for the right of defendants to bring witnesses for the defence before the magistrates.[72]

Depositions were forwarded to the attorney-general in Sydney. There were six NSW attorneys-general in the 1850s. John Hubert Plunkett had been appointed attorney-general in 1836 and would remain so until June 1856, when self-government resulted in an elected attorney-general, William Montagu Manning. Manning resigned in August 1856 because he did not want to serve in a Charles Cowper ministry. James Martin became attorney-general in August 1856 until October, when the Cowper ministry failed, and William Manning was again attorney-general until ill health forced him to resign in May 1857. The mercurial John Darvall was attorney-general until September 1857, when James Martin returned to the position within a Cowper ministry, staying until November 1858. He was followed by the democratic Alfred Lutwyche until February 1859, when the latter was appointed judge at Moreton Bay. The newly arrived Lyttleton Holyoake Bayley obtained the position of attorney-general that year, much to the disgust of the legal fraternity, particularly Daniel Deniehy, who published a satire about Lyttleton Bayley. When the Cowper ministry was defeated, Lyttleton Bayley resigned and the position of attorney-general was taken by the brother-in-law of William Manning, the social reformer Edward Wise. He was attorney-general until February 1860 when he resigned to be replaced with William Manning.[73] The criminal Crown solicitor during

---

69 *Sydney Morning Herald*, 25 October 1859.
70 *R v Cornelius Burke* 1850, 8, SR 9/6368.
71 *Sydney Morning Herald*, 23 April 1853.
72 ibid.
73 *Australian Dictionary of Biography*, [Online] (Canberra: National Centre of Biography, The Australian National University), adb.anu.edu.au/; Max M.H. Thompson, *The Seeds of Democracy: Early Elections in Colonial New South Wales* (Sydney: The Federation Press, 2006), 216–75.

the whole of the 1850s was John Moore Dillon. When the positions of civil and criminal Crown solicitor were combined in June 1859, Dillon lost his position to the much younger John Williams.[74] The place of Crown prosecutor, only active at the assizes, was sometimes taken by the solicitor-general or a member of the bar. To act in this way, a barrister had to obtain a commission from the governor and present it at the beginning of the assize session.[75] The attorney-general instructed the criminal Crown solicitor to draw up information or indictments and these separate documents were written out by the clerks of the office.

In cases before the Supreme Court and assizes, the deposition was of singular importance. Crown prosecutors noted whether witnesses strayed from their depositions and there were arguments about witnesses contradicting themselves.[76] Counsel would stress the discrepancies between the deposition and the oral account given in court.[77] This only occurred, however, if a prisoner obtained representation. There are indications in cases discussed in this book that the status of the deposition was changing in the 1850s and judges would allow oral evidence to differ in some cases but not in others. Depositions became public if they were printed and coroners' inquests were sent to the newspapers before 1857, when the Crown solicitor ordered the practice to stop.[78] Depositions were also sent to the press by individuals and they were thanked by the editors of newspapers for this service.[79] Such customs made depositions part of public debate and further underlined their importance.

Close research into documents can unsettle legal readings. T43 in the NSW State Archives Collection holds documents relating to the case *The King against Murral (Murrell)*,[80] a watershed case whereby Aboriginal people came under the jurisdiction of English law. This case established that Aboriginal

---

74 John M. Bennett, *A History of Solicitors in New South Wales* (Sydney: Legal Books, 1984), 314–17.
75 *Sydney Morning Herald*, 18 March 1858.
76 *People's Advocate and New South Wales Vindicator*, [hereinafter *People's Advocate*], 13 April 1850; *Sydney Morning Herald*, 3 May 1857, 14 May 1857.
77 'The learned Judge should have confined the proof on the part of the Crown to the specific act complained of and not have permitted the Attorney General to influence the jury by allusions and evidence to which the attention of the defendant had not been called.' Motion for a new trial, William Almond, 3 April 1850, Supreme Court Informations, State Archives Collection, SR T73; *Goulburn Herald*, 10 July 1852.
78 *Empire*, 23 January 1858.
79 *Bathurst Free Press and Mining Journal*, 6 June 1857; *Maitland Mercury and Hunter River Advertiser*, [hereinafter *Maitland Mercury*], 15 October 1857; *Empire*, 15 January 1858.
80 'The King' is the terminology on the front of the case, which also has another spelling of Murrell ('Murral').

people were not a conquered people with whom treaties should have been made but were subjects of the Crown to be provided with the sanctuary of English law.[81]

The case had been instigated in 1836 by an Aboriginal man, Bowen Bungaree, who wanted George Bummaree and Jack Congo Murrell 'tried by the English' as they had killed his cousin. The barrister Sidney Stephen argued there was no jurisdiction over Aboriginal disputes and the case was referred to the judges, who decided that there was jurisdiction. Aboriginal people could indeed be tried because otherwise 'our laws would be no sanctuary to them'. The case is considered a watershed in the history of jurisdiction over Aboriginal people, its importance underlined by the authority of a unanimous full bench.[82] That it was only adopted slowly has been suggested by Heather Douglas and Mark Finnane.[83] In the 1850s it was not adopted at all. Next to the case is a tiny note from Justice Therry to Chief Justice Stephen. Undated, the note was directed in pencil, to John Gurner, a commissioner of the court after 1844, who had been clerk of the court in 1836. The note reads:

> If the case relates to the Aboriginal—I spoke to Plunkett upon it and he tells me that about 1836–7 your brother Sydney defended an aborigine for the murder of another—and himself pleaded he was not amenable to our laws—that there was a law <u>inter se</u> by which Abs were liable to be punished by their own tribe and not punishable by death—the full court overruled all these pleas—and P says the Ab was executed. It would be well to find this case out from Plunkett if it occurred. RT[84]

---

81 Lisa Ford, *Settler Sovereignty: Jurisdiction and Indigenous People in America and Australia, 1788–1836* (Cambridge: Harvard University Press, 2011), 2.
82 'Australian Law as Applied to the Aborigines', in Australian Law Reform Commission, *Recognition of Aboriginal Customary Laws*, ALRC Report 31 (Melbourne: Australian Law Reform Commission, 18 August 2010), www.alrc.gov.au/publication/recognition-of-aboriginal-customary-laws-alrc-report-31/4-aboriginal-customary-laws-and-anglo-australian-law-after-1788/australian-law-as-applied-to-aborigines/; see also Ford, *Settler Sovereignty*; Henry Reynolds, *Aboriginal Sovereignty: Reflections On Race, State and Nation* (Sydney: Allen & Unwin, 2006); Shaunnagh Dorsett, 'Burton and the Draft Act for the Protection and Amelioration of the Aborigines 1838 (NSW)', in *Legal Histories of the British Empire: Laws, Engagements, Legacies*, eds Shaunnagh Dorsett and John McLaren (New York: Routledge, 2014), 171–86; Douglas and Finnane, *Indigenous Crime and Settler Law*, 50–51.
83 Douglas and Finnane, *Indigenous Crime and Settler Law*, 50–51.
84 *The King against Jack Congo Murral* [sic.] 25, Supreme Court Informations, SR T43.

This note shows three major legal personages of the late 1840s and 1850s with no memory of *Murrell*. The Chief Justice of New South Wales Alfred Stephen had no idea of his brother's earlier contribution to a milestone legal decision. The mild Roger Therry, who would preside over a similar argument to Sidney Stephen's in *Cuppy*, as we shall see, also had no memory; in fact, he doubted the case ever occurred. John Hubert Plunkett, attorney-general—that 'friend to the Aborigines'—had only vague recall of the case: Bummaree had been found to have no case against him and Murrell was acquitted; no-one was executed.

A tiny note between judges has the capacity to change how we perceive our history and opens a terrain of inquiry. Judges of the 1850s who appear in this note would not have thought of *Murrell* each time an Aboriginal man came before them as defendant and judgements continued in the same erratic manner for Aboriginal people as they had prior to Gurner finding the case. Uncertainty about Aboriginal status in *inter se* cases has been shown by Heather Douglas and Mark Finnane to have existed well into the twentieth century.[85] My point, however, lies not with such uncertainty but with the capacity of the note to change our view of the past: 'blind' judges appear where we thought there were none; a hesitant Attorney-General Plunkett, one of the most diligent of men with the most legal mind of his period, wavers and is plain wrong in his recall. Moreover, the legal point cannot be neatly applied to Australian history. While in law the 1836 case was a watershed, in the 1850s, no-one thought it was significant.

There were four sites for courts of assize in this period: Maitland, Goulburn, Bathurst and Brisbane. In 1859 Armidale and Deniliquin joined that list. The geographical approach used here is shaped by those jurisdictions. Selectivity means that this is a study of variables in the way law was practised in the colony of New South Wales. It is not new to say that English law in its transplantations was utterly malleable and responsive to local cultures and conditions. Niels Brimnes terms this 'layered sovereignties' in his study of Madras. Santanu Sengupta identified 'an agency of the local in shaping the colonial regime and its legal structure' in a study of the mayor's courts of Madras and Bombay. Leonard Hodges, and Lauren Benton and Richard

---

85 Douglas and Finnane, *Indigenous Crime and Settler Law*, 10.

Ross have discussed such layering. *The Cambridge Legal History of Australia* discusses the uncertainties of the transplanting of law to the colonies, essay after essay in that book dealing with uncertainties.[86]

This book does not seek out uncertainties in the transmission of the *Jervis Acts* to the colony, though that is plainly apparent in depositions. It is an ethnography of conflicting perceptions of what law was and what it was for at a time of political transformation.

---

86 Niels Brimnes, 'Beyond Colonial Law: Indigenous Litigation and the Contestation of Property in the Mayor's Court in Late Eighteenth-Century Madras', *Modern Asian Studies* 37, no. 3 (2003): 513–50; Leonard Hodges 'Between Litigation and Arbitration: Administering Legal Pluralism in Eighteenth Century Bombay', *Itineiro* 43, no. 3 (2018): 490–515; Santanu Sengupta, *Trade, Politics and the English Mayor's Court: Law and Trading Practices in the 18th Century Bay of Bengal*, The History Project Research Report (Cambridge: Center for History and Economics, Harvard University, n.d.), www.histproj.org/completed/Sengupta.pdf; Lauren Benton and Richard Ross, 'Empires and Legal Pluralism: Jurisdiction, Sovereignty and Political Imagination in the Early Modern World', in *Legal Pluralism and Empires, 1500–1850*, eds Lauren Benton and Richard Ross (New York: NYU Press, 2013), 1–18; Byrne, *Criminal Law and Colonial Subject*; Douglas and Finnane, *Indigenous Crime and Settler Law*. See essays by Amanda Kearney, Raynor Thwaites, Maureen Tehan, Shaunnagh Dorset, Mark Lunny, Ruth Morgan and Judith S. Jones, and Brendan Lim in Peter Crane, Lisa Ford, and Mark McMillan, eds, *The Cambridge Legal History of Australia* (Cambridge: Cambridge University Press, 2022).

1

Democracy

The choreography of democracy

New South Wales was colonised in 1788. Power rested with the governor of the colony, and relations with First Nations people alternated between diplomatic overtures and aggression. The governor ruled through proclamations and government and general orders. In 1823, the Legislative Council was established, consisting initially of government officials. It was later extended to include private individuals. In 1836, the law in *Murrell* ostensibly incorporated First Nations people as subjects of the Crown, although diplomacy and aggression continued. In 1843, the first elections for the council were held and, in 1856, a system of responsible government was established. The Legislative Council, appointed by the governor, was then complemented by an elected assembly. Initially there was a property-qualified franchise and, in 1859, universal suffrage. This did not specifically exclude First Nations people, but it did not distinctly include them either; they remained subjects without influence. The same diplomacy and aggression continued. All the political changes from 1788 had come about through pressure from colonial officials and legal officers, private representations and public meetings. The colony had represented itself to England and demanded change in the manner in which it was governed. The 1850s saw an escalation of pressure on England; the atmosphere in the colony was belligerent and at times revolutionary.[1]

---

1   Bongiorno, *Dreamers and Schemers*; Peter Cochrane, *Colonial Ambition: Foundations of Australian Democracy* (Melbourne: Melbourne University Press, 2006); Thompson, *The Seeds of Democracy*; Terry Irving, *The Southern Tree of Liberty* (Sydney: The Federation Press, 2006).

In the rhetoric[2] of the early democracy law was positioned not as something of reverence but as intricately bound up with deceits practised by the Crown. Legal officials and English law were tainted by that connection and the disrespect afforded the attorneys-general derived from such concerns. This rhetoric surrounding the place of law was transmitted through press accounts and read out in the public houses of the colony. This was the environment in which the clerks of the court took out their pens and papers and began to listen to complaints. The instability of the early democracy contributed to the way law was understood and the way it worked.

The first government of the new Legislative Assembly of 1856 in New South Wales was formed by Stuart Donaldson. How this government and the wider Legislative Assembly described itself at this crucial time gives the contemporary rhetoric of democracy. The government had, according to Terence Murray, member for the Southern Boroughs, 'stolen into office by the window when the proper way would have been to have come through the doors of the House'.[3] The governor-general had appointed Stuart Donaldson to form a ministry before the House convened because he wished the business of the country to continue. Former office holders had been asked but they declined, wishing to keep their pensions. Such a move was the prerogative of the governor-general under the terms of the Constitution, but it grated badly with those who sought to see the House as exempt from the control of the Crown.

The action of the governor-general in appointing Donaldson to create a ministry would open a perimeter of debate where the 'House' at times became synonymous with the British House of Commons. Yet, each prerogative of the House had to be fought for in elaborate choreographed references to the spatial confines of the building. What could' come in the window' had to be confronted, who tried to place papers 'on the table' would be argued, the walls of the building were brought into consciousness and the House had to squeeze itself into existence by stressing its independence from

---

2   I use rhetoric here in the same manner as Lynn Hunt, to describe shifting meanings and terminology in politics, to 'read it as a text in the manner of literary criticism'. Lynn Hunt, *Politics, Culture and Class in the French Revolution* (Berkeley: University of California Press, 1988), 25. See also Nancy Wright and Andrew Richard Buck, 'The Transformation of Colonial Property: A Study of the Law of Dower in New South Wales, 1836 to 1863', *University of Tasmania Law Review* 23, no. 1 (2004): 97–127. Although I do not use it in the same terms as these writers, who divide it according to origin.

3   New South Wales Legislative Assembly [hereinafter Assembly], *Sydney Morning Herald*, 30 May 1856.

the Crown and attempting to distance itself from 'party'—that combination of individual members in interest groups that was deemed corrosive and dangerous in the early nineteenth century.[4]

What happened in the House is available to the historian only through the reports of the *Sydney Morning Herald* and other newspapers. The *Sydney Morning Herald* has been adopted by the Parliament of New South Wales as an early form of *Hansard* and its reports will be followed here. That reports were sometimes inaccurate was suggested by James Macarthur, who complained his speech had been misrepresented by the *Herald*.[5] A reference to Donaldson challenging Charles Cowper to 'mortal combat' was made by Plunkett in April 1856. Donaldson replied to Plunkett that 'he challenged me'.[6] Yet, such an event cannot be found in earlier minutes. The reporter sometimes noted that a speaker was 'inaudible'.[7] William Forster apologised for his words 'in the heat of debate yesterday' in May 1856; these words do not appear in the previous day's report.[8] The records give a partial picture of the thinking of the House, and the content of this thinking shows an uncertain and hesitant environment, highly sensitive to its own right to exist. It is a partial picture that we share with the public of the mid-nineteenth century; they, too, could not 'hear' inaudible comments, they, too, would wonder whether a speech was accurately recorded.

The members of the Legislative Assembly often used the words 'the House' to indicate a democratic space that was breached by unconstitutional and illiberal actions. That it was the House that should be the centre of politics was stressed in the criticism of Charles Cowper, who had held a dinner at Rose Bay in May 1856 'to form a political party at which Mr Cowper was the leader … [E]very attempt was made by Mr Cowper and his friends to bias the minds of the newer and younger members of the Assembly'.[9] Too many things had gone on in drawing rooms, there was secrecy afoot. Private communications were read out in the House so that the positions of

---

4   Paula Jane Byrne, *Judge Advocate Ellis Bent: Letters and Diaries 1809–1811* (Sydney: Desert Pea Press, 2012), 6–10.
5   James Macarthur, Assembly, *Sydney Morning Herald*, 30 May 1856.
6   Plunkett, Assembly, *Sydney Morning Herald*, 30 May 1856.
7   Assembly, *Sydney Morning Herald*, 15 August 1856.
8   Forster, Assembly, *Sydney Morning Herald*, 5 June 1856.
9   Assembly, *Sydney Morning Herald*, 27 May 1856.

both 'sides' could be understood.[10] Henry Parkes spoke of members 'being brought within the influence of some combination inimical to the interests of the country'. He was 'independent and unconnected'.[11]

This was the old language of 'party' brought into the new assembly. Frank Bongiorno has pointed out that 'voice' is synonymous with 'noise' in the 1850s. Politics was made up of shifting and dissolving factions.[12] Charles Cowper was claimed to be an 'anythingarian': his views shifted to suit his aims for political power.[13] No-one in this first House of 1856 was a 'conservative', all were 'liberal' in the rhetoric of the House. Governor Denison in his speech on the opening of the House had 'out liberalled the liberals'.[14] Some had got into the House 'under the guise of liberals'.[15] This was a common language of a new parliament. Classical references, Greek, Latin (John Darvall gave part of a speech in Latin in September 1856), references to French and English history, to the reign of George III and to Pitt and Fox also linked the gentlemen of the House. Performance was for each other, for 'the people' and then 'the country'—two imaginary realms. Six long, bitter years of struggle for representative government in which the Crown was the avowed enemy left a hiatus. Feint and counter-feint followed from these men who had formerly had such a clear and potent opponent in the Crown, yet to be a 'republican' was frowned upon.[16]

The House was not a steady place. When the governor-general asked Cowper to form a government after Donaldson was successfully hunted out in September 1856, it was another instance of a ministry 'coming in through the window'.[17] The Crown would be seen to make incursions into the House through those legal officials viewed to be its representatives alongside the colonial secretary and the governor-general. Chief justice Sir Alfred Stephen thought his appointment as President of the Legislative Council was 'not political' and even though he knew the governor appointed him with the ministry he felt the appointment was 'peculiarly that of the Governor'. The governor concurred, saying he never would have appointed

---

10 Donaldson, Assembly, *Sydney Morning Herald*, 27 May 1856; Arnold, Assembly, *Sydney Morning Herald*, 30 May 1856.
11 Parkes, Assembly, *Sydney Morning Herald*, 27 May 1865.
12 Bongiorno, *Dreamers and Schemers*, 50.
13 Thompson, *The Seeds of Democracy*, 48.
14 Donaldson, Assembly, *Sydney Morning Herald*, 30 May 1856.
15 Arnold, Assembly, *Empire*, 11 September 1856.
16 Donaldson, Assembly, *Sydney Morning Herald*, 26 May 1856; Darvall, Assembly, *Empire*, 11 September 1856.
17 Hay, Assembly, *Sydney Morning Herald*, 18 September 1856, 24 September 1856.

Stephen if the position was 'political' and linked with the ministry of the day.[18] Stephen introduced the argument that 'party' and contests between individuals for the 'possession of power' were opposed to the 'interests of the advancement of the community generally'. Stephen would not be 'debased' by the 'uneducated'.[19]

One can see that the governor-general and the chief justice held perceptions of 'government' outside 'democracy'. When Donaldson stated he was going 'to take no action' in the matter of the chief justice, the House was clearly in uproar, the reporter noting that speakers were 'inaudible'.[20] In June 1856 James Martin informed the House that the governor-general had given a pardon in a criminal case 'without consulting the Executive Council … Were the Governor General's Instructions at variance with principles of Responsible Government?' Donaldson replied that he found the tone of the question insulting, but that they were entering 'a new state of things' and he found the governor-general's instructions 'incomprehensible'. The governor-general could not use his prerogative of remitting a sentence without communicating with the Executive Council, but the nineteenth clause gave him the power to resist and differ from the Executive Council if he pleased. There was an absurdity in the twentieth clause and the governor-general had sent the very question of both clauses to the secretary of state. There had been only one case of remission and that concerned 'an Aboriginal', which had been communicated to the executive.[21] The word 'Aboriginal' here was significant as responsibility for Aboriginal people by Britain or New South Wales had only been recently clarified, in 1854.[22] Martin persisted: two deputations of the public about the railways had gone to the governor-general with a petition *and he received them*. What was the point of the House having the name 'responsible government' if it was not responsible? Had anyone heard of the Queen receiving deputations? Donaldson replied that the petition had been sent to Cabinet, which wrote the governor's answer for him.[23]

---

18 Stephen, Legislative Council [hereinafter Council], *Sydney Morning Herald*, 13 August 1856.
19 ibid.
20 Assembly, *Sydney Morning Herald*, 14 August 1856.
21 Donaldson, Assembly, *Sydney Morning Herald*, 7 June 1856.
22 Curthoys and Mitchell, *Taking Liberty*, 10.
23 Martin, Donaldson, Assembly, *Sydney Morning Herald*, 8 August 1856.

The rhetoric of the House showed this need to push itself into the space of representative democracy despite tactics of 'throwing opposition' or distinct and 'dark' ploys by the dupes of the governor-general.[24] This was the primary message of all members of the House in the diverse actions they took to make the new space of government. Newspapers were read out in public houses and some of this language may be found in the records of the speech of ordinary people in the courts. The reference to 'longhair' by a witness before the Yass bench could have derived from speeches that referred to the English Civil War. Jemmy Darcy's claim that English law had nothing to do with Blackfellows' quarrels may be related to the arguments of judges and barristers that found their way into the Legislative Council. 'The people'—such a potent referent in the council and early assembly—were certainly present in the words of constables and magistrates on the South Coast of New South Wales. Rhetoric has a life of its own and is generative of multiple readings and interpretations.

In August 1856 the House sought to intervene in the membership of the Legislative Council. The judges should go, they should not be 'public figures'. Their judicial independence would be 'unfavourably' affected. It had been intended that the parliament should exercise 'supervision over the office of judges'. Forster quoted Montesquieu: '[T]here is no liberty in judging, if the judge takes part in legislation.' The fault lay in the ministry, Donaldson's, who had appointed them. Donaldson interpreted this as an expression of no confidence in his ministry.[25] In opposition, the idea that the judges would not be 'political' was 'perfectly absurd', said John Hubert Plunkett, the former attorney-general.[26] The Donaldson ministry would resign in September, two weeks after this debate, essentially over the incursions of the Crown into the House.

Uncertainties

Forster claimed in May 1856 that the Legislative Assembly existed only by statute; it had no right to assume parliamentary privileges by common law. The common law applied to parliament but not to the colonial legislature.

---

24 '[T]hrowing opposition', Donaldson, Assembly, *Sydney Morning Herald*, 8 August 1856; 'dark', Murray, Assembly, *Sydney Morning Herald*, 24 May 1856.
25 Donaldson, Assembly, *Sydney Morning Herald*, 5 June 1856.
26 Plunkett, Assembly, *Sydney Morning Herald*, 15 August 1856.

The House needed to pass an act on the rights and privileges of the House.[27] In August 1856, the word 'Honourable' was struck from the names of the members appointed to the Library Committee. They were 'elected', said Martin; only members of the Executive Council could be called 'Honourable'.[28] John Hay, member for Murrumbidgee, decried the means by which the first Cowper ministry had been appointed—again, by the governor-general. It seemed they were to have 'a series of revolutions'. This was 'extremely dangerous' and 'would run the risk of upsetting constitutional government altogether'.[29] Martin, the incoming and unpopular attorney-general, said the Donaldson ministry had 'obstructed the country going out when they did'.[30] Darvall claimed the very position of the attorney-general was dangerous in New South Wales. He could 'send the whole of the members of that House to trial' and 'instances were not wanting in the history of England'.[31] Certainties became hollow.

The standard of debate rapidly declined in the first Cowper ministry, and all admitted it was so—'horrible', according to Robertson. The personal reputation of Martin and his unsuitability for the position of attorney-general was accompanied with the throwing of invitation cards across the table, intimations of meeting in a field with swords and guns and frequent reference—perhaps in response to the drawing rooms brought into discussion in the House—to 'manliness' and 'unmanliness'.[32]

'The people' made a renewed appearance in these heated debates over who should govern or who should be attorney-general. The people 'knew nothing' of the barristers who had signed a petition against the appointment of Martin as attorney-general. Why should barristers 'govern the country'?[33] The position of 'the public man' was spoken of; his private life was to be interrogated. The emphasis on personal history resulted in William Macleay making the statement that 'the character of every public man was public property'.[34] It had become so in this session when women's calling cards were thrown across the table and it was suggested that Martin would be forgiven for such an act by 'the ladies of New South Wales'.[35] The female

---

27 Forster, Assembly, *Sydney Morning Herald*, 5 June 1856.
28 Martin, Assembly, *Sydney Morning Herald*, 13 August 1856.
29 Assembly, *Sydney Morning Herald*, 18 September 1856.
30 Martin, Assembly, *Sydney Morning Herald*, 18 September 1856.
31 Darvall, Assembly, *Empire*, 23 September 1856.
32 Robertson, Assembly, *Sydney Morning Herald*, 18 September 1856, 19 September 1856.
33 Robertson, Assembly, *Empire*, 23 September 1856.
34 Macleay, Assembly, *Empire*, 23 September 1856.
35 Flood, Assembly, *Sydney Morning Herald*, 24 September 1856.

was invoked in reference to the behaviour of members: they resembled 'housemaids' quarrelling, they were 'an old lady's tea party'.[36] The idea of manliness invoked by members of the House was related to 'fair play'. It was the opposite of the underhanded work of 'party'.[37] It was related to 'sympathy and good feeling' by Plunkett.[38] The 'public man' was also addressed: the proper 'test of fitness for office should be intelligence, industry and virtue', according to Robertson.[39] Instead, according to Arnold, it had been determined 'by the cut of the coat, the fall of the necktie, some trick of millinery'.[40] The shift between both ministries was one of discourse. Both had 'come in the window', but the appointment of Martin as attorney-general had introduced ideas of what had formerly been thought to be private into the language of the House and this resulted in vitriol and supposed threats of violence. Though the House behaved in a more orderly manner after 1857, when it began to demonstrate a sense of itself as a House with 'rules' and 'feelings', it could quickly revert to this realm of violence and emotion.[41]

Even though the House remained porous to the Crown after 1857, 'party' was completely accepted and, when Martin claimed that Cowper had a 'cabinet' that met regularly to determine the business of the government, there was no uproar at all; his complaint was ignored.[42] However, there were other threats, and these were internal. Members of both houses were individual occupiers of squatting land or members of squatting firms and in terms of questions related to land there were calls for such interests to be registered and made publicly available. Piddington referred to these men as 'the squattocracy'. The vote for a register of land was lost nine

---

36 Holt, Assembly, *Sydney Morning Herald*, 24 September 1856.
37 Nichols, Assembly, *Sydney Morning Herald*, 24 September 1856.
38 Plunkett, Assembly, *Sydney Morning Herald*, 19 September 1856.
39 Robertson, Assembly, *Empire*, 24 September 1856.
40 Arnold, Assembly, *Empire*, 24 September 1856.
41 'Irregular debate would be satisfactory to no-one', Speaker, Assembly, *Sydney Morning Herald*, 14 January 1857. Yet, in the same session, Solicitor-General Darvall threatened Mr Murray, walking up to where he sat, saying something inaudible and leaving the chamber, 'provoking a duel'. Cowper and Donaldson clashed in 1858 over religious ministers being 'pests to society'. *Empire*, 27 March 1858. An 'unparliamentary and degrading discussion', in which Donaldson stated that he would never attack a man 'except he would meet him face-to-face', was had in January 1859. *Sydney Morning Herald*, 7 January 1859. 'Hanging would be too good' for a government accused of corruption, claimed Dickinson. Assembly, *Sydney Morning Herald*, 8 October 1859. 'Rules': Cowper referred to 'the practice of Parliament laid down in May with regard to giving delinquents into custody of the serjeant at arms until apology', *Sydney Morning Herald*, 14 January 1857. 'In accordance with Parliamentary usage questions should be asked only either for the purposes of eliciting a fact from the Government or for ascertaining its intention upon any issue.' Martin, Assembly, *Empire*, 18 December 1857.
42 Martin, Assembly, *Freeman's Journal*, 20 November 1858.

to 18 votes, the opposing argument expressed by Darvall that these were 'private affairs'.[43] Squatters were asked not to vote in legislation that would benefit their interests in 1857 in a vote on the Assessment Bill. Forster responded that this would include most people in the House and very few would be able to vote; why should not such a request apply in other cases? Robertson said 36 members of the House held pastoral lands and there were only 54 members of the House in total; the House could not attempt to vote without 20 members.[44] Though the threat was considerably lessened by the willingness of many of the squatter members to accept the legislation, considering it was the best that could be obtained and without it worse might be in store, this debate did break up the sense of the House as something above private interests. Something of the rhetorical claims involving 'the people' or 'the country' was lost in favour of pragmatism. The rhetoric was becoming tempered and the House shifting to stable ground.

Of equal threat, and perhaps more representative of the House protecting itself, were the 'uneducated' who might be brought into the House by the introduction of universal suffrage in 1858. There was 'a great fear' of these men, according to Murray. Far from defending them, the democratic Daniel Deniehy stated that 'democracy should be established on the basis of education and refinement'. There was 'no greater test of liberals than education and all that was most dear to him would recognize education'. On his sitting down, he was loudly cheered by both sides of the House.[45] Donaldson did not want the franchise to be in the hands of 'the most unthinking portion of the population'. Henry Parkes also supported a plan that would admit a 'number of educated persons—born and educated in the colony'.[46] Gentlemen, faced with universal suffrage, responded by reifying the only asset they had outside money and land: education, from which had come the classical quotes and the Latin. A new kind of snobbery would influence generations of Australians who would see education as essential for advancement. Reading the newspapers in the public houses would give democratic man the desolate feeling that he was inadequate in comparison with the educated members of the House.

---

43 Piddington, Assembly, *Sydney Morning Herald*, 14 January 1857.
44 Piddington, Forster, Robertson, Assembly, *Empire*, 27 December 1857.
45 Deniehy, Assembly, *Northern Times*, 11 November 1858.
46 Donaldson, Parkes, Assembly, *Empire*, 7 May 1858.

Legal officials

At the centre of acrimony were officers of the law. Judges in the council, barristers with their petitions against Martin and the position of attorney-general himself—a man with far too much power who could put them all in gaol if he wished. Forster suggested in 1857 that it was not 'absolutely necessary' under the *Constitution Act* that the attorney-general or solicitor-general should be a barrister or attorney; 'it was quite competent for a layman to hold either of these offices'.[47] In August 1858, he claimed that 'the sooner they got rid of the connection between the Crown Law Officers and the government the better'.[48] By 1859 it was argued neither of these officers needed to be part of the ministry. They could both simply be replaced with a minister for justice, the only concern being the House would not want to be 'saddled with the salaries of two Crown Law Officers, (hear, hear)'.[49] In 1858 Deniehy said he could not understand why they needed two Crown law solicitors; their duties could be performed by 'any clerk'.[50]

Readers of the language of the House would see the attorneys-general did not command respect and at times were regarded with suspicion. This was not improved by Attorney-General Martin's resignation from the Cowper ministry in November 1858, when he stated he had felt obligated to stay with the ministry—'coerced' even. He was increasingly at odds with them and quite often absent from the House.[51] The appointment of Lyttleton Holyoake Bayley as attorney-general two months after he arrived in the colony resulted in another petition from the Bar. He was 'pitchforked' into the House, said Deniehy, 'local politics sprang out of local ties' and this grandson of English justice Bayley was a 'matter of convenience'. Plunkett said that Bayley was 'sprung from that dark antiquated race, the old Tories of England and he came here to join an ultra-radical government'.[52] The spectre of the Crown was invoked in such comparisons. In 1860 Manning only accepted the position of attorney-general in the proposed Forster ministry if he was 'in no way identified with the general policy of the Government or to take part in any political matters'. He would only advise the Crown on legal questions and give attention to the public justice of the

---

47 Forster, Assembly, *Sydney Morning Herald*, 28 August 1857.
48 Forster, Assembly, *Sydney Morning Herald*, 10 November 1858.
49 Rotton, Assembly, *Sydney Morning Herald*, 22 September 1859.
50 Deniehy, Assembly, *Sydney Morning Herald*, 30 July 1858.
51 Martin, Assembly, *Freeman's Journal*, 20 November 1858.
52 Deniehy, Plunkett, Assembly, *Sydney Morning Herald*, 9 February 1859.

country.[53] The main duties of the attorney-general were to be kept 'sacredly clear from all political influences or the suspicion of them'.[54] This would prove untenable without alteration of the law and Denison suggested that Manning resign. Manning was attempting to create an independent role, in much the same way as Stephen had suggested; he wished to be above politics. Denison wrote: 'I leave it to you whether you would send me a formal resignation from your office as Attorney General or leave me quietly to infer that in the resignation of Forster and his colleagues you were included.'[55] The new Cowper government was forced to offer Manning a commission to attend the Bathurst Assizes since he would not accept the position of attorney-general in the Cabinet. Manning would act as attorney-general until the end of the assizes.[56] The uncertainty of the position of attorney-general was the uncertainty of the place of law in the new democracy. This instability in government, evident in Martin and Manning, would also make the legal system seem wobbly, unable to properly find its feet in relation to the people.

Certainly, the House did not always trust the magistrates either. Flood, in the debates over the *Masters and Servants Act*, stated in August 1856 that he 'was disinclined to delegate any further power to the magistrates of the interior than they at present possessed. They paid very little attention to the law and less to the justice of cases brought before them.'[57]

Antecedents: The table and the council

Though 'the people' were referred to in the House in times of crisis, they had more presence in the earlier Legislative Council. The business of that body consisted of asking the governor to 'lay papers on the table' respecting an issue that might concern them and working in committee on particular issues. Kerry Mills argues that committees broadened democratic processes through the invitation of witnesses to participate.[58] The council also recorded numbers of petitions from the inhabitants of different districts

---

53 Manning to Forster, 18 February 1860, Papers of William Montagu Manning, ML, MSS 942/3.
54 Denison to Manning, 20 February 1860, Papers of William Montagu Manning.
55 Denison to Manning, 8 March 1860, Papers of William Montagu Manning.
56 Cowper to Manning, 9 March 1860, Papers of William Montagu Manning.
57 Flood, Assembly, *Sydney Morning Herald*, 14 August 1856.
58 Kerry Mills, 'Lawmakers, Select Committees and the Birth of Democracy in New South Wales, 1843–1855', *Journal of Australian Colonial History* 14 (2012): 131–54.

on local and colonial concerns. These petitions represented the voice of the people, regardless of how much 'rampant democracy' was distrusted by William Charles Wentworth.[59]

The table in the council became a point of contestation in 1850–56. This elected body could needle the governor for information to be 'placed on the table'. In many incidences, this involved law. In 1850 the governor had appointed William Whaley Billyard as civil Crown solicitor and Darvall stated that 'no recommendation from the authority of the Mother Country should give any person the right to be appointed to any office'. This was the first strand of references to law—that concerning the authority of the governor. The language was forthright. The system of appointments that prevailed was 'productive of injury to the public service and of unnecessary expenditure of revenue'.[60] The second strand involved individual cases in which inconsistencies and injustices of magistrates and police were discussed.[61] The governor answered for the failings of justice in the colony. Law was identified as being not only of English derivation, but also closely tied to the Crown's interests.

The 1854 debate over the Law of Evidence Bill followed a similar pattern, in which what was representative of the interests of England was contested. Darvall claimed that the solicitor-general seemed 'prepared to push the adoption of the reforms in the law of England to the greatest extent and the principle was bad'. Murray stated that 'they ought to be very cautious in the policy to which they had hitherto adhered of adopting the law of England without reference to the differences of circumstances in this colony'. The heat of the debate concerned the provision that wives be allowed to give evidence in cases involving their husbands. 'There was something rotten in it,' claimed Broadhurst. The solicitor-general replied that wives in the colony were involved in business and to say that a wife had no right to interfere with the affairs of her husband was to argue that 'women be kept in a perpetual state of slavery'. Manning unfortunately referred to England in his response: the intelligent weight of the legal profession in England supported the Bill, the 'public feeling of the people in England' supported the Bill.[62] This was

---

59 Wentworth, Minutes of the Legislative Council, 1 May 1851, Parliament of New South Wales, *Hansard & House Papers*, www.parliament.nsw.gov.au/hansard/Pages/Comprehensive-index-to-all-parliamentary-document.aspx [hereinafter *Hansard*].
60 Darvall, 16 July 1850, *Hansard*.
61 Isabella Osbourne, 28 June 1854; William John King, 7 July 1854; William Walker, 14 September 1854; Mary Singleton, 2 August 1854; John Walker, 14 September 1854.
62 Murray, Broadhurst, Manning, Council, 21 July 1854.

not what the council wanted to hear; the motion to recommend the Bill was defeated 16 to ten.[63] The solicitor-general returned with the Bill a week later. The offensive clauses concerning husband and wife, he said, were to be abandoned. The Bill was passed on 2 August 1854.

It is difficult to see the activities of the council outside this permanent tension with England and its representative. The needling would continue and the language become more aggressive. In September 1854 Cowper moved that 'the Government of the Colony as at present administered does not possess the confidence of this house'. Also: '[T]he Council resolves to postpone the estimation of the Estimates for the year 1855, until it is assured the Public Expenditure will be made under a Government formed upon the principle of ministerial responsibility.' Cowper's targets were the inefficiency and carelessness of the government in managing public funds, but 'the painful feeling of separation between the representative portion of the Legislature was increasing every week'. The colonial secretary had thrown a return to a member rather than place it on the table of the House; he spoke in such a subdued voice it was hard to hear his explanations. A report had been submitted to the secretary of state without coming before the council. The government of the colony was 'the most inefficient, the most profligate and, he must add, the most corrupt in the world'.[64] Cowper claimed he did not include the attorney-general or the solicitor-general in his accusations but the solicitor-general stated that all members of the government were included in the critique, thereby aligning both legal officers with the executive. The colonial secretary brought the weight of the imperial administration into the chamber: the motion brought by Cowper was 'illegal', the council had 'no right' and it was the product of 'a decided and wilful opposition'. There was 'some reason in the background'.[65] In the ensuing debate, Campbell claimed that only 'a manifestation out doors' had opposed the government, which 'wished to retain this colony as a penal settlement'. To replace the convict system, they had introduced the *Assisted Immigration Act*; yet another form of slavery, the *Masters and Servants Act*; and the *Seaman's Act*, which produced the same effect: 'the condition of serfdom'.[66] This was an appeal to the streets. The governor had been guilty of the 'grossest misrepresentation, he would say lying and deceit to maintain

---

63 Council, 21 July 1854.
64 Cowper, Council, 30 September 1854.
65 Manning, Cowper, Council, *Sydney Morning Herald*, 21 October 1854.
66 Campbell, Council, *Sydney Morning Herald*, 21 October 1854.

his policy'.[67] Henry Parkes saw no chance of the resolution being passed but it was brought up 'with the view of stirring up a wholesome and proper public spirit, and for the purpose of vindicating the grandeur and majesty of moral truth'. He stated that 'all great events arise out of small ones—even revolutions have their origin in this way'.[68]

The no-confidence motion was lost 29 votes to 10, but something more ominous was suggested by Parkes, who asked a week after the debate why constables 'dressed as gentlemen' were placed within the vicinity of the council. The inspector of police replied that his 'attention had been drawn to the infringement of the rules of the house. The speaker had expressed his opinion of the recurrence of sentiments which had occurred [if it] was renewed he should require the gallery to be cleared.'[69] The matter was not further taken up and the issue was defused by humour over the New Zealand Parliament and similar occurrences. The feint of discussion, the performance of rhetoric, becomes apparent in such a lack of interest in pursuing the executive further on this. The rhetoric, however, was how ordinary people understood the urgency of truly representative government.

First Nations

Into such a rhetoric came descriptions of Aboriginal people. They were more present in the debates of the council than the later assembly and the ways in which they appeared were bound up with the estimates. English reaction to colonial representations was often lukewarm. When William Charles Wentworth and Edward Deas Thomson went to England to oversee the Constitution Bill, they were largely ignored. Great interest was expressed in the defence capacity of the colony and the 59th Regiment was dispatched from Hong Kong, but attempts to meet with officials were met with claims that there was too much business to make time for the delegation from New South Wales.[70] This ignoring of colonial issues, particularly around Aboriginal people, was responsible for an ad hoc approach to their plight, according to Ann Curthoys and Jessie Mitchell.[71] Yet, in the rhetoric of the House, discussions of First Nations people occurred in close proximity to

---

67 ibid.
68 Parkes, Council, *Sydney Morning Herald*, 21 October 1854.
69 Inspector-General of Police, 26 September 1854, *Hansard*.
70 Deas Thomson, Assembly, 24 September 1856.
71 Curthoys and Mitchell, *Taking Liberty*, 10.

discussions about imperial control and particularly the battleground of the estimates. The executive was meant to provide the estimates of expenditure for the coming year to be approved by the council and, in October 1854, the estimates were delayed by Cowper's motion of no confidence. The increase in Native Police near the Victorian border because of large numbers of travellers was a measure undertaken by the executive,[72] but it was also a fiscal matter, and money, particularly the money belonging to the taxpaying colonists, was a sore point and would continue to be in the assembly. In August 1856 Buckley asked for information on the management of the Native Police and, in November, Forster asked about claims by individuals who supplied the Native Police under Frederick Walker and how the rations had been disposed of.[73]

Cowper, on 7 September 1854, brought up a report in the *Englishman*, which he read out. An eyewitness was at a squatter's homestead during the process of sheep washing. Suddenly the Native Police rode up under the command of a European officer and attacked several peaceful and unarmed Aboriginal people in the presence of the master of the station. When all were killed, mutilated or dispersed, a man who had hidden was discovered and dragged forth and shot. The newspaper claimed that 'the outrage was perpetuated under the authority of the British uniform and before the eyes of English witnesses'.[74] This report in Cowper's hands became a conflation of incompetence, murder and the administration together, particularly since the uniform was 'British'. Thus, the Native Police represented more than the force itself and the subsequent calls for inquiry came from that conflation. Cowper mentioned the Native Police again in his no-confidence motion speech: 'Every member who spoke afterwards and who was connected with the district in which the officer was employed, seemed quite aware of the reports of which the Government professed to be entirely ignorant.'[75] Government incompetence was underlined.

The Native Police was uncertainly established. The initial idea was neither military nor police in its conception and, at times, not at all 'Native'. It had a loose relationship to the state and emerged out of two conflicting pressures. The first involved the relationship to England, shown by Zoe Laidlaw to be

---

72 Council, 10 May 1853.
73 Buckley, Assembly, *Sydney Morning Herald*, 20 August 1856; Forster, Assembly, *Sydney Morning Herald*, 5 November 1856.
74 Cowper, Assembly, *Sydney Morning Herald*, 7 September 1854.
75 Cowper, Assembly, *Sydney Morning Herald*, 30 September 1854.

influenced by private connections and a new interest in efficiency.[76] Ann Curthoys and Jessie Mitchell have shown there were concerns in England about colonial brutality and requests from the Australian colonies for troops made through private letters as much as public representation.[77] The other concern was expenditure: neither the British Government nor the Australian colonies wanted to spend any money on solving the problems of the violence of expansion. Expenditure was fair game for any political opponent of these governments. Consequently, the administration was answerable for violence.[78] Into this environment came Frederick Walker with his 'scheme' of Native Police in 1849.[79] This involved recruiting young Aboriginal men. He received accolades for its effectiveness at first. He recruited from the Murray River and later the Clarence River. The relationship between government and the Native Police was uncertain because the Native Police were not administered by the police or by the regiments but by the colonial secretary, who appeared to be uncertain of their movements and appointments as early as 1855.[80] Squatter disunity at the inquiry into the Dawson River murders in 1858 showed that Walker had lifted the Native Police well out of the controls of the colonial secretary.[81] The Native Police went from run to run being entertained and fed by selected squatters. So, a quasi-state of Walker's operated by favour. This follows the selective pattern of squatters generally in their violent attacks.[82]

Walker's Aboriginal troopers were about the Condamine River in 1858 'committing depredations' and 'stealing ammunition' after Walker was dismissed. Some of them joined the Condamine contingent of the Native Police but they 'behaved badly' and the officer there 'did not know where the others had gone'.[83] But Walker himself did not leave his profession after

---

76   Zoë Laidlaw, *Colonial Connections, 1815–45: Patronage, the Information Revolution and Colonial Government* (Manchester: Manchester University Press, 2005), 72.
77   Curthoys and Mitchell, *Taking Liberty*, 172.
78   ibid., 30.
79   Paul Dillon, *Frederick Walker* (Sydney: Self-published, 2017), 65–71; *Sydney Morning Herald*, 4 February 1857.
80   Colonial Secretary to Native Police, 19 June 1855; Colonial Secretary to John Connell Bligh, 27 June 1855; Colonial Secretary to Native Police Commandant Fraylan, 26 June 1855; Colonial Secretary Letters to Judicial Establishment, State Records, SR 4/3858.
81   Evidence of Maurice Charles O'Connell, *Select Committee of the Legislative Assembly on Murders by the Aborigines on the Dawson River*, New South Wales Legislative Council, *Votes and Proceedings*, 1858, vol. 2, State Library of NSW, Q328.9106/6, 2 [hereinafter *Select Committee on Dawson River Murders*].
82   Edmond Morey, 'Reminiscences of a Pioneer in New South Wales', extracted from *Sydney Mail*, 30 October 1907 to 29 January 1908, ML, State Library of NSW, DS MSQ326; Charles Grant Tindal to Charles Tindal, 21 August 1853, Tindal Family Papers, ML, A2068.
83   Evidence of Maurice O'Connell, *Select Committee on Dawson River Murders*, 28.

his dismissal; rather, he set himself up with 'a small native force of his own about Euroombah and Hornet Bank', William Archer explained that 'some of the neighbouring squatters keep him to patrol about their stations'.[84]

Maurice O'Connell envisaged that the Native Police should have been reformed:

> Laws should be passed authorizing enlistment, constituting tribunals for the trial of offences and enacting summary punishments for infractions of discipline and crimes which are more dangerous to the community when liable to be committed by men with arms in their hands and assembled together in large numbers than when springing from the actions of isolated individuals.[85]

William Archer, in his evidence before the inquiry, said that the Native Police would be very much better 'if the whole thing was put on a legal footing—making their embodiment and giving them fire arms, legal'.[86] Archer had unwittingly pointed out how far from state control the idea of the Native Police had become by 1858.

The estimates brought the Native Police into political rhetoric, their persons representing the maladministration of the Crown. Yet, Aboriginal people were also represented in other ways. Attorney-General Plunkett brought up in discussion of the *Masters and Servants Act* the fact that he had long argued 'for the furtherance of the administration of justice' that Aboriginal people should be allowed to make statements in courts of justice, 'where their testimony might tend to corroborate that of other and Christian men, or like approvers', but 'the idea was scouted out of the house'. Plunkett believed the Aborigines were innocent and 'more worthy of credit' than the Chinese, who were 'allowed to be sworn on their cups and saucers'.[87] Plunkett was here utilising Aboriginal people in an argument against Chinese and Indian immigration. British people would not come to the colony if they were to be put on the same footing as 'Chinese or Hindoos'. Henry Parkes replied that he was not 'so illiberal' as to 'dislike a man on account of his complexion' and 'he knew of no more affecting a sight than that of the Aboriginal Jacky Jacky kneeling over his dying master'.[88] There was loud and prolonged cheering at this sentimental image, but it too was

---

84 Evidence of William Archer, *Select Committee on Dawson River Murders*, 62.
85 Appendix A, Maurice O'Connell, *Select Committee on Dawson River Murders*.
86 Evidence of William Archer, *Select Committee on Dawson River Murders*, 121.
87 Plunkett, Assembly, *Sydney Morning Herald*, 7 July 1854.
88 Parkes, Assembly, *Sydney Morning Herald*, 7 July 1854.

used against the Chinese, who were, according to Parkes, a cause of 'crime'. What was needed in the colony were Germans and Britons. The innocent and sentimentalised Aboriginal person in these references may be linked to romantic racism and early Victorian notions of sentimentality.[89] An image of Aboriginal people was created in the council and the assembly. It was not an Exeter Hall dialogue, emphasising a common humanity, which may have been found in elements of the press; rather, there was this romantic and sentimental perspective. There were elements of this in how Aboriginal people would figure in the courts.

Democracy on the ground

All historians of this period in Australia have stressed the participatory nature of democracy.[90] But democracy was also highly ritualised in local areas, not only at election time but also in public meetings and discussions. Election processions included colours and banners.[91] Lynn Hunt has discussed the symbolism and Mona Ozouf the pageantry of the French Revolution. Politics carried symbol and ritual.[92] Even corruption had its rituals in England: distributing money in public houses in exchange for votes was highly formalised.[93] What marked democratic ideals in New South Wales was the formality surrounding petitions, meetings and elections.[94] At the goldfields and in Armidale, people without the franchise requested that local members come each year and explain what they had done for the local population.[95] The work of democracy involved public meetings, called for any purpose, with voting and a series of recommendations to government. Public houses were the site of such meetings. Form was rigorously adhered to, there was always a chairman and a pre-arranged number of speakers. While crowds could call out and attempt to interrupt, they could not speak from the floor.[96]

---

89   Walter E. Houghton, *The Victorian Frame of Mind, 1830–1870* (New Haven: Yale University Press, 1957), 416.
90   Bongiorno and Messner, 'New England'; Hirst, *Freedom on the Fatal Shore*; Atkinson, *The Europeans in Australia*; Thompson, *The Seeds of Democracy*; Irving, *The Southern Tree of Liberty*.
91   *Maitland Mercury*, 14 January 1843, 20 May 1843, 24 June 1843. 'Mr Dangar was escorted to the hustings by a number of electors on horseback carrying his colours true blue and currency blue.'
92   Lynn Hunt, *Politics, Culture and Class in the French Revolution* (Berkeley: University of California Press, 1988); Mona Ozouf, *Festivals and the French Revolution*, trans. Alan Sheridan (Cambridge: Harvard University Press, 1988).
93   Frank O'Gorman, *Voters, Patrons and Parties: The Unreformed Electoral System of Hanoverian England, 1734–1832* (Oxford: Clarendon Press, 1989).
94   *Armidale Express and New England Advertiser*, [hereinafter *Armidale Express*], 16 May 1857.
95   *Armidale Express*, 22 August 1857.
96   Thompson, *The Seeds of Democracy*, 216–75; *Northern Times*, 16 June 1858; *Moreton Bay Courier*, 11 November 1854; *Empire*, 6 April 1853.

Elections themselves were rowdy and difficult occasions. This was largely because of the presence of electoral agents, who were employed to obtain votes for a candidate. In 1856 the candidate Byrnes at Parramatta claimed that payments had been made by agents to voters in favour of his opponent, Parker. This 'was not to blame Parker himself', implying that agents acted independently to assure the election of candidates.[97] At the Gwydir and Liverpool Plains election in May 1856, Mr Morris 'or his agents' gave instructions to publicans at the diggings to keep open on polling day and a sum was placed in their hands to treat those who would vote in Morris's favour.[98] That publicans encouraged contests and rivalry to make profit was suggested by temperance organisations in 1859. Political meetings always took place at public houses and thirsty listeners were obliged by a grasping publican; 'the wider the gap we can create between politics and public houses the better'.[99] This ability to be agents further extended the power of publicans; their management of credit and debt and money was entangled with electioneering.

The rhetoric of the early democracy would influence the way law was interpreted by local populations, by constables and by magistrates. Legal officials in Sydney were not necessarily to be respected. They were linked to England, they sought to introduce laws unsuitable for the colony and they did not mind their place in the House. Before 1859 people who did not have the franchise felt themselves to be represented and wished to keep those representatives to task; they did this through the highly formalised meeting structure as well as in the drinking and pageantry around elections. These were also the people who made use of law.

---

97 *Empire*, 15 October 1856.
98 *Empire*, 8 May 1856.
99 *Australian Home Companion and Band of Hope Journal*, 18 June 1859.

2

South

In August 1850, Hugh Hamon Massie, Justice of the Peace, wrote to the attorney-general about a quarrel between Thomas Smyth and William Thomas of Pambula. Thomas had stolen a watch from Smyth. This letter opens a kind of fruit in which we comprehend some of the purposes to which law was put. The magistrate Massie had both the inclination and the time to carefully explain the history of an argument:

> [T]he Prosecutor *did* give a watch to the prisoner in exchange for a horse alleged to have gone astray, but which had been sold with the knowledge of Thomas, out of the Queanbeyan pound some time previous to the exchange.[1]

When Smyth found out the horse had been sold, he 'was very indignant … and made no secret of his intention of proceeding against Thomas for having made the illegal sale of a horse'. He claimed that while drinking together Smyth had stolen his watch. The watch 'having no glass' was 'kept in a tin box, wrapped up in a silk handkerchief' and, together with 12 receipts, was snatched off the table at Hibberd's public house by Thomas. Magistrate Massie thought the real purpose of the theft was to obtain the receipt that Thomas had written when selling the horse. The next day Thomas gave all the receipts back except for the crucial one and did not return the watch. He said his child had found the receipts in the creek. Smyth claimed he went for Constable Whelan the moment after he was robbed, but Whelan in his evidence said that he came the next day. Massie thought that Whelan was drunk and had forgotten the incident.

---

1   *R v William Thomas* 1850, 4, SR 9/6397.

Map 2.1: The South Coast and hinterland of New South Wales
Source: W. Hughes, London G. Phillip and Son, circa 1858, State Library of New South Wales, MLZ/M1 806/1858/1.

Massie's beautifully written cover letter jarred with the information provided in the deposition in which Smyth acknowledged under cross-examination by Thomas that he did wait a day to go to the constable. He said, 'I wanted to keep it quiet till I had a chance of getting my property out of your house.'

Far from being easily explained by Constable Whelan being drunk and forgetting the day, as Massie suggested, the case was a muddle of claims and counterclaims, all of which sit side by side in the depositions. This confusion was intensified in the evidence of Whelan, who had 'heard' that Smyth had been robbed by 'two exiles from the Adelaide' and had proceeded in pursuit, searching for the two men, taking their money and showing it to Smyth. 'They are innocent men,' said Smyth; it was Thomas who had robbed him. Called back from Bega to execute a search warrant, Whelan found a watch in a desk in Thomas's house. He had heard both parties arguing over a watch and a horse, 'but the watch they were talking about was a different one altogether from the one with which the prisoner is charged'.

Constable Whelan was utterly at the service of Smyth, both in returning from Bega and in holding off his pursuit of Thomas at Smyth's request. Smyth was a labourer working with a shoemaker, yet in this case, involving a watch without a glass cover wrapped in a silk handkerchief, he commanded the power of the legal system. The components of this case—the erroneous long letter of explanation, the cross-examination of the defendant by the accused, the constable at the service of the local population, no matter how poor—characterise the majority of the 37 cases from the coastal area stretching from Wollongong to Eden. Law was accessed through threads of local dispute and ill feeling and constables were called for rather than acting independently. Massie's letter is markedly intimate in tone; he wrote to the attorney-general as though they jointly had a problem to solve, and this was also common to the region. The depositions were perfect, with little crossing out, which may suggest copying but they have not been edited by Massie, the language remains that of the people.

Asides in this case give some idea of the region's culture. Economic life stretched inland to Queanbeyan and receipts were important to keep as proof of ownership or sale. Constable Whelan travelled up and down the coast, from Pambula to Eden and to Bega. Mrs Thomas could imply that the desk found in her bedroom belonged to the wealthy Mr Imlay. No-one thought it unusual she should be minding it. There was suggestion of a 'Blackfellow' in Hibbard's public house; it was quite believable that he would be there. Everyone in this case is described as drunk at one time or other, apart from Massie himself. At Robertson's public house, Constable Whelan took all of Smyth's money, receipts and a watch and gave them to the wife of Robertson to keep for Smyth. The next morning, Mrs Robertson returned all the money apart from 3 shillings that Smyth had spent on drink, and he then took the money to another public house. The 'exiles from the Adelaide', convicts, were travelling to Mr Walker's 'Wallumla' and had money in their possession and called for three bottles of rum to travel with. Smyth was to travel with them up the country. The case gives a snapshot of the look and feel of European colonisation.

Aboriginal people of the South Coast (see Map 2.1) come from several different groups but at the time of writing refer to themselves generally as Yuin or the Yuin Nation. Websites give their history and what they think important to understand about their history.[2] To keep to the coast as this chapter does is to contradict the inland links of Yuin people, whose traditional country extends far further inland. This chapter follows the colonised coast, which saw itself as a separate region.

The South Coast from Wollongong to Eden was well-watered country, according to J.C. Byrne in 1848, but along the sea coast, Twofold Bay and Broulee were the only points where goods could be shipped and landed with safety.[3] Land was originally occupied for sheep and cattle runs. Whaling parties were described at Eden in 1858, though this was a seasonal industry.[4] Twofold Bay was 'originally occupied by Dr Imlay' and 'Mr Boyd purchased some sections of land where he founded a township' servicing the steamer trade as a port.[5] Mark McKenna has set out some of the early history of the Imlays and other squatting families in the district.[6] Four Manning brothers, including the solicitor-general and later attorney-general William Montagu Manning and Edwin and Robert Tooth formed the Twofold Bay Pastoral Association on 400,000 acres (1,619 square kilometres) around Pambula in 1854.[7] The Shoalhaven had been occupied from 1822 by the company Berry and Wollstonecraft, which obtained government grants of land. By 1850 Alexander Berry had carved up parts of the estate into small blocks, which he rented to tenants.[8] The *Illawarra Mercury* could report in

---

2   walc.com.au/our-culture-and-heritage/ [page discontinued]; Eden Local Aboriginal Land Council website: alc.org.au/land_council/eden/; Yuin & Monaro: Eden Community website: yuin-monaro.storylines.com.au/.
3   J.C. Byrne, *Twelve Years' Wandering in the British Colonies from 1835 to 1847*, 2 vols (London: Richard Bentley, 1848), 156–57.
4   *Illawarra Mercury*, 2 August 1858.
5   Byrne, *Twelve Years' Wandering in the British Colonies*, 156.
6   Mark McKenna, *Looking for Blackfellows Point: An Australian History of Place* (Sydney: UNSW Press, 2002), 38–40.
7   Angela George and Pat Raymond, 'Oakland's Oak Trees', Heritage Report (Pambula, NSW, n.d.), hiddenheritage.com.au/heritage-object/?object_id=82 [page discontinued].
8   Thomas M. Perry, 'Alexander Berry (1781–1873)', *Australian Dictionary of Biography* (Canberra: National Centre of Biography, The Australian National University, 1966), adb.anu.edu.au/biography/berry-alexander-1773/text1987.

1857 that 'the navigable portion of the Shoalhaven extends about 35 miles [56 kilometres] from the heads … and every available inch on each side of the river bank the whole length is in the hands of private individuals, and nearly all under cultivation'.[9]

This pattern could be found along the coast and small farmers cultivated crops for their Sydney agents, but the newspaper suggested many of these agents were unscrupulous.[10] Magistrates travelled up and down the coast and there were two benches that covered the region.[11] The servants of the larger estates, these farmers and the service industries of stores, tradesmen and public houses made up the non-Aboriginal population. The *Illawarra Mercury* was first published in 1855 in Wollongong and had correspondents from Bega and the Shoalhaven. Settlements were at Eden, Bombala, Kiama, Wollongong, Pambula and Broulee. Justices were Henry Hamon Massie, the Commissioner of Crown Lands and police magistrate; Arthur Manning, brother of the solicitor-general and later attorney-general, William Montagu Manning; James Walker, William Walker, Andrew de Mestre, Andrew Alcorn, Robert Menzies, Kenneth Mackenzie, George Hibb, Robert Perrot and Thomas Chapman. In 1854 the Sydney-based *People's Advocate* Shoalhaven correspondent wrote: '[S]o little is there to occupy the attention of the Magistrates that they only are required to attend the Bench once a month, and the Court of Requests once in three months.'[12]

In 1857 Patrick Murray, clerk of the bench at Eden, was appointed police magistrate, combining the duties of clerk with that of magistrate.[13]

Aboriginal subjects

The *Illawarra Mercury* reported the body of an Aboriginal woman being found near Mr McCarthy's inn on the Shoalhaven River in 1856. From marks on her body, it appeared she was murdered but 'by white or black is unknown'.[14] In 1858 an Aboriginal man named Billy Bailey was murdered in Terara Brush on the Shoalhaven and it was suspected that it

---

9   *Illawarra Mercury*, 2 November 1857.
10 ibid.
11 Eden Bench Book, State Archives Collection, SR 4/6501; and Kiama Bench Book, State Archives Collection, SR 4/5575, part 4/5576-77.
12 *People's Advocate*, 16 September 1854.
13 *Illawarra Mercury*, 21 December 1857.
14 *Illawarra Mercury*, 15 September 1856.

was 'the handiwork of Blackfellows' because the farm labourers of Terara 'heard the yells of the Blacks but supposed it was their usual drinking rows'.[15] There was no inquiry into either of these deaths and they indicate how dangerous the landscape was for individual Aboriginal people and how many uncounted deaths there were of Aboriginal people living close to or with non-Aboriginal people. Aboriginal people were not subjects of the law in these two incidents and Lisa Ford, and Heather Douglas and Mark Finnane would see this as part of the halting and uncertain nature of legal sovereignty.[16] That these deaths were reported in the local newspaper, however, is of significance because they became 'public', more than talk or rumour. The newspaper shows some kind of conscience over Aboriginal death despite its blasé assumption that, of course, no case would be held. This curious combination of public concern for deaths alongside brutality itself is the face of the occupation of Aboriginal country on the South Coast and would be evinced in the kinds of cases in which Aboriginal people appeared in the 1850s.

There was one inquest into the death of an Aboriginal man, Cabawn Mickey, on the South Coast, at Broulee in 1852, instituted by the man who shot him, the publican Robert Jones. After the shot, he quickly turned to Joseph White and said that he must go and get a constable: 'I have shot a Blackfellow.'[17] Constable McAllister attended. A coroner's jury was assembled, the case was heard and Jones was committed to the Supreme Court in Sydney.

Robert Jones in the deposition did not say he had shot Cabawn Mickey but that he had shot 'a Blackfellow' and, despite his initial calling of the constable and his admission that he was the perpetrator, he did not plead guilty before the Supreme Court. The language of all the witnesses in the depositions fitted the trope of the violent and aggressive Aboriginal person who had or had not been seen with a tomahawk and was terrorising a great many 'frightened' whites. But the case emerged from very close living and all the Aboriginal people outside the public house were well known to the whites inside it. Mickie Landie, Tommy Bonoringle, Miliga Dickie, Mickie Winger, Bobby Ullallie, Andy and Matilda were names easily recited by the people inside the inn. Robert Jones was indicted by the jury for manslaughter. He refused to sign his defence statement in which he said

---

15 *Illawarra Mercury*, 30 August 1858.
16 Ford, *Settler Sovereignty*, 205; Douglas and Finnane, *Indigenous Crime and Settler Law*, 3.
17 *R v Robert Jones* 1852, 9, SR 9/6361.

he 'did not take aim, did not raise it [the gun] to his shoulder and had no malice or ill will'.[18] Some of the jurors wished to add a rider to the decision saying they thought Robert Jones was justified in firing at the deceased 'as we are of the opinion he did so in defence of his life'.[19] According to Plunkett's *Australian Magistrate*, the crime of manslaughter did involve the killing of another 'without malice, either express or implied'.[20] Jones perhaps thought he would be indicted for murder, and this shows a familiarity with Plunkett that we find in other cases on the South Coast. The minority coroner's jurors, however, argued the shot was 'justifiable' and this was the language of the frontier that saturates the case to the point of the reader being unable to deduce what actually happened.

The argument that the shot was 'justifiable' was also made before the Supreme Court in Sydney by the barrister Darvall, who called the shooting 'admirable'. Chief Justice Stephen described the law of manslaughter and its penalties, from a fine of 1 shilling to transportation for life, but ended his address with the statement that if a man was assaulted in his own house, he was justified in killing his assailants, thus invoking from Plunkett 'a man may kill a trespasser who would forcibly dispossess him of' his house.[21] The sections of the depositions dealing precisely with an attack on the door had been marked by attorney-general John Hubert Plunkett, so one must assume this was Plunkett's position as well. The jury found Jones not guilty, and Stephen said he 'concurred'.[22] It is not possible to deduce *why* the jury in Sydney made such a decision, as a judge's advice was not always followed, but Stephen's position was clear. Cabawn Mickey, however, was not in the house nor a trespasser, he was outside with a crowd of Aboriginal people though a witness heard a bang on the door immediately before the shot. John Smith said that Cabawn Mickey tried to 'burst open' the door and Edward Heffernan said Mickey 'passed … towards the kitchen door'. In emphasising the house, when the defendant was not in the house, Stephen, too, was effectively following the perspective of the frontier in his advice to the jury that the killing could be justifiable.

That the case appeared at all is representative of the kind of combination of concern and brutality evident in newspaper reports of the South Coast. Yet, the language of the frontier dominates the depositions. Joseph White

---

18 ibid.
19 Rider, in *R v Jones*.
20 *Plunkett's Australian Magistrate*, 292.
21 *Sydney Morning Herald*, 9 April 1852; *Plunkett's Australian Magistrate*, 319.
22 *Sydney Morning Herald*, 9 April 1852.

said 'the blacks were outrageous ... threatening the whitefellows'. Cabawn Mickey 'seemed desirous to quarrel with the white people', said Henry Case, who was 'alarmed by the Blacks'. Both Edward Heffernan and William Long said Cabawn Mickey 'seemed determined on mischief'. While Mary Storeman did not see Cabawn Mickey with a tomahawk, everyone else did, and Michael Connell saw him trying to get in the door. This is embroidered by the time everyone gets to court in Sydney. In court, Joseph White said he heard Cabawn Mickey say 'bail me kill you' to Jones, when he had not mentioned it before.[23] Yet, it must be remembered that Robert Jones himself sent for the constable and he put the incident into the purview of the law; all the witnesses were the ones who sought to locate it elsewhere. That an Aboriginal man was subject to a coroner's inquiry at all was at the instance of a perpetrator who perceived he should be subject to law. There was an Aboriginal subject in this case, he was dealt with using the language and perspectives of the frontier and it is possible to argue that the frontier was present on the South Coast even though there may have been little report of violence between Aboriginal and non-Aboriginal people and there was close living and socialising.

Close living appeared in magistrates' letters and in depositions. In *Joseph Imlay alias Black Joe*, the defendant had been, according to the magistrates, 'brought up amongst white people' at Boyd Town.[24] Jackie Namlan, Mongel Mickie and Tommy Moggei at Moruya, despite needing an interpreter, were well known to all the witnesses against them and the victim was not at all afraid of them when they helped her over a creek.[25] Of Davy, charged with assaulting Elizabeth McKeon, the magistrate Campbell wrote that he was 'the most inoffensive of the natives and brought into his present position by intoxication'.[26] Two 'Blacks' camps' were mentioned during the period. One was near Boyd Town, with Joseph Imlay being arrested from there. One was mentioned near Broulee from which Jackie Namlan and Moggei were arrested.[27] There is no sense from these court records of a clearly divided society of Aboriginal camp and non-Aboriginal houses. Cases emerge from the same realm as do cases between non-Aboriginal people and that was while socialising or living closely. Joseph Imlay was accused of robbing a Sydney merchant, Samuel Browning, at a residence that used to be the Sea Horse

---

23 ibid.
24 *R v Joseph Imlay alias Black Joe* 1851, 19, SR 9/6361.
25 *R v Jackie Namlan, Mongel Mickie, and Tommy Moggei* 1854, 7, SR 9/6374.
26 *R v Davy alias Thandy* 1855, 14, SR 9/6389.
27 *R v Imlay*; *R v Namlan & Others*.

Hotel at Boyd Town. Adolphus Seidler saw an Aboriginal man running away from the hotel and assumed it was 'Paddy the Scamp', as Black Joe 'was known to wear a cabbage tree hat'. Similarly, in the case of the assault of Johanna Bolan, William Jackson explained that Aboriginal people wore the same article of clothing for a long time and Moggei could be identified by the comforter he always wore that was produced in court. Davy, according to Elizabeth McKeon, came around the side of the house with her brother's gun and said she should give him money, tea and sugar, matches, powder and shot and that he had killed people and was a bushranger. Mary Jane Richards, a girl of 11, said that earlier Davy grabbed her by the throat and said he wanted 'a white gin'. He got bread and beef from her and made both women walk down to the creek to show him where to cross. At a neighbour's, Flanagan's, he went in for a drink and told them to stand; they ran off. Flanagan caught him by the collar, but he escaped.[28]

The word 'white' was used by magistrates and victims alike and the word 'Blacks' was used by non-Aboriginal people to describe Aboriginal people. This was in keeping with press descriptions and links to reports of violence in the outlying areas of the state. Magistrates of the south were also likely to use the words 'Aboriginal' or 'Natives'—milder forms of description—and, in some depositions, we find the milder 'Blackfellow' used by deponents. The language referring to First Nations people in the records of the South Coast thus shifts in and out of frontier language. In cases involving Aboriginal people, both magistrates and local people went to law to manage incidents. This, however, did not mean an absence of hostility and there can be no neat dichotomy between living side by side and the idea of the frontier. The manner of Namlan and Moggei's arrest at midnight from an Aboriginal camp by a constable, his son and an innkeeper resembled a punitive raid. Jackie Namlan, Mongel Mickie and Tommy Moggei had to be taken quickly away from Moruya after their arrest for their attack on Johanna Bolan because of 'the excited state of the populace and the want of a proper place of security for the prisoners'. In the case against the men, Alfred Alliton said he saw two Aboriginal men, but 'many more might have been there without my seeing them'.[29] These well-known Aboriginal people, in his view, became part of a much larger, hidden and unknown group.

---

28   *R v Davy alias Thandy*.
29   *R v Namlan & Others*.

Joseph Imlay was the only Aboriginal defendant who did not confess. He declined saying anything in court. The others all incriminated themselves in their confessions. Davy said he attacked Elizabeth McKeon's house because 'he was drunk'. Moggei's confession was the only evidence against him, and the other defendants admitted part of their roles but claimed they were innocent of others. It is difficult to know whether any part of this confession is in fact what they did say as they required the services of an interpreter in the Supreme Court and their confessions were in pidgin English.[30] Accounts of the Supreme Court case in Sydney are very brief in all newspapers. The three men were charged with assault with intent to rape. Tommy Moggei was acquitted and Jackie and Mickie were sentenced to two years' imprisonment with hard labour.[31]

Aboriginal people were incorporated into the legal process at South Coast benches. They appeared in the same way as non-Aboriginal people in that they were well known and easily named. This existed alongside language in depositions that would associate them with an idea of the frontier, where there were 'outrages' and 'Blacks' and 'whites' and 'mischief'.

'The people'

'The people' were continual players in the language surrounding the courts on the South Coast in the 1850s. In 1853, Joshua Waddington, an overseer on Alexander Berry's run, sent his own appraisal of the varying perspectives on Lim Law or Jimla, who was charged with assaulting a boy:

> With regard to the caricter of the boy some of the nabours say that he is very imputenet Some of the peoples opinyon Chinie man commit offence boy no resistance, name of chinie man make a great maney of the small settlers shudder, he the gratest tairror as if all the men also like him.[32]

Waddington added that Lim Law had behaved very well under his charge. This letter was directed to W.G. Matthews, Alexander Berry's overseer in Sydney. It had begun with correct English, as though written by a far more literate person, but is written in the vernacular after the first paragraph.

---

30 *R v Davy alias Thandy*.
31 *Sydney Morning Herald*, 7 October 1854.
32 *R v Jimla* 1853, 1, SR 9/6374.

The letter was included in the depositions, possibly sent by Alexander Berry himself. Waddington thought it important to give an idea of the general feeling of 'the people'.

Alexander Berry himself wrote to the attorney-general about his first Chinese employee. He had been away from 'Gerringong' when the offence was committed:

> The people of the Shoalhaven do not believe there is any foundation for the charge against the man who rendered himself very useful in reaping the harvest. I shall therefore feel obliged if you will be kind enough to allow my clerk Mr Matthews to see the depositions and take notice of the same.[33]

Attorney-General Plunkett wrote on the back of this letter, 'I see no objection', and the case was made available not to a solicitor but to the clerk of Alexander Berry, W.G. Matthews. Plunkett jealously guarded depositions in other cases, so this was a matter of largesse and a response to the request of a fellow gentleman. It was in reference to 'the people' that Berry made the request. In this case, however, the people were of two minds—first, that the boy did not resist, but also that perhaps all 'chinee' were like the defendant and they were in terror of him and shuddered at his name. The *Sydney Morning Herald* used the committal to rail against 'Mr Berry's dangerous experiment to introduce such a race among his people and tenants … [T]hese Pagans know nothing of a God, or heaven and hell and consequently possess no idea of moral responsibility.'[34] This was also the manner in which the 'people' of the Shoalhaven spoke. Berry's own interests in defending his employee were contradicted by the local population. The details of the case were not reported but the jury found Lim Law guilty, and he was sentenced to death.[35]

If there were conflicts between a gentleman and the people in this case, there was also conflict in the relationship of the coroner's jury to the coroner and the magistrates on the South Coast.

---

33 ibid.
34 *Sydney Morning Herald*, 7 February 1853.
35 Criminal Crown Solicitor Judgement Books, Supreme Court, State Archives Collection, SR 4/5733.

The office of coroner was one of the oldest in English history. A coroner

> upon information shall go to the place where any be slain or suddenly dead and wounded ... [T]he Coroner ... shall inquire in this manner, that is to wit, if it concerns a man slain, whether it were in any house, field, bed, tavern, or company and if any and who were there.[36]

Marc Trabsky notes that British coronial law was transported in 1788, but was not codified until 1828, and coroners were appointed by the governor rather than elected.[37] Bennett writes that the sheriff assisted the coroner in establishing the names of 24 men in each region to serve on coroners' juries.[38] However, Ian Barker QC writes that the informalities surrounding coroners' juries were made statutory in 1847 and this change allowed juries with as few as five men in sparsely settled areas.[39] In rural New South Wales chief constables subpoenaed jurors from a list sent to the magistrates for approval by the local clerk of the bench.[40] Catie Gilchrist, in discussing the early colony of New South Wales, describes the coroner's inquiry as public and public access was a long-held 'civic liberty dear to the heart of every Englishman'.[41] In the 1850s both coroners and magistrates in New South Wales inquired into incidents that became murder or manslaughter cases.[42] Sometimes coroners were also magistrates and could conduct inquiry without a jury and sometimes a bench took depositions after they considered the coroner's conclusions inadequate.[43] In a coronial inquiry into a death, the names of the coroner's jury were listed in each case and their signatures or marks taken. They were the small shopkeepers and tradesmen of the region, the storekeepers and publicans of the settlements. They were core

---

36 De officio Coronatoris, 4 Edward 1st 2, quoted in W.N. Welsby, *Sir John Jervis, Office and Duties of Coroners with Form and Precedents* (London: H. Sweet, W. Maxwell Stevens and Son, 1866), 31–32.
37 Marc Trabsky, *Law and the Dead: Technology, Relations and Institutions* (New York: Routledge, 2020), 1.
38 John M. Bennett, 'The Establishment of Jury Trial in New South Wales', *Sydney Law Review* 4 (1961): 463–85.
39 Ian Barker QC, 'Sorely Tried: Democracy and Trial by Jury in New South Wales' (Francis Forbes Lecture, 2002), forbessociety.org.au/wp-content/uploads/2013/03/trial_jury.pdf, 209.
40 *Plunkett's Australian Magistrate*, 189–90.
41 Catie Gilchrist, '"Mystery Always Begets Suspicion": Defending the Open and Public Nature of the Coronial Inquest', *The Female Factory Online* (Sydney: Parramatta Female Factory, 2018), femalefactory online.org/essays/mystery-always-begets-suspicion/.
42 Though this is not clearly set out, it appears to have been under the magistrate's jurisdiction to investigate 'any felony'. *Plunkett's Australian Magistrate*, 246. There are accounts of conflicts over who should conduct an inquiry in 1824. Byrne, *Criminal Law and Colonial Subject*, 89.
43 This happened in *R v James Emmanuel Brace* 1858, 14, SR 9/6415. The Shoalhaven police magistrate P.J. Murray and magistrate Keon had a 'subsequent inquiry' after the coroner's inquiry was completed.

to the development of democracy in the regions and their participation in coroners' work was one of the avenues of participation alongside petitions, public meetings and involvement in Presbyterianism or Methodism.

Their views controlled the results of an inquiry. When he forwarded *Simms*, coroner Alick Osbourne wrote: 'I did not concur with the jury in thinking the evidence sufficient to convict Simms of Manslaughter, however I have committed him in accordance with the findings of the jury.'[44] Andrew de Mestre, justice of the peace at Shoalhaven, was critical of the coroner's jury in the case against Matthias Duncombe in 1857, which decided that Duncombe was to be discharged. The evidence of Duncombe's son was not, according to de Mestre, properly considered at the inquest. He wrote: '[I]t is supposed the Coroner's jury nullified the boy's evidence altogether, as the Coroner did not consider that he understood the obligations of an oath, we however, on examination of the boy do not coincide in his opinion.'[45] The coroner in the case was fellow magistrate Kenneth Mackenzie. This was a difference between gentlemen, but there was to be more controversy in the case concerning the make-up of the jury.

John Smith, Shoalhaven constable and lockup keeper, was highly critical in his own letter to the attorney-general:

> [Duncombe] was largely indebted to one Michael Hyam, a publican and storekeeper here, and it was important to Hyam to get such a jury impanelled as would be likely to discharge Duncombe, for in the event of a murder—he Hyam might not get his bill paid for drink supplied. Mr Brown, the District Constable who is intimate with Hyam only subpoenaed the Jury at the last moment, and then had Hyam there as one of the jurors—also Hyam's clerk Henry Moss or Moses who is brother-in-law to Hyam and who was also convicted for perjury at Goulburn and has been under sentence for the crime. Also, a Mr Rose, National Schoolmaster who was nominated foreman by Brown and who is under fear and influence of Hyam as being one of his patrons and a son of Hyam's with him as a boarder.[46]

---

44 *R v John Simms* 1851, 7, SR 9/6361.
45 Andrew de Mestre to Attorney-General, 19 May 1857, in *R v Matthias Duncombe* 1857, 10, SR 9/6412.
46 John Smith to Attorney-General, 25 May 1857, in *R v Duncombe*.

John Smith further wrote that he had been discharged from his duty because he had bought a mare of Duncombe's while Duncombe was in custody. When discharged from the coroner's hearing, Duncombe had drunkenly signed a bill of sale for all his goods and chattels, naming Chief Constable Brown as trustee. Hyam urged Duncombe to go to Sydney with his children and, when Duncombe was away, Hyam sold off all his goods at auction. He claimed the mare Smith had bought and Smith was sued for it. Smith's portrayal of the process of jury selection was put to the magistrates, who described it as 'true though highly coloured'.[47] The attorney-general John Darvall did not comment further, writing in pencil that Duncombe was to be tried for manslaughter.[48] All Smith's claims were, according to John Moore Dillon in a pencil note, 'not material to the prosecution'. Smith in his letter wrote that in response to his discharge from duty 'the public appear dissatisfied with this and are getting up a petition and signatures praying the magistrates to have me reinstated'.[49]

John Smith invoked several ideas in his letter that would be ignored. He thought that a coroner's jury should not be open to such opportunism as shown by Hyam. The subpoenas to appear as a juror should not have been manipulated so that Hyam could secure his financial hold over Duncombe. That is, the system should have operated as described in legal texts. In writing of the petition to reinstate him, Smith invoked a 'public' which was capable of dissatisfaction and which could seek remedy through petition. Smith claimed law as answerable to that public; it needed to be 'satisfied'.

That Hyam's manipulation of the jury system was 'true' according to the magistrates meant that they were unsurprised in dealing with a public and constabulary who were characterised by such manipulation. They assured Attorney-General Darvall that Smith had been dismissed but it was for 'other reasons'.[50] Nor was the attorney-general overly concerned by the manipulation that had been carried on by Chief Constable Brown.

That the people had opinions and needed to be satisfied worked alongside law on the South Coast. A public sometimes supported law and sometimes defined it themselves. It is necessary to see how this public lived to understand where cases emerged.

---

47 Andrew de Mestre to Attorney-General, 19 May 1857, in *R v Duncombe*.
48 *R v Duncombe*.
49 John Smith to Attorney-General, 25 May 1857, in *R v Duncombe*.
50 Andrew de Mestre to Attorney-General, 19 May 1857, in *R v Duncombe*.

Ways of life

Depositions give an idea of what life was like on the colonising South Coast in the 1850s through examination of 'incidentals'—that is, objects and items that were mentioned in passing by witnesses and defendants. South Coast magistrates, who may have copied their records, did not change the language deponents gave them. Consequently, this set of depositions provides some insight into everyday life.

The South Coast was carved into large runs for sheep farming. Sheep work was based on counting and re-counting to assure that none of the sheep had been lost; numeracy was important in shepherding. Associated with this were 'the books' in which numbers of sheep were entered regularly, and this work was done by overseers. Flock size was quite large. Peter Shaunnagahn had a flock of 2,037 sheep in 1850 at 'Bibbenluke', a property owned by the Royal Bank of Australia.[51] Sixteen-year-old Johanna A'Leary/O'Lary had nearly 3,000 sheep in her stepfather's flock on 'Bibbenluke' in 1858.[52] When out, shepherds could see each other and say whether they recognised those nearest. Johanna O'Lary recognised one other shepherd but 'none of the others', so sheep flocks were not grazed far apart. Shepherds were employed on contract and wages were paid at the end of the contract— usually six months. Sheep losses and the incorporation of other sheep into a flock would affect contracts and wages, so the work was not without stress. If sheep were lost, they were tracked and one could see from the tracks whether horses were with them, rounding them up. Such attention pervaded all sheep runs and there is a sense of close surveillance in this business.

This surveillance is apparent in all forms of work. At Jambaroo, Thomas Hart explained that his miller, James Greenslade, was his 'hired servant' and that he was paid 30 shillings a week and rations. His 'duty' was to 'receive wheat and deliver flour and to receive payment for the grinding etc'. There were 'no accounts necessary' between Hart and Greenslade as 'any monies he had received on my account during the week were handed over to me by him on the Saturday'.[53] An account book was kept of the money coming in and the flour exchanged for it and this account book was carefully perused by Hart and the discrepancies between the entries and local versions of the wheat they had bought resulted in a charge of embezzlement for Greenslade.

---

51 *R v George Clay and Thomas Baxon* 1850, 11, SR 9/6357.
52 *R v Hugh McNee* 1858, 5, SR 9/6415.
53 *R v James Greenslade* 1857, 16, SR 9/6410.

He argued that he knew he was 'using Captain Hart's money' but thought it would be resolved in the wages reckoning on 'the day first' (meaning the first of the month). Greenslade gave each farmer a receipt for the wheat they brought to the mill. The mill was referred to as 'Captain Hart's Mill'. James Paul paid Greenslade 42 shillings for 'grinding wheat for myself and two other parties beside myself'. He had the lots weighed separately and entered in the account book in three different names. Growing wheat, therefore, was a business involving as much accounting and reckoning as shepherding.

The pattern of settlement was not dispersed on a run. There were numbers of huts built quite close together and these huts were watched during the day by a hut keeper, who also cooked for the workers. On the run belonging to Alexander Berry, there was a 'barn' with a 'grindstone' and several huts nearby. One was occupied by William Smith, another by Mr and Mrs Harkness, another by Mrs Lamond and another by Jimla or Lim Law. No distances were given apart from 20 yards (18 metres) between Jimla's hut and Mrs Lamond's. Jimla's hut was 'a double one' with a 'slight partition'. It contained a 'bed'. Such partitions of huts and doors between them were described in other cases.[54] Another hut contained a 'swing rope' on which children played, indicating some huts were empty. Children were expected to work, and the children of shepherds tended sheep.[55] James Bundy, a boy, was charged with stealing a letter from the mailbag he was delivering, and his employer held him to high standards.[56] James Harkness was called by his father to turn the grindstone. Joshua Waddington described this run as growing 'bread stuff'; he was worried what the nine further Chinese workers could possibly do when they arrived; the run needed 'Britons' to grow crops. Chinese could not possibly drive the bullocks because the bullocks 'had not lernt german yet and never will exhachly [exactly], the old ones'.[57] This indicates the presence of German workers and Berry, like so many other squatters, may have employed German immigrants obtained in groups from immigration agents in Sydney. At 'Old Maharatta' near Bombala, the hut of Thomas Chambers and his wife, Isabella, was quite close to a shepherd's watch-box, which was also used for travellers to sleep in. These were boxes with wheels, long enough to contain bedding. Three kilometres away was the hut of the Eltons; it, too, had a watch-box close to the hut.[58] This combination of huts and watch-boxes was at 'Numba' near

---

54 *R v Patrick Ringwood* 1857, 2, SR 9/6412.
55 *R v McNee*.
56 *R v James Bundy* 1857, 11, SR 9/6412.
57 *R v Jimla*.
58 *R v James Fitzpatrick* 1855, 3, SR 9/6389.

the Shoalhaven in 1858.[59] Duncan Rankin described a store and a house with a number of huts nearby on 'Fountaindale' near Kiama in 1858, with numbers of people 'about the place'.[60] Runs were not isolated. Notable also in cases from runs are the references to dogs used to guard and give warning of anyone approaching.[61]

Travellers and labourers shared beds. A traveller slept with Thomas Chambers and Isabella Chambers slept in the watch-box with a woman who was travelling alone.[62] A labourer at 'Jimandez' slept with a younger worker for 'a fortnight'.[63] Chambers also had 'an inner room' and a 'sofa', though the word 'bedroom' does not seem to be used. At Catherine Dillon's 'house' on 'Minnamurra' run at Jambaroo, household objects were kept 'under the sofa' and this sofa was in the kitchen 'or outer room'.[64]

Huts in towns were referred to as 'houses'. At Eden, James Brace the shoemaker's house was divided into two: one room had his bench with his leather apron and another room was 'where the bed was'.[65] The word 'bedroom' was used for this room by a neighbour, Ellen Schultz, who described a door to it. There were front and back doors to this house, and it had a 'watercloset'. Next-door was Jonathon Schultz, a storekeeper, and his wife, Ellen. The shop had a 'counter' and a 'garden' that Jonathon Schultz worked, planting potatoes. On the other side of Brace's was Mrs Caznew, living with her son and her servant, Sarah Mitchell, who washed clothes in her employer's yard. Another person who described herself as living 'next door' was Maria Thomas, the wife of Henry Thomas, resident engineer at Eden, so there would have been two houses on one piece of ground. Mr Barclay's Store was nearby. Articles bought at shops were described. Mrs Brace bought 'sardines and eggs' at Mrs Shultz's shop and came back later to buy 'cakes for the children'. At Bega, James Kenny, shoemaker, lived in a hut also referred to as a 'house' that was '171 paces' from shoemaker James Crossley's 'house'. Behind Crossley's was the river and in front was 'Mr Judge's stockyard'. 'Down' from this was Mr Othow's shop. Mrs Childs lived nearby, and she could see Kenny's 'through the slabs'. She took in students, whom she described as 'in school'. Over the river lived

---

59 *R v John Egan* 1858, 6, SR 9/6416.
60 *R v Malcolm Ferguson* 1858, 10, SR 9/6416.
61 For example, *R v Clay and Baxon*. Clay 'tied up the kangaroo dog'.
62 *R v Fitzpatrick*.
63 *R v Ringwood*.
64 *R v Brace*.
65 *R v Lot Flannery* 1857, 8, SR 9/6412.

Mrs McGregor and in another house was Thomas Smith, a sawyer.[66] There is not a sense of clearly demarcated streets in these ways of self-locating and the manner of settlement seems disorganised.

Gates and fences were mentioned in cases involving small settlements, even if irrelevant to the case. At Hibberd's public house at Bega, there were two fences 'that go from Hibberd's to the creek'.[67] At Eden, Brace's house had a 'fence' and a 'gate' and much was made of the spatial relationship to them in the case by witnesses, as though this was a way of looking at movement in the street.[68] Demarcations of property through fencing were particularly important to small farmers, and two cases resulted from boundary disputes. James Emery said Richard Armstrong 'stood on his fence' to threaten his neighbour and Emery cut down a tree to prevent use of a roadway near his property.[69] These disputes were major parts of the activity of the bench and the quarter sessions.[70]

The furniture most commonly mentioned in houses both on runs and in the settlements was the 'sofa' and there were sofas in one-room huts as well as in kitchens. Public houses had more than the two rooms that we find in workshops and huts. John Murray was drinking at Rixon's public house at Kiama and got drunk so went to lie down 'in a place near the kitchen' referred to by Sarah Ogle as 'the drawing room'.[71] Toole's public house had newspapers for people to read.[72] Public houses were important political centres and public meetings were held at them but they also served as a kind of bank, managing credit and debt. Matthias Duncombe became so financially entangled with the publican Hyam that he lost all his money. William Thomas gave all his money to the publican's wife to mind.[73]

Of value inside houses were cups and drinking implements. *Crossley* began with an argument over a cup and basin being dropped by James Kenny in Crossley's house and it was suggested in the case that there were other cups in a cupboard. Rum was on the table, but it was in a pint pot; though people in the house drank out of the pint pot and the cup, they referred to

---

66 *R v James Crossley* 1852, 4, SR 9/6361.
67 *R v Thomas.*
68 *R v Brace.*
69 *R v James Emery* 1854, SR 9/6381 [tree felling]; *R v James Emery* 1855, SR 9/6389.
70 Quarter sessions depositions do not survive. *R v John Riley* 1853, 21, 9/6374.
71 *R v John McDermott* 1854, 3, SR 9/6381; *R v Charles Price* 1854, 11, SR 9/6381.
72 *R v Edward Goodwin* 1859, 11, SR 9/6423.
73 *R v Thomas.*

it as 'having a glass'.⁷⁴ At Shoalhaven, John Simms drank 'honey beer' from a jar.⁷⁵ There was very little detail given for clothing on the South Coast and seemingly little interest in describing clothes. There was, however, discussion of hats. An Aboriginal man at Eden usually wore a cabbage-tree hat and it was referred to in the case against Joseph Imlay.⁷⁶ That hats were worn at night is suggested by Patrick Harpur, in *Namlan & Others* he wore his hat at midnight to go to the Aboriginal camp with the constable to arrest Tommy Moggei.⁷⁷

Policing

In any part of New South Wales, the relationship between constables and the local population expressed a relationship to legality. Constables could harass a local population, they could ignore it, they could zealously conduct searches on their own initiative or they could, as on the South Coast, be its servants. This effectively positions law in a particular arena; it changes its meaning; law 'lands' in a particular way in local communities.

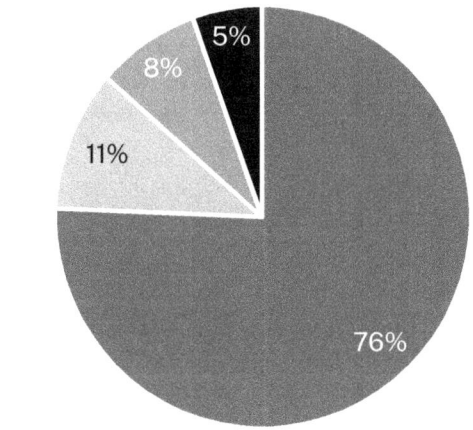

■ Neighbour/same status   ▪ Employer   ▪ Publican   ■ Constable

Figure 2.1: Origin of cases: South Coast

---

74   *R v Crossley*.
75   *R v Simms*.
76   *R v Imlay alias Black Joe*.
77   *R v Namlan & Others*, 9.

South Coast constables in these felony cases did very little policing on their own (see Figure 2.1).[78] Rather, they were called upon, sent for and waited on. In *Price*, both the defendant and the victim called on the district constable of Kiama Thomas Farrell. Charles Price called at Farrell's house very late at night when Farrell was sleeping to say that James Smith 'nearly murdered him'. Farrell stated that he did not make 'any distinct charge' and that Price went away saying he would see him in the morning. But James Smith also made a complaint in the morning: Price had tried to rob him on the road and had beaten him badly. The publican supported his account, saying Price had seemed interested in Smith's money. Thomas Farrell said he arrested Price at nine in the morning. He stated in court in response to Price's attorney that he had 'no warrant'.[79] The constable had a choice as to whom to charge with an offence; he was at the service of one complainant or another. Both the defendant and the victim went to law; it was the constable who was thought of first, so law was dragged into dispute.

There were 11 cases of murder in the period from 1850 to 1859 and an interest in calling for constables and assisting the constable is apparent in the surviving nine depositions. This means a high reliance on law in such cases because in other regions there was no such interest and rumours of deaths with no investigations, hence, low rates of murder. James Kirkland told the people standing around the body of the shoemaker at Bega, James Kenny, 'to leave the body as it was—and to write to Mr Walker JP to come and see it'.[80] This shows considerable awareness of the law when the usual practice elsewhere was to take a body into a house, lay it out naked and proceed to wash it. Kirkland sent for constable John Smith, who arrested James Crossley 'without a warrant'.[81] At Shoalhaven there was an intensive search for the body of Dick Hampton, who had disappeared from a boat being rowed to Pig Island by John Simms alias Jack the Lagger. Charles Comerfield said: 'I told the Lagger to report the case to Mr Brown the

---

78 Petty Sessions cases survive for Eden, which covers the southern part of the coast, for 1854–60 and for Kiama for 1852–56—a total of 480 cases. Of these, 221 (or 46 per cent) were instituted by constables for drunkenness, obscene language or vagrancy. Constable Ballantyne at Eden was active in bringing these offences and, at Kiama, constables Farrell and Goddard. Constables were here resisted and assaulted more than in other areas. Members of the public also brought vagrancy, drunkenness and obscene language cases against their neighbours, indicating an interest in policing one another. Some 259 cases (54 per cent) involved disputes between persons who were not constables. Very few of these were work-related apart from wage cases and most were concerned with assault, disputes over fences and roads and theft. There is a marked absence of convict policing. Eden Bench Book, SR 4/6501; Kiama Bench Book, SR 4/5575, part 4/5576–77.
79 *R v Price*.
80 *R v Crossley*.
81 ibid.

constable … [H]e never went for the constable.'⁸² When a woman was killed at the house of Thomas Chambers on 'Old Maharatta' near Bombala, Chambers said:

> I asked young Leonard to go for a constable, as he would not go, I went myself, the constable came at 12 o'clock at night … I pointed in the direction I saw the man go and the constable went after him.

Alden Wills, that constable, 'became convinced in my mind that James Fitzpatrick was the perpetrator' and he 'wrote a few lines to Mr Hebden and gave them to Constable Hipwell to take to that gentleman while me and Cameron proceeded in search of James Fitzpatrick'. Fitzpatrick was arrested by Constable Cameron five days later.[83] In these cases, the constables were directed by the local population as to who was the perpetrator; in a sense, the investigating had been done before constables arrived. In *Egan*, an attorney, Thomas Morton Richards, arrived at the scene of the murder of a shepherd and began investigating by himself.[84] Charles Comerford searched for the body of Dick Hampton and looked through all the contents of Jack the Lagger's boat, taking out an axe to see whether there was blood on it.[85]

Constables acted as adjuncts to local interests in felony cases and were called for rather than involved in policing themselves. The absence of intensive policing is most apparent in *Thomas*. Constable Whelan did pursue two exiles but was at the service of Smyth, who directed him to let them go.[86] There was only one felony case in the period that involved a constable instigating a case and there is strong indication that he was directed to do so. In 1853 James Emery was brought to court by Thomas Farrell, the district constable at Kiama, because Farrell 'saw a tree lying on the road'—the main post road between Kiama and the Shoalhaven River. He believed that James Emery had put it there. However, the case had already been heard before the quarter sessions, where it had been proved that the land in fact belonged to Emery and that there was no public road. The magistrates were hearing a case twice on the advice of Plunkett—this time with reference to nuisance.[87] Farrell had been sent to instigate the case. He did not act as sleuth, nor did he suspect anyone.

---

82 *R v Simms*.
83 *R v Fitzpatrick*.
84 *R v Egan*.
85 *R v Simms*.
86 *R v Thomas*.
87 *R v Emery* (1854).

In court, constables answered they did not have a warrant when they arrested suspects. This was criticised by the accused or an attorney, even though it was permissible that a constable did not have a warrant according to Plunkett.[88] Critics were holding constables to a particular standard. Yet, the language that constables used in their descriptions of taking a person into custody was not the formal language of constables elsewhere. There were no warnings by constables that anything said could be used in evidence. Suspects were only told they were being arrested; only Constable Smith told Charles Price 'the charge'.[89] This occurs throughout the period and there appears to be no criticism of policing methods by the attorneys-general.

In *Duncombe*, John Smith represented himself as a constable only interested in the welfare of Duncombe and his children. Duncombe wrote a statement for him on 23 April 1857:

> John Smith did not Bye the Mar one [owned by] me in the Wochous [Watchhouse]. Nor Nither did he Ask such athing of me … But I ask him if he New of eny one that He could sell the mar to for me that I [did not have] one shillin in the Hous Nor did Not know wear to Get one to Pay for the Childrens washing nor macking clos for them was almost Nacked.[90]

Duncombe was willing to support a constable and was thankful for his help. In *Namlan & Others*, the victim, Johanna Bolan, was so distraught she could not speak. John McAllister, chief constable, said he 'bled her and she spoke'.[91] This level of care is where the constable was generally placed in the public mind. Such an entrenched relationship could give rise to John Smith's accusation against the chief constable that he assisted in organising the membership of the coroner's jury in *Duncombe*. The contradictory statements of witnesses and the absence of police investigation are glaring to the modern reader, but we find they are ignored by the legal officials of the metropolis.

---

88 *Plunkett's Australian Magistrate*, 478.
89 *R v Price*.
90 Statement, Matthias Duncombe Brumdeery, 23 April 1857, in *R v Duncombe*.
91 *R v Namlan & Others*.

Perfect depositions

South Coast depositions were perfectly presented. Recognisances were always sent, all depositions properly witnessed and signed and all conducted within the hearing of the accused. Questions were asked by defendants and the opportunity was given to make a statement at the end of the case. This perfect presentation may have been one of the reasons for the absence of criticism of the bench by the attorneys-general or the criminal Crown solicitor. The aesthetics of the depositions was important.

Difference in witnesses' evidence was not questioned by the magistrates or noted by attorneys-general. Isabella Chambers claimed that Margaret Paddock spoke before she died, accusing her killer. Thomas Chambers said she did not speak. Isabella Chambers did not mention that Margaret Paddock slept in the watch-box with her, but this was in her husband's evidence.[92] The defendants in the assault of Johanna Bolan were seen by Alfred Alliston, who said 'they were the size of Jackie Namlan and Moggei', whom he knew well. Constable McAllister said he 'suspected' that Mongel Mickey was involved and he was later able to obtain three confessions in pidgin English from men who needed an interpreter in the Supreme Court.[93] Accounts in *Jones* differed wildly as to the proximity of Cabawn Micky to the door of the house.

Long letters were written by magistrates to accompany cases. The tone of these letters was distinctive. Magistrates acted as though they and the attorneys-general had a mutual problem to solve. Robert Perrot JP wrote to attorney-general Lyttleton Bayley in 1859 concerning *Goodwin*: 'There are no features in the case which require particular notice from me'—implying that he normally would comment.[94] In *Thomas*, Henry Massie gave three explanations of incongruities in the case: first, that Thomas robbed Smyth to get a receipt because Smyth was threatening to take him to court over the sale of a horse that had already been sold; second, only 11 of 12 receipts were returned by Thomas because he kept the crucial one; and third, that Constable Whelan was too drunk to know what day it was. Thomas was also a man of bad character and he had been frequently had up for thefts and robberies that 'were difficult to prove'.[95] James Walker JP explained

---

92 *R v Fitzpatrick*.
93 *R v Namlan & Others*.
94 Robert Perrot to Attorney-General, 13 July 1859, in *R v William Goodwin* 1859, 16, SR 9/6423.
95 *R v Thomas*.

the marks on the face of the accused in *Crossley*: they were not made by the deceased man but by a witness.[96] The coroner Alick Osbourne wrote in 1852 that he did not concur with the jury in thinking the evidence sufficient to convict John Simms of the murder of Richard Hampton in his boat but he committed in accordance with the feeling of the jury.[97] While the bench was caused 'considerable embarrassment' by the contradictory evidence of Hannah Kent in 1859, they forwarded the depositions because she insisted she was assaulted by William Goodwin and he had admitted the attack to the arresting constable.[98]

Magistrates added information in their letters that did not appear in depositions. In *Namlan & Others*, they noted that 'three pair of trousers were found and are now in possession of the police strongly affirmative of the statement of the accused'.[99] There was no reference to trousers at all in the depositions, but to the magistrates, they signified that they had been taken off. In *Emery*, Robert Fry and David Waugh, JPs at Kiama, wrote that 'it may not be out of place to remark that the Solicitor General is acquainted with the circumstances'.[100] The solicitor-general was Manning, a major landholder in the area. In *Price*, James M. Gray wrote: 'I have been informed Price made more than one attempt to compromise the matter with Smith', this does not appear in the depositions.'[101]

South Coast magistrates could also vary in their approaches to the rights of defendants. So that Sarah Ogle attend the Supreme Court in 1853, the magistrate regretted that he had no power to bind her over: 'I thought it better to let her think she is compelled.'[102] In the case against Jimla/Lim Law in 1853, no translator was obtained by the bench and 'it is impossible to understand what the prisoner says in his defence, so none is entered'. Jimla also was not able to question each witness against him, nor comprehend the case.[103] In *McDermott*, magistrate James Gray wrote that the defendant had a defence witness, a boy, 'but he is scarcely competent to be sworn' in, so his evidence was not taken.[104] In June 1854 the bench at Kiama was taken aback when a solicitor appeared halfway through the case against

---

96 *R v Crossley*.
97 *R v Simms*.
98 Thomas Chapman to Attorney-General, 29 July 1859, in *R v William Goodwin*.
99 *R v Namlan & Others*.
100 *R v Emery*, 1855.
101 *R v Price*.
102 *R v Riley*.
103 *R v Jimla*.
104 *R v McDermott*.

Charles Price and 'wished for permission to cross examine the witnesses whose evidence was taken in the previous days'. The bench thought this 'a most irregular proceeding'. It refused permission, but the solicitor, who remained unnamed, was allowed to question witnesses who had not been heard before.[105]

The positioning of constables as servants of the population and the willingness of that population to go to law meant that depositions were often contradictory. This did not worry the magistrates of the South Coast, who did not attempt to streamline their cases, but rather wrote to the attorneys-general to explain their reasoning in detail. In response, the attorneys-general and the criminal Crown solicitor seem markedly tolerant and did not castigate the magistrates for mistakes.

Attorneys-general

When a witness claimed he had been shot and his leg broken, a pencil note on the cover of the case by William Moore Dillon reads: 'Mr Walker [the magistrate] says there was no appearance of any gun shot and the man's leg was not broken.'[106] In *Milford and Davis*, Plunkett wrote: 'I wish the Crown Solicitor to read the deposition to say what his opinion is on the last deposition, to prosecute it I think Mrs Davis might be committed if Milford is taken as an approver.'[107] In *Emery*, Plunkett wrote that 'this is a weak case but an example of a trial can do no harm', thereby working with the magistrates and invoking the purpose of law as moral example.[108]

Pencil marking on depositions shows how the attorneys-general and the criminal Crown solicitor approached cases. Markings are rare on cases from the South Coast and those that were made are significant. The case against Robert Jones for shooting Cabawn Mickey was underlined at points where the witnesses referred to the door of the inn being under attack, thereby assisting a defence of justifiable killing. The depositions were read for a defence argument by Attorney-General Plunkett. In 1838 Plunkett came under great criticism for his involvement in obtaining a retrial of the defendants in the Myall Creek case.[109] The word 'Plunkettian' was still being

---

105 *R v Price*.
106 *R v Crossley*.
107 *R v George Milford and Joseph Davis* 1855, 19, SR 9/6389.
108 *R v Emery*, 1855.
109 Lydon and Ryan, *Remembering the Myall Creek Massacre*, 7.

used in public inquiry and in the press in 1860 to indicate perspectives of sympathy for Aboriginal people.[110] In May 1846 in his opening address in *Mickey*, Plunkett

> alluded to the accusations that had been brought against him of eagerness to prosecute whites for acts against the Blacks and the reluctance to proceed against the Aborigines for outrages on whites. These accusations he indignantly repudiated and delivered his full determination at all times to act legally and according to the dictates of his own conscience.[111]

This was several years after Myall Creek, yet Plunkett showed some sensitivity to accusations against him, and his reactions may have led to a different approach to cases involving Aboriginal people. In *Jones*, he marked the depositions in a way that was contrary to the idea of sympathy or justice for Aboriginal people killed by settlers. The South Coast cases destabilise a dichotomous view of the courts and non-Aboriginal society where there are those who are influenced by Exeter Hall on one hand and those who opposed this perspective on the other. That dichotomy cannot be applied to Plunkett and later attorneys-general.

Attorney-General Manning in the 1857 case against James Greenslade for embezzlement underlined the phrase where the employer sets out the 'duty of Greenslade' and then the sentence regarding the receiving of money.[112] This word, 'duty', had significance for Manning, and it is a word related to proper behaviour and morality. It is the language of a landholder and employer. Manning also supported the hearing of the magistrates against the inquest in *Duncombe* and wrote in pencil that the magistrates should be written to and Duncombe charged with the manslaughter of his wife. The inquest had exonerated Duncombe.[113] Martin, one of the most unpopular of attorneys-general, carefully underlined the relevant evidence in *Brace* and *Egan*, murder cases, and *Ferguson*, a rape case. In these cases, the behaviour of the perpetrator according to witnesses, whether he was joking or arguing, was important to Martin. What was said at the time of apprehension was also underlined. Martin drew a small hand in the column of the deposition to these crucial points. Of relevance to him was also any reference to a weapon or what might seem to be a weapon. Martin, also at the end of

---

110 *Maitland Mercury*, 3 May 1860.
111 *Sydney Morning Herald*, 25 May 1853.
112 *R v Greenslade*.
113 *R v Duncombe*.

a case, was likely to refer to the relevant acts. In *Ferguson*, for example, he listed '9 Geo IV cap 31 sec 16 [Call 325]'.[114] Bayley insisted that a child witness attend the court in a rape case, even though she could not speak a word before the bench.[115]

Very little criticism of the South Coast magistrates meant there was only one case for which the words of a witness that did not support the case were marked. This was in 1853 by Plunkett in *Riley*, in which a witness, Mary Johns, said she was present at the time Riley was supposed to have robbed a man in a room of a public house and that Riley never entered the room.[116] Plunkett's underlining did not mean he marked 'no case' on the cover.

When he was charged with the murder of James Kenny in 1852, James Crossley had been searched by constable John Smith and four pages of Plunkett's *The Australian Magistrate* had been found on him. Plunkett wrote in the column: 'Pages from book Mutiny, Murder I think.'[117] This is humour and Plunkett was entertaining Dillon in his comment; he was not inclined to criticise the constable involved, who may or may not have found the pages. This largesse was reflected in all attorneys-general relating to the South Coast in the 1850s. 'The people' were influential in determining how law worked until the cases came before the Supreme Court in Sydney. This was enabled by the presentation of perfect depositions. The material presentation of documents opened a door to the 'people' that would be shut elsewhere.

The people and law

There were eight cases involving sexual assault or rape in the period and six sets of depositions survive. Cases were brought because of the persistence of the accusers or their families and the language in cases does not reflect notions of disgust or horror. John Harkness, a carpenter, went to court with his son and emphasised that his son 'goes to church can read and write and understands the nature of an oath'. He went to court, he said, because of the 'brutality' of Jimla/Lim Law's assault on his son. In this case, there was some suspicion of the boy by neighbours.[118] In *Namlan & Others*, a constable was

---

114 *R v Ferguson*.
115 *R v William Goodwin*.
116 *R v Riley*.
117 *R v Crossley*.
118 *R v Jimla*.

called by the neighbours and Johanna Bolan could not speak until the constable bled her; even then, he acted on suspicion of Namlan rather than any identification.[119] Patrick Ringwood's assault on three boys was brought by their overseer Mr Gregory after one of the other convicts witnessed an attack. The boys said they were 'ashamed' and 'frightened' of Ringwood, who had beaten one of them.[120] Johanna O'Lary's case was brought by her stepfather, who 'said he would go and see Mr Boucher and Mr Hebden', and did so. Johanna told her mother that 'her character was gone' and her mother said 'her child was ruined'. Her stepfather wanted to pursue the man, but his wife said, '[N]o, go for a magistrate.'[121] Jemima May Dale was afraid her mother would 'whip her' if she told about the man who locked her in a room with him and assaulted her. Her mother requested a warrant.[122] Harriet Kent, the servant of a schoolmaster, reported to him how a man had come into her room from the neighbouring public house to assault her. The schoolmaster reported it.[123] Cases appeared because of the wish of employers, families or neighbours to go to court and a confidence that cases would be heard. That children could give evidence if they understood the nature of the oath was important for the magistrates of the South Coast and key witnesses in cases of manslaughter and murder were the children of the house.[124] The law was something familiar on the South Coast and there is a thread of an idea of public opinion of girls and women in the bringing of cases. There was also a notion of care and concern for non-Aboriginal people channelled into law.

This familiarity is also apparent in the behaviour of accused persons in court. The South Coast is notable for long questioning of witnesses by defendants and long defence statements. Defendants were involved in jostling the bench for questions and did not hesitate to question constables. There was no fear of these men. Cross-examination by defendants shows astute understanding of law. James Crossley used several angles in the case against him for murder. Was there not a block of wood at his door that Kenny could have easily hit his head on? Were there not large stones further away from the door? Did anyone see him strike Kenny? How clear a view was there of his house from across the river? Could anyone hear from over there?

---

119 *R v Namlan & Others*.
120 *R v Ringwood*.
121 *R v McNee*.
122 *R v Ferguson*.
123 *R v William Goodwin*.
124 *R v Brace*; *R v Duncombe*.

Wasn't everyone too drunk to recall what exactly happened? Didn't Kenny fall frequently in his house because he drank so much? These questions may be implied in the answers given to him.[125] James Emery asked long and involved questions of witnesses in the two cases against him. The 1854 case saw him asking exactly the position of the tree in relation to his property, if there were any accidents because of the tree and who exactly contracted to build the public road from Kiama to Gerringong and what exactly were the terms of the contract concerning the width of the road. The 1855 case had his prosecutor say, 'I did not jump off the fence and call you a perjured scoundrel.'[126] Charles Price asked specific questions about his movements at the time of the assault on John Smith and how many times Smith had fallen off his horse.[127] In *McNee*, the defendant established that his victim had a long conversation with him before the rape by simply asking, 'Did we speak?'[128] Defendants engaged witnesses for a considerable time, asking question after question and inducing long and involved answers. All this was tolerated by the bench. Such questioning by the accused was long part of the common law that was reinforced by the *Justices Act* and the South Coast benches adhered to this right.

In two cases the prosecutor joined in asking questions of witnesses. Alex Emery was questioned by James Armstrong, who reiterated that Armstrong had called Emery a 'perjured scoundrel' and said his father walked away from the argument.[129] James Smith, the prosecutor in the case against Charles Price, asked a question about ownership of the horse that Price was riding.[130] That there was space given for the prosecutor as well as the defendant to ask questions in court supports an approachable bench with an openness to the local population.

A long defence shows a similar faith in the bench. Robert Jones had a long statement in his defence where Cabawn Mickey had thrown a tomahawk at him and was in the doorway when he shot him. Jones, however, refused to sign the defence when it was presented to him.[131] He perhaps realised he had incriminated himself. As Justice Stephen said at Jones's trial, there was no exact evidence that he did, in fact, fire the gun. In his long defence in

---

125 *R v Crossley*.
126 *R v Emery* (1855).
127 *R v Price*.
128 *R v McNee*.
129 *R v Emery* (1855).
130 *R v Price*.
131 *R v Jones*.

1850, William Thomas gave a history of transactions between himself and his prosecutor and how he obtained the broken watch he was charged with stealing.[132] Four other cases during the period gave long, elaborate defences.

There were three cases in which a solicitor appeared, but these solicitors were never named by the bench, showing a marked lack of respect. In 1854 Charles Price's solicitor was able to ask questions in the second half of the case against Price. In 1857 Matthias Duncombe employed a solicitor, who only asked one question involving Duncombe's question to a surgeon about whether his wife had 'burst a blood vessel'. Duncombe had asked this question himself.[133] In 1859 William Goodwin's solicitor cleverly asked about the number of young men his victim had been 'walking out with' and whether any had been 'on top of her'.[134] The magistrates were highly embarrassed by his skill and yet his victim still insisted she wanted to go to the Supreme Court, and they felt they had to pass on the case. This embarrassment and the low numbers of solicitor appearances as well as their rejection of Price's attorney's request and their description of him suddenly 'arriving' suggest they were unused to this profession and the law was a matter for them and the people.

It remains unclear whether James Crossley did indeed give the fatal blow to the shoemaker Kenny because the case rested on the dying words of Kenny, 'Crossley has murdered me', and following that James Kirkland tried to drag Crossley back to his house and, in a scuffle, a pistol was fired. The pistol was thrown into the river. On examination, it was found to have been never fired but half the witnesses claimed they heard a shot. There was a discussion of whether to leave the body where it was or take it in and wash it, preparing for burial. This was a case involving clamour and a local population enthusiastically joining in an action that resembles pursuit; like *Namlan & Others*, the constables were quickly called for. It remains unclear whether Charles Price really did rob Smith because it was Smith who got to the constable first. James Emery may or may not have pointed his gun at Richard Armstrong. There was a long history of litigation between the two men. Twenty-three cases in the period emerged from two or more people of equal status ending up before, or going to, the constable or the bench.

---

132 *R v Thomas*.
133 *R v Duncombe*.
134 *R v William Goodwin*.

The words 'the people' appear quite early in the history of the bench but they appeared also in the words of the press correspondent from Bega and Eden after 1857. This correspondent reported of the election at Eden in 1859 that 'the electors voted openly before the Returning officer, poll clerk, and scrutineers declining and in fact refusing to go into the private ballot room, they saying that secrecy was not required by them'.[135] One would expect no more of the inhabitants of the South Coast with their own ideas of law and legitimacy.

Right of reply

I read this as a woman of Ngāti Whātua/Ngāpuhi Māori descent who belongs to Yuin people and Country by adoption. My words do not speak for Yuin but as an Indigenous scholar with kinship to and knowledge of the relationalities in the area.

I feel for law historians, merely referring to and historicising of 'the law' contributes to the normalisation of the interloping authority of Western Roman law on Aboriginal lands. Getting into the minutiae of cases that are looking for justice at a microtransactional level can shift focus away from the gargantuan miscarriage of justice that created the backdrop for this study of 'the Law'. Chief Justice Stephen and Plunkett's statement of 'the (imported) Law' that 'a man may kill a trespasser who would forcibly dispossess him of [his house]' demonstrates this sickening irony. The disregard for the Law of the Land, commonly referred to as 'the Lore', is the foundation of settler society, a foundation that broke its own law of trespass, among other maxims.

Some of the questions that come to my mind when reading this history are: what are the Thomas' version of events passed down about the case brought about by Smyth? What are the stories held by the Moruya, Shoalhaven, Narooma and Eden families mentioned in this legal history? Did the Berrys ever have to face 'the (imported) Law' for grave robbing or bone collecting? An oral history I have been privy to by dispossessed people of that area.

This macro setting aside, Byrne has presented this history with an accuracy and awareness of how the law was stacked against its Aboriginal 'subjects' and open to corruption by those with varying levels of power.

Dr Lou Netana Glover
Postdoctoral Research Fellow, Department of Critical Indigenous Studies, Macquarie University

---

135 *Empire*, 14 July 1859.

3

North-West

'The people' disappear from vision when we examine the records of the north-west of the colony of New South Wales (Map 3.1), despite that centre of democratic thought, Rocky River Diggings.[1] The purview of the courts in the north-west involved the activities of gentlemen, the economy of the public house policed by aggressive constables and paternalistic relationships. Aboriginal people played a considerable role in a region where there was a system of informal surveillance that tracked each person across the landscape. Aggression against First Nations people appeared in cases, but through the prism of sentiment. Because we enter the society differently through these records and they are created differently by the magistrates and clerks, law works in what is a new way for us.

The diary of a clerk of the court

The clerk of the bench at Wee Waa, George Mitchell Harper, wrote his 1850–51 diary in a settlement that provided a stop along one of the colony's major travel arteries.[2] People passed through to and from Tamworth, Maitland, Murrurundi, Walgett station, Pilica, Liverpool Plains, Brigalo Creek, Narrabri, Cooyaberri and New England. The diary allows some access to the geography and lifestyle of the north-west of the colony.

---

1 Bongiorno and Messner, 'New England', 152.
2 George Mitchell Harper, Diary 1850–51, University of New England Archives, Armidale, NSW, 5721.

Map 3.1: The north-west of New South Wales
Source: W. Hughes, London G. Phillip and Son, circa 1858, State Library of New South Wales, MLZ/M1 806/1858/1.

In this part of New South Wales, the major industry was cattle raising. It was not a wealthy man's life that Harper described. He sometimes wrote that he was hungry and that others around him were hungry also. Harper lived with his wife, Janet, of the wealthy Snodgrass family. They whitewashed the rooms of their house, had a parlour, had Janet's sister Liz to tea, played draughts and went shooting and danced all night after the races. In October

1850, they appointed Catherine Gunn as a house servant for £12 a year. They carefully observed the ritual surrounding funerals, Janet sewing crepe to Harper's hat for one.

Aboriginal people were named in the diary. There were those who travelled through or stopped for work: Billy-go-Easily, who also carried mail; Mickey, Bunna Bunna Jackey, Tommy, Jacky Shorty, Mickey the Priest, Mickey the tootler, Sandy and Maria, servant to a constable and his wife. There were also non-Aboriginal men who travelled with 'their Blacks' unnamed. By contrast with the South Coast, Harper did not use the word 'white' at all in his diary, only using surnames. Those men who travel through with 'their' Blacks are Mr Glennie the magistrate and Bagot, whose 'blacks [are] here having breakfast';[3] J.W. Loder, who 'lent' his Blackfellow to Harper to go for flour;[4] and Ryan, who 'lent' his Blackfellow and horses to the constable Will 'to water his cattle'.[5] This possessive language—'his', 'their'—does not appear in records from the South Coast and the 'lending' seems to suggest ownership. This relationship to 'boys' was described by Charles Tindal on the Clarence River in 1853. He referred to his 'black slave' Jacky:

> Jacky whom we picked up in the bush at William Ogilvie's ... is very useful and intelligent—we had a great business with his tribe to get permission—at first they kept him concealed but terms being agreed upon his mother gave a signal and he appeared and put on our livery—Black trousers and blue shirt.[6]

In Wee Waa, one of the constables, Will, who was married, is described as having a 'gin' whose name was Maria and this implies a similar relationship.[7]

The language of the Wee Waa area is Kamilaroi/Gumeroi, and it is language related to food and the getting of it that is most apparent in Harper's diary. He spends a lot of his time shooting pigeon or kangaroo, which is then eaten by the family; *cootoo* were fish and were caught by Mickey; pigeons were shot at 'Ningalal'. *Woolooloo*, *boolee* and *tucki* were animals and birds shot, though the words may be from other regions. This hunting was done with First Nations people who also obtained flour and tobacco from Harper.

---

3   ibid., 4 September 1850.
4   ibid., 14 September 1850.
5   ibid., 29 August 1850.
6   Charles Tindal to Fred C. Tindal, 30 November 1850, Tindal Family Papers, ML, A2068.
7   Harper Diary, 13 October 1850.

There is much intimacy between Aboriginal and non-Aboriginal people apparent in Harper's diary. When Billy-go-Easily was ill, a doctor was called and he administered pills.[8] When Simon's wife had a baby, all non-Aboriginal people went over to the camp to see it and they did this also in 1851 when Billy-go-Easily's wife had a son.[9] Social life consisted of going to the Aboriginal camp to see 'corroborees'. At times, Harper went alone; at times, his wife, Janet, went with Grace, the wife of one of the constables. There were visits for corroborees on 10 September, 27 September, 19 October, 26 October and 31 October 1850. All these were at night, and all appear to have been in the same place. Camp corroborees seem to be the major source of entertainment for the non-Aboriginal inhabitants of Wee Waa.

Harper recorded disputes within the camp. In December 1850 Harper records: 'Blacks and gins fighting. Tommy hurt went with Will and Bob to see him—very bad.' A day after, he writes: 'Blacks fighting. Went down. Tommy dead. Blacks buried him on Pine Ridge.'[10] Unlike other murders at Wee Waa, there is no inquiry into this death and this is not felt to be the province of the law. However, when Mickey the Priest's dray is burned, two constables are dispatched to inquire into it, but the result is not reported.[11]

South Coast newspapers reported the bodies of First Nations people being found on runs and in the streets, but the *Armidale Express* is notable for not mentioning Aboriginal people as Aboriginal or mentioning any aspect of the frontier. It did not provide that framework for people to conceptualise their surrounds.

In August 1862 at Falconer, near Armidale, another newspaper, the *Advocate and Advertiser for the Clarence, Richmond and New England Districts*, reported:

> Some three weeks ago the Blacks assembled to the numbers of about 80 at Falconer with what object it is not known. After conducting themselves peaceably for a few days the greater party scattered into smaller parties ... [T]wo troopers came up from Armidale as a precaution ... [W]e are informed that Mr Reay of the Falconer Inn has an Aboriginal woman in his employ who is able to read and write

---

8   ibid., 14 August 1850.
9   ibid., 6 September 1850.
10 ibid., 2 December 1850.
11 ibid., 28 and 29 November 1850.

English and is a very good sempstress and domestic servant it was believed it was at her instance the Blacks were assembled, as she paid a visit to their camp.[12]

That the Aboriginal polity was in existence despite never appearing in the *Armidale Express* in the 1850s is apparent from that report. All Aboriginal people mentioned in this chapter had an involvement in complex law and ceremonial life that was largely 'not known' by whites, as the Falconer Inn report describes it. It is not white business to discuss it. There were two recorded massacres in the New England region. One was at Paddy's Land in 1850 and the other at Lagoon Creek in 1860. They were carried out by 'settlers', according to the Newcastle database compiled by Lyndall Ryan and others.[13] Again, this material is sensitive, but it is sufficient to say that, for Aboriginal people, the idea of being attacked and knowledge and memory of attack would have been present in the period.

Distance and surveillance

Witnesses and defendants in north-western cases give descriptions of travelling long distances and being aware of individuals in the landscape because they had 'heard' of their presence and movements. At Warialda in 1854, the clerk of the bench wrote that he could only serve subpoenas on two witnesses because the others 'had left the district for Drayton', 160 miles (257 kilometres) to the north-west. One of those men, Michael McManus, had been employed at 'Callandoon' station but 'had since left his employ, his time of service being expired. His present residence is unknown.'[14] The clerk obtained this information by letter from the Drayton bench; networks of magistrates could in this way track people who had committed no offence from one district to another. Employees travelled long distances from one of their employer's stations to another. George Gordon, a witness in *Sawyer*, told the bench he had been shearing at 'Goonoo Goonoo' and intended going to Port Stephens. In the same case, James Leonard said he had been shearing at the run and was from 'South Park', Maitland.[15] Dennis Moore was employed by Charles Macdonald of Falconer, near Armidale, in 1851

---

12 *Advocate and Advertiser for the Clarence, Richmond and New England District*, 11 August 1862.
13 *Colonial Frontier Massacres, Australia, 1788 to 1930*, c21ch.newcastle.edu.au/colonialmassacres/map.php.
14 *R v Sippy* 1854, 2, SR 9/6388.
15 *R v Joseph Sawyer* 1857, 13, SR 9/6411.

and from there travelled to Macdonald's run on the Burnett River, 440 miles (710 kilometres) to the north-east. He travelled back from the Burnett 'to get a statement'.[16] In his defence for a charge of forgery at Tamworth in 1850, James Kelly could claim to have received one cheque in the Burnett district and another on the Condamine River, Darling Downs.[17] This kind of long-distance travel created networks of recognition. When Ellen Coole's 13-year-old daughter was taken by Thomas Marshall, she went first to Mr Morris's station where Marshall was employed and asked the cook and then got information from a shepherd of Mr Marks at Black Rock that Marshall had called. She obtained a warrant and then received a letter to say that Marshall had been at the cedar tents there.[18] Word of mouth traced Marshall across country before the constables became involved. William Rourke and John McGuiness traced a horse from Bundarra to Narrabri because they 'heard' it had been sold at Warialda.[19] Similarly, Hugh Roland Labatt at 'Gragan', near Warialda, received information from a fellow squatter, James Edward Davys, that a herd of cattle being driven along the road between Muswellbrook and Maitland had two of his cattle in it.[20] Constables reported 'hearing' of the movements of a horse thief or forger and followed such information and rumour until they obtained their quarry.[21] The Namoi was notable for such recognition. Wee Waa constables could not go there in hope of finding a defendant as word was quickly passed from station to station.[22]

Aboriginal people were crucial to such a climate of surveillance. When John McGuiness and Billy Rourke were searching for a stolen horse, they 'met a Black boy and gave him a present and put him on the track'.[23] Mrs Jean McKillop of the Woolpack Inn Wellingrove was robbed and two of her stools were 'found by a Black'.[24] When Henry Romaine was avoiding the Wee Waa police, the magistrate at Wee Waa reported that an Aboriginal woman said that a 'white paper' had been taken by her people between the stations informing Romaine of the constables' whereabouts.[25] The system of awareness or surveillance, the traceability of non-Aboriginal persons,

16 *R v James Jeffries* 1851, 3, SR 9/6367.
17 *R v John Kennedy alias James Kelly alias James Johnson* 1851, 5, 6, SR 9/6361.
18 *R v Thomas Marshall* 1851, 1, SR 9/6367.
19 *R v Burke*.
20 *R v William Nowland* 1856, 7, SR 9/6404.
21 *R v Michael Sullivan* 1853, 17, SR 9/6388; *R v Burke*.
22 Letters concerning McLaughlin, Wee Waa, SR 9/6388.
23 *R v Burke*.
24 *R v George Williams* 1855, 1, SR9/6397.
25 Letters concerning McLaughlin.

mimics Aboriginal ways of knowing about movement, and the two converge in criminal law (see Figure 3.1). These different cultures worked together in making law work in this region. In comparison with the South Coast, here Aboriginal people played a role in the construction of cases.

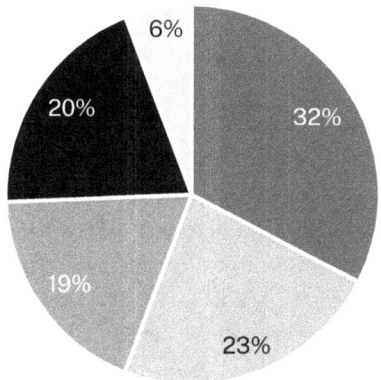

■ Neighbour/same status ■ Publican ■ Employer ■ Constable   Not Known

Figure 3.1: Origin of cases: North-west

Public houses

Public houses in the north-west were conglomerations of small rooms leading into each other. There was one 'tap room' and another room, 'the bar', and leading from these were 'parlours' and 'bedrooms'. At the back of the public house was the kitchen. Informal public houses also existed in the detached kitchens of houses on runs and people would arrive there to drink.[26] Drays were parked next to the public house at Carlisle Gully and people slept under them rather than pay for accommodation.[27] Aboriginal people were present and drinking in public houses.[28] Two kinds of offences emerged from public houses in the north-west: forgery and murder. In both, financial transactions were recounted closely by the publican and he or she distinguished between giving and buying.

---

26   *R v Cubby* 1856, 6, SR 9/6404.
27   *R v John Connor* 1854, 11, SR 9/6396; *R v Roger and Jemmy* 1858, 8, SR 9/6418.
28   *R v Cubby*; *R v Roger and Jemmy*.

Illiteracy meant that many people carried cheques with them that they could not read. Lewis Salomon, 'acting as agent for Phillip Cohen', had charge of The Traveller's Rest at Armidale and received a cheque from Neil O'Donnell, who asked him whether it 'was alright'. Salomon 'retained the cheque but did not give him the change', telling O'Donnell to come back next morning. This demonstrates the power of a publican to hold money and to take time to consider its validity. O'Donnell also was prepared to wait and to trust the publican. Next morning storekeeper Phillip Cohen pronounced the cheque a forgery and O'Donnell and the man from whom he said he got the cheque, Patrick Cullen, found themselves before the bench.[29] At John Martin Davis's public house at Currumbubula near Tamworth, Joseph Griffiths refused to pay Mrs Davis the 16 shillings he owed her. Constable Russell, who happened to be in the public house at the time, came to her assistance, and Griffiths was charged with forgery of the cheque he produced.[30] Fifteen cases emerged directly from a publican calling for a constable or just happening to have them on the premises. There was a strong link between publicans and legitimacy; the centrality of their role in managing the region's money and translating that money to customers made them powerful.

Publicans before the benches did not need to have witnesses to support their claims. William Stitt of Carlisle Gully brought a case against John Burns and Robert Alexander, who he said came to his public house and drew a knife on him, telling him to 'bail up'. Stitt claimed to have tackled Burns and knocked Alexander out with the barrel of a shotgun.[31] He gave the prisoners to Armidale constable John Hancock. His description of his valiant defence was the only evidence in the case. When Constable Threadgold was harassed at McFarlane's Inn on the Namoi River, McFarlane thought he would add on a charge of forgery. He said he 'should have obtained a warrant … had I not been informed by John Croker JP he thought there was already a warrant'.[32] At the Dumbarten Castle Inn on Beardy Plains in 1850, the publican became annoyed that James Daley was 'treating all present' when he only gave an order for 6 shillings. He consequently looked closely at the order's signature and pronounced it a forgery.[33]

---

29 *R v Cullen and O'Donnell* 1850, 7, SR 9/6360.
30 *R v Joseph Griffiths* 1850, 4, SR 9/6396.
31 *R v John Burns and Joseph Alexander* 1851, 7, SR 9/6367.
32 *R v James Clarke* 1855, 3, SR 9/6388.
33 *R v James Daley* 1850, 15, SR 9/6361.

Forgery seems to be a matter of choice for the publican. Perhaps indicating one had to take care around them, gifts were part of a relationship. Mary Cott gave the cook's wife at Mr Cock's in Tamworth in 1855 'a present' of two nuggets of gold.[34] In the case against Thomas Dent alias Gardiner, publican Samuel McCrossin distinguished carefully between what was given and what was sold:

> I gave you two gallons of rum and a bottle of wine and you gave me a cheque for three pounds six shillings and you gave me some cheese and you took away a piece but you started home with the keg. You came back to my place with your wife and child in the afternoon—you gave us some liquor, you asked for supper and you asked for a bed and you called for a glass of wine and I took a glass and drank health to you and your wife.[35]

McCrossin also received a white shawl and a petticoat wrapped up in a bundle when Thomas Gardiner woke him, though the purpose of such giving was not explained. Publicans and storekeepers worked together. At Wellingrove, the miller John Dixson asked publican Elijah Loveday whether he had given away a cheque given to him by Dixson and drawn by Mr Gardiner 'because I have seen it in the hand of Paddy Heggarty'.[36]

Public houses were the sites of murders during the period. Harold Chennier was travelling with his servant, an Aboriginal man, Roger, to 'Burbengate' run for stores and they camped half a mile from the Rock Inn on the Namoi. Jemmy had worked at the Rock Inn for 10 years. Another Aboriginal man, Baan Ba Billy, was also drinking at the inn. Roger, Jemmy and Chennier went to the dray to sleep and during the night Chennier rolled into the fire. He went to the inn, naked and in terrible condition. Mr Doyle the magistrate, who was travelling and stayed at the inn, 'said to the dying man that he had better state how he got burnt' and Chennier first accused Roger and Baan Ba Billy of throwing him on the fire. Frederick Chase, butcher, also staying at the inn, claimed that Chennier said 'Roger and Jemmy', not 'Baan Ba Billy'.

Chase acted as investigator and went to the camp where Roger and Jemmy 'were quite ignorant of the charge'. There were no marks of a struggle. Roger declined to make a defence, but Jemmy said that Chennier was quarrelling

---

34   *R v Mary Cott* 1856, 7, SR 9/6404.
35   *R v Thomas Dent alias Gardiner* 1853, 4, SR 9/6368.
36   *R v Richard Bigge* 1857, 1, SR 9/6411.

with Roger and Roger took his boomerangs and spears from the dray. Jemmy told him to put them back and not to run.[37] At trial at Maitland, according to Dickinson's account in the reserved case, the butcher Chase or Chaver was far more lyrical in his statement that the dying man had accused Jemmy and Roger.[38] Both men were sentenced to death. There was public uproar. The *Sydney Morning Herald* wrote that there was not a 'tittle of evidence' in the case. The evidence was the word of a dying man alone. Furthermore, one of the jurors at Maitland had threatened to kick the others unless a verdict of guilty was returned. The entire NSW Bar signed a petition along with members of the public on behalf of Roger.[39] It was the climate of the public house with its gentleman visitors, its intrigue and uncertainty that had resulted in the case.

That public houses were sites of murder in the north-west did not mean there were no murders in other sites that did not appear before the court. William Gardiner said he had killed 'a gin' by drowning her when he reported the death of his wife. This was not commented on by the court.

Publicans exerted control over exchange in their region, they made use of constables in bringing cases and the law 'landed' in the north-west around their establishments.

Constables

At Armidale in 1864 constables took buttons off their uniforms and replaced them with new ones.[40] This seems to express an independence from government controls. The records of the assizes in the 1850s show that constables of the north-west were by no means the servants of the local population; they acted independently and were influenced by publicans. As well, a bench book survives for Warialda, a police record book from Armidale and a letter book from the Wee Waa bench. These records by no means give a consistent record of all police activity in the region and they tend to resist statistical analysis, but they do show aspects of the style of policing, which, combined with the records of the assizes, show how police involved themselves in their work.

---

37 *R v Roger and Jemmy*.
38 Dickinson, *R v Roger*, Reserved Case, SR T78.
39 *Sydney Morning Herald*, 11 October 1858.
40 J.T. Browne, Superintendent of Police, Armidale, to Superintendent of Police, 1 November 1864, Police Superintendent of Western Districts, Copies of Letters Sent, State Archives Collection, SR 4/10757.

In *Connor*, chief constable Lloyd Bradshaw was woken in the early hours to be told that a woman had been found dead at Carlisle Gully beside Stitt's public house. James Polley came from Stitt's. He was, according to Bradshaw, a 'total stranger bringing no letter from any person I know'. Bradshaw 'did not proceed'. Next day, he received a letter from Mr Stitt and proceeded immediately.[41] Bradshaw required a particular approach.

Wee Waa constables would not go outside their district in 1856. The magistrates Thomas Dangar and Andrew Doyle wrote to the Inspector-General of Police wanting an extension of the police district:

> The present dividing line between Tamworth and Wee Waa police districts on the east is formed by the Narraby Creek 27 miles [43 kilometres] distant from Wee Waa and 130 miles [209 kilometres] from Tamworth. Within 12 miles [19 kilometres] on the further side of this boundary and consequently under the jurisdiction of the Tamworth Bench of Magistrates is a public house much frequented but quite beyond the observation of the constabulary of that district … Were this locality brought within the Police District of Wee Waa a considerable loss of time would be saved, a great deal of crime would be prevented which is now committed with impunity.[42]

Police elsewhere travelled widely, often well out of their own district, but these constables would not.

At Armidale Chief Constable Bradshaw was active in a particular manner. A great deal of his time was spent policing drunkenness offences in the streets of Armidale. The town's police record book shows a marked increase in the numbers arrested between 1852 and 1854 when the volume ends. There were 37 cases of 'drunk and disorderly' between 1850 and 1851 and 426 between January 1852 and November 1854. In this kind of policing, the status of defendants was clearly given, whether 'Exile', 'Free by Servitude' or 'Free'. Intimately bound up with the convict system, the first two categories gave the name of the ship on which the prisoner had been transported. Arrests for drunkenness or disorderly behaviour included Aboriginal people. Magistrates imposed a fine, the lowest being 6 shillings, and, if this could not be paid, 24 or 48 hours in the lockup resulted. They sometimes discharged offenders of all four statuses and cautioned them not to appear again, indicating a disjunction between themselves and constables. Being

---

41   *R v Connor*.
42   Thomas Dangar and Andrew Doyle to Inspector-General of Police, 15 October 1856, Wee Waa Letter Book, State Archives Collection, SR 4/7547.

without 'an abode' and having no 'fixed means of living' were also among the offences found in the record book. Constables also apprehended persons under warrant, usually deriving from the *Masters and Servants Act*. These persons were advertised for in the *Hue and Cry* or the newspapers.

Lloyd Bradshaw and other constables decided what constituted an offence. Matilda Feyson, holding a ticket of leave, was charged in 1851 with 'gross irregular and immoral conduct'. Bradshaw said he knew her well; she was perpetually drunk and disorderly and 'frequently at the tap of the Public Houses'. Bradshaw confined her 'a week ago at the request of her husband who stated he could get no good out of her'. For the 'well-being and order of the township', Bradshaw asked 'that she be removed'. He told her that 'if she promises to go away from the district and break off her connections her ticket might be returned'. There was no comment on this entry in the police record book and a pencil note in the margin requested that it be copied. This was possibly for the Principal Superintendent of Convicts as only he could remove persons from the district, but Bradshaw here was representing himself as interested in banishment because of the wellbeing of the township, as though it were an entity, not simply a conglomeration of shops and houses. He was also acting on behalf of the husband and there is one other case where a husband brought his wife, Margaret Butler, before the court for drunkenness.[43] This seems to be an informal manner of divorce from ticket-of-leave women.

That such policing was intensive is shown in several entries. Lloyd Bradshaw approached Joseph Martin in December 1851 asking him 'if he had anything to show', meaning proof of status. Martin said he arrived on the *Robert Stuart* and had been in the colony 10 years. Bradshaw thought his account of himself was not satisfactory and apprehended him. Martin was discharged by the magistrate.[44] Two days later four men were brought in 'suspected' of being illegally at large. They were discharged and told not to leave the district until word had arrived from the Principal Superintendent of Convicts. Bradshaw's initiative in intense policing was not reflected in the magistrates' determinations. This policing happened within Armidale itself, not on the roads leading to and from it. Road constables or mounted police are absent.

---

43 Margaret Butler, 19 April 1853, Armidale Police Record Book, State Archives Collection, SR 4/5488 [hereinafter APRB].
44 Joseph Martin, 2 December 1851, APRB.

The Warialda bench book for 1850–57 includes 59 cases during this period when constables arrested non-Aboriginal people for drunkenness in the street and seven arrests of Aboriginal people for the same offence. Aboriginal people received the same fine and sentence as non-Aboriginal people, with offences resulting in a fine of £1 or 48 hours in the lockup. In 1855 constables began to take money from offenders as a surety for their appearance in court and that evolved into constables taking all the money offenders had in their possession, which was then forfeited as a fine. Mickie, an Aboriginal man, lost 5 shillings in this way in December 1853.[45] Policing of drunkenness began in the early 1850s in the area immediately in front of the courthouse, where the clerk of the bench James Snape lived, and around 'Mr Geddes' Inn'. From 1853 constables arrested people for being drunk inside public houses.[46] Such policing was carried out by chief constable Thomas McGee, who in 1854 arrested John Geddes for having drunk people on the verandah of the inn.[47] Warialda police also extended the policing of drunkenness to the Aboriginal camp near the town. They arrested non-Aboriginal men for being drunk at the camp and for selling alcohol there.

Street policing was complemented by creative use of the *Vagrant Act. An Act for the more effectual prevention of Vagrancy and for the punishment of idle and disorderly Persons, Rogues, and Vagabonds, and incorrigible Rogues in the Colony of New South Wales* was published on 1 December 1851. This was for those deemed to be a habitual drunkard or wandering idle or a prostitute or in company with Aboriginal people:

> Any Justice of the Peace [is] to commit such offender (being thereof convicted before him by his own view or by the confession of such offender or by the evidence on oath of one or more credible witness or witnesses) to Her Majesty's nearest gaol or house of correction there to be kept to hard labour for any time not exceeding two years.[48]

This Act was first invoked by James Snape, clerk of the bench, when a man claimed that Snape owed him money. 'I owe him nothing,' said Snape and sought to have him charged under the *Vagrant Act*.[49] An orderly attached

---

45 Mickie, 15 December 1853, WBB.
46 Geddes Public House; Stephen Hogg's, the shoemaker's; Clebburn's; in WBB.
47 *McGee v Geddes*, 11 May 1854, WBB.
48 *No. IV. An Act for the more effectual prevention of Vagrancy and for the punishment of idle and disorderly Persons, Rogues, and Vagabonds, and incorrigible Rogues in the Colony of New South Wales* [1 December 1851], classic.austlii.edu.au/au/legis/nsw/num_act/va1851n9131.pdf.
49 Patrick Reed, 8 January 1853, WBB.

to the Commissioner of Crown Lands who had finished his contract and had no food and who tried to pay for his rations with a non-negotiable note was described by the bench as a 'rogue and vagabond'.[50] The fifth clause of the *Vagrant Act* involved the use of obscene language in a public place. Constables arrested persons who were arguing loudly outside or in their own houses or were at the door of the lockup or on the goldfields;[51] Aboriginal people were brought forward for exposing themselves in the street when they were having sex.[52] A Chinese man was brought forward because he was 'incapacitated from getting a living and unfit to be publicly at large'.[53] Warialda shows a similar connection to publicans that is apparent at Armidale but it intervenes in Aboriginal life more closely and incorporates the Aboriginal camp into such policing. This is not a uniform adoption of the *Vagrant Act*, but one determined by the interests of local constables.

Cases before the assizes involving constables resulted from publicans calling for them in instances of violence, forgery or theft. The assizes only represented activity by constables in very specific circumstances, involving very little exertion on their part. Six cases between 1850 and 1851 involved constables who either happened to be in a public house when called upon or close by. In fact, trying to involve a constable could result in a member of the public being arrested himself or herself. When James Johnson went to a constable with half a £10 note he had found on the Armidale racecourse in 1855, Lloyd Bradshaw promptly arrested him for theft of the note.[54] Before the bench, Johnson pleaded guilty, even though the bench was not to take pleas. Why he did so when there was no other evidence against him other than that of Bradshaw's is unclear, but it is notable that in all cross-examinations by defendants at Armidale, a constable was only questioned once.[55]

Constables may have been acting in their own interest. Henry Blanchargen was brought before the court by constable James Doyle in Tamworth in 1854. It was one year after he had paid an order by Sercold of the A.A. Company for £11.10 and the storekeeper Catherine McKidd said she 'saw the prisoner before in the police force. I know him by the name of

---

50   George Cook, 15 March 1855, WBB.
51   Outside House: Mary Shepherd, 5 April 1854; Betsy Clark, 19 July 1855. Lockup: James Corcoran, 17 October 1853. Courthouse: Gillan, 11 March 1857. Goldfields: William Horton, 13 September 1853.
52   Kitty, 1 August 1854; Tommy, 4 October 1855; in WBB.
53   Sam a Chinaman, 19 January 1854, WBB.
54   *R v James Johnson* 1855, 3, SR 9/6396.
55   *R v Michael Cunnyham* 1855, 19, SR 9/6396.

Hering.'⁵⁶ Mrs McKidd found the order was a forgery, but it would not have taken her a year to do so, nor did Doyle say there was a warrant for Blanchargen.

Notable in records from the north-west is the absence of accounts of formalities of arrests to be found elsewhere. David McGrail, chief constable at Wellingrove, gave evidence in 1850 that he proceeded to the Dumbarton Castle Inn at Beardy Plains because he was called for. James Daley was pointed out to him as presenting a forged order. He stated: 'I arrested James Daley and told him what I arrested him for' and the prisoner 'was cautioned not to tell anything to criminate himself'.⁵⁷ This was the only case from Wellingrove that mentioned the requirements of arrest set out in the *Justices Act*.

Warnings appear in few cases. In Armidale, on the arrest of Thomas Gardiner, Chief Constable Bradshaw said: 'I cautioned him before he spoke not to make any statement and said I would repeat anything.'⁵⁸ At Tamworth in 1858, Constable Bullock told John Beresford he 'was my prisoner, he asked me what I took him in charge for, I told him "You know well enough"'. Beresford said 'he might as well drown myself and put an end to his existence as be persecuted the way he was in Tamworth'. When they had walked to Cock's public house, Bullock 'told him what I apprehended him for'.⁵⁹ At Warialda, Sippy, arrested by the Native Police, was given no warning before he confessed to them that he had killed Ann Eliza Bott.⁶⁰

Constables acted at the behest of publicans. Magistrates at Armidale may have rejected many of Lloyd Bradshaw's cases, dismissing them or giving only a caution to defendants, but they did not confront this persistent connection between publicans and police.

---

56   *R v Henry Blanchargen* 1854, 13, SR 9/6397.
57   *R v Daley*.
58   *R v Dent alias Gardiner*.
59   *R v John Beresford* 1858, 1, SR 9/6418.
60   *R v Sippy*.

Gentlemen

The records of the north-west benches include cases involving gentlemen, and the purview of the courts incorporates the language by which they referred to employees and each other. Thomas Rusden said of his employee at 'Europeambella':

> Joseph Lowndes was to pay me 30/- for breaking [a mare] in. On the 15 November Safe requested me to buy the filly from Lowndes he told me £4 10/- was all the money I would require to give for her and Safe agreed to give me £6 for the mare when he had the money. I told him he should have the filly at £5.5/- if he behaved himself well and got out of my debt.[61]

Safe left his employment, taking the horse. Rusden speaks the language of paternalism, the worker's 'behaviour' was subject to scrutiny and was part of the exchange. Yet, court agreement could not be assumed and this would characterise the north-west. Rusden was asked by Robert Massie JP if he had actually seen the horse being taken by Safe and had to admit he did not. He was asked difficult questions by another servant, Wheatley, and he said he did not ask Wheatley to come to court as a witness.[62] The benches did not always favour fellow gentlemen. Ill feeling 'on both sides' resulted in a flock of David William Jameison's sheep being bludgeoned to death on Rusden's run in 1852. Jameison explained that 'if you were on Mr Rusden's head station you would soon be inculcated with a bad feeling against me'.[63] Thomas Vivers in 1857 thought his status would protect him from a charge of horse theft from one of Francis Wyndham's servants. The chief constable at Wellingrove John Proctor told Vivers, 'I did not think a warrant would be granted, it would be a summons case. I would not execute it', but two of Vivers' servants gave evidence against him. Vivers had branded the horse after being told it belonged to Robert Meredith, Wyndham's overseer. Vivers said he 'didn't care'. Despite Wyndham not being willing to 'positively swear' it was Meredith's horse, the case was committed to the assizes.[64] At the first trial at the Maitland Assizes in March 1857, the jury was locked up all night because they could not agree and were discharged by the court.[65] In September 1857 Vivers was found not guilty, yet in the same sessions

---

61 *R v Richard Safe* 1856, 6, SR 9/6397.
62 ibid.
63 *R v Frederick Moreton, William Cornish, Francis Millar, and Josiah Saunders* 1852, 8, SR 9/6380.
64 *R v Thomas Vivers* 1857, 2, SR 9/6411.
65 Criminal Crown Solicitor Judgement Books, Maitland Circuit, March 1857, SR 4/5755.

he was listed to be tried again. This time the chief constable was the first witness against him and the depositions appear not to have survived. The solicitor-general ordered the case not be tried. No reason was given.[66] These cases indicate that conflict between gentlemen surfaced in the criminal courts in a manner that is not found on the South Coast. Gentlemen were not secure in the kind of superiority they expressed. In *Vivers*, the local chief constable attempted to support him, to no avail. The cases reveal a complex interaction of legal authority and the status of a gentleman where rivalry, generally expressed in the civil courts, produced criminal cases.

Such rivalry was blatantly apparent in the case against Charles Wentworth Bucknell and Francis (Frank) Newham Bucknell of 'Mongyer' on the Gwydir River initiated by Henry Dangar in 1858. Discussed by the Legislative Assembly, it was the subject of much public debate. The case is a perfect demonstration of how local magistrates managed law and there are a great many faults in the deposition that were ignored by attorney-general James Martin, who was criticised for not finding a 'no case'.

The case was begun by Aboriginal people who informed Arthur Hunter Palmer, Dangar's manager, that the Bucknells were taking Dangar's cattle. Managers and overseers were fellow gentlemen on runs, using their time to learn the management of a station.[67] Aboriginal people were portrayed as active in law and such activity may be compared to Paul Fox's perspective on gossip, where First Nations people were able to play landholders against each other.[68] Arthur Hunter Palmer said that as a consequence of this report, 'two detective constables were sent up to *Mongyer* by the Inspector General of Police at the instigation of Robert Fitzgerald David Ryan'; the words 'and myself' on the deposition were crossed out by an unknown hand. Robert Fitzgerald and David Ryan were squatters. They were able to obtain the services of two detectives, John Abigail and Edward Lloyd Lewis, who proceeded to 'Mongyer' in disguise and asked for work. They worked 'undercover' to see whether they could obtain proof that the Bucknells were stealing cattle.[69] Six months after the offence had been investigated, chief constable George Hopper of Wee Waa proceeded to 'Mongyer' on the advice of the detectives and arrested the two brothers. Before the bench, Lewis described how, on 16 October 'last year' (1857), Frank Newham Bucknell

---

66 Criminal Crown Solicitor Judgement Books, Maitland, September 1857, SR 4/5758.
67 Byrne, 'Australian Squatter Space 1850–1880'.
68 Paul Fox, *Sweet Damper and Gossip* (Benalla, Vic.: Benalla Art Gallery, 1994).
69 *Northern Times*, 22 September 1858.

had driven a bullock into the slaughtering yard at 'Mongyer', shot it and skinned it. Bucknell and 'one of his gins' dragged the skin away towards the hut and Bucknell cut out the 'HD' brand and threw it in the fire. The bench, comprising Thomas Dangar, nephew of Henry, Andrew Doyle and Arthur Rose, wanted to know why the detectives did not reach into the fire and pull out the brand as evidence. Lewis replied that there were 'a large number of Blacks around the yard, and we considered that if we attempted to get the brand we should have been killed'. The detective was here using the language of the frontier. Despite being in the yard of a squatter, he characterised Aboriginal people as threatening. Lewis claimed 'Billy Hippi' had driven the cattle into the yard with Frank Bucknell. George Waller said two Aboriginal people, 'Billy and Hippi', had travelled to the Big River with him and Hippi was away until 23 October; you could not mistake one for the other. Furthermore, there were only two young Aboriginal men on the station, so Lewis's story was false, he implied.

It is clear there were two groups of Aboriginal people represented in the case: those who informed on the Bucknells and those who were on the Bucknells' run. Both groups were represented as players in the case. There was no evidence apart from Lewis's word as a detective, but as we have seen, one deposition was often enough for the north-western benches to commit. The Bucknells were extremely active before the bench, questioning witnesses, making extensive defence statements and producing witnesses of their own. Arthur Hunter Palmer questioned the defence witness John Worthington Lloyd. He showed John James Brown had bought William Bucknell's share in 'Yarrawaa' station. Brown sold his station to Charles and Francis Bucknell. He said: 'I know no reason why Brown sold out excepting his having sufficient inducement of a pecuniary nature.' This question seems irrelevant to the case, but it shows the whole history of relations with the Bucknells had influenced the prosecution. The Bucknells had been disliked for some time and had been targeted for reasons more than cattle theft. The Bucknells, with their bail of £500, fought their case before the bench themselves, to no avail. They were committed to the assizes at Maitland.

In July 1858 the Bucknells appeared before the bench at Wee Waa again to insist their witnesses be heard. Their partner John Worthington Lloyd said that he had heard Edward Lloyd Lewis state that 'it was not until after his return from *Gulligul* that he was received into the confidence of the Messrs Bucknell'. George White gave evidence that HD cattle had been sold by the Bucknells and that they had been authorised by Palmer to do so. While he was giving evidence, William Bucknell, brother of the accused, came up and 'whispered something in his ear' before the bench could stop him. White then refused to sign his statement. In their defence, the Bucknells produced a cheque book and a black-covered memorandum book. These were seized and kept as part of prosecution evidence. No other defendant in the north-west would have been given such a privilege of calling back the court and producing new evidence 'at the earnest request of the accused' after they had been committed for trial. That this was unorthodox is suggested by the drawing of a hand by the attorney-general pointing to the magistrate's inclusion of the new evidence.

The new passages were marked by attorney-general James Martin in pencil, and he was influenced in his reading of the case by the 'earnest appeal'. But he proceeded to trial, saying that the detective Abigail was also to give evidence; the attorney-general needed more evidence that the bullock was marked HD, not 'HE', as the Bucknells claimed. The attorney-general marked passages where it was stated that the bullock 'was not a working bullock'. He underlined the statement made by Arthur Hunter Palmer: 'I should most certainly have considered it a felony had they retained any [of Dangar's] cattle and killed it.' He marked the defence of Frank Bucknell where he stated he bought the cattle from a man named Egar, 'who is in New Zealand now', and that they were branded at 'Mongyer' seven to eight years previously. His brother purchased the entire brand 'two years and a quarter since'. There were five or six cattle left. Martin also marked John Worthington Lloyd's statement when he produced the memorandum book that entries there related to Ned and that they were there when he received the book from the Bucknells. Martin marked with an 'x' the statement made by George Waller that there were 'fifteen persons on the station, white and black' and that two years ago the HE brand had been purchased. Martin was looking for fault in the defence argument rather than clarity in the prosecution, so it seems he was already partial to the prosecution case. Partiality was also apparent in the criminal Crown solicitor, who wrote alongside the account of the rope slipping on the gallows when the bullock was hung for slaughtering: 'Lewis says he let go of the rope on purpose to impress on those present the fact of the killing.' He clearly had discussions with the detective after the case arrived in Sydney.

Faults in the depositions, the crossing out of contradictory statements and the unsigned altering of evidence were not questioned by Martin, and his perusal of this case seems erratic. He underlined points that do not seem pertinent to the case: the 'working bullock' made no difference, the 'felony' was someone's opinion, the memorandum book with its '2 years' did not contradict Bucknell's 'two and a quarter years' since the HE bullocks were purchased.

The nervousness of the Bucknells is apparent in the great effort they put into the hearing before the bench: their long defence statement, their defence witnesses and their presentation to the court of their memorandum and cheque books, seized in court and later having to be requested by Charles Bucknell.[70] The Bucknells made the bench matter. Even though they did not engage a defence solicitor, they argued every point in their case, even those irrelevant to the substance of it—how many Aboriginal people were on the station, for example. The effort would continue as they approached the assizes.

At the assizes in Maitland on 16 September 1858, the Bucknells were defended by the barristers Mr Isaacs and Mr Faucett and the attorneys Joseph O' Meagher and Robert Deane. Detective Edward Lloyd Lewis was closely cross-examined by Isaacs, who wished to establish 'a contradiction' between Lewis's evidence in court and what had been said before the bench at Wee Waa. Detective Lewis stated that the magistrate Rose had taken the depositions and that he was not certain exactly whether he had given all the details to him. The barrister Isaacs' mode of argument was objecting to irrelevant evidence. Justice Dickinson did not proceed to defence witnesses. He instructed the jury that their safest course was to acquit as there was no proof that the animal killed belonged to Henry Dangar; it may have previously been purchased by someone else and then sold to the Bucknells. It could not be told. The jury decided on a not guilty verdict. The *Sydney Morning Herald* wrote that the case had 'broken down'.[71] The Bucknells moved to charge both detectives with perjury.

The Bucknell case was discussed in the Legislative Assembly and reported in the *Sydney Morning Herald*. The Bucknells had petitioned the House about the case and William Forster spoke of 'a state of facts discreditable to a civilised community'. Detectives entered the employment of two gentlemen and gave information before a police magistrate in Sydney. The Bucknells 'were arrested and dragged in handcuffs a distance of seventy-five miles to the Wee Waa bench'. There had never been any proof of the ownership of the bullock and the police magistrate in Sydney had 'gone beyond his

---

70   *R v Charles and William Bucknell* 1858, 2, SR 9/6419.
71   *Sydney Morning Herald*, 21 September 1858.

power in granting the information … four hundred miles from the place of the alleged offence and six months after it had been said to have been committed'. A magistrate at Wee Waa 'was nephew to the supposed owner of the bullock'. Forster also stated that the prisoner, who requested that portions of his evidence that were in his favour might be written down, 'was refused' and he handed in a written protest against the decisions of the bench. The committal was 'in opposition to justice, to the facts of the case and to law itself'. The attorney-general was not without blame; he exhibited neglect and he showed 'undue animus' in the trial. Forster was not opposed to detectives, but there needed to be an offence or something that showed prima facie evidence of guilt.[72]

Attorney-General Martin replied to Forster, stating that the result of the case was that 'cattle could be driven off a run with impunity'. The other judges did not agree with Justice Dickinson's advice to the jury in this case. He hoped Forster would have a copy of the depositions printed 'so that the public might be able to form opinion on the subject'.[73] William Wentworth Bucknell, brother to the defendants, in a letter to the *Herald*, claimed that much more had been said in the House by the attorney-general and not published. Charles Bucknell's petition contained a grave allegation against the attorney-general, 'Mr Martin, acting in his capacity of grand jury in the colony'. In his letter, Bucknell argued that the magistrates at Wee Waa had no just and legal ground for committal; *a fortiori* the attorney-general had no just and legal grounds to send the case to a jury.[74]

This public aspect of the case challenged the whole system by which the Bucknells had been committed, the process of the initial hearing and the decision of the attorney-general to allow the case to proceed. This was not addressed in the assizes; rather, the contradictions of the detectives were brought up by Isaacs. The *Herald* also printed a petition by squatters on behalf of the Bucknells attesting to their honesty in business.[75] The signatories were the opponents of the gentlemen who had combined to contact the Inspector-General of Police to obtain two detectives to investigate the Bucknells. The cases evolved from local skirmishes between gentlemen as much as the actions of Aboriginal people.

---

72 *Sydney Morning Herald*, 5 October 1858.
73 ibid.
74 *Sydney Morning Herald*, 4 October 1858.
75 ibid.

Many opportunities were open to the Bucknells that were not available to other defendants. They spent £1,000 on the case and it was they who initiated the charges of perjury against the two detectives. The Maitland magistrates dismissed the first case and discharged Abigail, saying there was not the slightest imputation on his character in respect of the charge.[76] The second case, concerning Lewis, was heard in the Sydney Central Police Court on 26 September 1858. It was as though the Bucknells were being tried again. We find some of the history of the detectives. Lewis had been working as a detective in Hobart, Victoria and New Zealand. He was an exile, being transported for 'robbing a Jew'. The Aboriginal woman in the yard at Bucknells was Lucy—the first time she had been named.[77] Lewis was committed by the Sydney bench but the attorney-general did not prosecute the case. When Forster asked why in the House in September 1859, Mr Batley said he was unable to secure a witness and that consequently he was 'impelled to abandon the prosecution'.[78]

Representative government had been brought into play in the defence of the Bucknells but attitudes opposed to them proved as strong. The Wee Waa magistrates were only questioned in the press and the House. Links and disputes between gentlemen proved stronger than any ideas of justice brought up in the rhetoric around the case. This intersection of democracy and law was utterly in the service of the gentlemen involved. There was not a secure 'squattocracy'. More importantly, we find all levels of law utterly at the service of gentlemen, from the detectives to the magistrates and the attorney-general himself.

Servants

Runs in the north-west were referred to as 'stations' and there was one 'head station' and other named stations some miles away.[79] People located themselves by the names of these runs and stations, coming and going from them, stopping some time without being employed. The word 'stranger' is rarely found in north-western cases, as though new faces were expected

---

76 *Northern Times*, 22 September 1858.
77 *Sydney Morning Herald*, 8 October 1858.
78 *Maitland Mercury*, 17 September 1859.
79 *Hugh Baird v Peter Evans*, 21 February 1850, WBB.

on runs.⁸⁰ Cases involving servants were instituted by squatters or their managers or superintendents and they show paternalistic relations between employee and employer. In 1850 Albert Norton, grazier, said his carpenter, Cameron, came to him because he wanted his wife to come home to his hut. She had moved into a hut with another man on the run.⁸¹ At a time when work agreements were carefully noted and wages owed clearly understood, the servants in these cases seem emotionally dependent on their employers.

In cases between persons of equal status, 17 assize cases involved non-Aboriginal station servants or persons visiting a run. David Walker stabbed a man named 'Jimmy the Jockey' in a hut at 'Wee Ta Wah' after 'skylarking' and drinking grog 'out of a cup'. Mr Bryan, the overseer, sent to Wee Waa for the constable.⁸² Michael Ellis was playing cards in a hut on 'Clairevaux' when James Binnsely was commenting from the bed and Ellis stabbed him. The overseer sent for a constable.⁸³ When Patrick Walsh stabbed Thomas Reynolds or 'Towsey' at the washpool on 'Wallangra', it resulted from a work environment in which 'the men were in a habit of chaffing one another'.⁸⁴ The overseer Gerald Raymond informed the magistrates. Jemmy, 'a chinaman', stabbed Sam Pong near Gunnedah. Charley Imee had just come from the stores and became frightened. He 'told police and the Doctor'.⁸⁵ Mark Gray was a traveller, who was allowed to sleep under a dray on Mr Orr's run. He slept with an axe 'in dread of fairies' and inexplicably attacked one of the stockmen, James Hardinge. He seemed 'a little out of his mind'. James Orr 'started a man to give information'.⁸⁶ True hostility appeared in *Callaghan and Johnstone*, when James Hunt asked the two men 'how they were getting on with Telfer'. Johnstone said he 'did not like him as a hut mate, he called him names, said he was nothing more than cow's droppings, one of Lord Ashton's ragged arsed schoolboys'. Telfer was later found dead, 'both his eyes knocked out', and Hunt 'rode to the nearest magistrate'.⁸⁷ While there may have been killings where the superintendent

---

80   There are two examples from depositions. Edward Glenn claimed he received a foal from 'strangers'. *R v Edward Glenn* 1855, 1, SR 9/6404. And David Walker was told 'not to make a row with strange men' by James Reed, a fellow stockman, who was referring to cattlemen who had come to transport cattle. *R v Walker* 1856, 17, SR 9/6404.
81   *R v Thomas Crane and Eliza Cameron* 1850, 6, SR 9/6388.
82   *R v Walker*.
83   *R v Michael Ellis* 1855, 30, SR 9/6397.
84   *R v Patrick Walsh* 1857, 15, SR 9/6411.
85   *R v Jemmy* 1859, 2, SR 9/6426.
86   *R v Mark Gray* 1858, 3, SR 9/6418.
87   *R v David Callaghan and Hugh Johnstone* 1859, 11, SR 9/6430.

or overseer did not send for the constables at all and there was no hearing into a death, those that do appear stress this servant reliance on the hierarchical nature of stations. On the South Coast, such relations remain opaque to us.

The financial relations on runs were complex. The purpose of the store is demonstrated by James Hunt, the superintendent at 'Baan Ba' in 1859. Callaghan and Johnstone came with their sheep to Hunt and said they wanted to 'get a few things from the store'. Callaghan was asked whether he could watch Johnstone's sheep and Johnstone went into the store to get boots and 4 ounces of 'negro-head' tobacco. He then asked for money. Hunt said: 'I gave him 2 orders for £1—[numbered] 274 and 275. Callaghan then came and asked for £1 which he was given, [number] 276.'[88] At the end of their contract, such expenses would be deducted from their wages and careful accounting was undertaken. This way of managing money was mirrored in public houses, where money was held and, at the end of the visit, which might take several days, expenses were weighed up against the money that had been held. The rituals of money in public houses thus mimic those on runs. In both cases, financial dependency was entangled with a kind of emotional dependence, even though workers may have been on short-term contracts.

Goldfields

Like an oasis, the Rocky River Diggings near Armidale was a landscape of tents. It was also a place of what seems continuous entertainment. A 'circus' was referred to in 1856 that went on all night until six in the morning. There was also a bowling alley and public houses, while opium could be obtained from the Chinese, who had their own section of the diggings named 'the Chinese tents'.[89] Obtaining opium was done socially, with a visit to a tent in which opium was bought and smoked and then card games were played. The Chinese tents—'Hong Kong Chinaman's'—were described as 'big', indicating they were larger than tents elsewhere. Gambling took place there all night. All these activities cost money; opium cost 'a few shillings'.[90] Cash was mentioned on the goldfields more than elsewhere, together with silver dust and gold dust, and the goldfields allowed a man to describe himself as a 'gold digger'. Like public houses, the goldfields were places where liberality of spending combined with alcohol. Armidale in 1859, like Rocky River,

---

88 ibid.
89 *R vs Ling Lieu, Tiro Swee, and Johnny* 1856, 5, SR 9/6404.
90 ibid.

had a circus that sold 'seats' on forms or benches. 'Cakes' and 'glasses of liquor' were obtained by 'tickets for refreshments given out'. In the circus a 'play actor shot the dog', indicating that the 'circus' had elements of a theatre performance.[91]

Five cases came from Rocky River, one from Hanging Rock and one from the Peel River Diggings. They stress the sociability of the diggings and the insecurity of personal property in tents. Charles Columbing or Kallenberg went to the accommodation house of William Moran at Rocky River between 11 and 12 pm. A man 'asked him to bet' and he did so, betting that he could hold a candle to his mouth. Someone knocked the candle out of his hand, he was dragged out of the tent and robbed. He said: 'I am a foreigner, none of the bystanders attempted to prevent the robbery.'[92] Though the newspapers liked to stress the divisions between different immigrants on the fields—the 'Australians' versus the English, for instance—this was the only case where such divisions appeared.[93] Kallenberg claimed no-one watching helped him, as though he assumed they would. It was more likely that offences emerged from crowded social conditions. At Hanging Rock Diggings, Skelton Head was involved in a game of tossing half-pence when the coin fell onto the back of another man and a challenge to fight ensued.[94] One has the impression of entertainment-hungry groups of people. The rooming-house tent at Rocky River had 'doors' that were 'put up', indicating a need to restrict entry. Fitches store on Bungarra goldfields was also a site of sociability, as were designated public houses, which may also have been tents.[95] There were hierarchies inside tents. James Mitchell employed Michael Sullivan and left him in charge of the tent at Hanging Rock Diggings, and in the magistrates' hearing into Jemmy at Armidale, there was a servant girl working in one of the tents.[96]

Gatherings of people at all hours of the night meant there was some assistance or witnesses to be had. Sam Sun had his tent cut open while he was sleeping at Rocky River and his carpet bag was taken out. It contained 15 sovereigns, white shirts, a pair of trousers and a silver watch.[97] He called out and 'two

---

91 *R vs Kenneth Matheison* 1859, 8, SR 9/6426.
92 *R v John White and William Smith* 1857, 3, SR 9/6411.
93 Divisions, for example: *Goulburn Herald*, 12 May 1855; *Empire*, 4 August 1853; *Sydney Morning Herald*, 9 January 1852; *Northern Times*, 29 April 1857.
94 *R v Skelton Head* 1853, 14, SR 9/6381.
95 *R v Brennan* 1856, 11, SR 9/6404.
96 *R v Sullivan*; Jemmy, 26 September 1854, APRB.
97 *R v Ling and Others*.

white men' came, both of whom had been smoking opium in a nearby Chinese tent. One of them, Charles Elliott, 'went to the Commissioner's Camp to report the incident'.[98]

Cases from the goldfields emerged from this realm of entertainment available and demanded all night. Yet, there is no trace of 'the people' in these most democratic of places. Nor do 'the people' appear in cases surrounding public houses, where electioneering was carried out via publicans as agents of gentlemen. Rather, the heady nature of entertainment dominated, and one would venture that the pageantry of elections would form part of that entertainment at election time. Paternalism and overseers dominated cases from runs, though servants gave evidence against gentlemen, implying the sentiment may not have been mutual. We do not find stability in the north-west, a secure alternative state of squatters and servants. Aboriginal people also shaped a role in policing and cases were brought on their behalf.

The Aboriginal subject

An Aboriginal man, Jemmy, was killed at Rocky River in September 1854 and an inquiry was held into his death. This contained contradictory evidence from witnesses. Jemmy, dressed in a guernsey and trousers and riding a horse, had stopped at a tent to ask for a light of a pipe. He either 'tumbled down the hill' or was beaten severely by the inhabitants of the tent. He may have 'fallen in the creek' and had difficulty getting out, having to be helped. He was found the next morning, naked, under bark and branches near the tent at which he had stopped. Constables were called. Thomas Markham conducted an autopsy and could find no sign of the cause of death. Markham decided that he had died 'of the cold' and some 'humanity' on the part of others could have prevented it. There was to be no case.[99] Assize cases involving Aboriginal victims emerged from the same sentiment expressed by Henry Parkes when he spoke of the 'faithful' Jacky.

In April 1854 Charles Frederick Hamilton Smith of the Wee Waa bench wrote to the attorney-general about an Aboriginal man named Major Walker. He was 'an intelligent and faithful servant' of Peter Eckford of 'Burren Burren' and he had been shot—'a foul wanton act' by a 'mulatto' named Henry Romaine or 'Black Harry', aided by another man, Daniel

---
98 ibid.
99 Jemmy, 26 September 1854, APRB.

McLaughlin. Jacob Noel—'Blind Jacob'—a 'sly grog seller', was present 'but the Blacks say he took no part'. The magistrate Smith had dispatched the constables to arrest Romaine and Jacob Noel, but the Wee Waa police were too well known on the Barwon River and Mooni Creek. Also: 'The white people assist the murderer and engage blackfellows to carry notes to Blind Jacob. Many persons in the district think it no crime to kill a Black Fellow deeming them no better than beasts of the forest.'[100]

There were two groups of Aboriginal people apparent in this quote: those who carried notes and those who were involved in the bringing of the murder charge. At Mungindi, Constable Hopper had seen Jacob Noel in the distance armed with a gun. An Aboriginal woman told Hopper she had brought a note from Mr Lance for Noel. He estimated the letter was conveyed 50 miles (80 kilometres) in 24 hours from station to station. The news could not have been sent without the knowledge of the Lawries at 'Towindi' and the Webbers at 'Caidmurray'. There was no doubt Noel was being harboured by some of the Barwon squatters. William Webber at 'Caidmurray' said he sold a horse to Noel, but Smith said his impression was that it was not sold at all—it was only a 'ruse'.

John Callaghan, one of the witnesses, was seen by Aboriginal people 'rigged out like a blackfellow' and 'travelling with a Black gin'; he had gone towards the Darling Downs, where he had been living for years with 'the wild blacks'. Networks of knowledge and rumour supported both sides in the dispute over the murder of Major Walker.[101]

The depositions in the case had been taken at 'Burren Burren' on the Barwon River, where Major Walker had been killed. John Callaghan gave evidence that he was a hutkeeper of Peter Eckford's and a fortnight after his first arrival on the run, Jacob Noel came in his cart with rum 'or brandy' on his dray. Callaghan kept himself 'sober and solid', but Black Harry and McLaughlin drank. Callaghan left the hut to go to Dick Lewes on the next run and returned to go to bed. The three men, Noel, Romaine and McLaughlin, 'started out of the hut' before he went to bed. Callaghan was in bed when a Black boy, Mick, came, saying 'open the door and let me in'; he said McLaughlin had cut him with a knife. Callaghan rubbed ointment in the cut and went to sleep. In the morning 'Black Billy Murray' came and told him that Major Walker was killed, that 'Black Harry had shot

---

100 Charles Hamilton Smith to Attorney-General, 18 April 1854, correspondence in SR 9/6388.
101 ibid.

him'. Callaghan asked what 'was the occasion of the row but received no intelligence'. Callaghan added: 'I am not aware who wounded the Black gin.' That more than one person was attacked is clear in this account: the boy Mick was wounded and an Aboriginal woman was wounded. There was no mention of these people in any of Smith's letters to the attorney-general and Plunkett did not indicate that he would consider these acts. The focus of the case was one man: Major Walker. Next day, Harry Romaine and Donald McLaughlin left the station, going towards Namoi Creek. Callaghan mentioned the incident to a man passing with cattle and Dick Lewes. When Mr Ryan came to the run, he did not mention it to him. Callaghan said he did not know Ryan was a magistrate.[102]

Peter Eckford had been travelling up the country when Major Walker was killed. He said that 'on hearing it I immediately proceeded to Wee Waa and gave intelligence to the police'. His hutkeeper, Callaghan, had 'sent him a note'. Eckford was able to tap into the same network of communication that had benefited Jacob Noel. It was Eckford who instigated the case and Hamilton Smith who pursued it. Eckford described Major Walker as 'a faithful servant of mine'. It was this sentimental attachment that produced the case, not any idea of justice or defence of those at the Aboriginal camp. Eckford and Hamilton disinterred Major Walker and found the bullet hole in his jacket.[103]

Constable Threadgate continued a pursuit of McLaughlin. On Thursday, 18 June 1854, he and Constable Gills went up to Mr Loder's place at Wee Waa. They went into the sitting room, where McLaughlin was 'sitting there at tea'. McLaughlin was arrested; he was with 'Mr John Eckford', who told Threadgate that McLaughlin had come on purpose 'to give himself up'.[104] One can see in this account the divisions between squatters over the case, including the Eckford brothers. McLaughlin was in the sitting room at tea as though he was a gentleman. When arrested, he said 'very well', as though imitating the gentlemen whom he was with.

Jacob Noel appeared before the bench on 30 October. From his evidence, the hut described in the first deposition was filled with other people. Besides Mrs Lewes, who had not been mentioned by Callaghan, there were two Aboriginal women present and both Callaghan and Romaine left the hut

---

102 *R v Donald McLaughlin* 1854, 1, SR 9/6397.
103 ibid.
104 ibid.

with the two Aboriginal women and Mrs Lewes to go to 'Mogil Mogil', where Mrs Lewes lived. On the way 'coming or going', Black Harry 'lost his gin'. He 'came running home' and told McLaughlin that 'he would make some of the blacks find her'. He took the gun, gave McLaughlin the cutlass and proceeded to the camp, which was 710 yards (650 metres) from the hut. When they got to the camp, however, there were 'some Marren Blacks' there. Noel heard the report of a gun and went to the camp. McLaughlin and Black Harry had a man on the ground. Asking who it was, Noel was told it was 'old Walker'. Noel got hold of McLaughlin's arm and told him to leave Major Walker alone. McLaughlin and Harry got up and left. Noel held Walker and asked whether he was hurt. Walker could not answer and Noel felt something warm under his jacket. Then Noel left the camp and went back to his dray to sleep. Next morning, he asked Callaghan where Romaine and McLaughlin were; they were asleep. He bid Callaghan 'good morning' and went away. The next day 'some of the Blacks told my Blackfellow that McLaughlin and Black Harry had killed "old Walker"'.

Noel's version of the event was far more detailed than Callaghan's. It suggests that the shooting was wrong. He gave the bench to understand that Romaine and McLaughlin knew they were not able to stay on the run and proceeded to attempt to evade the authorities for three months, McLaughlin in disguise. Noel did not explain why he disappeared from the district himself.

Charles Hamilton Smith took the statements of two Aboriginal people, Mickey Coffee and Billy Murray, on 10 April 1854. They were included in the depositions in October. As such, Charles Hamilton Smith was challenging the law that stated that Aboriginal people could not give evidence in court because they could not understand the nature of an oath. An even more complex rendering of the events of the shooting was presented in these two accounts. Mrs Lewes was at the Aboriginal camp the whole time of the shooting. Billy Murray, who was at the hut, claimed Noel and Harry took guns from the hut and Donald took the sword. Harry challenged Walker with 'where's Mary Ann?'. Walker said: 'I don't know.' Harry said: '[Y]ou must find her, or I'll shoot you.' Walker went down to the creek. Harry followed and shot him. McLaughlin cut Walker over the head with the cutlass. Walker was lying dead, Jacky covered him with an opossum cloak and McLaughlin cut old man Jacky over the head. McLaughlin then stabbed Kitty between the shoulder blades on the left side. She ran away and hid. The three men left and Billy Murray hid near the river. When Harry left, he took a horse, the brand of which Billy Murray identified to the magistrate.

The Aboriginal people all went to 'Mogil Mogil' in the morning. Mickey Coffee said Donald McLaughlin had given him a blow with the cutlass across his face at the camp and Mickey had returned to Callaghan's hut, where he stopped in the room at the back all night. He had left Mrs Lewes at the Aboriginal camp. Mickey did not know when the men left but they 'were gone for good'.[105]

The brutality in this account does not appear in the register of massacres set out by Lyndall Ryan and others because the numbers of dead cannot be quantified at six.[106] There were four people cut with McLaughlin's cutlass: one woman severely, the old men Major Walker and Jacky and two young men. Major Walker was shot, not by McLaughlin but by Romaine. The law could not take account of this Aboriginal evidence. The event could not be said to have legally taken place.

However, that the case appeared at all is significant. It was Peter Eckford in defence of his 'faithful servant' who instigated the case. This is the realm of sentimental attachment to an Aboriginal man. This sentiment did not extend to those in the camp who were attacked with a cutlass. It intersected with law through Charles Hamilton Smith, who described a 'foul wanton act'. Filtered through the relations between squatters, the case was drained of any accuracy or legal sense.

Written in pencil beside the statements of Mickey Coffee and Billy Murray were the words 'not evidence'. On John Callaghan's evidence was the pencil note 'this witness has absconded and cannot be found'; John Moore Dillon wrote: '[H]e knows nothing of the facts attending the death of Major Walker.' The evidence relating to Mrs Lewes' argument with McLaughlin was marked by Plunkett. Peter Eckford's evidence was pencil marked by Dillon: '[I]t only identifies the body after it was taken from the grave—was not in the neighbourhood at the time of the death of Major Walker and knows nothing of the facts.' Where Mickey Coffee stated that Mrs Lewes was at the camp when he left there was pencil marked but no attempt was made to obtain any deposition from her.

Despite being described as an 'outrage' by both the *Freeman's Journal* and the *Maitland Mercury*, the case was not continued with by the attorney-general and McLaughlin was bailed, much to the disgust of the Wee Waa

---

105 ibid.
106 *Colonial Frontier Massacres.*

magistrates.[107] Thomas Bagot wrote to Attorney-General Manning in January 1857 about 'the little trouble taken over the case' and 'the lawless set of men who reside in that part of the colony'. He argued that 'it is feared that similar, if not worse acts may result'.[108] Manning wrote back in January 1857 that he had carefully perused the depositions and had communicated with the criminal Crown solicitor John Moore Dillon:

> We are all of the opinion that the evidence available to the Crown is not as such as would be able to secure a conviction, and unless new facts are discovered and the evidence of such facts would be available it would be useless to attempt to proceed.[109]

John Moore Dillon had written to Manning that at the February 1856 Maitland Assizes, McLaughlin was allowed out on bail. The number of letters sent and replied to relating to the case indicated that 'Mr Bagot's statement that "little trouble" has ever been taken etc seems to be without foundation'.[110]

Despite the alacrity of the Wee Waa magistrates and the diligence of the police, this case might be said to emerge from the same sets of conflicts apparent in the Bucknell case. Groups of squatters opposed each other and sought to utilise the appearance and mechanism of the law to bring their opponents to court.[111] The Loder household had no doubt been told that there could be no case because Aboriginal evidence was unacceptable, so they proceeded with a deposition in the parlour. Nevertheless, the Wee Waa magistrates took evidence of Aboriginal people, in the first instance as 'memoranda' and in the second as a deposition, even though they were not to do so. There was much playing of law on both sides of this dispute.

The case against David Storr at Armidale in 1856 followed the same pattern. It was set in the arena of public dispute and it involved the closeness of an Aboriginal servant to his employer. An Aboriginal boy, Tommy, 'belonging to John Gallegos' or 'Jack the Spaniard', was at Armidale Creek, 2 miles from the town, when two non-Aboriginal boys came along playing with

---

107 *Maitland Mercury*, 25 February 1854; *Freeman's Journal*, 25 February 1854.
108 Thomas Bagot to the Attorney-General, 1 January 1856, SR 9/6410.
109 Attorney-General to Thomas Bagot, 1 January 1857, SR 9/6410.
110 Criminal Crown Solicitor to Attorney-General, 7 January 1856, SR 9/6410.
111 Apparent in C.T. Hamilton to Inspector-General of Police, 12 January 1852, in which Mr C.M. Doyle's letter was quoted stating a letter from the Wee Waa bench only referred to Smith and 'other members of the Bench were not consulted at all'. Hamilton stated that Mr Glennie had 'gone down the country', Mr Browne was not present and Mr Ryan and Mr Selwyn 'have long left the district'. Wee Waa Letter Book.

pistols. One boy was 'young Mossman', the other was Davy Storr. Hugh Mossman became an approver in the case and said Davy Storr was teasing Tommy about 'having a Black gin for a mother'. Tommy told him to 'be quiet' and Davy Storr jokingly said, '[W]hat if I was to shoot you?' Hugh Mossman walked towards the creek, but Davy followed Tommy and Mossman heard a shot. Davy came running: 'Oh I have shot the poor boy I must run home and tell my mother.' Though it has been argued that the case bears the signature of the frontier, that it appeared before the bench is significant. It was brought because of community pressure by one group of Armidale citizens, including Bazle Dumas and the farmer James Moore. In response, another group wrote a petition arguing that the shooting was an accident and that Bazle Dumas, with his evidence of a quarrel between Tommy and Davy Storr, had committed perjury. He had confused Davy with his brother James. Twenty-seven residents signed the petition. James Storr included a letter saying that Tommy had thrown stones at him, not his brother.[112] The case was not prosecuted by order of the solicitor-general. His reasons were not given.[113]

In these cases, local magistrates heard depositions only for them to be rejected by the attorney-general. While in *McLaughlin* the Aboriginal evidence could not be accepted, Mrs Lewes could have been called upon to make a deposition. In *Storr* there was clearly a case of manslaughter, but the solicitor-general decided not to proceed. It was the metropolis rather than the distant frontier that rejected the opportunity for Aboriginal people to obtain justice and local magistrates and sections of local communities were the ones who made use of law in defence of Aboriginal people. This is a reverse of the trope of the frontier—further out, lawless and uncontrolled. Struggles between members of local populations opened an opportunity for law to be meaningful. However, it is through the prism of sentiment and attachment that the cases appear. Aboriginal people show signs of negotiating local disputes among non-Aboriginal people, however unsuccessfully. They were willing to assist to bring cases and they were willing to help people avoid arrest. They had uses for law and they, in combination with non-Aboriginal people, were closely involved in the motor of the law in the north-west.

---

112 *R v David Storr* 1856, 5, SR 9/6397.
113 Criminal Crown Solicitor Judgement Books, Maitland, 1856, SR 4/5754.

That Aboriginal law was also active in the north-west is apparent in *Cuppy*, in which two different groups of Aboriginal people were involved in a case of an Aboriginal man murdered on the floor of a public house on the Namoi River. One group was involved in the attack, the others were feared by that group because it was expected they would arrive to defend the victim. That Billy Cuppy was present in the house was unremarked upon; Aboriginal people were often in public houses in this region. The judgement in the case recognised Aboriginal law.[114]

Warialda magistrates Richard Bligh and Richard Ottley and Armidale magistrates Robert Massie and Thomas Markham refused to send cases involving Aboriginal defendants forward to the attorney-general if there was not enough evidence. Tommy, 'an Aboriginal native of the Macintyre', had been confined by constables on suspicion of having been concerned in the murder of Edward Bradley at 'Minnimee'. Bligh and Ottley decided 'no evidence is produced beyond that given at the inquest and search having been made without success for the witness Edward Parsons the said Tommy is now discharged'.[115]

Lack of evidence also resulted in the discharge of Cobbo Jimmy for the same murder in 1851.[116] John Callaghan came before the Armidale bench in 1852 to say he was walking towards Mrs Kennedy's when she came out to say 'there was a Black gin in her house who says she knows who murdered the white woman'. Callaghan went and asked the Aboriginal woman, and she said an Aboriginal man named Charley was over towards Mrs Taylor's house. Callaghan and two other men then went over and apprehended Charley. The magistrate Markham wrote:

> I am satisfied the prisoner has had nothing to do with the murder but has merely told what he has heard from the actual murderer who happened to meet him, when camped in the bush. The murderers are known and the blacks will I have no doubt bring them in alive.[117]

In Markham's note there are two groups of Aboriginal people: one that has murdered and another who will act in concert with law. This is a partial recognition of an Aboriginal polity with its differing and diverse groups

---

114 Paula Jane Byrne, 'An Archival Find', *Criminal Law Journal* 46, no. 2 (2022): 110–12.
115 *Tommy* 1851, 7, SR 4/5679.
116 Cobbo Jimmy, 15 September 1851, WBB.
117 Copy of deposition, 16 August 1852, APRB. In December 1852, magistrate Robert Massie dismissed a similar case against Scotchy and Riley, who had been apprehended for the murder of Mrs Mason. No details were given. 3 December 1852, APRB.

expressing distinct interests in English law. The north-western benches were closest in working with this polity, both in the use of the Aboriginal messaging system and in the acceptance of Aboriginal accounts of events.

Three contradictory and confusing depositions were given to Markham at Armidale in 1852 concerning Bony alias Parry, an Aboriginal man. He was first accused of walking into a hut on 'Aberfoil' station, asking for Mr Bogan, saying he was contracted by him to cut bark and then attempting to seize a gun. Michael Horan said he had got off the bed in the hut and picked up a gun while doing so. Parry seized the gun and attempted to wrestle it from him. Henry Allingham, rather than supporting the story of Parry seeking work, said that all the non-Aboriginal men had met in the hut in consequence 'of a report that the Blacks had let the sheep out of the hurdles'. Mr Bogan 'had some sort of struggle with the prisoner'. He had 'commenced the affray' with Parry 'by catching hold' of him. Parry, said Allingham, seized the gun because he was 'actuated by fear'. Joshua Bogan, the overseer of 'Aberfoil', had yet another story. He had received a report from a shepherd named Welsh 'that the Blacks were in possession of the hut'. He and the two other men proceeded to the hut to find there were no Aboriginal people in the hut. Parry came to the door, knocked and Bogan asked him to cut bark. Welsh went into the bedroom and whispered to Allingham, Parry 'heard the whispering and endeavoured to bolt out of the hut' but Bogan 'caught him by the hair of the head'. Bogan called for the others, who came out of the bedroom and Parry took up a hurdle fork. Horan, seeing this, gave Parry a blow 'that knocked him down'. Horan threatened to shoot Parry: 'we secured him by binding him', though Allingham mentioned 'chains'. Bogan said: 'I think I had a right to catch him by the hair of the head because he had been represented to me as being one of the murderers of Mrs Sullivan' and 'it is generally believed that three different Blacks named Jack, Jacky Charlie and the prisoner were the murderers of Mrs Sullivan'.[118] This was Ellen Sullivan, the wife of a shepherd on 'Aberfoil'. She had left her house in July and was not heard of until her body was found on 10 September 1852. She had been killed by a spear to the throat. She had 'a general antipathy to the Blacks', claimed the *Goulburn Herald*.[119]

---

118 16 August 1852, APRB.
119 *Goulburn Herald*, 4 September 1852. In September 1852, a reward was offered—£20 or a conditional pardon—for the capture of Jemmy and Charley for the murder. Jemmy was 6 feet 11 inches (210 centimetres) tall and wore a blue swallow tailcoat with one skirt off. Charley was 5 feet 7 inches (170 centimetres) tall with no beard and did not understand English. They were natives of the Clarence River. *Maitland Mercury*, 4 September 1852.

Parry was taken to the courthouse, cautioned and the clerk wrote:

> [A]s far as I could understand from his imperfect knowledge of the English language, that he struggled for the gun in consequence of being frightened at Michael Horan's pointing it at him, he further said that he was severely kicked in the legs by Michael Horan and the marks still remain.

Markham wrote: '[T]he prisoner is discharged; I do not consider there is sufficient evidence to warrant his committal for trial.'[120]

These divergent stories do not suggest a reprisal mentality; the three deponents each bore a different relationship to Parry, from exonerating him to entrapment. All reverted to law rather than conduct their own punishment for the killing of Mrs Sullivan. They chained Parry and took him to the magistrate. They do not use any of the language of the frontier found on the South Coast. The Aboriginal camp was 100 yards (90 metres) from the hut and no-one expressed any fear related to its presence when Parry was being beaten and chained. This was also the case in *McLaughlin*, where, despite the presence of numbers of Aboriginal people and 'the Marren Blacks', no reprisals were expected or spoken of. Deponents in the north-west were not 'translating' their experiences into the language of the frontier. This does not mean that Aboriginal camps were not attacked or that Aboriginal people were not killed outside the purview of the law; rather that the law was interpreted differently in this region than it was on the South Coast. The experience of constables, the relationship of the magistrates to the attorneys-general and the attitudes of accused and witnesses were also different.

Though the Native Police were active in the region, they appeared only in *Sippy*. The case concerned the death of Ann Eliza Bott, a murder that occurred on the Darling Downs. Depositions were taken at Warialda. Alexander Graham, a serjeant of the Native Police, secured Sippy at 'Bulla Bulla' and obtained a confession from him.[121] Though this was a Darling Downs case that would be heard at Moreton Bay, it was transferred by the bench at Warialda. In this case, the primary evidence was a confession obtained by the Native Police. There was very little other evidence.

---

120 25 August 1852, APRB.
121 *R v Sippy*.

There is a particular axis of power regarding Aboriginal people in the north-west that derives from sentiment and attachment between gentlemen and their Aboriginal servants. It is as though Henry Parkes with his description of 'Jacky Jacky' has entered the law in this region. This sentiment refracts through the press and it gives status to particular Aboriginal men.

Magistrates and the attorneys-general

The Armidale and Tamworth magistrates took pleas. This was both before the bench in drunkenness cases, for example, and in cases that would be committed. A defendant would be asked for a plea—'guilty' or 'not guilty'—and this would be entered at the beginning of the hearing of depositions. Magistrates should not have taken pleas at all; this was the task of the assizes, where the prisoner would be asked how he or she would plead. If the plea was 'guilty', the prisoner was not subjected to trial and would be held over for sentencing.[122] Despite the taking of pleas and the sending of inadequate depositions with which the attorneys-general would not proceed, the Armidale and Tamworth benches were never reprimanded.[123] Where there should have been interventions there were none. Cases also contained contradictory statements by different witnesses and long depositions were sent in which witnesses claimed they saw nothing.[124] In *Blanchargen*, the case began with constable James Doyle saying that 'the information I have provided is correct' but no earlier deposition appears in the documents sent to the attorney-general. This is despite the fact the case was sent a year after the original offence of forgery was committed.[125] In *Mary Cott*, the surname of the victim is left blank in two sections of the deposition.[126] There is an account of criticism of the Tamworth bench in 1855 in a reply to a letter that asked where the recognisances in *Beresford* were. Police Magistrate Massie wrote to the attorney-general:

> Adverting to the last paragraph of your letter in which you state 'and I beg to remark where there is a resident Police Magistrate I would expect irregularities would not occur.' I have the honour to remind [struck through] state that altho' I am a Police Magistrate

---

122 *Plunkett's Australian Magistrate*, 271–72.
123 *R v Abraham O'Dell and John Beale* 1853, 3, SR 9/6380; *R v William Foley* 1853, 7, SR 9/6380; *R v McLaughlin*; *R v John Shepherd* 1854, 13, SR 9/6396.
124 *R v Walsh*.
125 *R v Dent alias Gardiner*; *R v Bucknell and Bucknell*; *R v White and Smith*; *R v Blanchargen*.
126 *R v Cott*.

of this territory my duties as such are in no way to interfere with those I perform as Commissioner of Crown Lands which absorb the greatest portion of my time. It is the duty of the clerk of petty sessions to forward the necessary documents to the proper department.[127]

Massie was not at all in awe of the authority of the attorney-general and his tone reflects the attitude that could be established in letters from the north-western benches. The benches all sought to direct the attorneys-general. Letters they sent often referred to the distances involved in obtaining witnesses. In *Griffiths*, the Tamworth bench wrote that it did not subpoena Mr Gramorne, who lived 'a great distance' at 'Talgan' on the Darling Downs.[128] Benches were particularly reluctant to send constables to Maitland as witnesses due to 'the expenses' involved.[129]

Magistrates instructed the attorney-general. Thomas Markham of the Armidale bench informed Plunkett that he had decided to receive the evidence of John Beale as an approver in *O'Dell and Beard*, but 'his committal for trial is ordered to secure his evidence against the other prisoner'.[130] In *Frederick Moreton and Others*, the Tamworth bench informed Plunkett that 'the case is somewhat novel in nature and the Bench were divided in opinion on the propriety of committal'.[131] In *Mason*, Durbin wrote from Tamworth that he believed

> Mason and McKenzie with sundry others had been mixed up in a general system of horse stealing. McKenzie was put on his trial but I had to dismiss the case against him and make use of him as a witness.[132]

In *Johnson*, J.B. Fellowes, police magistrate at Armidale, wrote that 'upon being asked the prisoner pleaded guilty but I deemed it advisable that depositions should be taken'.[133] In *Beresford*, the clerk of the bench informed the attorney-general that 'the Bench of Magistrates did not consider the Chief Constable's evidence of sufficient importance to cause him to leave the district for sixteen days thereby causing great inconvenience to the public'. The attorney-general replied that in murder cases all witnesses were

---

127 *R v George Beresford* 1855, 14, SR 9/6397.
128 *R v Griffiths*.
129 *R v Burke*.
130 *R v O'Dell and Beale*.
131 *R v Moreton and Others*.
132 *R v Alexander Mason* 1853, 21, SR 9/6388.
133 *R v Johnson*.

of importance.[134] All these letters to the attorney-general show an immense looseness of interpretation of the requirements of law, yet the benches were allowed to do what they pleased, mainly without interference.

In *Mattheison*, the coroner's jury included a rider after they entered a guilty verdict—'that the authorities be requested to put the strongest security measures that the law will admit of with force towards the improvement of the neighbourhood in which the murder was committed'.[135] They were referring to Beardy Street with its public houses and travelling circus. This is more than a rider on a case would allow, but it reflects Armidale and the north-west's free interpretation of the law and its superiority over the metropolis, unchecked as it was by the attorneys-general.

Wellingrove sits in stark contrast and the reasoning for that bench becoming subject to the wrath and displeasure of the attorneys-general is difficult to discover. The magistrate who received such reproaches was Captain Phillip Ditmas. In *Castle*, the depositions were returned to the bench, 'the groundwork of perjury utterly wanting'.[136] *Stephenson* was also returned: it needed the clerk of the bench or 'whoever was in attendance' to prove that the prisoner had indeed no account at the bank upon which a forgery was attempted.[137] In *Ellis*, the attorney-general requested 'the original depositions be sent to Maitland, these must be had at trial'.[138] Ditmas wrote to the attorney-general in *Williams*: '[H]ad I been aware of the custom that you mention of writing an explanatory letter I should have done so, though in this case little is left for explanation.' This was in response to a letter from the criminal Crown solicitor demanding an answer as to why no recognisances had come in and that 'until they come, I am at a loss to determine what court a trial should take place … I would beg to remind them [the bench] that it is usual to write an explanatory letter.'[139] In *Vivers*, the magistrates wanted to know 'which of the witnesses you will require for trial'. The criminal Crown solicitor wrote to the attorney-general of

---

134 *R v John Beresford*.
135 *R v Matheison*.
136 *R v Charles Castle* 1850, 10, SR 9/6361.
137 *R v Matthew Stephenson* 1851, 1, SR 9/6368.
138 *R v Ellis*.
139 *R v Williams*.

the extraordinary question put by the clerk of the bench when he asks in the event of a case being sent to a jury will it be necessary for him to send down the original depositions or will the copies be sent (and which should be returned) be sufficient?[140]

At Wellingrove, the clerk drew attention to himself, but there is more than this in the absence of reproaches to the other benches. They comprised the wealthiest men in the colony, who had considerable power in managing their regions, if not the colony. It is necessary to see the attorneys-general as players in the disputes between gentlemen and the courts as sometimes subservient to these disputes. It is not as though there is a centralised law embodied in the attorneys-general or the criminal Crown solicitor and wayward magistrates being brought into line in the name of justice and impartiality. Rather, law was thoroughly imbricated with a system of manners by which some gentlemen thought themselves better than others, some gentlemen came into conflict with others and these conflicts showed themselves in the criminal courts.

Defences and questions in court

Roughly one-third of cases at Tamworth and half the cases heard before the Armidale bench included questions by the accused of witnesses. The Warialda bench was most formal in its entries in the bench book, listing the acts under which the defendant was charged and always including questions and cross-examination by both the bench and the defendant. Cases sent to the attorney-general included such cross-examination.[141] At Wellingrove, there were eight out of a total of nine cases in which the defendant asked questions. Defence statements were far fewer at other north-western benches and the absence of defences may be related to the warnings given by the benches that information could be used in the prosecution at the assizes—a practice not followed by all benches. There were solicitors present in *Storr* and in *Ling and Others* in Armidale, but these cases were in the same session and the unnamed lawyer perhaps worked both cases.[142] In *White and Smith* at Armidale, a case from the Rocky River, an unnamed 'defence counsel' asked questions of witnesses on behalf of Smith.[143] Two Armidale

---

140 *R v Vivers*.
141 *R v Glenn*; *R v Brennan*, 11, 12; *R v Nowland*.
142 *R v Storr*; *R v Ling and Others*.
143 *R v White and Smith*.

cases in 1859 included questions by the solicitor Mr Forster.[144] Compared with other regions discussed in this book, representation was rare. In 1859 Thomas Smith said in his defence statement that 'as you have declined to allow my attorney to examine the witnesses, I decline to say anything'.[145] He implied solicitors were actively discouraged by some Armidale magistrates.

There were two coroner's inquests during the period. The first was on the body of Mary Ann Martin. The jurors in the case asked questions of witnesses and contradictory evidence was given as to the level of consciousness shown by the deceased. Her daughter said she was never sensible after George Martin hit her for 'going about too much'. Other witnesses said she was up and talking the next day. There were two defence witnesses who gave evidence of Martin's kindness to his wife and her constant drinking from anything she could get—a 'tumbler, pint pot, anything'. The case was accompanied by a letter to 'His Honour the Judge presiding at the Maitland Assizes' from the jury foreman. The coroner Thomas Markham JP had refused to bind over two witnesses. They had, it was feared, given information designed to assure they would not have to go to Maitland for the trial. Markham had given the original depositions to a solicitor engaged for the defendant, 'which appears to be unprecedented and tending to frustrate the ends of justice'. The judge suggested to the attorney-general that there should be

> a communication with the Coroner that it was irregular to hand the original depositions to a private solicitor—though probably it was done to save expense and delay in obtaining copies. Dr Markham should have given his own evidence [of the autopsy] before a magistrate.[146]

The foreman was correct that the depositions should not have been given to the solicitor and the attorney-general was the only person with such power to allow copying of depositions. The other points concerning concocted stories to avoid the assizes were left unaddressed. This inquest was the only time that contradictory evidence was questioned, and it was done by what those on the South Coast would call 'the people'. The approachability of the jury was suggested by Kenneth Mattheison in 1859 when he told Constable Callaghan to 'tell the jury not to try me today, I am in liquor—I wish to tell the truth tomorrow'.[147]

---

144 *R v George Swann* 1859, 1, SR 9/6426; *R v Francis Foot* 1859, 3, SR 9/6426.
145 *R v Thomas Smith* 1859, 5, SR 9/6426.
146 *R v George Martin* 1859, 5, SR 9/6426.
147 *R v Kenneth Mattheison* 1859, 8, SR 9/6426.

Questions by the accused in bench hearings indicate varying approaches. John Boyle said that Matthew Considine told him he did not report a theft to the bench. Boyle was reproaching his accuser for bringing the case.[148] Michael Cunnyham asked chief constable Lloyd Bradshaw whether he did not ask him to make a pair of shoes, which was either an indication of reproach or a suggestion that Bradshaw was corrupt.[149] John Campion replied to the accused: '[Y]ou did buy two bottles of rum the night before [the robbery] for 10/- from the Blacks—I was at the Blacks' camp with you.'[150] This was not at all relevant to the robbery.

Another angle of questioning involved the behaviour of the accused at the time of or before the offence. Moreton was asked whether any scabby sheep of Rusden's had ever been brought onto the run, thereby implying the slaughtering of sheep was because of fear of disease.[151] James Clarke asked his accuser whether he had assaulted him.[152] This questioning suggested that the offence was misinterpreted and actions misread. It is the major form of defence from north-western benches. Unlike the South Coast, no suggestion was made in any series of questions that there had been a number of criminal or civil cases involving persons of the same status and this is borne out by the records of the two benches in which such local disputes do not appear.

Questions also involved descriptions of the perpetrator's exact movements at the time of the offence. John Connor asked where and when he was in the tap room of Stitt's public house.[153] Thomas Gardiner asked where exactly he had been seen on the night his wife was killed.[154] Of more complexity was the suggestion in *Ashby* to constables that they were out of their district when they arrested Ashby and the defendant offered to come quietly if a warrant would be shown.[155] Cornelius Burke simply asked how he was found.[156] In *Leach* at Wellingrove, 'in answer to a question by prisoner' was crossed out.[157] These were copied depositions but the absence of the offer made to question witnesses in many cases implied that some accused were never asked.

---

148 *R v John Boyle* 1850, 8, SR 9/6361.
149 *R v Cunnyham*.
150 *R v George Beresford*.
151 *R v Moreton and Others*.
152 *R v Clarke*.
153 *R v Connor*.
154 *R v Dent alias Gardiner*.
155 *R v Robert Ashby* 1854, 3, SR 9/6388.
156 *R v Burke*.
157 *R v Daniel Leach* 1850, 17, SR 9/6361.

There were defence witnesses in cases involving gentlemen and in *Lieu and Others*. Two white men on the goldfields vouched in the latter case that Johnny and Tiro Swee were at the circus and at the bowling alley at Rocky River and then at Dr Fook's public house. The defendants had a solicitor, and any appearance of defence witnesses may be associated with his presence.[158] Defence witnesses were not usual in other cases. *Storr* had no defence witnesses. In *Leach*, Hugh Connor JP wrote to the attorney-general: 'Do you consider defence witnesses necessary?'[159]

Defence statements did not necessarily show familiarity with law. Robert Ashby claimed he had been drunk and bought the horse he was charged with stealing from 'a place called Gowrie near Gougil'.[160] Alexander Mason was 'about to sell the filly when he found it had been stolen'. He had a receipt. This defence was prefaced with 'the prisoner was warned before writing his defence'.[161] It is not clear why the defence was not spoken as it was recorded as such in the depositions—an indication that the Tamworth bench copied the depositions and sent copies to the attorneys-general. That writing defences might have been usual at Tamworth is indicated in *Beresford*, in which 'having made a statement *viva voce* the prisoner was committed to trial'. The defence statement was not written out by the clerk.[162] In *Sawyer*, the defendant said he was 'not guilty I can't help what the witnesses have said' and then gave an account of his evening just before he was apprehended and his walk from 'the big hut' to his own hut and his cooking of three eggs. This had no bearing on the case. He produced a defence witness who seemed more aware of what was required and said that the defendant had been singing with him all night, but this was quickly demolished by the magistrates when he admitted the prisoner was out of the hut at the time of the assault.[163] At Armidale in 1856, Lieu contradicted the evidence against him for theft of a carpet bag, saying he had been at the 'Hong Kong Chinamen's tent' gambling and went to another tent where he bought opium. He smoked it, drank and left. Next morning, he returned to give some opium back and was caught, held and tied up. The prosecutor offered him £100 to swear against the other prisoners. That amount of

---

158 *R v Ling and Others*.
159 *R v Leach*.
160 *R v Ashby*.
161 *R v Mason*.
162 *R v John Beresford*.
163 *R v Sawyer*.

money hints the case may have been about far more than the carpet bag that had been stolen from the gambling tent. That stolen property was never found and not presented in court.[164]

The kinds of questions asked and defences given in the north-west do not indicate great familiarity with the processes of law and this may have been because of the absence of solicitors whose style could be mimicked before other benches. The benches of the north-west did not at all belong to 'the people'; rather, they belonged to the publicans and their close cohorts, the constables. Because magistrates and constables were not reprimanded, a particular kind of surveillance centring on publicans dominated the region. This was not state surveillance, and it was in concert with Aboriginal people. An awareness of movements across different areas of country created a strong net of a kind of policing like control. Despite being on the frontier, on the edges of settlement, the language of the frontier did not appear in criminal cases. Aboriginal subjects appeared as victims and perpetrators, mainly through a notion of sentimental attachment by non-Aboriginal people. The landscape was violent and part of violent occupation, but this related to law in specific ways. The central authority of the attorneys-general made no attempt, apart from in Wellingrove, to discipline the system of law present in the north-west.

Right of reply

Through the blurred and selective lens of colonial records, this paper reveals the indispensable yet unacknowledged role of Indigenous people in shaping the social and legal fabric of New South Wales' north-west. Acting as informants, mediators, and trackers, they were foundational to frontier life, even as colonial systems sought to erase their contributions. Their quiet resilience reveals a lasting influence, reminding us that history often lies in the margins as much as in the mainstream.

Serene Fernando
Curator, State Library of Queensland

---

164 *R v Ling and Others.*

4

West

Factors in the transmission of documents from local benches involved the aesthetics of the deposition and the inclusion of correct information in the correct order, but they also involved manners. The South Coast benches approached the attorney-general as though they had a mutual problem to solve. Letters from the north-western benches were, on the other hand, imperious, directing the attorneys-general. What is notable is the sheer effort that went into First Nations cases. The Armidale and Warialda benches kept cases down involving Aboriginal aggression. A man at Shoalhaven called for the constable because he had shot a 'Black man', yet the case was swept up into the language of the frontier, which was most prominent in the metropolis. In cases from the north-west, it was the criminal Crown solicitor as well as the attorneys-general who not only refused to accept Aboriginal evidence, but also were critical of the content of that evidence. The frontier had traction in Sydney. The culture around law empowered different groups and in its very selectivity was a motor of colonisation. Gentlemen had power in the north-west, skirmishes between them utilised the language of democracy, while 'the people' had power in the South Coast region. When we open a door to the cultures of the west of New South Wales, the diversity we have seen means we do not expect to find similar patterns there (Map 4.1).

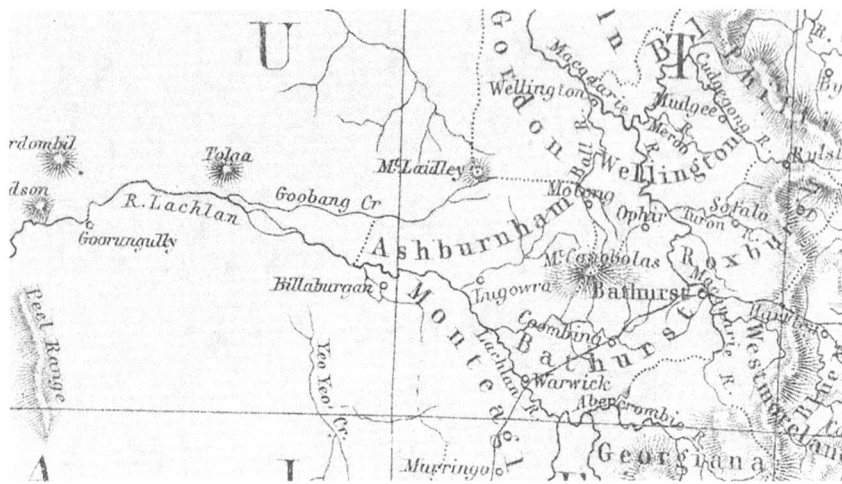

Map 4.1: Western New South Wales
Source: W. Hughes, London G. Phillip and Son, circa 1858, State Library of New South Wales, MLZ/M1 806/1858/1.

Three benches exhibited distinct relations to law. The Orange, Molong and Carcoar benches show the existence of popular utilisation of law alongside strong policing structures and diligent magistrates. They are in stark contrast to the laxness of the north-west and south. Because two of these benches present accurate depositions with great detail, they show a different aspect of the practice of law in New South Wales. The law has a different footprint in this region; it delves and intervenes in a different way. The movement through the three benches is a move towards an unsettling perspective of law—one that cannot be ascribed to laxness or self-interest among wealthy men. Molong, with its strangers and its adherence to the new *Justices Act*, shows that distance from Sydney had little bearing on conformity to the requirements of legal textbooks. Orange, 22 miles (35 kilometres) from Molong, introduces notions of crime and more extensive manipulation of the courts by an active public, so the law begins to be taken away from its purpose. Carcoar, further west and court for the unruly Lachlan River region, demonstrates that this interest in manipulation became extreme through a concern for 'evidence'. The bench at Carcoar was entirely 'lawful' and the local population took law as far as it liked. Though the language of 'the people' did not appear, this was the ultimate swallowing of law by democracy.

4. WEST

Molong

The town of Molong was established in 1835. Its population was 1,446 in 1856, growing to 1,871 in 1861.[1] The *Empire* in 1859 gave the following description:

> Molong is situated on the main Western road of the colony, is distant from Bathurst about 80 miles [130 kilometres] and is surrounded by a large increasing population, having Orange distant about 22 miles on the south east, Stoney Creek, Iron Barks, Mookerwara, all within 30 miles [48 kilometres] on the eastern side, Wellington 40 miles [65 kilometres] on the northern side and the large pastoral district of the Bogan and Lachlan on the west.[2]

All the magistrates at Molong, Robert Barton, J.H. Hood, Charles Hood, Benjamin Darby, Henry Kater, Jonathon Maugham, Alexander Hood, John Smith, John Douglas, William Palms and Jonathon Wood, were squatters—that is, landholders of significant acreages who had obtained recognition as landholders after 1837.[3] In 1857 a police magistrate appeared, Henry Whitty. All through the period, however, it was Robert Barton who wrote to the attorneys-general on behalf of the magistrates and was present in the majority of cases. Like most squatters, he obtained other properties besides 'Boree', reaching as far as the Barkly Tableland, north of Cloncurry in Queensland. Barton was considered an authority on pastoral matters.[4] He was perhaps interested in scientific thinking and this may have shaped how he saw the law.

Twenty-three sets of depositions survive for the Molong bench for 1850–60. Cases were initiated by constables and then employers and neighbours in equal proportion, in contrast, for example, to north-western New South Wales, where most cases were begun by publicans or overseers (see Figure 4.1). They show considerable effort by the clerk of petty sessions and magistrates to produce what they understood to be legal documents.

---

1   *Empire*, 21 June 1861.
2   *Empire*, 31 October 1859.
3   Stephen Roberts, *The Squatting Age in Australia* (Melbourne: Melbourne University Press, 1964).
4   *Sydney Morning Herald*, 19 August 1924; Obituaries Australia, 'Barton, Robert Darvall (1842–1924)', *Obituaries Australia*, National Centre of Biography, The Australian National University, oa.anu.edu.au/obituary/barton-robert-darvall-73/text1562.

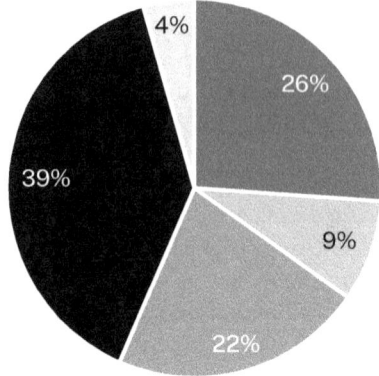

- Neighbour/same status
- Publican
- Employer
- Constable
- Not Known

Figure 4.1: Origin of cases: Molong

Aboriginal people

Press references to large gatherings of Aboriginal people in this region give an indication of the existence of an Aboriginal polity. In 1853 Peter, an Aboriginal man accused of murder, was arrested 'at a gathering of 300 to 400 aboriginals on the Bogan' River.[5] In 1850 the *Bathurst Free Press* described:

> [A] party of the Goulburn blacks who have lately been sneaking hereabouts commenced a murderous onslaught upon the Boree blacks on the 27th ult. near Boree Nyrang the residence of R.J Barton Esq. and killed three of them.[6]

Though Barton was a magistrate, there was no additional information as to pursuit or retribution by whites. The political landscape of different Aboriginal groups was here shown to exist alongside the occupation of their country; printed in the newspaper, such an account widens understanding of how colonisation occurred. It also was the society comprehended by the newspaper reader: there were two systems of governance existing side by side.

---

5   *Bathurst Free Press and Mining Journal*, 31 December 1853.
6   *Bathurst Free Press and Mining Journal*, 7 December 1850.

Newspapers stress Aboriginal involvement in industries including mining, shepherding and pastoral work. In 1851 a correspondent to the *Sydney Morning Herald* reported:

> Nearly all the Cowra, Carcoar and Molong blacks are camped at the [Ophir] diggings together with their gins and picaninnies, and I believe these sable gentlemen make a good thing of it by cutting bark, bringing firewood and water and looking after stray horses.[7]

The high standard of living enjoyed by Aboriginal people at the mines was also commented on by this writer as well as their further services in skinning wallabies for themselves and others. Such employment and Aboriginal mining are noted by Fred Cahir in his work on the Victorian goldfields.[8] Aboriginal people were also miners on NSW fields even though the Commissioner of Crown Lands decided in 1851 that they were not to mine without a licence. Gold was referred to as '*budgeree*'.[9] Peter Read has written of the history of Wiradjuri and has discussed the resource base created for Aboriginal people by the missions at Wellington and, later, Nanima from 1830 to 1850. He deals with the failure of the missions due to the removal of children and the Wiradjuri exit from both settlements in the late 1840s to 1850.[10] He does not discuss the goldfields or pastoral work in the period from 1850 to 1859. Missionaries concentrated on literacy and produced numbers of readers and writers.[11] A list of donors to the Patriotic Fund in 1855 gives 17 people from 'the Wellington Aboriginal mission'. Donations were collected by Reverend William Watson. These ranged from 2 shillings to £1.[12] The Patriotic Fund was for the widows of the Crimean War, and we cannot tell the circumstances by which this money was collected. What we can tell is that Aboriginal men and women had substantial amounts of money to hand, so were working to obtain such funds. Their listing in the newspaper alongside nearly 200 others gives them a status of equality in the press.

---

7   *Sydney Morning Herald*, 23 June 1851. The word 'gin' refers to an Aboriginal woman and is derogatory today. The word 'picaninny' for 'child' comes from the West Indies.
8   Fred Cahir, *Aboriginal People on the Goldfields of Victoria* (Canberra: ANU E Press, 2012), 9–10.
9   *Maitland Mercury*, 27 August 1851.
10 Peter Read, *A Hundred Years War: Wiradjuri People and the State* (Canberra: Australian National University Press, 1988), 15–16.
11 ibid., 14–15.
12 *Sydney Morning Herald*, 16 August 1855. Donations from James Mitchell, Jane, Ann, Clara, Thomas Taylor, Biddy, Fanny, Henry, Johanna, Richard Davis, Alexander Davis, Matthew, Tobias, Martha, T.C. Watson, Mary Campbell, Edward Campbell.

Documents: Transcription

Molong presented original depositions as the common law required. The clerk at Molong also had an eye for precision. In *Palmer*, the case refers to a nulla-nulla[13] 'now produced'. In the surgeon Patrick Charlton's evidence, 'the nulla nulla now produced is the one' is crossed out to be replaced with 'the nulla nulla would make such a wound as the one I saw'.[14] In *Powell*, Oliver Beadle was explaining exactly where his son took the sheep and proceeded to clarify further with the word 'usually'. This was crossed out and replaced with 'half an hour after he came', meaning the clerk took down only evidence related to the offence.[15] Corrections were done while the deposition was being taken.

Additional information appears rarely in Molong depositions and only to establish meaning. In *Cornelius and Cummins*, the words 'I went there' were replaced with 'I went to Burrawong'.[16] Such marking indicates that depositions taken at Molong conformed to the proper legal requirements; they were original documents.[17]

Diligent magistrates and the attorneys-general

The tone the Molong bench used in their letters to the attorneys-general was one of supplication. In 1850 in *McDonald*, they wrote:

> We have sent to the Dubbo Bench to cause Mr Kinghorne to appear before them and be bound over to appear at the QS [quarter sessions] at Bathurst on 21 Feb but hearing that it will not reach him in time, we wish to let you know, as if you think it necessary to put off the case until the Quarter Sessions we will in the meantime secure Mr Kinghorne's statement of the necessary facts.[18]

In *McGrath*, magistrates were conducting inquiries into the prisoner's name, 'but fearing these inquiries would not be developed by the time of the sitting of the Quarter Sessions was our reason (with your approval) to

---

13 A nulla-nulla is a club hewn from wood by Aboriginal people. The word was adopted by non-Aboriginal people.
14 *R v Billy Palmer* 1854, 14, SR 9/6386.
15 *R v William Powell* 1855, 5, SR 9/6394.
16 *R v Kearn Cornelius and Augustus Cummins* 1858, unnumbered, SR 9/6417.
17 Chitty and Chitty, *Richard Burn's Justice of the Peace and Parish Officer*, 118.
18 J.H. Hood and Charles Hood to the Crown Prosecutor, in *R v William McDonald* 1850, 16, SR 9/6359.

commit him to the Circuit Court'.[19] The blurring of quarter sessions and assize cases is apparent in other benches. There is no comment on these two requests for the moving of cases between jurisdictions, but in 1850 in *Peisley*, the attorney-general wrote in pencil on the cover 'inform the bench that the Quarter Sessions have no jurisdiction to try cases of forgery'.[20] The bench seems to have viewed the courts as interchangeable. In 1858 the clerk of the quarter sessions was asked to forward to the attorney-general a set of depositions for a case of stabbing. Criminal Crown Solicitor Dillon noted in pencil that the date for the recognisances was the date of the quarter sessions.[21] Mistakes indicate the bench was not perfect in managing depositions, but their letters indicate they asked for advice.

Zealousness and 'improving' cases

Molong magistrates were zealous. They wondered 'how to proceed against persons who having taken out warrants and offered rewards for the apprehension of horse stealers refuse to proceed against them when apprehended'. Attorney-General Plunkett wrote in pencil on the case: 'I can only recommend that a summons be issued for the parties to give evidence and then they must come forward as witnesses.'[22]

The bench's concern for accuracy, however, also resulted in them making creative decisions of their own. In 1850, for example, they wrote that 'many cases in which McGuiness has been concerned have been brought before us and we have selected two of the clearest cases to bring him to trial'.[23] All cases of felony should have been sent to the attorney-general.[24] In 1850 the magistrates had been reprimanded for not forwarding a forged document with the depositions they had sent. They wrote in an initial letter that 'the cheque alluded to in the Peisley case will be produced by the chief constable in whose possession it remains'.[25] Three weeks after the first letter, they wrote again: '[W]e have the honour to enclose the required document and will attend to your instructions in future cases of the like nature.'[26]

---

19 Robert Barton to Attorney-General, 24 March 1851, in *R v Richard McGrath* 1851, 7, SR 9/6365.
20 *R v Henry Peisley* 1850, 12, SR 9/6359.
21 R.B. Mitchell to Attorney-General, 23 December 1858, in *R v Dan* 1859, 17, SR 9/2624.
22 Robert Barton to Attorney-General, in *R v John McGuiness alias McGee* 1850, 9, SR 9/6359.
23 ibid.
24 *Plunkett's Australian Magistrate*, 150.
25 Henry H. Walter to Attorney-General, 7 January 1850, in *R v Peisley*.
26 J.H. Hood to Criminal Crown Solicitor, 28 January 1850, in *R v Peisley*.

They had not realised crucial evidence was not to be given to a chief constable for safekeeping. In 1857 they were asked to forward recognisances they had not included in a case.[27] In 1858 they wrote concerning another omission:

> In reply to your letter of the 30th ult. Stating that an explanatory letter ought to be sent with depositions and requesting the return of the depositions in the case of Donovan vs Cummings (cattle stealing) required as collateral evidence in the case named in the margin [*R v Donovan*, perjury] we do ourselves the honour to enclose the depositions in question.[28]

Despite such mistakes, the Molong magistrates worked diligently to put the attorney-general 'in possession of the facts'.[29] John McGuiness was 'a most determined horse stealer'.[30] In the case of an Aboriginal man tried for rape, they wrote:

> We beg further to inform you that two women, one at Montefines, Wellington, and one at the copper mine, Molong were about the same time similarly assaulted by an Aboriginal native, on both these occasions 'Peter' was encamped with Agland and the dray was at the places the assaults happened ... [I]n our minds he was the perpetrator tho' not justified. Peter for many years lived with small settlers and speaks English well and before he went to live with the Agland's was sent away from the service of a farmer living near Summer Hill, for putting the females of the family in bodily fear, considering it our duty to put you in possession of these facts.[31]

Further letters reveal the urge not only to include more information about the accused but also to embellish the case. Magistrate Robert Barton wrote to the attorney-general in 1853 that John Robinson came to see him and asked his advice about a horse he'd bought from Mrs Phillips which had belonged to 'old Mr Constable'. The horse was branded 'MC'. Robinson then sold the horse to Mr Matthews and afterwards discovered it was branded 'WL' on the near shoulder, 'which he had not seen at the time'. Barton asked Robinson if he had a receipt from Mrs Phillips, he said no, and whether he had shown the horse to Mrs Phillips before he took it away; he had not.

---

27 H. Whitty to Crown Solicitor for Criminal Business, Sydney, 24 February 1857, in *R v William Johnson* 1857, 20, SR 9/6408.
28 H. Whitty, Police Magistrate, to Attorney-General, 5 February 1858, in *R v Cornelius and Cummins*.
29 *R v McGuiness alias McGee*.
30 Robert Barton to Attorney-General, in *R v McGuiness alias McGee*.
31 Robert Barton to Attorney-General, 27 January 1851, in *R v Peter* 1850, 7, SR 9/6359.

I then told him I suspected he had made away with somebody's horse who had got wind of it, and that I should hear something further about it presently, this I am ready to swear in court when called upon, and also told Robinson in open court that this was one of my reasons for committing him.[32]

It was:

> a very barefaced affair nearly every Body examined being more or less culpable, particularly Phillips and Johnson … I also do not believe the sale of the JS horse to Robinson ever took place—it having been an afterthought when they conceived too many people were talking about Clancy's horse being made away with.[33]

As well as committing, magistrate Barton was prepared to be a witness, but he was not deposed in court before another magistrate, nor were recognisances given; he imagined he could arrive at the assizes and give evidence there. This is contrary to the place and purpose of a deposition expressed in *Plunkett*: all evidence was to be sworn and depositions were read at trial to ensure there were no divergences in information and the case was not 'concocted' or the tale 'improved'.[34] 'Improving' on the depositions in a letter was exactly what the Molong magistrates were doing.

In 1854 Barton claimed a defendant called upon him the evening before the examination before the bench. He 'admitted that he had slaughtered the heifer … and admitted he had done wrong by doing so'. The defendant, Keenan, 'asked me to get him out of it and use my endeavours to prevent him having to appear at the Police Office the following day'.[35] Barton did remand the case for a week so Keenan could produce a cow relevant to the case, but instead Keenan went to Bathurst and brought back a lawyer. Before the bench, his attorney argued that there was no evidence that the slaughtered animal belonged to the person who instituted the case. Barton then stated that Keenan had told him he had done it and what he said was immediately corroborated by the chief constable.[36] Further, Barton decided that the depositions had not been faithfully taken down: 'I shall make it my duty to be present at the Assizes when I can explain the case more fully.' A set of statements accompanying the letter contained no signatures before

---

32 Robert Barton to Attorney-General, 12 December 1852, in *R v John Robinson* 1853, 19, SR 9/6378.
33 ibid.
34 *Plunkett's Australian Magistrate*, 95.
35 Robert Barton to Attorney-General, in *R v James Keenan* 1854, 2, SR 9/6364.
36 ibid.

a magistrate, no date and were headed 'what Robert Barton knows about Keenan's affair'. They were received by the attorney-general on 31 August 1854. The witnesses for the defence statements made at the end of the hearing in May that year also were not dated. Again, this was not a sworn statement and it was a considerable 'improvement' on the deposition. These were immense informalities, but the letters are not pencil marked. The prisoner was remanded and bailed in September 1854. It was the labour of producing depositions and the sheer involvement of Barton in wishing to present 'all the facts' that produced how the court worked at Molong. The wish also, evident in *McGuiness*, to bring reluctant prosecutors into court and the concern as to exactly how to do this were signs of a diligent magistracy working with their own version of the law.

That the magistrates had a propensity to add information or statements of witnesses to depositions is apparent in other cases besides Keenan's. Depositions were legally meant to be taken in the presence of the prisoner and if he or she was not present such depositions should have been taken again.[37] The magistrates added a letter including evidence at the end of *Pickup* without it being sworn to.[38] They added a deposition to *Pienell and Peters* saying 'this witness James Lee of Larry's Lake can give the following evidence if called upon in Bathurst'.[39] At the end of *Robinson*, there are two entries by magistrates that are not depositions and are not signed. One was by a man named Martel that he had been asked to come to the courthouse by John Robinson to give evidence on Robinson's behalf that 'he saw Robinson take old Mick away'. Robinson stood accused of taking a far better horse after buying 'old Mick'. Martel told Robinson that 'if he summoned him he would speak the truth, he did not see him take old Mick away'. This account was neither signed nor dated. James Rue 'can prove' the identity of the horse taken, and great detail was provided, but again, no signatures or dates were given.[40] In the case of *Peter*, they sent an additional deposition a month after the initial hearing, not indicating that the accused was present during the hearing.[41] The magistrates clearly believed that these additional witnesses could simply be called up in Bathurst. While in South Coast and north-western cases magistrates added information in letters, at Molong, they extended the depositions with evidence that was not sworn.

---

37 *Plunkett's Australian Magistrate*, 150–53.
38 *R v John Pickup* 1854, 8, SR 9/6394.
39 *R v Robert Pienell and James Peters* 1854, 6, SR 9/6364.
40 *R v John Robinson*.
41 *R v Peter*.

That the attorneys-general castigated the Molong magistrates for their mistakes is apparent in the letters sent by the magistrates to them. Like all other depositions of the period the most intensive marking in pencil came from attorney-general John Hubert Plunkett, but these for Molong were few. The most scathing criticism of the Molong bench came from the criminal Crown solicitor. John Moore Dillon wrote in pencil on the depositions supplied by magistrates Barton and Whitty, which claimed that Donovan had committed perjury 'by swearing that Augustus Cummins had stolen a bullock':

> But he has not sworn any such thing as will be seen by the evidence—on the contrary he describes all he <u>heard</u> and prays a warrant which the magistrate very improperly granted on such a statement and as it turns out McCrae does not identify the bullock in question as one he received from Cummings. He noticed the bullock first when Donovan pointed him out.[42]

Dillon wrote:

> I have gone through the whole of these proceedings and cannot discover any materials from which to draw an information for 'perjury.' Both cases (cattle stealing and perjury) appear to have originated out of the reckless manner in which Mr Whitty [police magistrate] issued the warrants in both cases for the apprehension of the parties. Cummings may have had good grounds of action against Donovan for commencing Criminal proceedings at all, and against the magistrate for issuing a 'warrant' on such an insufficient information as Donovan swore in the first instance, but in fact none of all the persons examined differ materially as to what took place after the bullock was first noticed.[43]

The attorney-general James Martin thought there was 'ample evidence' for Donovan to be charged and overruled Dillon.[44] The jury at Bathurst agreed, though barrister Holroyd's argument was not given in the press report, and Donovan was found guilty.[45] This disagreement between Dillon and Martin seems unresolved. Dillon's criticism, however, was of the enthusiasm of the police magistrate, who had decided that perjury had occurred in the petty sessions and Whitty's actions were in keeping with the enthusiasm apparent in other magistrates. The assumption in the drafting of the 1853 amendment

---

42   *R v Donovan* 1857, 16, SR 9/6417.
43   ibid.
44   ibid.
45   *Sydney Morning Herald*, 22 March 1858.

to the *Justices Act* was that police magistrates, as paid individuals, would understand more of the requirements of law and thus they were enabled to hear cases alone, without other magistrates.[46] John Moore Dillon argued otherwise in terms of Henry Whitty, who was 'reckless' and overenthusiastic in his granting of warrants in this case. Whitty had been Commissioner of Crown Lands on the Maranoa from 1851 and was not legally trained.[47] His actions in *Donovan* were in keeping with the culture of the bench but they were not distinctively related to the supposed greater skill of a police magistrate.

The culture of the bench showed zealousness and a wish to embellish cases. This came partly from magisterial ignorance of the requirements of the deposition and partly from the enthusiasm demonstrated by Robert Barton. Informalities in adding evidence and presuming they could simply appear at the assizes were not noted by the attorneys-general. The mannered nature of the interaction is therefore stressed. The attorneys-general did not in all instances enforce the requirements of law concerning depositions. Their methods distinguished between benches.

Constables and diligence

Detail provided in cases gives access to the structure and style of policing. Constable Longbottom of the mounted police noticed 'some persons' with horses on the Kings Plains and rode up to ascertain their identity.[48] He recognised John McGuiness. Constable Chidsworth, who was with Longbottom, could identify the horse. No-one questioned the mounted police being able to stop persons they met on the road, and this is related to the convict system with its passes and identifications. This mode of policing encompassed all travelling persons.

Constables were as transparent as they could be in their depositions. Constables elsewhere would simply say they tracked a stolen horse, but in Molong exactly who tracked and where they tracked were clearly stated. Their failing was in the absence of recordings of warnings at the point of arrest. The *Justices Act* required that persons being arrested were to be warned that anything they said could be used in evidence and that they

---

46 Schofield-Georgeson, *By What Authority?*, 103–4.
47 *Maitland Mercury*, 26 May 1852.
48 *R v McGuiness alias McGee*.

should not incriminate themselves.[49] There was only one instance of such a warning being given at Molong and that was in the case of Thomas Chew, accused of grievously assaulting his wife in 1857. John Davis claimed that:

> before stripping the prisoner I asked him have you anything to tell me as I was going to Gamboola respecting the charge you are in for but I said don't say anything as it might be given in evidence against you.[50]

Given the propensity of constables to record any statements they made and to give as much detail as possible, it may be concluded that warnings were not given in all the other cases. Like magistrates, they were diligent in the pursuit of their duty, but this duty was skewed slightly away from the requirements of the law.

Constables were also relied upon by the local population. They were sent for by publicans and storekeepers on first sight of a suspicious note.[51] They were also called upon by employers and by servants and persons of equal status to the accused.[52] Warrants and the methods of setting them out, determining evidence and issuing them were set out in Plunkett's *Australian Magistrate*:

> When a complaint is made to a Justice of the Peace that an indictable offence has been committed by any person within the district to which his commission extends his duty is to issue a summons or warrant to bring the party before him, in order that he may examine and enquire into the matter of the charge and commit, or bail, or discharge the party.[53]

Warrants were also obtained by constables in pursuit of defendants. Chief constable John Davis obtained a warrant to apprehend Richard McGrath, who had escaped from custody in 1851; he searched for McGrath for 'thirty hours'. In 1855 he obtained a warrant against Robert Pienell and James Peters after he had inspected the hides at Peters' residence.[54]

---

49   *Plunkett's Australian Magistrate*, 89.
50   *R v Thomas Chew* 1858, 15, SR 9/6417.
51   *R v Peisley*; *R v John Ryan* 1855, 10, SR 9/6394.
52   Employers: *R v McGrath*; *R v John Hushan* 1855, 7, SR 9/6394; *R v Peter*. Same status: *R v William Powell*; *R v William Johnson*; *R v Palmer*.
53   *Plunkett's Australian Magistrate*, 89.
54   *R v McGrath*; *R v Pienell and Peters*.

Warrants were obtained by the public in five cases by persons who claimed cattle or horses had been stolen from them. These were formally given, as required in *Plunkett*, and included in depositions.[55] James Budge Clymo obtained a warrant against his former servant.[56] Patrick Clancy had 'just reasons' that James Robinson 'late of Molong in the said colony did on or about the morning of the 7 May steal a bay gelding the same being my property and therefore pray that justice may be done'.[57] Joseph Irvine claimed James Keenan had stolen his heifer and 'pray that he be made to answer for the same according to law'.[58] James Donovan came to court to say: 'I charge Cummins with stealing my bullock.'

There were no inquests at Molong, meaning that the opportunity for members of the public to control an investigation through a coroner was not available. Nor was an inquest even mentioned by the magistrates. There were two deaths during the period. *Palmer* and *Hushan* did not include a surgeon to establish the cause of death. In 1858 Andrew Ross, a 'legally qualified medical practitioner', gave evidence in the assault case *Dan* and he appeared also in the assault case against Thomas Chew, who cut his wife's throat. He must have been a newcomer to the area. It seems unusual that Molong did not have the services of a person who acted as a surgeon, even if not qualified; they do appear in inquests 20 miles away at Orange. The absence of this information means that the work of inquiry was not properly done at Molong. The magistrates made no comment on this point and it seems were not requested for information about such an absence by the attorney-general. The cases were tried despite there being no proper evidence of cause of death.

Constables' diligence and the willingness of the public to utilise the services of constables indicate a high level of popular interest in the law at Molong. There was a tight net of control on the roads and in police searches of property. The absence of concern for warnings implies that the law was not entirely understood but the use of warrants indicates adherence to the requirements of law. In cases involving death, the close procedure of the coroner's jury did not appear at Molong, nor did the key witness in any case of death anywhere in the colony, the surgeon, appear at all. Diligence had its blind spots.

---

55   *Plunkett's Australian Magistrate*, 89.
56   *R v McGrath*.
57   *R v John Robinson*.
58   *R v Keenan*.

The Molong public and depositions

Molong includes a kind of person who appears rarely before other benches, and this is the 'stranger'. Both Aboriginal people appearing as defendants were described as strangers to the people they attacked. William Powell was a stranger to the boy he assaulted, and horse thieves were unknown to those from whom they stole.[59] The work of constables became important in these cases. The use of the word 'stranger' indicates a close community that identified outsiders, Aboriginal or white.

Cases brought by persons of equal status were long and complex and show the use of the criminal court alongside other courts to obtain redress, ruin a rival or institute proceedings they later regretted. John Robinson went to the constable for help in placing an advertisement in the *Bathurst Free Press* saying he had accidentally sold a horse not belonging to him. Patrick Clancy obtained a warrant on the strength of the advertisement and refused the offer of £8 for the horse. He had been searching for six weeks for the horse and had told a lot of people, including the constable who had helped with the advertisement. The horse was worth £30, he claimed.[60] Diverse witnesses appeared against Robinson, all of whom gave detailed evidence as to horses they had sold and thought they saw on the street in possession of someone else. If evidence was seen to contradict a former witness, the person was recalled and questions asked and in this way the depositions were streamlined, all being tailored to the point of the case. This was the work of magistrates who were thorough, but it was also the willingness of witnesses to include detail themselves.

The inclusion of detail and the dovetailing of the evidence of witnesses distinguish Molong. On the South Coast, contradictory statements were simply put side by side into the depositions. The north-western benches allowed witnesses to contradict themselves without comment. It seems that Molong deponents were guided through a case. The attorney-general's critique was thus warded off by the careful attention to detail. We gain information on the behaviour of cows, the nature of butchering, the way in which Aboriginal people were treated when they called at the door of a house, the behaviour of shepherds, the trading positions held by women— all in service of the case. Was that the nulla-nulla that killed Jane Bradley or

---

59   *R v Powell*, *R v William Johnson*, *R v Palmer* and *R v Peter* were all cases in which the words 'strange' or 'stranger' were applied to the defendant.
60   *R v John Robinson*.

was it another just like it? This had to be made clear in the deposition. Was the strawberry cow exactly the same strawberry cow that the heifer bothered or was it another? Several witnesses were needed to answer this question.

Thus, the *work* of the law was undertaken by the Molong magistrates under Barton, a JP, not a police magistrate, and hearings were closely and accurately documented. Excesses came from diligence rather than carelessness or disinterest.

While there was enthusiasm for law and a willingness to go into detail to secure a conviction, there was also a propensity present at Molong to play the law. Attempts at this were made plain before the bench and negotiations to resolve disputes outside the law were circumvented. The detail and the openness to an *idea* of law that may have been quite far from the actual requirements of law are something the Molong public, the constables and the magistrates had in common. Such perspectives incorporated Aboriginal people, and this is apparent in cases involving Aboriginal defendants. Molong was distinct in this incorporation, as in other areas no Aboriginal people appeared before the courts or they appeared because of their close relations with an employer.

Molong Aboriginal subjects

There were two cases against Aboriginal men for attacks on white women at Molong in the 1850s. Peter 'spoke very good English and was dressed in a check shirt, cabbage tree hat, broken, and trousers'.[61] Billy Palmer also could speak 'pretty good English' and carried a nulla-nulla.[62] Both visited huts asking for directions, according to the depositions, and both were unknown to the persons they assaulted and the white people around them, fitting the idea of the stranger. They were both given food: Peter was given 'tea, bread and tobacco' and Billy Palmer 'grog and bread'. Billy Palmer asked for the road to 'Wandowendong'; Peter asked Diana Elms whether 'she had seen a blackfellow from Mr Barton's named Jacky who had lost a horse at Blackman's swamp'.

Peter was referred to by Edward Atkinson, who worked for James Keenan, as 'a strange blackfellow', who 'was seen about here … [T]he blackfellow was a stranger, not one of the Boree tribe.' Billy Palmer was the only Aboriginal

---

61   *R v Peter*.
62   *R v Palmer*.

person in the neighbourhood of 'Galgullardo' station, according to William Murray, superintendent of Archibald Campbell's station, 'Wandla Wandla'. John Bradley, a shepherd of that station, gave evidence that a

> blackfellow had come to his hut, the prisoner at the bar resembles the blackfellow but I cannot swear to him—he told me he was going to Mr Sherry's—that the blackfellows at Balderadgery were going to kill him and that he would go to the Murray.[63]

The only witness to the murder of Jane Bradley by Billy Palmer was a Chinese man, On Qweu, who did not speak English and had mimed to constable Patrick Charlton of Molong police what he had seen through a crack in the door. He had tied up Billy Palmer very tightly and had put clay on the wound on Jane Bradley's head. There was no interpreter at the bench and so his deposition did not appear. William Murray, the superintendent of Campbell's station, bathed Jane Bradley's head in warm water; she was alive but unconscious and Murray told On Qweu to untie Billy Palmer and let him go. He thought Jane Bradley had been drinking and her 'insensible state was partly to be attributed to this cause'.

It is the arrest of Billy Palmer that creates difficulty with the veracity of the descriptions of On Qweu's account. There are three accounts of the arrest. The first by constable Patrick Charlton stated that William Smith, chief constable, gave him directions to 'follow the man':

> I had no description of him but when I got to Mr Palmer's station at Cudgerie I heard there was a wounded black with his arm in a sling and a friend of mine on the station induced him to come up to the hut to have supper and to look for lost sheep and on his coming in I apprehended him, it was Sunday night I apprehended him from suspicion from the marks of the cords on his wrists and on passing Baldan-dgery Mr William Murray identified the black as the one that he let loose in the hut.[64]

Billy Palmer confessed to him on the road to Molong, as was the wont of many defendants at Molong. The second account involves the *Bathurst Free Press and Mining Journal*:

> A Chinaman in Mr Campbell's service saw the whole transaction through the chinks of the door, seized a paling and rushed upon the ravisher whom he felled to the ground, and subsequently tied in

63 ibid.
64 ibid.

such a manner, wrists, ancles [sic] and neck to a cross beam, there, but for the timely arrival of Mr Murray he would have been hanged. By some means or other he managed to escape but was taken by a Molong policeman, who identified him by the incision made by the cord in his wrists, from a gathering of 300–400 aboriginals on the Bogan … [T]he perseverance and bravery of the policeman whose name has not transpired in capturing the sable ruffian under such circumstances are worthy of recognition.[65]

John Bayliss, however, placed an advertisement in the *Bathurst Free Press and Mining Journal*:

I understand that the Constable at Molong has stated that he apprehended Billy Palmer the aboriginal, who is sentenced to death for the murder of June Bradley, in the night time. I beg through your paper to state such is not the fact. I myself apprehended the blackfellow at his camp and delivered him to the Constable at the hut about 10 o'clock of the night in the presence of three men. The Constable never visited the camp nor saw the blacks.[66]

John Bayliss was, it may be assumed, Patrick Charlton's 'friend' in his account. The newspaper account of how Palmer was tied is not corroborated in the Murray account. Murray untied Billy Palmer because he thought the woman was drunk and Palmer was innocent. Constable Charlton arrested a man with a sling and marks of cords on his wrists, who had a nulla-nulla. He was identified in court by William Murray as being the man he untied. There remains some doubt over conflicting accounts. No-one could identify the nulla-nulla as the exact weapon used.[67] On Qweu gave evidence at the assizes, despite his deposition not being forwarded. He killed a cock in court to indicate he was telling the truth. The barrister Holroyd, watching the case, questioned On Qweu's capability to give evidence at all, but the jury found Billy Palmer guilty and he was executed.[68]

Peter was accused of raping Deanna Elms, who resided on James Keenan's station. The chief constable at Molong Joseph Samuel Evans 'followed' Peter, meaning he was presumably tracked and apprehended at Summer Hill Creek and on the Monday following he was identified by Deanna Elms.[69] Elms was also wounded on the back of the head. Peter's employer,

---

65 *Bathurst Free Press and Mining Journal*, 31 December 1853.
66 *Bathurst Free Press and Mining Journal*, 18 March 1854.
67 *R v Palmer*.
68 *Bathurst Free Press and Mining Journal*, 18 March 1854; *Bell's Life*, 18 May 1854.
69 *R v Peter*.

a bullock drover, called at the hut and, on Deanna Elm's request, reported the assault to Keenan. He met Peter at Keenan's swamp and spoke to him about Mrs Elms, but Peter denied the attack.[70]

At the assizes, Peter received the death sentence for rape and was about to be executed when a letter to the colonial secretary asked why New South Wales had not followed England, where the punishment of death for rape had been abolished. The Act of Parliament had been silent on New South Wales, Dickinson contended, therefore the death penalty still applied. The colonial secretary requested the opinion of a full bench, which decided after 'wading through every Act of Parliament and every Act of the Colonial Legislature' that execution still applied in New South Wales. The executive, however, decided that Peter would not be executed.[71]

The terms on which these two cases appeared in court were different to other areas where Aboriginal people lived closely with the persons who brought them to court and were well known, or they were brought at the instigation of Aboriginal people themselves. These men were strangers and described as such. The untying of Billy Palmer suggests that there were indeed perceptions of Aboriginal innocence at Molong and there was such detail given over the nulla-nulla and its possible use as a murder weapon, with two persons claiming it was 'like' the weapon they saw. This does not ensnare Aboriginal people in an immediate realm of suspicion and hostility, even if they were seen as strangers.

The Aboriginal subject at Molong emerged, then, from the same kind of close living that also brought Aboriginal people on the South Coast before the bench, but this was through them being 'outside' and 'unknown'. They were brought through constables' activity in either tricking them or following their traces.

The three elements in Aboriginal cases—the stranger, the close detail required by magistrates and the pursuit by constables—are apparent in all Molong cases and these three components of the culture bring people into the purview of law. Once people got into court, they further expressed and showed their relationship to law.

---

70 ibid.
71 *Geelong Advertiser*, 23 April 1851.

Questions in court

In keeping with the efficiency of the clerk at Molong, answers to the questions asked of witnesses by defendants were written out and sometimes the question was also rendered. The defence statements were also given. This means the *Justices Act* was clearly followed in the courtroom at Molong and whether the defendant had questions was noted. Other benches do not record such questions and, at Hartley, a defence statement was made a day after the hearing of depositions and the magistrate was not present.[72]

Questions and answers give some idea of the way the law was understood by the ordinary population of the district of Molong. John McGuiness had the following exchange with the sheep overseer of John Woods' station, 'Brudendon':

> Question by Prisoner
>
> When you met me did I not ask you if you had a chestnut colt on the run?
>
> Answer, you did.
>
> Question, Did I not ask you if Mr Woods was at home and if he was would he lend me one horse?
>
> Answer, you might have said so.[73]

McGuiness was suggesting that he did not intend to steal the horse, or why would he have asked after it in this manner. This had no bearing on the fact of being found in possession of the horse by corporal Thomas Longbottom of the mounted police on the Wellington Road, but McGuiness thought it did. William Johnson posed a similar question to a witness, asking why he would speak of a horse if he was about to steal it.[74] The idea of intent was also used by James Sutherland, who asked a storekeeper: 'Did I not offer you another cheque before I gave you the five pounds order?' The storekeeper answered: '[Y]es you did offer me a one pound five order which I gave you back.'[75] The forged order was among other orders and Sutherland, if intending to pass a forged order, would surely only have had one.

---

72 *R v Ambrose Graves* 1851, 11, SR 9/6365.
73 *R v McGuiness alias McGee*.
74 *R v William Johnson*.
75 *R v James Sutherland* 1851, 11, SR 9/6365.

Defendants also tried to discredit evidence. John Robinson asked exactly where the horse he was accused of stealing had been taken from and how long ago one witness had sold the horse.[76] William Powell asked his victim whether he could look him in the face in court and say that all he said was true.[77] This kind of questioning was closer to the manner of attorneys in the colony. Only two cases suggest that there was a solicitor present and the first was *Cornelius and Cummins*. Donald McCrae, a grazier 'to some extent', was questioned 'by the defence'. The questioning related to the circumstances of the cattle being identified as belonging to the accused by the key prosecution witness. The case was halted by the magistrates and a charge of perjury brought against the main prosecution witness.[78] In *Keenan*, magistrate Barton suggested that Keenan 'brought back an attorney' from Bathurst. This case had defence witnesses, one of whom was the clerk of petty sessions Archimedes Byrne Luscombe, testifying that the prosecutor had also gone to the Court of Requests, indicating that legal advice was taken or the attorney was present, though questions were asked 'by the prisoner' in the case.[79] The *Bathurst Free Press* reported the hearing and the presence of Mr McIntosh, attorney, who argued there was 'no case to go to a jury'.[80]

James Keenan, the prisoner, sought comments on the public nature of his talking of slaughtering a cow. Nothing was 'kept concealed', he claimed, and the questions about the slaughtering were asked 'in public'. There was 'a room full of people' even though 'I would not swear if they all heard'.[81] Such public statements would suggest the defendant thought he was acting legally. Being 'public' implied innocence and such public speaking protected the defendant. In this way, the import of the words 'the public' in the House, as the realm of goodness and decency, appeared also in a criminal case.

Thomas Chew, before he asked questions of witnesses in his case concerning the assault of his wife, 'asked that all females be ordered from the court'. His questions of Michael Donnelly concerned Donnelly's presence in his hut at night during the week before Chew assaulted his wife. He also asked whether a man named Caulfield said of Chew 'that's the bugger as soon as we can see him off we are right' or 'the bugger is too quiet to live'. Nor had Donnelly heard anyone say of Chew's wife 'put her on the bed and shove the

---

76　*R v John Robinson*.
77　*R v Powell*.
78　*R v Cornelius and Cummins*.
79　*R v Keenan*.
80　*Bathurst Free Press and Mining Journal*, 17 June 1854.
81　*R v Keenan*.

bugger outside'.[82] Though Thomas Chew was said to be mentally impaired, these questions related exactly to intent, as did the question relating to how drunk he was at the time of the offence.[83]

More complex was the question asked by John Ryan to a man who was sleeping in the same room as him and who claimed Ryan had stolen a cheque out of his trousers pocket. The answer was: 'You did not tell me that you brought tea and sugar with you.'[84] This is related to the customs of giving and treating in the colony and seems more a reproach to the prosecutor than any defence.

Defences

After the end of 1850 prisoners generally were asked at Molong whether they had anything to say in their defence. This was sometimes 'nothing' and this was duly noted.[85] One mode of defence involved the property or part of the property being the possession of the accused and not stolen. Such property included a saddle and bridle, a heifer and coat straps.[86] In Richard McGrath's case, he claimed 'he knew nothing of the horse, good or bad', but the saddle and bridle were his own and he accused his employer, the innkeeper James Budge Clymo, of having 'perjured himself'.[87] All these cases imply that the evidence against the accused was false and that the case was concocted— something common where the accused and defendant were living closely or of equal status. There was the implication that the law was being played. This was proven in the 1858 Kearn Cornelius and Augustus Cummins case of bullock theft, where the accuser, James Donovan, who 'had not been on speaking terms for some time' with the defendant Cummins, was shown to have recognised that the 'stolen' bullock actually did belong to Cummins.[88]

In defences, cheques, orders and money had been 'found' or given by someone else and women seem to be mentioned in this context. Mrs Bloomfield and Mrs Martel were responsible for giving forged orders to James Sutherland.[89]

---

82 *R v Chew*.
83 ibid.
84 *R v Ryan*.
85 *R v Peter*; *R v John Robinson*: 'I decline making any statement at present.' *R v Pienell and Peters*; *R v John Hushan*, though this is recorded as 'no questions', as is *R v Ryan* and *R v Chew*: 'I do not wish to say anything'; *R v Keenan*: 'I reserve my defence.'
86 *R v McGrath*, saddle and bridle; *R v Keenan*, heifer; *R v William Johnson*, coat straps.
87 *R v McGrath*.
88 *R v Cornelius and Cummins*.
89 *R v McDonald*, 'found the cheque near Sheehan's station'; *R v Sutherland*.

In a case of horse theft, the innocence of William Johnson was claimed because 'I went on the road to look for work, feeling fatigued I went in the bush, laid down and did not wake till approached by the constables'.[90] Dan or 'Tan' was employing a shear blade to cut his boot when attacked by a man he stabbed. It was accidental, the shear blade was in his hand when he tried to defend himself.[91] John Pickup sold a bullock belonging to his employer because it was lame and was told to sell another four.[92] A letter he wrote was included in the case. He wrote to his employer, Mr Hawker, that he 'was lying in Molong lockup' and that he had sold a lame bullock belonging to Hawker and some of the cattle he was droving belonging to Patrick McMahon. He gave a receipt for all of them.[93] The information about the sale was underlined but not the point of the receipts. For Pickup, requesting that Hawker come to Molong as soon as possible, this letter would mean he was exonerated. Hawker, however, came to court to say he had never given permission to sell, the cattle were not his, he was running them for others.[94] It is difficult to tell at what point the letter came to the attention of the magistrates, whether it was intercepted by the lockup keeper or given by Hawker. It was simply added to the case, as Molong magistrates, as we have seen, were wont to do.

Only one case, *Keenan*, provided witnesses for the defendant—James Keenan's employees: one 'engaged' with Keenan, the other a 'hired servant', indicating the status difference. Neal Angus, the man who was engaged, gave evidence that a heifer was sucking on Keenan's cow. It was branded 'JI' and there was discussion over what to do with the heifer. 'First they thought of branding her but decided on killing her.' Patrick McAvoy, the hired servant, claimed that the prosecutor James Irwin made an offer to take 'a pound' and another heifer to settle the case. Irwin was recalled and said that Patrick McAvoy offered the pound 'to compromise the case' and that Keenan offered him a cow and heifer as an equivalent for the one he had killed. Keenan's defence statement was confusing: '[T]he beast I killed was my own, the brand which was on it I did not know and I thought it better to kill it as I could not send word, not knowing the brand.'[95] The clerk of

---

90 *R v William Johnson*.
91 *R v Dan*.
92 *R v Pickup*.
93 John Pickup to George Hawker, 14 November 1854, enclosed in *R v Pickup*.
94 *R v Pickup*.
95 *R v Keenan*.

petty sessions also gave evidence that Irvine took Keenan to the Court of Requests to recover the sum of 5/- in pounds sterling for the value of the beast slaughtered.[96] Again, playing the courts was suggested.

The right to silence deriving from *Warickshall's Case* (1738) evolved slowly in the colony, beginning from 1824, when Chief Justice Forbes refused to receive a confession he deemed involuntary in *Stack and Hand*.[97] Confessions were to be voluntary and made on oath, according to Plunkett's guide in 1847, and no inducement was to be offered or else the confession was involuntary.[98] Some Molong defendants admit guilt to a witness or in notes added at the end of a case that they had in fact done what they were accused of. Such confessions should have been sworn documents, yet the attorneys-general placed great weight on this kind of informal confession. John Pickup's letter was underlined by the attorney-general because it could be used against him because he admitted to selling the cattle.[99] John Robinson, in inveigling Martel to give evidence on his behalf, admitted that he did indeed take a horse that he knew did not belong to him.[100] Billy Palmer told constable Patrick Charleton both that he had murdered Jane Bradley and that 'they would hang him as the woman had tumbled down'.[101] John McGuiness, alias McGee, confessed, on the road to the lockup, to the arresting Trooper Chidsworth of the mounted police that the horse with which he was found did not belong to him.[102] Such confessions strengthened the case against the defendant and their inclusions may be part of the diligence shown by magistrates. They also may be a result of the lack of awareness elsewhere evident among defendants at Molong. Their weight for the attorneys-general meant that, despite the *Justices Act* and the common law set out in legal texts, voluntary confession was not a settled matter in the colony.

While the clerk of petty sessions with his accuracy and clarity may give the reader confidence in the legality of deposition taking at Molong, the actions of magistrates bring it into question. Their diligence was in part their failing. The attorneys-general also did not always follow the requirements of the law in their reviewing of depositions.

---

96 ibid.
97 Schofield-Georgeson, *By What Authority?*, 136.
98 *Plunkett's Australian Magistrate*, 167.
99 *R v Pickup*.
100 *R v John Robinson*.
101 *R v Palmer*.
102 *R v McGuiness alias McGee*.

It was possible to work beyond the scope of the law in the name of law. The diligent magistrates and constables of Molong were aware of some requirements, and they presented detail after detail in long-running initial hearings. Such activity sometimes ensnared the local community in a manner in which they were unwilling, but it was 'out of their hands' and the case had to proceed to the assizes.

The attorneys-general often ignored the inadequacies of this bench. This ignoring, where other benches were castigated, was a mannered process. The attorneys-general were approached in exactly the right way by the Molong Bench: they were asked for advice. What examination of depositions throughout the colony shows is that manners of one kind or another—obsequiousness, imperiousness or obsessiveness—helped determine the fate of those accused of offences in New South Wales.

Molong shows also how the Aboriginal polity existed alongside non-Aboriginal law and how particular mechanisms, such as the idea of the 'stranger', resulted in Aboriginal people being accused of an offence. It is not a case of Aboriginal people being subjects of law but rather an example of law reaching into the Aboriginal polity in particular ways.

Orange

Orange unsettles any study of law. The depositions invite the researcher's suspicion because there was so much awareness of law in the town. There was such a great willingness to inform, to 'pull', as the locals termed it, that one wonders what exactly appeared before a jury—real events or concocted tangles of stories in which constables and magistrates seem complicit because of an idea of duty or intense policing. Law at Orange crossed into feud and the bench played along with this, forwarding as many witnesses as possible and incomplete cases. Magistrates' sense of their 'duty'—a word not found in letters elsewhere—often overrode legal requirements. There was also a great reluctance to bail any prisoner, and solicitors at the Bathurst Assizes had to seek a judge's bail. It is difficult not to see law at Orange as being gnarled or soured by enthusiasms expressed by local people, constables and magistrates; certainly it was manipulated. Aboriginal people appeared in the courts because of the dynamic of sentiment—close relations between white men and Aboriginal men 'owned' by them. The cases, however, allow the reader to glimpse the Aboriginal polity. Magistrates forwarded evidence of Aboriginal witnesses, deeming it part of their duty although such evidence was not legally acceptable. Orange was also the place where Wiradjuri man Jemmy Darcy made the strong statement that Aboriginal disputes were not the business of the 'white fellow', indicating the strong and continued presence of Aboriginal law in the region.

Region and policing

Orange, in Wiradjuri Country, sits on the slopes of an extinct volcano, Mt Canobolas, and lies 100 miles (160 kilometres) west of Sydney over the Blue Mountains on undulating tablelands. Numbers of swamps existed there in the nineteenth century. The Aboriginal history of Orange, available online, has been written in close consultation with local Wiradjuri people.[103] The town was gazetted in 1836, but town lots were not sold until 1849 and it was eclipsed in the 1850s by the goldfields' settlements of stores, butchering establishments and informal public houses further west.[104] In 1858 the correspondent of the *Bathurst Free Press and Mining Journal* wrote:

> But a few years back Orange, known only as Blackman's Swamp consisted of a few scattered huts. But now she numbers from sixty to seventy buildings, principally brick with a population from five to six hundred residents in the town distinguished for their industry and indomitable perseverance.[105]

From accounts of 1851, the town was bypassed by traffic to the Turon fields in the south.[106]

Cases heard in Orange came from 'Blackman's Swamp', the original name of the town, deriving from the surname of Bathurst constable Blackman. They came also from runs or settlements around it where there were small groups of people living in huts: Summer Hill, to the north-east, the Heifer Station, the Valley and 'Long Swamp'. People living in these places sent for a constable at the time of a robbery or after an act of violence. There was considerable public involvement in bringing people to justice and we also read the evidence of informers—something rarely found in other benches. There were 31 assize cases heard in this period and cases initiated by ordinary people number more than those initiated by constables and employers (see Figure 4.2).

---

103 Orange City Council, *Orange Aboriginal Heritage Report*, February (Prepared for Orange City Council by NTS Corp, 2012), orange.nsw.gov.au/wp-content/uploads/2018/07/Orange-Aboriginal-Heritage-Report.pdf.
104 Orange Regional Museum, *A Short History of Orange* (2018), www.orange.nsw.gov.au/wp-content/uploads/2018/08/Short-History-of-Orange.pdf.
105 *Bathurst Free Press and Mining Journal*, 28 April 1858.
106 *Sydney Morning Herald*, 28 October 1851, 5 August 1851, 5 August 1857.

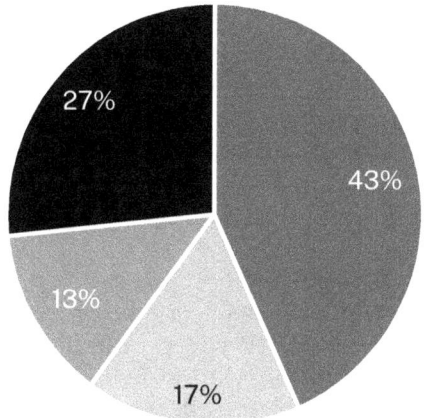

- Neighbour/same status   - Publican   - Employer   - Constable

Figure 4.2: Origin of cases: Orange

'Freedom' or the category describing a person as 'free' was part of the convict system. The Orange bench referenced the convict system in the early 1850s in its construction of assize cases while other places did not. This capacity of the convict system to wax and wane has not been recognised by Australian historians who have preferred to map the system and resistances to it.[107] The Orange magistrates categorised defendants until 1853. James Jewell was 'free by servitude' in 1850, Richard Lees was 'a native of the colony' and Richard Pepper was 'free by servitude' in 1851. James Tom was 'free' in 1852 while Morgan Davis had a 'Ticket of Leave' and John Butler was described as 'Free by Servitude' in the same year.[108] Such naming does not appear to affect the rights of the defendant in court, but it did affect ticket-of-leave holders, those who held a pass to travel and work. They, like convicts, were to lose all their property on conviction and it is these ticket-of-leave holders who further show the reader the erratic and partial nature of the convict system.

---

107 Alan G.L. Shaw, *Convicts and the Colonies: A Study of Penal Transportation from Great Britain and Ireland to Australia and Other Parts of the British Empire* (Melbourne: Melbourne University Press, 1966); John B. Hirst, *Convict Society and its Enemies: A History of Early New South Wales* (Sydney: Allen & Unwin, 1983); Stephen Nicholas, ed., *Convict Workers: Reinterpreting Australia's Past* (Melbourne: Cambridge University Press, 1988).
108 *R v James Jewell* 1850, 13, SR 9/6359; *R v Richard Lees* 1851, 17, SR 9/6365; *R v Richard Pepper* 1851, 4, SR 9/6365; *R v James Tom* 1852, 4, SR 9/6371; *R v Morgan Davis and John Butler* 1852, 18, SR 9/6371.

Ticket-of-leave holders were bound in this period to remain in the district to which they were allocated, and they were required to obtain passes to move around the country. They were to report their names, masters, means of supporting themselves and their trades quarterly to the clerk of petty sessions.[109] A person out of the district would lose his or her ticket and be returned to the superintendent of convicts. The case against Daniel Howard in 1851 underlines the informalities of administration at the local level. The magistrates wrote:

> We have the honour to report to you that the sum of £58 was found in possession of the prisoner Howard and request you will be kind enough to instruct us on its disposal we have received information that he is a ticket of leave holder for the district of Wellington.[110]

It was the Crown solicitor Dillon who discovered the difficulty with such a letter:

> The prisoner is not [sic] a Ticket of Leave Holder, having obtained his certificate of freedom on the 9th (see Colonial History annexed) January last. The offence of passing a forged cheque … is said to have been committed on or about the 10th or 12th of January last.[111]

Howard had travelled from another bench's jurisdiction into Orange district and his status was determined as ticket of leave. Dillon had obtained the entire police history of Howard from the Principal Superintendent of Convicts. His history was:

> Per ship Lloyds arrived 17 July 1837 was tried at Essex Assizes 7 March 1836 for horse stealing, Sentence 14 years
>
> 11 November 1839, 50 lashes drunk and absent
>
> 11 November, 25 lashes contempt of court
>
> 11 November, 12 months in irons, violently assaulting a constable
>
> Obtained ticket of leave 43/2874 dated 12/12/43 district of Wellington

---

109 This was under the fourth clause of the regulations of 1841. *Sydney Morning Herald*, 22 October 1841. See also notices in *New South Wales Government Gazette*, 11 December 1849, 8 July 1850, 22 November 1850.
110 Orange Bench to Attorney-General, 13 March 1851, enclosure, *R v Daniel Howard* 1851, 5, SR 9/6365.
111 Criminal Crown Solicitor to Attorney-General, 17 April 1851, enclosure, *R v Howard*.

Obtained Certificate of Freedom No. 51/13, 9/1/51

Principal Superintendent of Convicts' Office 3 April 1851.[112]

The attorney-general wrote in pencil that £10 of the £58 be given to the solicitor McIntosh, who was engaged in the defence of Howard, and requested the money be released to him as it did not form any part of the charge. Plunkett wrote that 'the rest should be kept safe until the results of the trial are known'.[113]

The depositions claimed 'Howard, Lloyd 1837 14 years, states himself Free by servitude'.[114] Howard was aware of the date of his freedom, but the magistrates chose not to believe him. In the first pages of the deposition, then, the status of the defendant wavers. This elasticity derived from the regional identification of convicts and ticket-of-leave holders and the magistrates' interest in retaining the convict system's way of referring to defendants. This gave them considerable power over individuals, but such power was erratically applied. Documentation by the superintendent of convicts could follow a person from district to district but the import and meaning of that documentation were determined by the magistrates.

Constables at Orange were careful to state that they had warned defendants before arrest and in this way were in keeping with the *Justices Act*. 'I told you I did take you legally,' said chief constable Daniel Fitzpatrick in the case against James Tom in 1852.[115] There were two cases of bribes being offered to constables at the time of arrest. John Ryan offered £5 and Rachel Stanbury offered 'five pounds and a new Tweed coat' if a constable would ignore evidence.[116] In a suggestion that constables could be considerably inventive, James Corbitt in his evidence in the case against Thomas Birkin suggested that the constable who came to search his hut 'might have put something into the bundle besides the beef for all I know'.[117] These cases indicate that constables were not simply at the service of the local population but had their own enthusiasm in pursuing cases. The relationship was not one in which they were simply called for at the time of a crisis.

---

112 ibid.
113 Jonathon to Beverley at the Attorney-General's Office, 15 April 1851, pencil note by Plunkett, enclosure, *R v Howard*.
114 *R v Howard*.
115 *R v Tom*.
116 *R v Ryan*; *R v Rachel Stanbury* 1853, 15, SR 9/6378.
117 *R v Thomas Birkin* 1856, 20, SR 9/6402.

There was evidence of sleuthing at Orange. In *Wilbrahim*, Richard Weily, a constable searching for evidence of cattle theft, said: 'I examined the fire outside, but it was not a fresh fire, it appeared to have been used for burning bones.'[118] He followed the tracks of Charles Finch in 1855 and took a boot from him, which 'corresponded with the track except that the boots had nails in them and the track has none'.[119] John Herrick also searched for tracks in Nicholl's store in Orange, which had been robbed. He put the suspect into the watchhouse and removed one of his boots to return and compare it with tracks: '[I]t is an extraordinarily nailed boot, having four rows with five nails in each row in the centre of the boot and the same nail track was plainly visible in the ground.'[120] This reference to detail indicates constables may have been castigated for lack of evidence and consequently they and magistrates included as much as they could in depositions.

Without such a need for detail, we would not be able to see the detective work of the most aggressive constable of the period, Thomas Fennerly. In 1857 he told the court that he had been watching the workers in the Wentworth goldmine 'for a very long time past'. He said it was in consequence of 'whole sale robbery being carried on there'.[121] He was similarly investigative in cases of cattle and horse theft. He visited Rudd's paddock in 1857; seeing three saddles and bridles on the ground and only two men present, he asked where the third man was: 'Smith said he (the owner of the saddle) bolted when he saw me coming that he thought it was Ive Brims, that was sending us after him. Afterwards he said it was Bob Lamb.'[122] In another case, Fennerly wanted the ears of an animal that was killed and went back the next day and found the hide of a heifer, but there was no brand on it. There should have been an 'A' if the heifer had been bought by the men who killed it. The absence of a brand was evidence to Fennerly.

Chief Constable Fennerly's methods drew the attention of the *Bathurst Free Press and Mining Journal* in January 1857. He had represented himself as a digger and was given a ride in a dray to obtain an arrest for illegal sale of spirits at a house where the two draymen stopped. He offered to pay for a glass of spirits at the house and payment was accepted, ensuring a summons for illegal sale of alcohol. He also ensured that the contents of the two drays were seized. The goods on one of the drays belonged to Mr Kator,

---

118 *R v William Wilbrahim* 1855, 1, SR 9/6393.
119 *R v Charles Finch* 1855, 16, SR 9/6393.
120 *R v Birkin*.
121 *R v Henry Rembart* 1857, 9, SR 9/6408.
122 *R v James Smith, William Perkins, and Robert Lamb* 1857, 8, SR 9/6408.

4. WEST

a magistrate, 'who had the mystic letters JP after his name', according to the newspaper. He 'demanded the restoration of his property', which occurred. The two draymen were fined £30 'without the slightest evidence'.[123] Fennerly conducted the same method of policing in three other cases before the petty sessions, disguising himself as a digger and trapping draymen into arrest. The editor of the newspaper was sure 'other motives than a desire to promote the public good' had inspired Fennerly.[124]

There does not appear to be close surveillance of the streets in Orange. When the mounted police appeared in depositions, they did so in terms of the arrest of Aboriginal people.[125] What the absence of such surveillance suggests is that constables were drawn closely into local disputes.

Detail

Orange cases contain considerable detail as though all relevant information was sought and included in the hope of obtaining a conviction. It is possible to picture at the workshop with a window that swung open as a counter,[126] the inn, the persons with nicknames living there, Dorsey Billy and Nick the Flat.[127] The manner in which gold was extracted at the Wentworth mine—by a shaft, which was a totally new way of mining—was elaborately detailed in the cases against Thomas Dalton for receiving stolen gold. A metallurgist gave the court the exact feel of the gold in one's fingers.[128] Orange defendants and witnesses noted clothing: a pair of tweed trousers, strapped, and a pair of black striped trousers,[129] a waistcoat, blue pants and clean shirt and a shawl wrapped round the head,[130] and the opossum cloak placed over Billy Morgan's wife.[131] It is also possible to ascertain customs: the playing of Bagatelle,[132] the singing and dancing in public houses,[133] the hand shaking[134] and the meeting and befriending of people on the same road

---

123 *Bathurst Free Press and Mining Journal*, 17 January 1857.
124 ibid.
125 *R v Darcy*.
126 *R v Jewell*.
127 *R v Lees*.
128 *R v Thomas Dalton and Henry Curren* 1858, 2, SR 9/6417.
129 *R v Howard*.
130 *R v John Arrow* 1859, 7, SR 9/2624.
131 *R v Billy Morgan* 1856, 13, SR 9/6402.
132 *R v William Young* 1856, 5, SR 9/6402.
133 *R v Arrow*; *R v Langham* 1855, 11, SR 9/6393.
134 *R v Howard*; *R v Tom*; *R v Patrick Holdess* 1856, 5, SR 9/6402.

as yourself.[135] The noting of the absence of 'a hat, coat or vest'[136] suggests the etiquette of travelling, and the certainty of a 'watch'[137] indicates the presence of these objects among poorer people.

Orange witnesses were good at recounting exactly what they heard. Hence, Elizabeth Bower said of James Jewell that 'he took the silver, I heard it rattle in his hand. He says bugger the subscription this will pay the fine this time.'[138] John Lester, son of an innkeeper at Guyong, heard a conversation between two men who were thought to be jointly responsible for passing forged cheques:

> [T]he prisoner at the bar recognized the other man and shook hands with him, he said he was sorry he had not returned the shears he had borrowed of him and that he had got a very good job at Smith's at Burrendong. His friend asked the prisoner to meet him at Dubbo near Mr Maughan's.[139]

Samuel Dickson related the entire conversation he had with James Tom: 'I asked him who he was, he said Tom, I asked if he was the Mr Tom, he answered, I am.' Dickson said he apologised to Tom, but asked why he didn't come to the hut to explain the presence of himself and his horses in the paddock belonging to Dickson. 'He asked where my hut was, I told him he knew well where my hut was.' Dickson said that he told Tom if he 'knew the parties' he would not have come to see who was in the paddock, 'but I had taken him for a different person'. Tom then said: '[Y]ou be f----d, take them [the horses] if you dare.' Dickson said: 'I did not want to take them, he said "you dare not take them", well now, [I said], I will.' The breakdown of a mannered hierarchy resulted in an affray, according to Tom, but a single stabbing, according to Dickson.

Rachel Stanbury was heard to say that her neighbour Garvin 'would not make a penny while he was there' and, when accused of burning Garvin's wheat stack, her husband said that 'they would pull them and make them prove what they had said about charging Mrs Stanbury for setting the wheat on fire'.[140] Thomas Smith said to Crombie Irwin, who had stopped him stabbing the publican David Bonce, that 'he knew I had claims at Ophir

---

135 *R v William Farrell* 1852, 20, SR 9/6371; *R v Finch*; *R v Ryan*; *R v Young*.
136 *R v Thomas Gleeson* 1856, 20, SR 9/6402.
137 *R v Young*.
138 *R v Jewell*.
139 *R v Howard*.
140 *R v Stanbury*.

and he would get me murdered'.[141] None of such overhearing was irrelevant; Plunkett underlined each statement that Rachel Stanbury was alleged to have made.[142] When Henry Heylin asked what was the matter with his hired servant, who had attacked him with a spade, the servant said 'nothing'.[143]

The popularity of tracking at Orange may be related to the willingness of victims to investigate. William Garvin found the track of a woman's shoe leading directly to Rachel Stanbury's hut. Mr Burfitt also saw the tracks and said 'that will do they are quite plain'. James Burfitt junior said they had better come away 'for if Mrs Stanbury got up she would most likely destroy the tracks'.[144] All the deponents believed the tracking was key to the prosecution. The constable supported this by getting all Rachel Stanbury's shoes and measuring them against the track, and Rachel Stanbury offered £5, a tweed coat, a pair of trousers and a hat to the constable if he would say that Peg Garvin's shoes were the same size as hers.[145] Edward Nicholls said he and the constable he called 'found some foot tracks' on the floor of his store and afterwards saw a boot that corresponded. He had no doubt that the 'tracks were made by that boot'.[146]

Complainants received help from informers. Edward Brennan lost his horse at Muckerenna diggings and proceeded towards Orange to look for him. On the way he 'heard' the man who had the horse 'had the look of a foreigner and spoke broken English'.[147] Joseph Lucas gave very detailed evidence against Thomas Dalton that he wanted kept secret until the assizes at Bathurst. Though the case was for receiving stolen gold, it included the statement: 'I recollect Dalton paying some money to a man I do not know the man, it was for a horse.'[148] William Hallet gave evidence against Thomas Gleeson that consisted solely of the information that Gleeson arrived at his house without 'a coat vest or hat', asking the way to the Canobolas.[149] Similarly, Edward Raine gave evidence against Thomas Dalton and Henry Curren in 1857, saying he had been at Dalton's store several days during May of that year and he saw 'both the prisoners going toward Bathurst,

---

141 *R v Thomas Smith* 1856, 23, SR 9/6402.
142 *R v Stanbury*.
143 *R v Holdess*.
144 *R v Stanbury*.
145 ibid.
146 *R v Birkin*.
147 *R v John Hennessey* 1856, 16, SR 9/6402.
148 *R v Dalton and Curren*.
149 *R v Gleeson*.

I understand they were going to Sydney'.[150] Henry Miers told the bench that when John Arrow came to the public house after his wife was killed, he was 'singing and dancing at the time, he said "I hit but did not kill her"'.[151]

The word 'pulled' was used in *Stanbury*, when Rachel Stanbury's husband said he would have the neighbours 'pulled', meaning to bring them before the courts.[152] It was used again in *Gleeson* by Michael Conway, who said he would have Gleeson 'pulled' for stabbing a man at a house where people were drinking.[153] The word indicates a propensity to use the courts against a rival or opponent.

Orange bench is notable for a number of cases of extreme violence by persons who were otherwise 'quiet' and 'good tempered' and some of whom appeared not to have remembered their violence after the event. An explanation might be found in a particular form of alcohol sold in the public houses after 1855, but not all persons were described as drunk in the accounts of their acts of violence and in Billy Morgan's case pale brandy was only mentioned in the assize hearing, not at all before the bench.

Patrick Holdess appeared at his employer's bedside with a shovel and hit his employer's wife. He then set fire to the house. He suffered from fits but had never been violent. Manning noted on the case:

> It will be proper to enquire whether the prisoner is sane at the time of his arraignment. He will probably be found to be so at that time that it is equally probable that he will be acquitted on the ground of having been insane at the time of committing offence. In that case he can be put under treatment.[154]

Edward Fowler, with 'nothing remarkable in his manner', took out his gun and shot George Washington at McKay's public house in Orange. He had been sitting on the verandah talking 'quite foolishly so that I could not make out what he was talking about', said James Corbett. He was just back from 'a concert' he had attended.[155] Thomas Gleeson stabbed a man at Buckley's house. He rushed past Michael Conway and 'stabbed him, immediately

---

150 *R v Dalton and Curren*.
151 *R v Arrow*.
152 *R v Stanbury*.
153 *R v Gleeson*.
154 *R v Holdess*.
155 *R v Edward Fowler* 1856, 5, SR 9/6402.

after he ran away'.[156] John Arrow was rushing to the house he shared with his wife, but 'he did not appear to be excited'. He had never abused his wife before that afternoon.[157] In 'talking foolishly' and 'singing and dancing', the behaviour of defendants was thought unusual. At Buckley's house, where illegal alcohol was certainly sold, there was much interference with the deceased. Before he died, he was given castor oil and water and a new shirt was put on him. He was moved from one bed onto the floor and then to another bed and no-one sent for a surgeon until after he died. 'A body ought not to be disturbed for the ends of justice might be defeated,' said the attending surgeon, Henry Warren.[158]

Constructing depositions

Orange depositions are in the same handwriting and this handwriting is very poor—something remarked upon by the attorney-general in letters sent later in the 1860s.[159] Depositions present only a few corrections and nearly all were marked while writing. That they were actual transcriptions and not copies is apparent in words being crossed out and exactly the same words written again.[160] Spelling mistakes were corrected, 'metallurgist' was corrected on top of the word and 'was' was replaced with 'were', indicating a second reader of the depositions. The word 'hopples' was replaced with 'hobbles', indicating the witness's pronunciation; using 'p' for 'b' was Kamilaroi/Gumeroi English.[161] There was also an interest in precision in constructing depositions. In *Davis and Butler*, in the words of a witness, the 'met' in 'I was met', was replaced with 'overtaken', indicating that the prisoners came on the road behind the victim.[162] The word 'glass' was replaced with 'drink' in *Gleeson*, indicating there was no glass involved.[163] Irrelevant details provided by witnesses were also crossed out. Mary Buckley went into great detail about what spirits were actually in the house where a violent assault occurred. This was no doubt because of the fear of fines,

---

156 *R v Gleeson*.
157 *R v Arrow*.
158 *R v Gleeson*.
159 Attorney General to Orange Bench, 11 June 1866, 4 February 1867, Criminal Crown Solicitor's Letter Book, State Library of New South Wales, CY 2753.
160 *R v Farrell*; *R v Wilbrahim*; *R v Gleeson*.
161 *R v Tom*. For Kamilaroi pronunciation, see Anna Ash, John Giacon, and Amanda Lissarrague, eds, *Gamilaraay/Yuwaalaraay/Yuwaalayaay Dictionary* (Alice Springs: IAD Press, 2003). See also 'Dhaalan: Pronunciation', in *Garay Guwaala: Talk the Language* (Armidale: Catholic Schools Office, 2018).
162 *R v Davis and Butler*.
163 *R v Gleeson*.

but all this detail was crossed out.[164] The order referred to in *Howard* was not 'signed by the' defendant, which was crossed out.[165] This method of presenting depositions was exactly what was recommended in *Blackstone*, the main legal text of the period, so the clerk and the magistrates were diligent in the production of documents.[166] It was by no means, however, a perfect bench. At Orange there were significant differences in the attitude of magistrates to the attorneys-general, the absence of coroners meant murder cases were not fully investigated and there was an acute awareness of legal technicality among ordinary people that suggests concoction of cases.

The magistrates and the attorneys-general

Orange magistrates sought to advise the attorneys-general about local conditions, the character of defendants and the technicalities of cases. They did this because, they informed the attorney-general, it was their 'duty'. They deemed it their duty to commit John Ryan even though they did not have enough evidence of horse theft.[167] The magistrate Andrew Kerr wrote that:

> [while William Young] was in prison on suspicion of horse stealing and during the time he was in custody waiting for evidence against him for that charge, a claimant made his appearance for the blankets on which charge I deemed it my duty to convict him.[168]

That a man was held in gaol waiting for evidence against him for some time was not remarked upon by the attorney-general and it is apparent that such 'duty' was considered to be of greater importance than the opinion of the attorney-general. Indeed, the bench made their own opinions clear to him. In *Howard*, they wrote:

> Although the cases are separate yet they are to a certain extent dovetailed in each other, the prisoners having been identified as having been in company when one of the forgeries was uttered at Stanton's Inn, and as a past many cheques similar to those for which the prisoners have been committed were present in this and the Wellington district, we have no doubt that a regularly organized plan was in operation to pass them on the different innkeepers at

---

164 ibid.
165 *R v Howard*.
166 *Blackstone's Commentaries*, 70–71.
167 Orange Magistrates to Attorney-General, 14 February 1856, in *R v Ryan*.
168 Orange Magistrates to Attorney-General, 13 December 1855, in *R v Young*.

the same time. The prisoner Pepper endeavours to prove an alibi, we have been informed the witnesses are some of the worst characters in Bathurst.[169]

The magistrates had 'no doubt' that the offence for which they had evidence was part of a much larger operation and that the alibi was a false one. But none of this evidence was in the case. Trying to incorporate opinions created some frustration on the part of magistrates. Orange magistrates used the word 'crime',[170] indicating that they saw an underlying stratum of criminal activity for which they could not find evidence to suit the law. John Ryan was a 'notoriously bad character', they advised the attorney-general, even though they did not have enough evidence for the charge of horse stealing.[171] In 1857 they wrote of a reluctant witness that 'there is little or no heed in the sacredness of our oath'.[172]

That the Orange bench was castigated for their mistakes in presenting depositions is apparent in letters included in cases. They had neglected to include the original subpoenas in *Wilbraham*,[173] their recognisances were inadequate in *Stanbury*[174] and in *Ryan* they had to return the depositions sent back to them by the attorney-general 'together with the warrant under which the Prisoner was in custody, also the hour he was last seen in his cell'.[175] More complex debate was entered into when depositions against James Smith, William Perkins and Robert Lamb were returned by the attorney-general. The magistrates wrote that they had committed the persons accused 'for the following reasons' and listed the contents of the case. They returned the case to the attorney-general, saying they had underlined the relevant passages and begged to 'call your attention to' them.[176] Such temerity was ignored by the attorney-general.

The magistrates went further in *Dalton and Curren*. They produced a witness who would not give evidence in Orange 'for certain private reasons' but would before the Bathurst Assizes. Joseph Hill of Summerhill, 'in the presence of Captain Battye JP and Chief Constable Fennerly said that if put

---

169 Orange Magistrates to Attorney-General, 15 March 1851, in *R v Howard*.
170 Orange Magistrates to Attorney-General, 28 April 1857, in *R v Smith and Others*.
171 Orange Magistrates to Attorney-General, 6 March 1856, in *R v Ryan*.
172 Orange Magistrates to Attorney-General, 28 April 1857, in *R v Smith and Others*.
173 Orange Magistrates to Attorney-General, 12 February 1855, in *R v Wilbraham*.
174 Orange Magistrates to Attorney-General, 3 March 1855, in *R v Stanbury*.
175 Orange Magistrates to Attorney-General, 6 March 1856, in *R v Ryan*.
176 Postscript Orange Magistrates to Criminal Crown Solicitor, 22 May 1857, in *R v Smith and Others*.

into the witness box at Bathurst he would astonish them (the prisoners)'.[177] Joseph Hill was undermining the whole process of law. The magistrates did not comprehend this. It was John Moore Dillon, criminal Crown solicitor, who made a comment in pencil:

> Surely the magistrates have allowed some thing or other to astray them with such a suggestion. How could the Crown ask any JURY to believe such a man? A conviction at any price seems all that is aimed at in this case.[178]

Beside the word 'astonish', he wrote: 'He might astonish the Crown if put into the witness box without knowing what evidence he was to give.'[179]

The Orange magistrates' actions in constructing cases derived from the idea of duty and that they had a 'sacred oath'. Thus, the pursuit of detail was augmented in Orange by a moral purpose that allowed advising the attorney-general and sending incomplete cases to trial. Judges would grant bail that the magistrates had neglected. In *Howard*, John Moore Dillon, Crown solicitor, wrote in pencil, 'Judge Therry appears to have ordered the prisoner to be admitted to bail', and Therry had written on the cover of the case that 'the prisoner to be admitted to bail himself in £100 and 2 sureties of £50 each, bail may be taken before a magistrate'.[180] On the cover of *Stanbury*, 'Roger Therry admits prisoner to bail' was signed 'RT'.[181] In 1858 a note on the cover of *Smith and Others* reads 'letter to the Bench at Orange, all defendants on bail', indicating they, too, were bailed by the judge.[182] Chief constable Thomas Fennerly wrote to the clerk of sessions at Bathurst in August 1857 that Thomas Dalton and Henry Curren 'were about to apply for judge's bail':

> From information I have received I have just cause and reason to believe that they will both abscond if they obtain bail, the whole of Dalton's property is in the hands of the creditors. I have also information that Henry Curren's property is made over to some person, whom I cannot say.[183]

---

177 Orange Magistrates to Attorney-General, 6 September 1857, in *R v Dalton and Curren*.
178 *R v Dalton and Curren*.
179 ibid.
180 *R v Howard*.
181 *R v Stanbury*.
182 *R v Smith and Others*.
183 *R v Dalton and Curren*.

The bail was granted at £800.¹⁸⁴ It is unclear whether such judge's bail had always to be applied for or was decided by the judge himself at the beginning of sessions. Dalton had counsel and thus may have applied to the judge on the counsel's advice.¹⁸⁵ Orange magistrates did grant bail in some cases, but they were unclear in its administration. In *Tom*, they issued both a 'recognizance of remand on the adjournment of examination' (a printed form) and bail itself.¹⁸⁶ In *Finch*, they misused the form 'Memorandum of depositions' to record bail.¹⁸⁷ Recognisances for witnesses properly should have appeared at the front of a set of depositions, but at Orange they were at the back of cases. This is the fault of the clerk of the bench and indicates some inexperience on his part.

Witnesses were asked questions by the accused in court and defences were noted at Orange. However, cases at Orange specify distinct questions by the bench during depositions and these give some indication of how magistrates approached evidence. Precision was important to the bench. In *Tom*, how dark the night was and whether objects could be clearly seen at the time of a stabbing interested them and the same questions were asked in *Gleeson*.¹⁸⁸ When exactly a cow was swapped by the accused was demanded of a defence witness in *Wilbraham*.¹⁸⁹ The magistrates asked a surgeon in *Padbury* whether he could be sure that the child who died did belong to the woman accused of the killing.¹⁹⁰ In *Dalton and Curren*, the exact character of Wentworth gold compared with other gold was the object of their attention.¹⁹¹ In the complex case of *Tom*, the magistrates asked a whole series of questions of the victim's son as to whether he had taken any part in the scuffle that led to his father's stabbing, when he saw the wound, whether his father had been under the influence of liquor, if he knew why the men had camped with the horses next to his father's house without permission, how many minutes before the altercation started and whether he had heard anything about 'knocking something' out of the party camped near the house.¹⁹² In such questioning, the bench sought to ascertain the truth of the depositions and

---

184 ibid.
185 ibid.
186 *R v Tom*.
187 *R v Finch*.
188 *R v Tom*; *R v Gleeson*.
189 *R v Wilbraham*.
190 *R v Mary Ann Padbury* 1858, 1, SR 9/6417.
191 *R v Dalton and Curren*.
192 *R v Tom*.

were following the guidelines for magistrates in *Blackstone*.[193] Orange is one of the few benches where such questioning is listed in depositions and it may account for the canny approach of defendants in cases.

The underlining by magistrates in *Smith and Others* concerned a case in which chief constable Thomas Fennerly had used his detective skills to discover brands. The attorney-general had sent back the depositions, saying the evidence was inadequate. Magistrates underlined several passages in the deposition to indicate the guilt of the defendants. They underlined Fennerly's claim that Smith told him he had only killed one beast and that belonged to Agland. They underlined Fennerly's claim that he prepared the hide himself and discovered a brand of three 't's', they underlined the evidence by constable Thomas Harper that when a defendant was told he was being arrested he said, 'Oh I know about it' and that he said he 'was coming in this morning with the two Miss Joblings but'.[194] For the magistrates, the latter statement was a confession of guilt. Attorney-General Manning's marking of the depositions constructed signs of guilt quite differently. That one defendant had 'bolted' was marked, Perkins claiming he had bought the beast from Smith was marked and Chief Constable Fennerly saying 'I cannot say what sort the animal was. I believe it to be about 2 years old and a "poley" beast' was marked. Robert Lamb telling the constable that his name was 'Henry Sutton' was underlined three times. Ferdinand Brunswick Whitty saying he went to Bray's yard to look for his cattle was marked, as was his identification of a piece of hide and foreleg as being his lost heifer and him positively identifying the hide as his.[195] The behaviour of the defendants, the unsubstantiated claims of buying and the owner's identification were critical to Attorney-General Manning. While he did not concur with the magistrates' underlining, it was rare for Manning to mark depositions in this way, so he had gone through the depositions after the magistrates returned them. At the assizes, Manning intimated there was no case against Robert Lamb and he was acquitted by the jury. The defence counsel Mr Dalley suggested the other two prisoners be acquitted as well, 'but his Honour [Stephen] demurred'. He summed up and the jury found the other two defendants 'Not Guilty'.[196] The magistrates' underlining had come to nought.

---

193 *Blackstone's Commentaries*, 70–71.
194 *R v Smith and Others*.
195 ibid.
196 *Sydney Morning Herald*, 29 September 1857.

Orange magistrates put a great deal of effort into bringing cases before the assizes, but they neglected legal requirements in the hope of securing a conviction. Their strong sense of duty was more than matched by the cleverness of the local population.

Knowing the law

When James Jewell was claimed to have said 'where are your witnesses' to Elizabeth Boner after he had pelted her house with stones, he was referring directly to the court process.[197] This statement was obtained through his own cross-examination of her neighbour, who appeared to give evidence on her behalf. Orange defendants were, it seems, encouraged to ask questions and this is in keeping with the *Justices Act*. They, unlike defendants elsewhere, took the opportunity to cross-examine constables, surgeons, wealthy landowners and people of their own status, and 16 accused persons took the opportunity to ask questions. There is only one case involving a solicitor asking questions.[198]

The questions asked by defendants were not written down by the clerk, so answers indicate what was asked. One mode of questioning involved discrediting the witnesses' version of what had happened. Richard Lees suggested he had bought the mare he was accused of stealing and was able to have the witness say that the mare had been in the possession of a man with a patch on his eye.[199] Richard Pepper in 1851 and John Arrow in 1859 suggested they were not wearing the clothes described by witnesses.[200] James Tom's extensive questioning of his prosecutor resulted in the statements 'I did not whistle … I did not call for a pistol … I could not get up without help'. The victim's answers gave a cause for the dispute: 'Mr Nicholson the surveyor tells me it is a public road, I consider it a private road, there was no reserve made on the lease I purchased for a trade.'[201] The wealthy landowner Thomas Kite 'never marked any cattle by mistake to my knowledge, never marked any of the mill cattle by mistake, never … one at Molong pound by mistake by the stock keeper'.[202] Rachel Stanbury, accused of burning a hayrick and tracked to her house, was able to suggest in her questioning that the prosecutor's daughter had been at her hut on the Wednesday

---

197 *R v Jewell*.
198 *R v Lawrence Byrne* 1858, 7, SR 9/6417.
199 *R v Lees*.
200 *R v Pepper*.
201 *R v Tom*.
202 *R v Wilbraham*.

before the fire and that accounted for the tracks of women's shoes between properties.[203] William Young suggested a closer relationship between he and his prosecutor: 'I was playing Bagatelle at Wellington on Saturday, we had some drink at Wellington, you paid for some and I paid for mine … you never gave me any money.'[204] Thomas Gleeson's questioning was aimed at proving he was drunk at the time he stabbed his victim. Michael Connesley said, '[Y]ou might have got drunk without my knowing it' and 'in about half an hour after going to Buckley's I got stupidly drunk'.[205] Even though Patrick Holdess suffered from fits and was thought to be insane, he asked a series of astute questions of his victims.[206]

Orange defendants were willing to suggest the ineptness or corruptibility of constables. James Tom was able to get a constable to say, 'I thought you were coming to give yourself into custody … I told you I did take you legally … Dickson did not tell me that the prisoner said "you know it" when he asked him his name.' Tom was able to suggest that his accuser was involved with the constables and that he was not a complete stranger to Tom as was suggested.[207] Owen Maine was able to have the constable say, 'I think you told me there was 1309 in the flock. I took £8.1.0 from you when I apprehended you.'[208] He was able to suggest his own honesty and the constable's dishonesty. James Smith also suggested his innocence when he caused the constable to say that 'it was half 6 pm, it was dark, you could have escaped as well as Lamb'. Billy Mitchell, an Aboriginal man charged in the same case, had the constable state: '[Y]ou did not offer to escape.' Constable Harper was made to suggest Robert Lamb's innocence when he stated, '[Y]ou made for your horse when you saw me. You did not undo your horse quick.'[209] Charles Finch suggested the constable did not search the hut properly when the constable answered, 'I was at the hut where you live on the Sunday night. I did not see you there or go into the bedroom.' The constable inadvertently supported Finch's alibi.[210]

---

203 *R v Stanbury*.
204 *R v Young*.
205 *R v Gleeson*.
206 *R v Holdess*.
207 *R v Tom*.
208 *R v Owen Maine* 1856, 6, SR 9/6402.
209 *R v Smith and Others*.
210 *R v Finch*.

There was no hesitation either in questioning surgeons. James Tom asked the surgeon whether 'such a wound' could have been inflicted while an attacker was lying down. He also asked the surgeon about 'cuts on [my] trousers which appear to have been done by some cutting instrument'. The surgeon thus supported Tom's argument about a general melee, in which the fight included everyone present.[211] Wealthy landowners like Thomas Kite were also not spared cross-examination. The police magistrate Whitty was closely questioned by Robert Lamb and James Smith over his identification of an animal he claimed as his own that was not branded.[212]

Another line of questioning introduced the idea that the defendant had been trusted. Patrick Holdess had Elizabeth Heylin, whom he had attacked, say that she had always left the house in his charge 'without finding anything wrong'. His employer, Alexander Heylin, answered, '[Y]ou asked me if you had burnt the place, you said you were sorry for it and offered to give me Henry's coat at dinner time, you gave yourself up.' Henry Heylin answered, 'I have between £30 and £40 of yours in my keeping.'[213] The latter ensured that Holdess could claim that money as well as indicating a close relationship between accuser and defendant.

In their questioning, the defendants were acting in the same manner as a solicitor. The only solicitor mentioned in Orange cases tried to discredit the evidence of witnesses by asking whether they had been drunk at the time of the offence.[214] The defendants in these cases were managing their appearance before a magistrate. Such an astute population is not to be found elsewhere.

Defences

As well as being unclear on bail, the Orange magistrates did not give due attention to asking for a defence. Until 1856 each defendant was asked what they had to say in their defence and if they had nothing to say the clerk recorded it. Three persons during this period declined making a defence.[215] From 1856 there was no mention of the prisoner being offered to make a defence in 15 cases and only three persons made a defence from 1855 to 1859. Lawrence Byrne 'declined making a statement' in 1858.[216] In one

---

211 *R v Tom*.
212 *R v Smith and Others*.
213 *R v Holdess*.
214 *R v Byrne*.
215 *R v Howard*; *R v Farrell*; *R v Stanbury*.
216 *R v Byrne*.

instance the clerk made an addendum at the end of a case that the prisoner had no defence to make, as though he had forgotten to note it during his taking down of minutes.[217] The major mode of defence was to discredit the prosecution case. Richard Lees said he had purchased the mare from the prosecutor.[218] William Wilbraham said the beast he had killed was his own and 'Mr Kite must have marked it by mistake'. He produced three witnesses to show that such marking—'anything he could get'—was a habit of Mr Kite's overseer.[219] James Tom's defence shows his own mode of speaking. He was accused of stabbing a man who accused him of trespass:

> It was perfectly false them denying them being more than one opposed to me when in the affray and denying there was any weapons or any violence when down—and that I stabbed him while standing was also false, or that he endeavoured to get away from me while scuffling together and that they did not whistle.[220]

He produced a witness to support his account and surgeon William Bell testified of Tom's own injuries. Thomas Smith went further in his defence against his charge of stabbing. He said of the prosecution witnesses: 'Bonce and Cromber were both drunk and the charge has been trumped up against me as I threatened to take away his licence for his bad conduct.' He also explained how he came to be carrying a knife into the public house: he was cutting rawhide to pack his horse as he was going away, the victim attacked him and 'the man might have got stabbed but I had no intention of stabbing anyone'.[221] In 1859 John Arrow explained how he came home to find clothing burning in the fireplace, his wife came home 'stark naked' and fell at his feet, he put his clothes on, his 'waistcoat' and went to the public house, where he sent for the doctor.[222]

In the case against Morgan Davis and John Butler for robbery on the road, it read that the prisoner Davis 'declines to say anything' and Butler 'says he was drunk at the time'.[223] Richard Pepper used his defence to claim an alibi for his charge of passing forged notes. He was getting new shoes

---

217 'Memo the prisoner declined to say anything in his defence', James Wilkes, Clerk of Petty Sessions, in *R v Howard*.
218 *R v Lees*.
219 *R v Wilbraham*.
220 *R v Tom*.
221 *R v Smith* (1856).
222 *R v Arrow*.
223 *R v Davis and Butler*.

in Bathurst and produced witnesses to support him.[224] Jemmy Darcy in his defence explained that he had hit the victim 'once' and their dispute was an ongoing one. His victim was always taking his wife. This was interpreted by Attorney-General Plunkett as a confession.[225] Defences and inclusion of defence witnesses show a similar astute understanding of law apparent in questions of witnesses.

Aboriginal subjects

Three Aboriginal defendants appeared before the Orange bench and two cases concerned the crucial area of *inter se* murder. In *Darcy*, an Aboriginal comment on English sovereignty was made by Jemmy Darcy when he was overheard to shout, '[A]ll whitefellow go home and go to bed there is nothing to do here, one blackfellow's quarrel has nothing to do with English laws.'[226]

That non-Aboriginal people felt themselves to be living in an Aboriginal political landscape was reflected in the kind of position Jemmy Darcy held with his employer. Darcy was employed by Mr Burfitt on his sheep station as 'overseer for the purpose of protecting himself [Burfitt] from the Blacks'.[227] This was a specific position of mediator, as Mr Moulder, another wealthy landholder, stated: '[H]e understands English well … is an intelligent Blackfellow and has been living in the employ of white people.'[228] Though living with whites so long, he clearly rejected the English legal system and his use of the words 'English laws' suggests he had given the subject some thought.

That the magistrates operated differently in terms of the legal status of Aboriginal people is apparent in the case against Billy Mitchell, accused, alongside others, of cattle theft. The magistrates wrote to the attorney-general that Mitchell 'being an Aboriginal altho' a long time domesticated with a respectable family was not in a position to make such a statement in his defence, as would have justified in discharging him without your approval'.[229]

---

224 *R v Pepper*.
225 *R v Darcy*.
226 ibid.
227 ibid.
228 ibid.
229 Orange Magistrates to Attorney-General, 28 April 1857, in *R v Smith and Others*. Mitchell was not forwarded to the assizes.

The attorney-general discharged Billy Mitchell. In the case of Jemmy Darcy, the magistrates were aware they did not have enough evidence but 'we do not feel justified in discharging the prisoner without your sanction'.[230] Plunkett did not discharge Jemmy Darcy at all. He thought the 'statement of the prisoner was sufficient to put him on his trial' (Jemmy had stated before the court the reasons for his attacking the victim) and his case went to trial, at which he was found not guilty.[231] However, the magistrates had not always followed what they took as regulations. In *Darcy*, Orange magistrates 'took the evidence of the Blackfellow Jacky' and it is presented at the end of the case without signature but witnessed by two magistrates, Templer and Kerr. They also stated that they 'examined one other native Black but his evidence was the same as Jacky's'.[232] Grappling with separate status was difficult.

Cases against Aboriginal people in Orange were initiated by non-Aboriginal people. Port Phillip Shailley's employer, Joseph Moulder, went to the bench to make a complaint that Shailley had been killed by Jemmy Darcy.[233] Billy Morgan was brought for the murder of his wife, having been seen beating her.[234] The interest in detail shown by the Orange bench gives such information as Jemmy Darcy's speech, the fact that Moulder had just given Port Phillip Shailley 'the making of a dress for his gin' and that Billy Morgan placed an opossum cloak over his wife.

All these Aboriginal accused were living closely with employers. Billy Mitchell was bailed by the squatter Joseph Aarons junior.[235] Billy Morgan was employed by Andrew Kerr, the magistrate, who took Morgan into custody.[236] The killing of Port Phillip Shailley occurred at the Aboriginal camp, which was 140 yards (128 metres) from a public house called Hanrahan's at Orange. To the barman at Hanrahan's, two of the Aboriginal people, who were quarrelling so much he ordered them away from the public house, 'belonged to Mr Moulder'.[237] The name Port Phillip Shailley may or may not indicate that the victim came from the south-east. The word 'Shailley' used by his employer is rendered 'Charlie' by Battye of the

---

230 Orange Magistrates to Attorney-General, 6 May 1853, in *R v Darcy*.
231 *R v Darcy*.
232 Orange Magistrates to Attorney-General, 6 May 1853, in *R v Darcy*.
233 *R v Darcy*.
234 *R v Morgan*.
235 *R v Smith and Others*.
236 *R v Morgan*.
237 *R v Darcy*.

mounted police and by Shailley's brother 'Jacky', so it may be more closely connected to an Aboriginal name. That relations between employer and Aboriginal employee could be very close was illustrated by the *Bathurst Free Press and Mining Journal*'s account of the suicide of James Glazier on the Lachlan River, who:

> had been overland with horses to Melbourne, accompanied by an Aboriginal who had been many years with him and other settlers. The Aboriginal was murdered by the blacks on the Murray River, which seems to have played on Glazier's mind, as it appears to be partly the cause of his attempt on his own life.[238]

The local press represented such closeness alongside a picture of an Aboriginal political landscape in this account.

Jemmy Darcy was arrested by Captain Battye of the mounted police, who had captured him when he escaped. He claimed that Darcy had confessed to him.[239] Though the mounted police were apparent at Molong, this is the only reference to them in Orange depositions. Their role was 'totally unconnected with any body of Police in the colony', claimed the *Bathurst Free Press and Mining Journal* in 1857. It comprised 26 troopers in all and they were stationed at Bathurst, Orange, Carcoar, Cowra, Ballynor, Hartley and Blackheath.[240] Their involvement in the arrest of Jemmy Darcy suggests they were central to the policing of Aboriginal people in the 1850s, but their activities are not recorded.

Those who were at the camp when Jemmy Darcy killed Port Phillip Shailley were two Aboriginal men, Baibee and Jacky. Jacky said that he lived with Mr 'Morleens', which was his pronunciation of 'Moulder'. He said that he, Jemmy Darcy and Charlie (Port Phillip) Shailley went to Mr Hanrahan's. They were all drunk. He saw Charlie hit Darcy with a nulla-nulla and Darcy threw a spear at Charlie but did not hit him. Jacky said he then went away and saw Charlie dead the next morning. He knew there had been a quarrel some time before between Charlie and Darcy. The magistrates wrote:

> The evidence of the Blackfellow Jacky is quite different from what has been previously stated to his master (Moulder) and others, and it is evident from his hesitation, equivocation and reluctance that he had fully determined not to criminate the prisoner. We examined

---

238 *Bathurst Free Press and Mining Journal*, 21 December 1859.
239 *R v Darcy*.
240 *Bathurst Free Press and Mining Journal*, 4 November 1857.

> one other native black but his evidence was quite of the same nature as Jacky's. It appears to us it is the continuation of some quarrel terminating in one of the parties being killed, at the time all present being more or less under the influence of liquor.[241]

No other person had seen the incident. The magistrates did not think there was sufficient proof. Jemmy Darcy's own statement did not convince them:

> Some time ago he and Charlie had a quarrel at Ophir ever since then Charlie has wished to quarrel with him. The evening they met at Orange and went to Hanrahan's they had all been drinking. Charlie hit him a severe blow in self-defence he hit Charlie again, once Charlie always wanted to take away his gin.[242]

As stated, it did convince Attorney-General Plunkett. The magistrates here, in attempting to have Aboriginal deponents and in assuring Plunkett they thought there was no case, were perhaps operating partly within the paternalism expressed in the 'ownership' of Aboriginal employees—the sentimentality expressed by Glazier. The law was thus negotiated differently for Aboriginal defendants in these two ways: the altering of process for them and the existence of this sentiment.

The evidence in *Morgan* was brief and contradictory, bringing the case into line with many other Aboriginal cases. Orange, however, valued detail in pursuit of accuracy and streamlining of cases, unlike places such as the South Coast and Grafton, where contradictory depositions were forwarded for both Aboriginal and non-Aboriginal defendants, so *Morgan* was unusual. Andrew Kerr gave evidence that the prisoner was in his employment and the morning before the deposition he 'was very violent and threatened to take his wife's life and that he would kill anyone who attempted to prevent him'. Kerr put the woman in his kitchen and at 3 pm 'she went to the camp'. He heard nothing of her until he was informed 'that the prisoner had killed her I took him into custody'.[243]

The two other non-Aboriginal witnesses were contradictory. Denis Langham, a painter, was sitting on the wood heap near Mr Kerr's when he 'saw the prisoner hit a Black woman in the head with a large piece and drag her some distance, he covered her with an opossum cloak'.[244] Langham

---

241 *R v Darcy*.
242 ibid.
243 *R v Morgan*.
244 ibid.

then saw Morgan 'coming towards the creek with one of his children when he went back to where he left the woman and picked up the other child and was making away to the high road'. Langham went over to where the woman was and found her with her head drawn between her legs and bound: 'I immediately let the bondage loose, she fell back and appeared to breathe for a short time, after which she died.'[245] This binding was also part of Kamilaroi/Gumeroi burial practices: the body was buried sitting up and covered with their opossum cloak.[246] The next witness, the surgeon Henry Warren, 'could find no marks of wounds about the head'. He did find wounds that went as far as the bladder. This was how she was killed. Warren had been called to 'Wellwood', Kerr's property, so the body was moved there for examination. Langham's evidence has gaps concerning the movement of Billy Morgan, while the opossum cloak was not mentioned again. If he saw the assault, he did not see the tying up of the woman into, he said, the shape of a ball. It was extremely rare for the body of an Aboriginal woman to come before the courts though many were mentioned as asides in other cases. This woman appeared because of the magistrate Kerr.

What is also remarkable is the difference between the newspaper account of the trial and the depositions. Langham in the Bathurst Assizes said the whole event happened in the Aboriginal camp and that he stopped Billy Morgan burning his wife's digging sticks by getting them out of a hollow log. Kerr said, as though performing, that Billy Morgan 'would break out into his wild habits and go into the bush'; a great deal of detail was added regarding the woman 'requesting a warrant against her husband' and Billy Morgan being drunk. Much was made of the former good relationship between husband and wife and how the wife had been educated by Mr Watson, the missionary.[247] Such variation was referred to by the chief justice:

> Many material points had not been elicited from the witnesses at the time of the prisoner was committed to trial causing much embarrassment to the counsel by their having to combat evidence for which they were not previously prepared. To show more clearly the duty of magistrates in this respect, His Honour read extracts from various charges of Lord Denman and Barons Parke and Alderson.[248]

---

245 ibid.
246 Major Walker, notes, SR 9/6410.
247 Mentioned in the brief review of the case in *Sydney Morning Herald*, 24 March 1856.
248 *Bathurst Free Press and Mining Journal*, 2 April 1856.

Court evidence that contradicted depositions was generally not acceptable. Chief Justice Stephen was acting unusually in accepting these courtroom stories and it was not, as he suggested, the magistrates who were at fault, but himself. This point was not brought up by the defending barrister William Pring, who had been requested by the chief justice to watch the case of Billy Morgan. He 'contended that the case was a conspiracy between the prosecutor and the interpreter'.[249] Both Kerr and Langham had stressed in their evidence before the assizes that Billy Morgan perfectly understood English and Langham claimed to have seen Morgan and his wife reading a book.[250] An interpreter was employed, however, there seemed to be concerted attempts on the part of prosecution witnesses to assure the court that Billy Morgan had comprehended his trial. The whole case seems too carefully constructed and when we read Kerr's evidence to the assize that this Aboriginal woman who worked in the kitchen was the only woman working on the run, other scenarios suggest themselves. Langham, by the time of the assize, was described as working for Mr Kerr and everything he saw was relocated from near the wood heap at Kerr's to the Aboriginal camp on Kerr's run; the blows to the head were replaced with violent activity of an uncertain kind and both Billy Morgan and his wife were described as drunk.

Chief Justice Stephen stressed in his advice to the jury that Aboriginal people were 'British subjects' who needed protection from the law. Being drunk was no excuse as one chose to drink and aggravated the offence rather than ameliorated it. The jury found Billy Morgan guilty, and he was sentenced to be hanged. Later records show that the hanging did not take place because of the uncertainty of the status of Edward Wise, who was acting for the attorney-general. Morgan was sent to Cockatoo Island but key letters concerning the commutation are missing.[251]

This case seems sinister because of what it implies—that Aboriginal people were thought worth conspiring against to such an extent as is revealed by the alteration and embellishment of evidence and there are comparisons to be made with the Supreme Court case concerning Cabawn Mickey's death on the South Coast. Stephen's advice to the jury in *Morgan* suggests

---

249 ibid.
250 ibid.
251 Due to a legal technicality concerning the attorney-general not appearing at the assizes, Morgan's execution was delayed for one week and then six weeks. The next record related to him refers to his presence at Cockatoo Island penal station in 1857, where his sentence for the murder was 15 years on the roads, one year in five in irons. Colonial Secretary to Chief Justice, 4 April 1856, 16 April 1856, SR 4/3761; Colonial Secretary Letters to Judicial Establishment.

the 'Aboriginal subject' was pursued by the Crown despite faulty and inadequate evidence and what Pring called 'a conspiracy'. Rather than being impartial machinery, the law in this case was certainly manipulated to assure conviction. This is contrary to the perspective that justice was possible for Aboriginal people and shows that opposition to First Nations people appeared inside metropolitan legal administration, as it did in Major Walker's case and in the murder of Cabawn Mickey. To assume that absorption of *inter se* cases into the legal system was clean of further manipulation is belied by the Morgan case. There is intent by Kerr, by the attorney-general and by the chief justice to assure conviction.

All cases against Aboriginal people at Orange emerged from the sentimental relationship stressed by squatters towards the Aboriginal people who 'belonged' to them. This allowed the discharge of Billy Mitchell from the charge of cattle theft. But Billy Morgan's case shows how such sentiment and long descriptions around it could become part of a narrative in the constructing of the Aboriginal accused and ultimately the Aboriginal subject. Sentiment or close emotional connection would have implications in fields such as Aboriginal politics where non-Aboriginal support is given. It is a central component of Australian racism.[252] As these Aboriginal cases show in the informality of law, sentiment could have both negative and positive outcomes for Aboriginal defendants.

Surgeons

'No inquest on the body was held,' said John Kelly of the burial of Port Phillip Shailley.[253] There were no inquests among the Orange depositions. There was no coroner at Orange despite the presence of surgeons who appeared in almost every case of violence, investigating wounds and giving reports.

The surgeons mentioned in depositions were J.B. Shield, 'a medical practitioner'; William Bell, 'the surgeon'; and Henry Warren, 'a legally qualified medical practitioner'. Warren appeared in 1856 and was the only medical practitioner consulted in the years after. Surgeons were also called upon by the populace. James Tom called on William Bell so that

---

252 John Maynard, *Fight for Liberty and Freedom: The Origins of Australian Aboriginal Activism* (Canberra: Aboriginal Studies Press, 2007); Aileen Moreton-Robinson, *Talkin' Up to the White Woman: Aboriginal Women and Feminism* (Minneapolis: University of Minnesota Press, 2021).
253 *R v Darcy*.

his wounds could be detailed in the case against him, so the surgeon was a defence witness in this case.[254] John Arrow told a witness he 'was going for Dr Warren' concerning his wife's injuries.[255]

Surgeons appeared in assault cases as well as examining bodies of the deceased. In *Byrne*, the surgeon Warren stated that the victim was in 'a dangerous state, I do not consider him to be out of danger now'.[256] In *Fowler*, he was able to report that the victim 'was getting on favourably' and that he had removed a portion of shirt from the bullet wound.[257]

Warren gave evidence contrary to others in two cases. In *Padbury*, he stated that the baby had died 'from exhaustion', not from the head injuries others saw Padbury inflict.[258] In *Morgan*, he decided the victim had died from wounds to her lower body, not a head injury from being hit by her husband, of which there was no sign.[259] The magistrates did not comment on such discrepancies. That Henry Warren felt himself part of the court and that he was perhaps critical of the absence of inquests at Orange was apparent in *Gleeson*:

> The body had been washed and the shirt changed, had the body been left alone I could have judged better how long the man had been dead from the nature of the wound, he might have been dead for some hours. I do not know who washed the body, it is unusual for a body to be washed on an occasion of this nature, without previously being seen by a magistrate or Coroner.[260]

At Orange there were suggestions that locals would have preferred the formality of an inquest, even in Aboriginal deaths, and that it was wrong not to have them.

Variations in local understandings of law indicate how far the law can be manipulated by well-meaning magistrates, dogged in search of 'crime'— a word found at Orange and not in other places. This is despite considerable accuracy in depositions—something that was rarely present elsewhere. Popular understanding of law indicated a particular understanding of legal technicalities uncommon in New South Wales, yet Orange did not have

---

254 Maynard, *Fight for Liberty and Freedom*; Moreton-Robinson, *Talkin' Up to the White Woman*.
255 *R v Arrow*.
256 *R v Byrne*.
257 *R v Fowler*.
258 *R v Padbury*.
259 *R v Morgan*.
260 *R v Gleeson*.

solicitors arguing cases as did other benches. Notable also was the lack of concern for rank: constables, surgeons and gentlemen were questioned by defendants as closely as were peers. If Aboriginal subjects appeared, they came from a completely different arena to white fellows. They appeared because of the realm of sentiment, emotional links between white men and 'owned' Aborigines.

The picture we have of metropolitan law officers resisting the idea of an Aboriginal subject, refusing their evidence and treating them differently in the court process is strengthened in examination of Orange cases. As in the north-west, here there is an idea of close relations between a non-Aboriginal employer and his servant, and these relationships resulted in cases being heard. Like the north-west also, magistrates were willing to take Aboriginal evidence and forward it to the attorneys-general. However, unlike the north-west, there does not seem to be the mutual interest in policing shown by groups of Aboriginal people, leading to the network of surveillance that characterised that part of New South Wales. Cases emerging from Orange return to the idea of the people present at the Shoalhaven. There is an interest in 'pulling' an opponent. The erratic nature of the convict system appears at Orange as well as notions of 'crime' along with a set of diligent and sleuthing constables.

Carcoar

In 1850 Carcoar's non-Aboriginal population was 300; in 1857, it was 364. Though the geography of the region is mainly grassy sloping plains with low hills, Carcoar is situated in a relatively hilly area. Hilly and creeked country meant that the town was very close to goldfields. In 1851 there were 1,000 non-Aboriginal people camped on the Carcoar fields and across the creek were 600 Aboriginal people from the Lachlan River to the south-west and Molong to the east, camped and providing miners with wallaby, bark and other necessities. They were also engaged in mining.[261] References to Aboriginal people in the court records from Carcoar or east at Molong or Orange always include references to payment, to wages or work. Newspaper accounts provide some insight into the Aboriginal polity stretching long distances—for example, Lachlan Aboriginal people travelled to Goulburn

---

261 *Maitland Mercury*, 31 May 1851.

to fight in 1851.²⁶² In calling out Aboriginal names for blanket distribution in Carcoar in 1850, the newspaper noted there were Wentworths, Mitchells, Fultons and Sloanes, indicating the allocation or adoption of surnames from major squatting families. This was, according to the paper, one 'tribe' coming from different parts of the Lachlan River west of Carcoar.²⁶³

In the region under the control of the Carcoar bench, extending as far as Cowra, Canowindra and Blayney, rented property figures large. This includes ground, huts, cows, herds of cattle or sheep and horses. The settlement pattern described in the courts shows a public house or a house that was unlicensed but selling spirits, with numbers of rented huts around it. Public houses were controlled by women as much as men and women are referred to as being involved in transactions, paying money and signing documents. For example, Eliza Smith was 'selling potatoes down the Lachlan' in 1850 with her husband; Eliza carried the money.²⁶⁴ Rosannah Murray alias Rose Grady and her daughter ran cattle and had their own brands.²⁶⁵ Deborah Cooper ran her house as a public house. Her husband lived some distance away.²⁶⁶ Mrs Neville had the run 'Millburn Creek' and rented out milking cows.²⁶⁷ Catherine O'Brien was joining Mrs Ward 'from the next tent' at Oakey River goldfields 'to purchase a cow'.²⁶⁸ As in Orange, convict status was given on the depositions.

It was rare for a case at Carcoar to have no women in it as witnesses or defendants. The public houses were financial centres and one can see white women in huts trying to begin businesses as publicans while their partner or husband was at work.²⁶⁹ There is specific reference to the Irish made in Carcoar depositions. One woman's evidence was translated from Gaelic²⁷⁰ and in a murder case a witness said they told the defendant that 'the cross of Jesus be between you and me'.²⁷¹ A man insisted his real name was Tanteragee, not Charles Maguire,²⁷² the designation the court gave him. Tanderagee is a town in Armagh, Northern Ireland, and we hear his accent in the deposition.

---

262 *Cornwall Chronicle*, 5 February 1851.
263 *Sydney Morning Herald*, 3 June 1850.
264 *R v Richard Seldon and John Say* 1850, 5, SR 9/6538.
265 *R v Rosannah Murray alias Rose Grady* 1851, 9, SR 9/6365.
266 *R v Joseph Morris* 1853, 1, SR 9/6378.
267 *R v Daniel Neale* 1854, 36, SR 9/6385.
268 *R v Patrick Foley* 1853, 17, SR 9/6378.
269 *R v Morris*.
270 Julia Henley, in *R v Timothy Sullivan* 1852, 7, SR 9/6371.
271 *R v Timothy Sullivan*.
272 *R v Charles Maguire and John Malony* 1858, 1, SR 9/6416.

The Carcoar bench refers to broken down and old horses being sold and what seems to be a marked lack of awareness of slaughtering or care for cattle killed for consumption.[273] The words 'poor' and 'rich' appear at Carcoar and were used by the magistrate Samuel North as well as witnesses. In contrast to the coast, the word 'esquire' or 'gentleman' was not used for squatters; rather, the word 'grazier' was used for wealthy men and this word was porous because if you had a number of cattle, you would use the term to apply to yourself. There is an idea of upward mobility. Timothy Sullivan the publican and moneylender referred to himself as a grazier.

Benches in New South Wales were sometimes very localised, and constables would not travel to areas deemed out of their jurisdiction. At other times, their law sprawls into Victoria and very much further afield than the allocated police district. Carcoar constables travelled quite far in their pursuit of warrants—to Sydney, for example.[274] They also received information through the *Hue and Cry*, an early version of the police gazette, and suspects were sent to them from Sydney as they had been advertised in this paper circulated around New South Wales and into Victoria. Cases before the bench overlap with nearby Orange. They come from Cowra and Canowindra, on the Lachlan River, Mount Macquarie, Summerhill Creek, Kings Plains, Browns Plains, as well as the goldfields.

For the 10 years between 1850 and 1859, the Carcoar bench sent 54 depositions to the attorneys-general. This is quite high compared with other benches in the same region and it suggests the bench was sought out. When Helenus Scott arrived at Carcoar in 1854, one of his first questions to Attorney-General Plunkett was, '[I]s it necessary to copy all depositions?'[275] Depositions from Carcoar were copied documents, beautifully written, which explains their neatness and some of the inconsistencies found in language. For example, it is very rare elsewhere in New South Wales to find the word 'hut' used by the people who lived in them; rather, they say 'my house' or 'my place'. Hut is a word used by magistrates who cross

---

273 The victim in *R v Addison Mitchell* (1856, 12, SR 9/6408) was sold a broken-down horse. In *R v Henry Alexander* (1851, 11, SR 9/6358), a milking cow was killed and the meat not hung properly. In *R v Thomas Duce and John Jeffries* (1853, 6, SR 9/6385), a working bullock was killed; in *R v Thomas Cogan* (1855, 9, SR 9/6393), a cow was shot; and in *R v William Vane* (1859, 5, SR 9/6424), the slaughtered carcass was in 'a bloody state' when it was taken to the National School.
274 Daniel Fitzpatrick, constable, went to Canowindra and arrested a suspect he saw walking by. *R v John Reynolds* 1850, 4, SR 9/6358. Henry Fox went to Sydney to arrest Patrick Foley (*R v Patrick Foley*); in *R v Maguire and Malony*, the constable went to Dubbo to obtain a receipt; and in 1856, a constable went to Orange to find a suspect (*R v Kennedy alias Kelly alias Johnson*).
275 Helenus Scott to Attorney-General, 19 June 1854, in *R v John Hennessy* 1854, 11, SR 9/6381.

out 'house' and write 'hut'.[276] The landscape of the Carcoar region was populated by 'huts', according to these depositions. The depositions were acts of translation, they were also smooth and detailed accounts of what was said in court, without any of the crossing out and contradictory information found elsewhere. Samuel North was police magistrate in 1850 and his clerk was his son Samuel Charles Valentine North. The pattern of their taking depositions was briefly interrupted by Helenus Scott and was resumed by Edward North, Samuel North's son and a JP, in 1856. The Norths sometimes sat alongside William Watt, who was the local member of the Legislative Assembly, and William Rothery—both major squatters. James Dagell was appointed police magistrate in 1856, Nathanial Connolly in 1857 and, from 1858 to 1859, C.E. Smith. The style of deposition continued.

Reading these sets of depositions is like focusing and blurring with a camera. Sometimes the local community can be understood, sometimes it is blurred by the editing of the magistrates. To give an example of this kind of difficulty: numbers of hats were referred to in the depositions coming from Carcoar. Timothy Sullivan, a publican and wealthy lender of money, in 1852 wore a green California hat;[277] Henry Cheeseman, a stockman and overseer, 'generally wore a cabbage tree hat'[278] in 1853; and Charles Spink, the Carcoar pound keeper, had a 'black California hat' in 1856.[279] Looking closely at the depositions, one sees the witness is being asked about hats by the magistrates, and this makes it more difficult to see hats as something valued by witnesses. This is an obstacle for the reader looking through the case to discover local cultures. Hats left at a scene of robbery or violence were regarded as evidence for the magistrates. A whole case against the lawyer George Robinson depended upon a hat, reputed to be his, being found next to a stolen tarpaulin on the road, and in 1856, a hat found in the bedroom of Mrs Neville at Cowra was described in the deposition of a constable.[280] These hats reveal a distinct obsession of the Carcoar magistracy with evidence—one that is not found elsewhere. The word 'evidence' is crucial to understand the structure of power operating at Carcoar; there is scarcely a letter from the Carcoar bench to the attorney-general in which the word was not used. Because of this there was an interest in obtaining what was

---

276 Paula Jane Byrne, 'The Language of Space and Ownership in Rural New South Wales', *Rural History* 32, no. 2 (2021): 167–86.
277 *R v Timothy Sullivan*.
278 *R v Morris*.
279 *R v George Robinson* 1856, 16, SR 9/6401.
280 ibid.; *R v William Brown* 1856, 29, SR 9/6401.

termed 'enough' evidence, and the taking of depositions and the statements of victims and witnesses at Carcoar was got through very slowly throughout the 1850s, with cases sometimes lasting for weeks.[281]

The second aspect of cases at Carcoar was that most were initiated by a person coming to the magistrate making a complaint and asking for a warrant. This is a marked difference from other benches, where local populations went to constables, not the magistrate, and constables are the ones who bring the case together or who institute cases themselves. The major utilisers of the warrant were farmers and publicans (see Figure 4.3). They went to the court not with evidence but with suspicion, sometimes just a feeling that their neighbour was the culprit. After 1856 such suspicions were formally set out by Edward North JP: 'I have good reason to believe and suspect and do suspect.' A warrant was drawn up and a defendant diligently sought for by constables, sometimes for months or years before he or she was arrested and warned and brought back to be put in the watchhouse or bailed. Then depositions would be taken and taken over again in the presence of the prisoner, week after week, on Saturdays usually, the same witnesses would be brought up to be re-sworn and their evidence read out to them.

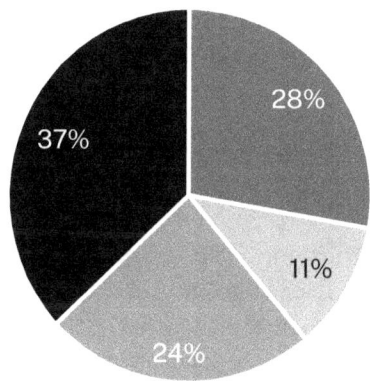

■ Neighbour/same status   ■ Publican   ■ Employer   ■ Constable

Figure 4.3: Origin of cases: Carcoar

---

281 *R v Seldon and Say*, two weeks; *R v John Reynolds* (1850, 23, SR 9/6358), two months; *R v Peisley*, seven months; *R v Patrick Maher* (1851, 5, SR 9/6365), three months.

This gave opportunity for a witness to embroider information or to retract it by claiming hazy recall or mistaken recognition. Sometimes people changed their mind about their former evidence or introduced new material when they came back into court. Daniel Healy said in 1852 that he wanted to change his evidence completely because he had been to Bathurst to confess to a priest and he did so by direction of the priest.[282] Thomas Haines came back into court a week after his first evidence and said he was 'determined to tell the truth now, [he would not] let his own good nature get him into trouble'.[283] There was no comment by the bench or the attorney-general on such changes of mind. Given the propensity of magistrates to streamline and edit cases and the willingness of the local population to add to information they gave, there is a dovetailing of interest. This is apparent in *Mitchell*, in which a local, agreed upon story was presented about the movements of a young, elegantly dressed man on his way to the goldfields and the surly servant who was accused of killing him. While the depositions were initially contradictory, later testimony ironed out differences and new evidence was presented at the Bathurst Assizes concerning a watch found by two 'concerned' witnesses where the prisoner had been staying.[284]

The aspects of the Carcoar bench that significantly distinguish it from others, even those 20 miles away, are the bench's dependence on the warrant and suspicion, this concern for evidence and the consequent power these gave to the communities from which cases emerged.

There were differences between gentlemen over the investigation of cases. William Rothery and Helenus Scott both refused to investigate the death of a man at the hands of a constable at the Cowra races in 1854, saying it was out of their jurisdiction, but Edward North undertook the inquest as a JP and returned the depositions to Carcoar, after which he sat on the bench. When we look at Scott's management of his early depositions, he acts in the manner of a coastal gentleman magistrate, taking depositions, not hearing 'evidence' and sending them to Sydney quite quickly; this was not the Carcoar way. Scott seems to have been quickly sidelined in the constructing of cases for the assizes.

---

282 *R v Timothy Sullivan*.
283 *R v Morris*.
284 *R v Mitchell*.

The Carcoar magistrates' idea of what constituted evidence occasionally differed from that held by the attorneys-general or the criminal Crown solicitor. In 1856 the criminal Crown solicitor wrote in the margin of *Dinger* that the evidence was 'insufficient'.[285] In 1858 the Carcoar bench retried a man whose case had not been proceeded with in the quarter sessions and found him guilty. Local petition and press reports resulted in a government inquiry and Edward North lost his position as JP.[286] In another case, the criminal Crown solicitor demanded to know what the detail in the deposition had to do with the case against the accused.[287] Attorney-General Bayley wrote in 1859 that 'some cattle were lost and some were traced' and the evidence against the defendant was 'wholly insufficient'.[288]

Unlike benches further east, the Carcoar bench bailed defendants, requested questions from the defendant after every deposition was taken and defence solicitors asked questions in court on the prisoner's behalf. There were eight cases in which a solicitor appeared for the defence in the 1850s.[289] The solicitors were Messrs Waddeson, Sergeant and Walsh. The local population was willing to engage these men and they were present at this distant part of the colony. Carcoar was of interest.

Questions were asked in court by defendants and they involved denial of the information given: the horse was loaned, the cow previously bought, the assailant nowhere near the victim. Scott was criticised for not allowing the opportunity for a defendant to question his accuser; this was the way of a coastal magistrate.[290] The presence of so many solicitors before the Carcoar bench must have contributed to the increasing professionalisation of the law because defendants frequently stated they would leave matters to their solicitor. The bench is erratic in recording whether questions were asked or the defendant was told he or she could ask questions. The Cody and Kennedy families asked questions of their defence witnesses, just to be safe.[291] When questions were asked, they were as astute as in Orange, despite the long, rangy depositions. Addison Mitchell was able to get a witness to

---

285 *R v Frederick Abraham Dinger* 1856, 11, SR 9/6393.
286 *Sydney Morning Herald*, 23 June 1858.
287 *R v Patrick Foley*.
288 *R v John Richards alias Jack the Butcher* 1859, 5, SR 9/6424.
289 *R v Reynolds*; *R v John Cody the Younger* 1852, 12, SR 9/6371; *R v John Cody, James Kennedy, and Catherine Kennedy* 1853, 13, SR 9/6378; *R v Duce and Jeffries*; *R v Colin Henby* 1853, 14, SR 9/6385; *R v Richard Stack or Portuguese Dick* 1853, 15, SR 9/6385; *R v John Cody* 1853, 9, SR 9/6385; *R v George Chester* 1855, 8, SR 9/6393.
290 *R v Neale*.
291 *R v Cody and Others*.

contradict her evidence completely. She had not seen him rushing along the road; her husband had told her to say she had. This skill did not transfer to the Goulburn Assizes, where, despite being charged with a capital offence, Mitchell had no counsel appointed to watch the case.[292]

Carcoar magistrates bailed when many other benches did not, and Catherine Kennedy in 1852 was told she could go home as long as she came back to court again.[293] On the surface, these depositions adhere to the requirements of the *Justices Act*.

The Carcoar bench provided opportunities for deals and false swearing. That they were suspected of falsification is suggested in depositions—for example, in 1854 Thomas Eagan, a mill worker at Carcoar, stated in a case involving the sexual assault of his two-year-old daughter that the defendant 'never supported me and my family. My wages are 30/- a week and what flour I can use.'[294] He felt it necessary to declare not only that he had no financial relationship to the defendant but also that he had sufficient wages to support his family and was not in need of money. Witnesses in other cases claimed they did not want 'court work', and accused persons offered money to constables and prosecutors so that the case might be forgotten.[295]

The requirements of the court created local behaviours. Cattle and horses were branded three times rather than once,[296] money was sewn into pockets,[297] receipts for animals that were purchased were always written by the nearest literate person even though the wrong brands might be written in.[298]

The Carcoar bench would have been the dream for the inhabitants of Orange and Molong, where such disputes were disturbed by constables' sleuthing and detective work, upsetting plans to 'pull', as informing was called. At Carcoar until 1858, when a style of policing really deriving from the road patrol began to appear, the local population virtually controlled

---

292 ibid.
293 *R v Cody and Others*.
294 *R v Stack or Portuguese Dick*.
295 *R v Michael Fox* 1851, 7, SR 9/6365; *R v Alexander*; *R v William Platt* 1852, SR 9/6371; *R v Patrick Foley*; *R v Vane*.
296 *R v Reynolds*; *R v Murray alias Grady*.
297 *R v Henby*.
298 *R v John Cody the Elder* 1854, 8, SR 9/6385.

the bench and the court intervened where they wanted it to.[299] This meant high dependence on law and a great willingness to make a complaint. It was a law-abiding community if one sees law in the use of it. What it meant was that a competitive community could effectively control what it understood to be law.

What also makes Carcoar distinct is the relationship to Aboriginal people expressed in depositions. There is an instance of an Aboriginal fight being interfered with by constables at the Cowra races in 1852.[300] Constables went down to the races to take waddies from the Aboriginal people there as they had begun to fight. The waddies were given to the constable and later returned to their owners. This interference was tolerated and is representative of the presence of an Aboriginal subject. This Aboriginal subjecthood existed alongside the Aboriginal polity at Carcoar. At Carcoar also, statements were taken from Aboriginal people and sent to Sydney as though they were depositions at a time when Aboriginal evidence was not accepted. Jacky Sloan is described as a 'half-caste' by the magistrate—a word I do not find used by magistrates elsewhere—and his evidence is taken as a statement.[301] In another case in which he was the prosecutor of a man who stole his saddle, his deposition was taken, signed and accepted by the attorney-general and by the jury at Bathurst, who found the defendant guilty. In 1859 Alix or Alex Leans, another man described as a 'half-caste', gave evidence as a witness in court in a deposition, even though his being Aboriginal was pointed out to the attorney-general.[302] We can't say that the further we move from Sydney, the more uncontrolled and the less lawful were the benches.

In the west, we find the benches acting as they should have in their presentation of depositions and their adherence to the *Justices Act*. Yet, they also overstepped the bounds of the law by diligently adding new information or providing background, assuring the attorneys-general that they had a 'duty'. Overzealousness at Carcoar with its concern for 'evidence' created a culture whereby the local population owned the law and felt itself to be obtaining 'justice' when it was obtaining nothing of the kind. Carcoar shows us another meaning of the word 'lawful'. Local populations on the South

---

299 A corporal of the mounted police arrested William Brown in 1856. *R v Brown*. A corporal of the western road patrol arrested Owen Fox in 1858. *R v Owen Fox* 1858, 5, SR 9/6408. In all cases from 1857 to 1859, constables arrested on their own accord.
300 *R v Patrick Green* 1855, 4, SR 9/6393.
301 ibid.
302 *R v Mary Burns* 1860, 4, SR 9/6431.

Coast would have influence over law but they did not pick it up and cart it off so successfully as those at Carcoar. When we have moved north-west and west, we have not found the language of the frontier in depositions; rather, it is present in the metropolitan attorneys-general, among some members of the bar and among the judges. We are not moving further away from law in our movements north-west and west, but closer to it, closer to attention to detail. The public and the people were never mentioned but ordinary persons were active in shaping what law was. A movement west has also brought us into contact with an active police force, sleuthing on its own account. As we move south-west, the landscape becomes increasingly policed and militarised.

Right of reply

A Wiradjuri reader thought right of reply or reading the chapters were not necessary but was pleased to have been asked.

5

South-West

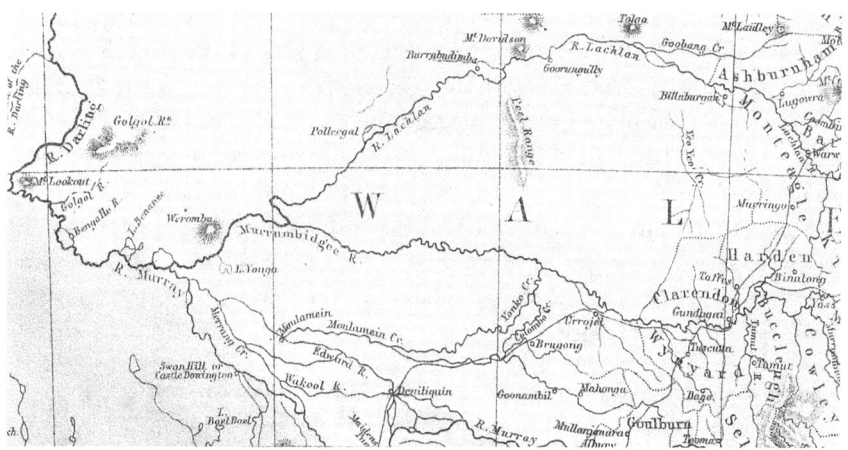

Map 5.1: The south-west of New South Wales
Source: W. Hughes, London G. Phillip and Son, circa 1858, State Library of New South Wales, MLZ/M1 806/1858/1.

Yass

Sixty-two cases were sent from the Yass bench in 1850–59 (Map 5.1). At Yass, ideas of the strict application of law and justice appeared alongside intensive policing. Perhaps because of adherence to the idea that Aboriginal people could not give evidence, there were no Aboriginal subjects at Yass for these 10 years and we must look elsewhere for records of Aboriginal people. The Aboriginal polity in Yass and south into Victoria is present in the press of the period; the law at Yass in felony cases neither covers nor interacts with it. Three Aboriginal people appear in the lower court records for being drunk and disorderly in Cooma Street, Yass, in 1856 and 1857, and for this they receive the same fines as non-Aboriginal people. Their distinct categorisation as Aboriginal indicates a separate status given by the arresting constable.[1] A vagrancy charge and the same fines as non-Aboriginal people indicate that the idea of the Aboriginal subject was present, but deposition records are silent and neither Aboriginal defendants nor witnesses appear.

Herbert King describes the Southern Tablelands as level and gently rolling plains interrupted in places by lines of low residual hills. Yass was planned in 1837 and, by the 1840s, had become a major staging post on the road between Sydney and Melbourne, with great demand for town housing lots.[2] In 1850 a correspondent to the *Goulburn Herald* explained that before the arrival of Chief Constable McJeanett, the town was 'a little paradise, music and harmonious concerts, without riot or debauchery, were nightly the theme', but McJeanett strictly enforced the *Publicans Act* and the liveliness of the town was disrupted.[3] An Aboriginal camp on a volcanic outcrop close to the town survived until the late 1950s and people from there, Ngunnawal, travelled widely in their country and beyond, some of them later moving to the reserve known as Hollywood, which continues today. Ngunnawal people have their own history, available on their website.[4] For all people, Yass was a place of transit.

The Yass bench of magistrates engaged with notions of justice. Such an attitude may have resulted from the intellectual life of surgeons who largely made up the bench. Yass magistrates irritated the attorneys-general, as they were both pedantic and lax in the questions they asked and the depositions they presented.

---

1   Bobby, 14 August 1856, fined 10/-, it being the first offence; Robert Carberry, 25 May 1857, bailed £2, does not appear when called, bail forfeited; Thomas Wright, 4 June 1857, reprimanded and discharged; Yass Bench Books, State Archives Collection, SR 4/5703.
2   Herbert Henry King, 'The Urban Hierarchy of the Southern Tableland of New South Wales' (PhD diss., The Australian National University, 1959), 220.
3   'Report from Yass', *Goulburn Herald and County of Argyle Advertiser*, 30 March 1850.
4   King, 'The Urban Hierarchy of the Southern Tableland', 226; for Ngunnawal history, see Buru Ngunawal Aboriginal Corporation website: www.buru-ngunawal.com/426484390.

Police

In Yass in the 1850s, the depositions of constables were placed at the front of the case. It was more common in New South Wales that police depositions appeared at the back of the case, so that they showed when police were called for and the subsequent actions they took.[5] Placing police depositions first makes the work of policing central to the document produced in Yass and central also to the way Yass magistrates saw the purpose of law (see Figure 5.1).

Yass constables were supplemented by constables from the road patrol under Mr Louche[6] and the mounted police, who also appeared to give evidence in court. Policing was greatly aided by the publication in 1855 of what was termed the *Hue and Cry*.[7] Constables also indicated that they occupied a landscape of suspicion, stopping travellers on the roads and searching them and making note of suspicious activity.[8] In 1858, William Roche, constable, saw a man on the road at Limestone Creek near Yass; he 'rode up to him and asked him his name'.[9] Some 49 per cent of all cases that were transferred to the assizes at Goulburn emerged from constables' activity.

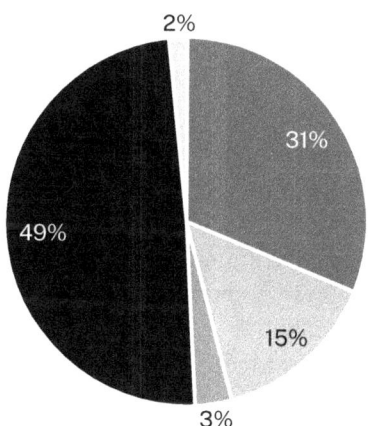

■ Neighbour/same status ▪ Publican ▪ Employer ■ Constable   Not Known

Figure 5.1: Origin of cases: Yass

---

5   This is the way of managing the compiling of depositions at Grafton, the South Coast benches, western NSW benches, Orange and Molong.
6   *R vs William McDonald* 1854, 8, SR 9/6388.
7   ibid.; *R v John Sheridan* 1856, 18, SR 9/6403; *R v Hang Kong* 1856, 14, SR 9/6388.
8   *R v William Connor* 1857, 18, SR 9/6410; *R vs Edward Flaherty* 1856, 15, SR 9/6403.
9   *R v Edward McGuiness* 1858, 12, SR 9/6426.

In 1855, the magistrate Hardy wrote to constables:

> To Chief constable McJeanett at Yass and his assistants and to all other Chief constables, their assistants. This is to command you to apprehend Cook, son of a publican, Cook of Bargo who stands charged on oath before me with stealing a Horse from Hardwicke— and to bring him before me or some other justice to be dealt with according to law.[10]

The horse and the saddle belonged to the magistrate himself. The defendant was a 14-year-old boy who had worked on the Hardy estate.[11] Such entanglement of interests shows that the Yass court was as complex as other places in distinguishing motives for the initiation of cases. Yet, the constables were consulted before the bench and in this and other cases they said they 'proceeded according to information'. Informants rarely appeared in court.[12]

Constables pursued suspects. In 1853 John Jenkins, constable, heard of the theft of a horse and obtained a description of the suspect. 'I followed and not finding him went to Gunning, I soon after heard of the prisoner being at Smith's public house in Gunning—I went and apprehended him there.'[13] William Cunningham, constable, 'proceeded with the Chief Constable to Bowning and from there to Mr Neil O'Brien's place at Bendimere' and 'there heard that the prisoner had gone in the direction of Burrowa ... I then proceeded to Burrowa'.[14] A great deal of constables' time was spent on the roads of the colony. This activity occurred alongside that of the 'road patrol' with its troopers who busily stopped and searched travellers. Constables from other towns such as Tumut and Albury were also combing the roads in pursuit of their own suspects. In such an environment, constables referred to themselves as 'troopers' and the militaristic derivation of such policing can be found in the district's prior history of bushranging, where great success had been achieved by the magistrate Hardy in the 1840s.[15] Constables were also aware of the movements of locals, the money they had and what they

---

10 *R v William Cook* 1855, 19, SR 9/6396.
11 ibid.
12 The informant was not usually named by constables. Under questioning, McJeanett revealed in *Dunn* that 'Mrs Matcher' gave the information. She did not appear in court at all. *R v Morris Dunn* 1858, 4, SR 9/6418.
13 *R v Alexander Thompson* 1853, 2, SR 9/6380.
14 *R v William Gardiner* 1853, 19, SR 9/6380.
15 James Adams referred to himself as 'a trooper in the Tumut police' in *R v Dunn*, 4. For Hardy, see Nancy Keesing, 'Hardy, John Richard (1807–1858)', *Australian Dictionary of Biography* (Canberra: National Centre of Biography, The Australian National University, 1972), adb.anu.edu.au/biography/hardy-john-richard-3715/text5831.

were capable of purchasing. In *Heffernan and Cummins*, a constable stated: 'I have observed the two men living at Douglas' public house for some days lately.'[16] 'I saw Wheeler and you knocking about the public houses for six- or seven-days,' said Constable Costello in his cross-examination by an accused man in 1853.[17]

Yass constables did not act in geographical isolation; they were closely linked to police in other towns, even across the border of the colony into Victoria. Letters and notes were included in cases. They referred to themselves as 'Yass Police Force'.[18] In 1859 chief constable Robert McJeanett sent 'a telegraphic message to Gundagai' to obtain descriptions of stolen horses.[19] The Ovens River was in Victoria, another colony, yet McJarnett in 1853 was pursuing a case there, well outside the jurisdiction of the Yass bench.[20] This was markedly different from police of the north-west of New South Wales.

Such practices remained throughout the 1850s. The creativity apparent in the policing of bushranging was apparent at Yass. The term 'bushranger' was used and the practices of bushranging involving masks and extreme violence in robbery on the roads appear in cases.[21]

As well as tracking offenders from descriptions given to them or read in the newspaper, constables undertook searches of prisoners and their surrounds. After tracing a description of 'robbers' to a hut at Wayalah near Yass, Robert McJarnett found two scotch twill shirts at a woman's hut nearby, 'given to her to wash'.[22] Searches of the person were carried out regardless of the charge made, so that we have lists of what was in the pockets of persons accused of murder.[23] There was also close attention to the reactions of the accused: 'I told prisoners I apprehended them on suspicion of robbery but they did not ask me what robbery,' said Robert McJarnett of Heffernan and Cummins in 1850.[24] John Costello, constable, in 1853 explained:

---

16   *R v Martin Heffernan and Michael Cummins* 1850, 10, SR 9/6360.
17   *R v Thompson*.
18   *R v Patrick Keys* 1854, 6, SR 9/6388; *R v McDonald* (1854) (to Tumut); *R v Dunn*, 2.
19   *R v William Moreton* 1859, 25, SR 9/6425.
20   *R v Thompson*.
21   ibid.; *R v Heffernan and Cummins*.
22   *R v Heffernan and Cummins*.
23   *R v Laurence Hing* 1855, 11, SR 9/6396: arrested for murder, searched in the watchhouse, 'found 2/9 in delivery against the agreement of Mr Barber with him'. The deceased was also searched and a purse found containing '10/6 in silver'.
24   *R v Heffernan and Cummins*.

> I apprehended George Wheeler on a charge of Highway Robbery, I took him partly on my own suspicion ... Kelleher told me he had been robbed but it was not on this charge of robbery that I took Wheeler—I took Wheeler on suspicion from information received from Kelleher knowing that this man Wheeler had been drinking with Doyle and having been informed by Kelleher that Doyle was one of the men who robbed him.[25]

There is the image of a thinking constable, a sleuth. 'I observed to Colls that if anyone had got the bridle and saddle his groom must have,' said constable Richard Hassnett in 1853, and he got a candle and searched the loft of the stable to find the saddle and bridle hidden between two bundles of hay.[26]

On the South Coast, constables were the servants of the local population, eagerly consulted and sent for at a time of crisis, even if the crisis was concocted. In Yass, constables gave evidence that they came across dead bodies in the street as though they were alone, when they were part of a crowd of people.[27] Their professionalism excluded the public. Constables described exactly how they arrested a suspect. 'I told him what I arrested him for—he ... told me to produce my warrant or he would not go with me ... [H]is wife incited him to resist us.'[28] In 1859 William Moreton told constable George Patrick he knew nothing about any horses, and he did not think that Patrick had any right to arrest him without 'shewing him a warrant'. 'I said I would see about that and put the handcuffs on him.'[29] Moreton was sure he had rights and Section 24 of the *Justices Act* did require warrants in removal of prisoners from one place to another.[30] More importantly, Patrick felt it necessary to mention this information in court.

Part of the reason for detailed information in constables' depositions was their wariness of the law. Chief constable Robert McJarnett was clear in a case of robbery that he had charged Michael Doyle 'on suspicion of the murder of Marcus at the Ovens diggings':

---

25 *R v Thompson*.
26 *R v William Nicholls* 1851, 1, SR 9/6367.
27 *R v Robert Burns* 1854, 24, SR 9/6388; *R v Laurence Hing*: Constable Hassnett gives evidence as though he was alone in examining a body, when he was surrounded by people.
28 *R v Keys*.
29 *R v Moreton*.
30 Schofield-Georgeson, *By What Authority?*, 100.

I had him in custody I asked him where he came from, he said from the Ovens diggings the Friday week before the 27 of December last—and it was after he had told me this that I apprehended him on suspicion of murder.[31]

Recalling exactly what was said was important. Constables' attentiveness to correct procedure was a response to the climate of the courtroom. This did not mean they were without the complexity of corruption to be found elsewhere. 'Jones offered Corporal Brennan £5 if he would apprehend the prisoner Russell,' claimed Patrick Brennan when cross-examined at Yass in 1856.[32] Two road constables were charged with robbing a prisoner, Isaac Johnson, whom they were taking to Yass in 1854. They had gone to several public houses on the journey and the constables closely watched where Johnson kept his money. The magistrate Campbell gave one of the constables into custody after Johnson complained. They were also charged with allowing two prisoners to escape, saying they had 'lost' them along with two parcels of money.[33]

The Yass bench worked within the definitions of policing created in an earlier period. The terms 'free' or 'freed', categories of the convict system, appeared throughout the period. In 1851 William Nicholls was 'free by servitude' and in 1853 Alexander Thompson appeared before the bench 'stating himself to be free'.[34] In 1854 James Waters, a private in the 11th Regiment and attached to Mr Louche's road patrol, was described as 'free', and in 1855, James Popham the younger was described as 'free'.[35] John Sheridan in 1856 was described as a 'native of the colony'.[36] Dennis Mineham the same year was described as 'free'.[37] Bernard McManus explained when giving his deposition in 1854 that he 'came to the colony a free man but am now a Ticket of Leave holder'.[38] That the convict system was erratic in execution is demonstrated by Thomas Edgeworth, a victim in the case against James Talbot:

---

31   *R v Thompson*.
32   *R v Sheridan*.
33   *R v James Waters* 1854, 21, SR 9/6388; *R v James Waters and John James* 1854, 22, SR 9/6388.
34   *R v Nicholls*; *R v Thompson*.
35   *R v Waters*; *R v James Popham, the Younger* 1855, 14, SR 9/6396.
36   *R v Sheridan*.
37   *R v Dennis Mineham* 1856, 12, SR 9/6403.
38   *R v Robert Burns*.

Edgeworth kept a sly grog shop and he has done so for the last two or three years, he is now fortunately in custody and has turned out to be a prisoner of the Crown illegally at large, he has been examined before the Yass Bench and states that he has a ticket of leave for Patrick's Plains … [W]hen Edgeworth first lost his ticket he boasted that he had a friend who would soon get it for him again and his wife now says she will have him up again within twelve months … Edgeworth has acquired some considerable property in horses, cattle, farming implements, spring cart etc etc, he seldom or never worked … [H]is wife is likely to pursue the same trade of grog selling if she is permitted to retain this property.[39]

It is not surprising that the regulations related to the convict system should also be applied erratically by the magistrates' bench at Yass. The terms 'convict' and 'free' were thus open to interpretation.

Working documents

Yass depositions show crossings out, asterisks and corrections as well as the usual pencil markings of the attorney-general and the criminal Crown solicitor. Yet, depositions were far from perfect. Yass was one of the benches written to and castigated by the attorneys-general in the 1840s and 1860s.[40] The transparency of document production and the lack of rewriting, however, attest to a bench interest in following the law.

Depositions were also corrected. Spelling and expression were altered, the word 'store', for instance, crossed out to be replaced with 'hut',[41] indicating a sense of accuracy by a person of reasonably high status. 'Was' becomes 'were' and syntax is crossed out and corrected.[42] The corrections, however, do not stop there. They affect the legality of the deposition in a number of ways. For example, Hugh Tunney's deposition reads, 'I left in Yass in evening of the same day, namely the 8 December instant', and it is altered to read, 'I left Yass Tuesday 4 December instant.'[43] After the *Justices Act*, mistakes in information or indictments were no longer to affect the case and

---

39 Nicholas R. Bernard, Commissioner of Crown Lands, Yass, to Attorney-General, in *R v James Talbot* 1853, 2, SR 9/6388.
40 Attorney-General Letters, State Archives Collection, SR 4/6659; New South Wales Crown Law Office Letter Book, State Library of New South Wales, CY 2753.
41 *R v Patrick Flynn* 1851, 9, SR 9/6367.
42 'Was' was replaced with 'were', in *R v John Costello* 1856, 25, SR 9/6388; 'showed any of my money' was replaced with 'had money', in *R v Flaherty*; 'and the prisoner ran after her' was replaced with 'and the prisoner after her', in *R v John Trapp* 1855, 8, SR 9/6403.
43 *R v Trapp*.

the former playground of the lawyers of the empire ceased to exist.[44] Such a mistake as this incorrect date would, though, materially affect the validity of a deposition: what day Tunney did in fact 'leave Yass' is open to question. Plunkett did not comment on this crossing out.

The depositions, however, go further. Key names were crossed out to be replaced with others. In *Murray and Hatfield* in 1858, an asterisk included new information by Margaret Reidy: '[W]e stopt a night at Bill James and came to Yass on Friday.'[45] The information is in the clerk's handwriting, but it is impossible to tell when this information was added to the margin of the case. Since Margaret Reidy's evidence contradicted that of her sister, who had said that the two of them had gone straight home and not stayed with Hatfield, who may or may not have promised to marry Mary Reidy, this new information was crucial. That the depositions were doubtful was not mentioned by the attorney-general.

Information was sometimes completely crossed out. In the case against Alexander Thompson in 1853, George Douglass, keeper of the Swann Inn in Yass, made the statement 'Mr Laidlow later informed', which was completely crossed out and the case moved on to cross-examination by the prisoner. A cheque had been paid to Swann that had been passed to Thomas Laidlow Esquire, a magistrate and storekeeper.[46] The reader wonders why the part-sentence has been crossed out. Similarly, in *Mineham*, Michael Delaney claimed he had a case against the defendant in the small debts court and 'I never told' was crossed out and may have suggested he was threatening to make a false criminal complaint.[47] More complex is when these crossed-out lines were replaced with new words: 'I do not know when' was replaced with 'I was told by a man' in *Holmes*.[48] 'I see a woman now in court, she was the only one in the house' was completely crossed out and replaced with 'There were no other persons in the house besides Riley' in *Keys*.[49] This streamlining may well have occurred in other benches, but the process is made clear for us in the wish to present an original deposition at Yass. For the purpose of law, this threatened the validity of depositions

---

44 Schofield-Georgeson, *By What Authority?*, 100.
45 *R v Dennis Murray and Charles Hatfield* 1858, 14, SR 9/6418.
46 *R v Thompson*.
47 *R v Mineham*.
48 *R v Isaac Holmes* 1857, 4, SR 9/6410.
49 *R v Keys*.

coming from Yass, but this was ignored by all the attorneys-general. In 1855 in a case against *Thompson alias McGuinness*, Plunkett wrote in pencil on the cover of the case:

> I feel bound to put the prisoner on his trial again—in the meantime let the Criminal Crown Solicitor issue subpoenas not only to the witnesses already examined but such others as he may discern, can make up the defective parts of the case pointed out by Mr Callaghan.[50]

The minute by the acting Crown prosecutor Callaghan does not survive. Callaghan's criticisms should have been picked up by Plunkett in his initial reading.

The attorneys-general were often irritated by the Yass bench. Magistrates wrote long and detailed letters to the attorney-general in which they worried legal points and attempted to advise him. Magistrates Isadore Blake and Charles Campbell were surgeons, Blake was also coroner. Hamilton Hume, like James Hardy, Frederick Allman and John George Davidson, held runs, and Thomas Laidlow held several economic interests in Yass, including a store. Nicholas Bernard was the Commissioner of Crown Lands and a police magistrate, though he signed himself JP. The attitude of correcting the attorney-general possibly came from Blake, as perhaps did the rigorous adherence to the new developments of the *Justices Act*. An article in the *Yass Tribune* of 1939 described Blake:

> When he made any decision on the evidence to the Bench he adhered to the attitude he adopted in public meetings and gave his ideas in a most emphatic manner as to what he considered justice and after giving voice to the same rose and left the court.[51]

This was part of the local story about Blake, yet it locates him as a pedantic member of the bench.

Plunkett wrote in pencil on the back of *Gardiner* about a receipt for bullocks: 'It does not appear what has become of the document shewn to the prisoner. It should be produced at the trial if necessary.' Another pencil note refers to the deposition in this case: 'Prosecutor states, in his evidence that it was lost in the late Gundagai flood.'[52] Manning wrote scathingly of a stolen horse that should have been exhibited at the courthouse door that

---

50   *R v James Thompson alias James McGuinness* 1854, 2, SR 9/6388.
51   'Looking Back, Early Medical Practitioners', *Yass Tribune*, 11 April 1939: 2.
52   *R v Gardiner*.

'it does not appear the police obtained possession of the horse'.[53] In 1854 Plunkett wrote in pencil on the back of a deposition concerning a constable robbing a prisoner he was transporting: 'I do not understand how it is Constable James is also not committed—the evidence appears to apply equally to both.'[54] Some tension is indicated in letters sent between Blake and Plunkett in 1851. Blake requested in 1851 that all the depositions in an inquest be returned to him by the attorney-general 'for the purpose of being re-sworn in the presence of the prisoner. Was he to resume the Jurors, as he was Coroner as well, or was he to act in the capacity of magistrate?' Plunkett wrote in pencil on the back of the letter for the information of the criminal Crown solicitor:

> The depositions [are] to be taken before the Bench ... as if the Inquest was not held at all. If Dr Blake had not suggested the taking of depositions to allow the Prisoner the opportunity of cross examination I should not have considered such a course necessary that I see no objection to it merely for more abundant caution.[55]

Plunkett was using the weight of his position; the re-swearing was either necessary or not. Blake, however, was distinctly referring to the *Justices Act*, which emphasised the prisoner's right to cross-examine.

The bench forwarded complex requests. In 1850 they asked that depositions of a victim of highway robbery be heard before a Sydney bench as she could not travel back to Yass.[56] The attorney-general did not reply to the letter. The bench wrote again, 'not having been as yet favoured with your reply we have thought it our duty under all the circumstances to commit the prisoner for trial'.[57] In *Bennett alias Carroll*, they wrote:

> Although the nature of the evidence in the cases was, and is, unsatisfactory as to the positive identification of the prisoner, we considered the strong suspicion which attached to Bennet rendered the course which we adopted necessary, namely that of sending him to trial.[58]

---

53 *R v Dunn*, 2.
54 *R v Waters*.
55 *R v Michael Coller* 1851, 10, SR 9/6367.
56 Police Office Yass to Criminal Crown Solicitor, 29 June 1850, in *R v Heffernan and Cummins*.
57 John Watson JP to Attorney-General, n.d., in *R v Heffernan and Cummins*.
58 F. Allman JP to Attorney-General, 19 July 1850, in *R v James Bennett alias Thomas Carroll* 1850, 11, SR 9/6360.

In other letters, the magistrates discuss cases in detail: 'It has occurred to me that it may be desirable to give evidence of Talbot's state of mind immediately before this most atrocious deed—Mrs Cheer and her husband speak of it shortly after the murder.'[59]

The magistrates did not write with due attention to the knowledge and authority of the attorney-general and the issues they discussed were framed not as mutual concerns but as independent legal opinion.

The depositions also give some idea of changes of mind or dispute between court officials. Written in pen on the front of the case against John Webber was a note initialled by Manning in 1854:

> There is no evidence of the completion of a rape the charge could be indecent assault under Mr Wentworth's Act. Probably the girl's appearance may enable some qualified person to give evidence to the effect of her being under 12.[60]

This note was completely crossed out in ink, and it appears no action was taken upon it. Such crossing out was not initialled. Conflict is also apparent in 1858. Attorney-General Bayley worked diligently on depositions from Yass, marking them in pen rather than pencil. In 1858 John Moore Dillon, Crown solicitor, commented on a case Bayley had already committed: '[T]he principal witness in the case, Sullivan, was under committal for stealing the same horses when he appears to have been allowed to give evidence by the Yass Bench.'[61] This may have been a criticism of Bayley allowing such an event to go without comment as much as the Yass bench.

What appears in Yass also is an emphasis on the legal requirements for married women. At Yass a married woman could not undertake a recognisance herself; her husband had to do it on her behalf. In 1853 the bench noted:

> Thomas Colls appeared as the bondsman of Bridget Macdonald and surrendered her to the court he being apprehensive that she being now married will not attend the Court of Assize as such witness ... Bridget McDonald now Bridget Hobcroft proposes as her surety in Colls place her husband John Hobcroft.[62]

---

59 Nicholas J. Bernard to Attorney-General, 18 October 1853, in *R v Talbot*.
60 *R v John Webber* 1854, 25, SR 9/6388.
61 *R v Murray and Hatfield*.
62 *R v Charles Wilson* 1857, 5, SR 9/6380.

When 'Miss Susan Potter' was abducted, her stepmother's new husband gave evidence: 'I have never since my marriage given my consent to Miss Susan Potter leaving my protection.'[63] This attentiveness to legal requirements derives from the bench's concern with the law independent of the attorneys-general.

Representation

The precision of the police at Yass in protocols surrounding arrest and in reporting what was said at the time of arrest may have resulted from experiences of cross-examination by prisoners in court. The operation of law at Yass was therefore structured by the accused as well as police and magistrates.

The accused was also able to make a statement at the end of a case and call witnesses in his or her defence. They were 'warned' before making any statement and many consequently 'had nothing to say' or made a brief statement as to the falsity of the accusations.[64] Longer explanations were also entered into and a man accused of murder claimed that the blood on his clothes was the result of both cutting up a sheep and a subsequent nosebleed.[65] Michael Cummins in his defence statement said he had won the purse he had been accused of stealing from two travelling men. Martin Heffernan stated he had received the order he was accused of stealing from 'a man who told me his name was William Brett' after he won a bet at the Collector races.[66] Heffernan was able to subpoena a man who would support his defence and the case was remanded twice until a letter from Robert Grant at Collector stated that he would 'not know the robers from any man on the Race Cours'.[67]

There were defence witnesses. In *Holmes*, the magistrate James Davidson appeared to give evidence that he knew one of the prosecution witnesses: 'I am almost certain he was brought before me as a magistrate for drinking.'[68] Davidson was not the magistrate hearing the case and such use of the magistracy by an accused person is in keeping with the bench's idea of justice.

---

63 *R v George Stephens* 1853, 15, SR 9/6388.
64 Alexander Thompson said, 'I know nothing of the matter with which I am charged, either good, bad or indifferent' and 'No statement, I reserve what statement I have to make', in *R v Thompson*.
65 *R v Hang*.
66 *R v Heffernan and Cummins*.
67 Robert Grant to Dr Blake and F. Allman JPs, in *R v Heffernan and Cummins*.
68 *R v Holmes*.

A major figure at the Yass bench was the solicitor George Allman, who appeared at both coroner's inquests and magisterial hearings. Allman appeared in 15 of 62 cases and Mr Ryall appeared in one. Allman's questions often invoke the idea that permission was given to take a horse or cow, that the prosecutor had some other quarrel with the defendant and that the case was a fabrication. He undermined the detail and the day or time when something was supposed to have happened. Many witnesses floundered under his questioning, but the cases still proceeded to Goulburn for the assizes and the attorneys-general seem unaffected by Allman's skill.

William Sawyer, licensed squatter, claimed under Allman's questioning in 1853:

> The prisoner was not in the habit of riding that horse by my permission—I requested him to go to Mr Bootes about some hay but he did not go ... [The] prisoner was not in the habit of taking the saddle and bridle by my permission he had one of his own. I never offered to lend him my hat.[69]

At times Allman was employed by one or two prisoners and a third remained undefended. In these cases, he would seek to establish his own client's innocence at the expense of the undefended man.[70] Allman's appearance at all in court attests to the community's interest in a justice more aligned with the textbook perspectives of law.

What Allman exploited in his defences was the feeling that cases were part of a continuum of court use by the local population, where justice was meaningless and courts were part of popular dispute. It is difficult not to see this element of false swearing in all benches and hints of it appear in most cases where defendants were of equal status.

Yass defendants, possibly because of the influence of the solicitor Allman, were most likely to decline asking questions of witnesses. The depositions were duly marked 'prisoner declines to ask any questions' after each deposition. The Yass bench made much of warning the prisoner that if they made a statement, it could be used in evidence, so perhaps silence was thought to be the best approach. Unlike the South Coast, here defendants seem wary. If questions were asked, they were most likely asked of the constables and, as in Orange, they were astute questions. Alexander Thompson was

---

69 *R v Gardiner.*
70 *R v Francis Clarke and Edward Prior* 1854, 27, SR 9/6388.

able to get the chief constable to say that he did not give Constable Lockett the authority to allow the prosecutor in the case to examine money reputed to be stolen. He undermined the whole basis of the case.[71]

The absence of the Aboriginal subject at Yass

The Aboriginal polity is apparent in press reports at Yass for the second half of the nineteenth century. In 1857 there was 'a Black's camp a short distance from the town',[72] and in August:

> A very large number of the Aborigines have camped about a mile and a half from Yass, and on Tuesday several of the townsfolk visited the camp for the purpose of witnessing a corroboree. The blacks are known as those of the Lachlan, Murrumbidgee and Binalong and large numbers of them are daily to be seen roaming the town. The reason of their gathering—if indeed they have any is not known.[73]

In August 1859 the *Sydney Morning Herald* reported that Mount Charcoal was visited 'by the last surviving remnants of the Aboriginal race in the Gundagai district':

> One of them was Sir Niger Varre whom the Reverend Dr Lang has immortalized and who saved so many lives during the great flood at Gundagai. He was accompanied by Tallboy, Boco and a few of their female friends from Wagga Wagga. On being interrogated as to their business on the Adelong they replied they had use for a reef.[74]

The camping place near the town remained during the rest of the century and was challenged in the early twentieth century.[75]

The second group of people came from the south. The border between New South Wales and Victoria was porous and people travelled back and forth to the goldfields and towns. Victorian newspapers were widely read, and Melbourne was regarded as the closest city. Victorian newspapers reported the development of a land agreement between a deputation of Aboriginal people and the Victorian Government in 1859. The deputation was introduced to the Commissioner of Crown Lands by William Thomas, the Victorian Protector of Aborigines. The names of the deputation were

---

71 *R v Thompson*.
72 *Bathurst Free Press and Mining Journal*, 9 September 1857.
73 'From the Yass Courier of Saturday', *Sydney Morning Herald*, 18 August 1857.
74 'Adelong Mining Journal', *Sydney Morning Herald*, 23 August 1859.
75 Read, *A Hundred Years War*, 57–58.

'Beaning' (a chieftain), Wonga, Munnarin, Murrin Murrin, Parngean, Baruppin and Koo-gurrin.[76] The reporter described the men 'attired in the same manner as sailors or labourers of an inferior class. They wore coarse jumpers and trousers, three of them had coats.' They were granted the land and after 'arrivals from the various parts including the Delatite, Broken River, Murray etc', came to see the grant. Later messengers were dispatched to the Yarra, lower Goulburn, Murray and Bendigo rivers and ceremonies held.[77] Despite the paternalism apparent in the granting of the land, the grant was fitted into the Aboriginal polity. News of these developments was read about in the press available at Yass. That Aboriginal people did not figure large in the criminal law in Yass compared with other areas means they were not incorporated into the notion of subject. It is difficult to find accounts of violence to Aboriginal people at Yass in the 1850s.[78] This does not mean they did not occur. The footprint of the Supreme Court in Yass did not incorporate Aboriginal people; it is not certain whether they remained in the non-Aboriginal mind a 'conquered people'.[79]

There was a case at Cooma, a bench some distance away, in 1858 in which Scabby Harry was pursued for rape. He went to the Corrowong and 'intelligence reached Bombala where a party augmented by Mr T Simpson, Mr B Allan, Mr Hayden, Mr Charles Bell, JP, [and] Mr John McLachlan' set out in pursuit. Four Aboriginal men gave information as to his whereabouts in exchange for money and Scabby Harry was captured.[80] The pursuit resembled a punitive raid, particularly in the involvement of gentlemen, but Harry was not shot. Also, in keeping with Victoria, there is some use of the law by the four men who informed.[81] This was also present in 1852 at Tumut when 'intelligence has just been received at the Crown Lands Head Quarters in Tumut, also a bench some distance from Yass, through the Tumut blacks' about the murder of 'a half caste' girl named Sally McLeod by an Aboriginal named Yaree or Coonong Deramundinna, son of Bobby, King of Adelong, who was her husband. Aboriginal people led the commissioner to the burial place of Sally McLeod. Warrants were issued by the Tumut

---

76 'The Aborigines of the Goulburn District', *Argus*, 8 March 1859.
77 'Aborigines at Goulburn', *Mount Alexander Mail*, 8 March 1959.
78 *R v Robert Ward alias Bob the Lawyer* 1857, 1, SR 9/6410; *R v McLaughlin* 1854, 7; *R v Davy Storr* 1856: Nymbodia, Wee Waa and Armidale cases, respectively.
79 The Supreme Court's response to the idea of recognising Aboriginal people as conquered rather than subjects was to thwart an exterminationist clique, according to Douglas and Finnane, *Indigenous Crime and Settler Law*, 45–47.
80 'New South Wales', *Brisbane Herald*, 16 October 1858.
81 Paula Jane Byrne, 'The New South Wales Bar and Aboriginal People: Making Aboriginal Subjects c. 1830–1866', *History Australia* 15 (2018): 413–29.

bench, but this is the last we hear of the case.[82] Those who initiated the case were Tumut Aboriginal people. At Yass, however, no such interest appears in bench or policing records. The researcher, then, is presented with a region in which the absence of Aboriginal subjects is an important component of the practice of the law and the newspaper evidence shows an idea of Aboriginal governance was present.

Non-Aboriginal culture and the law in Yass

Yass had a strong police culture and the word 'bushranger' appeared there when it did not yet appear in other regions.[83] There was a fine eye for cloth as well as dress at Yass that does not appear in the records of coastal benches. Two armed men who bailed up James Ward, landlord of the Golden Fleece, had 'white crepe or muslin' over their faces. 'Fustian or Tweed trousers', 'a light tweed coat and fustian trousers', said Richard Howarth in the same case. The men took a 'cashmiri shawl, [and] a black silk scarf'.[84] In 1858 'a shepherd's plaid cowl' was stolen from George Patrick; the thief put it on and was seen later 'in a kind of check coat'.[85] John Williams sold two 'scotch twilled shirts and moleskin trousers' to Martin Heffernan.[86] Hamilton Hume noted a man he saw galloping across his paddock had on 'a light coat'.[87] Being 'in shirtsleeves' was something to be noted and it seems the wearing of coats was a matter of etiquette.[88] When a man wanted to fight in the Royal Hotel, he 'took off his coat to fight'.[89] The coat was important to mention, and taking it off an act of aggression.

There is also an emphasis on eating together and of eating being part of the measurement of time during the day. 'Thompson came first and ordered tea for two,' says Thomas Colls of two men who came to his public house.[90] James Talbot called 'at Shine's lighted his pipe and drank some tea there'.[91] 'We eat the bread and fried the eggs and the pork,' said Isaac Johnson of he and the constables who were taking him to Yass.[92] Watches do not appear

---

82   *Goulburn Herald*, 11 September 1852.
83   'The bushrangers went toward Yass': evidence of Dennis Kelliher, in *R v Thompson*.
84   *R v Bennett alias Carroll*.
85   *R v Moreton*.
86   *R v Heffernan and Cummins*.
87   *R v McDonald* (1854).
88   *R v Talbot*.
89   *R v Charles Shearman* 1854, 23, SR 9/6388.
90   *R v Thompson alias McGuinness*.
91   *R v Talbot*.
92   *R v Waters*.

to be consulted as much as elsewhere, nor stolen or carried. Breakfast and 'after breakfast' were important to mention, as were dinner and tea.[93] Who ate where was an important indicator of where a person lived.

Inns and public houses figure large in the court records. Defendants are seen drinking in them and constables are contacted. When John Riley went to the house of Patrick Keys, he asked Keys to give his mate some rum: '[A] woman brought out a tumbler full, saying there was half a pint there, the woman demanded two shillings.'[94] This was not a public house but spirits were still being sold there and it seems many houses sold spirits despite not being licensed.

Illegal behaviour was influenced by what constituted evidence in a criminal case. If highway robbery was detected through appearance, a disguise should be worn and your voice should sound different. 'The prisoner was talking through his nose, a rag was hanging down on his forehead as low as his eyes,' said Mary Ann Tunney of a man who robbed her father's camp.[95] The brands should be cut out of cattle lest a carcass be identified.[96] Horses ran away and were caught; it was possible to say you were simply holding onto one until you got to the pound. Yass defendants seem more schooled in how to avoid detection. Together with constables, they shaped how law worked. 'I suppose this will be a Goulburn job,' said the prisoner Charles Turton on his way to the lockup in 1859.[97]

That the requirements of the *Justices Act* could be so quickly incorporated into ways of doing law at Yass is indicative of the importance of culture to legal change because elsewhere in the 1850s there were far fewer rights to be found in depositions. The Yass magistrates and clerks worried at the law, they challenged the attorneys-general in that worry and they produced complex documents with details altered as easily as spelling. This is not an example of improvement in legal practice, a forward movement in any sense, but rather an example of how curiously change in what is understood as law develops.

---

93 *R v Thompson*.
94 *R v Keys*.
95 *R v Trapp*.
96 *R v William James* 1856, 24, SR 9/6403.
97 *R v Joseph Turton and Charles Turton* 1859, 26, 27, SR 9/6425.

The movement south and west illuminates the policed nature of these regions, with mounted police and road patrols appearing as key players in the management of local populations. This was the result of localised interpretations of the convict system and all the terminology associated with it, including the word 'free'. Active constables made use of different sources of intelligence and their purview was well outside the towns in which they were based. The detail constables give us derives from the amount of criticism they received at the hands of the attorneys-general and the level of criticism was invited by local magistrates. While the personality of a single local magistrate could determine the personality of the bench, it is the capacity of law to be made so malleable that shaped local cultures of law.

Right of reply

Ngunnawal correspondent Michael Bell, Indigenous Liaison Officer at the Australian War Memorial, was happy with how Aboriginal people were represented.

Balranald

Balranald, on the Murrumbidgee River, is in semi-arid, flat far south-western New South Wales. Saltbush and mallee scrub predominate. The town was established in 1850 on an older major trading route for cattle and sheep for Adelaide markets.[98]

In 1859 the clerk of the Balranald bench George Edwards wrote to magistrate John Kelly:

> I have the honour to request you will inform me your opinion with respect to the legality of inserting in the list of electors for the Electoral District of Balranald the names of Aborigines resident in the District, a list of which has been handed to me.[99]

It is not apparent who gave the list to Edwards and Kelly's reply has not survived. Chief constable Simon McDonald had the responsibility of updating the electoral roll, but Edwards writes as though he has received a

---

98 Morey, 'Reminiscences of a Pioneer in New South Wales'.
99 George Edwards, CPS, to John Kelly, 31 January 1857, Balranald Letter Book, SR 4/5503.

separate list and this is of all the Aboriginal people in the district, not just those on one run. This district-wide approach also suggests that Aboriginal people gave their names for the electoral list and that they may have had an interest in voting. The incident was reported in the *Daily News* and reprinted in other newspapers.[100] This list has been discussed by Naomi Gabrielle Parkinson in her analysis of Aboriginal people and the franchise and appears also in Curthoys and Mitchell. The Balranald magistrate Augustus Morris had wanted to bring in a short act to disqualify Aboriginal people but was unsuccessful.[101] Morris may have been behind the creation of the list, but it is the clerk's response that is relevant here.

Edwards' precise concern with legality emerged from a culture in which magistrates felt they knew more about law than the attorneys-general. While there are very few assize cases emerging from Balranald, the bench books for the entire 1850s survive as well as the letter books. This idea of legality understood at Balranald incorporated information that was overheard, and talk was a major component of criminal cases. Emphasis on proper procedure and reporting meant that speech was accurately reported, and changes of mind and slang were included. This opens a terrain hidden in the north-western benches. Publicans controlled much of the way the court worked and took up most of its time, as they did in the north-west, but at Balranald their machinations are exposed.

Aboriginal subjects

First Nations people at Balranald have their own history, some of which was made available in the return of Mungo Man and Mungo Woman.[102] Aboriginal people were crucial in two cases sent to the attorney-general in the 1850s. William Taylor would not have been committed without the evidence of an Aboriginal man, Pompey, in 1857. The publican Mrs Lowcock sent for Constable Hannan to say a man in her public house had been robbed, having the pocket of his moleskin trousers cut off. All men in the house were searched and nothing found. From 'information received' from Pompey, who had been washing clothes near the inn, Hannan arrested three men whom Pompey had overheard talking about 'big one money'.

---

100 *Illawarra Mercury*, 3 February 1859.
101 Naomi Gabrielle Parkinson, 'Impersonating a Voter: Constructions of Race, and Conceptions of Subjecthood in the Franchise of Colonial New South Wales, c. 1850–1865', *The Journal of Imperial and Commonwealth History* 47, no. 4 (2019): 652–75; Curthoys and Mitchell, *Taking Liberty*, 340.
102 *Jajoo Warrngara: The Culture Classroom* (Brisbane: SharingStories Foundation, 2022), jajoowarrngara.org.

Pompey went to a tree, saw the marks of fingers on the ground and followed foot tracks to where he found a purse containing £20. The magistrates took the evidence of Pompey, which they included in the case. The criminal Crown solicitor noted in the column 'not evidence'. The magistrates' letter accompanying the case did not contemplate that Pompey would not be able to give evidence; rather, Chief Constable Hannan wrote that 'owing to the uncertainty of getting black fellows to come forward at the time wanted I Chief Constable Hannan hereby certify the evidence by the blackfellow Pompey'. The case had initially been sent not to the attorney-general but to the Inspector-General of Police. They had done this because, they wrote, they were not confident about the appearance of the man who had been robbed, Edward Stephens, before the assizes. They had no concerns about Pompey's evidence. Rather than the attorney-general replying to the bench, he replied to the Inspector-General of Police William Mayne. Mayne wrote to the bench that there was insufficient evidence for the prisoner Taylor to be tried for stealing but not for conviction under the *Vagrant Act*:

> The Aboriginal evidence cannot be received but facts ascertained by competent witnesses as to what he pointed out can be proved, this track though would not have been observed by a white man unaided, but which are seen when pointed out can be sworn to. The Chief Constable maybe can speak to the direction of the tracks—if there were any clearly visible he should have compared them with shoes worn by men under suspicion.[103]

The cross-purposes of the attorney-general and the bench are apparent here. The bench was not aware that Pompey's evidence was not legal and the person they asked about the attendance of the victim was the Inspector-General of Police, not the attorney-general. How deliberate was such ill recognition of the authority to which they directed their question is unclear. When castigated by the attorney-general for sending copies of depositions rather than the original, they wrote to him that they believed the case would not be proceeded with only because they could not secure the attendance of the victim.[104] They were making the attorney-general's task their own.

Pompey was central to this case and the magistrates accepted Aboriginal evidence in other cases. In the inquiry into the suicide of a white man working for John Lecky Phelps in 1852, an Aboriginal man, Bullen Bangy, who had loaned his gun to the victim, gave evidence and signed with an 'x'.

---

103 *R v William Taylor* 1857, 2, SR 9/6404.
104 ibid.

The inquiry was held so that Bullen Bangy would not be delayed in his wish to leave the locality. Jemmy the Ram, another Aboriginal man, gave evidence that he directed the deceased to 'Jimmy Buttubungy's camp' because he asked for 'the Blackfellow who had the musket'. He also signed with an 'x'. This case was sent to the attorney-general.[105] The case against James Johnson alias Cooper rested upon the evidence of Jessie Dare, who had 'heard from the Blacks that one man had murdered another in a billy bong near the Darling and he had burnt him in a fire. Dare said that he did not know the blackfellows name who told me but I know him by sight.'[106] He expected that the man would be called to give evidence. While the status given to Aboriginal evidence is apparent elsewhere in New South Wales, at Balranald, it is central to the construction of these cases. One can see in this environment how it would be possible for a clerk to check the legality of putting Aboriginal names on the electoral roll or how it was possible for someone to collect those names in a group.

Billy the Bull in 1851 and Billy, Aboriginal of Paika run, in 1854 were the only Aboriginal defendants in this period for whom cases were entered in the bench book. Nanang Cobra Billy was discharged in 1859 because there was no evidence against him. The charge was not given.[107] In the case against Billy the Bull, the evidence of constable William Eaton stated he had heard from another Aboriginal man, Happy Dingo, that Billy had killed two white men. William Darcy, constable of the Moulamein police, apprehended Billy 2 miles below Reynolds' station at the Aboriginal camp on the Murray River. Darcy asked Billy whether the account was true and he answered, '[O]nly a croppie' and that another Aboriginal man, Tommy Mitchell, was with him and cut out the victim's belly fat. Darcy fully believed that Billy understood the questions he asked. The case had begun with William Darcy's evidence that he heard from the magistrate George Morey that a warrant for Billy had been granted; he made no mention of Eaton or Happy Dingo. Nor was Tommy Mitchell ever mentioned again. In a deposition that gives yet another story in the case, the squatter William Ross said he had sent an Aboriginal man, Jacky Jacky, down to Commissioner McDonald to report what Jacky had told Ross—that Billy had murdered a 'croppie' whitefellow. There seems to be too many constables giving evidence, two magistrates were consulted in the case and everyone had been told something by an

---

105 Copy of Depositions Death of James Lavery, 30 October 1858, Balranald Bench Book, State Archives Collection, SR 4/5505.
106 James Johnson alias William Cooper, 6 September 1850, Balranald Bench Book.
107 Nanang Cobra Billy, 21 June 1859, Balranald Bench Book.

Aboriginal person. This elaborate approach is, however, in keeping with the Balranald style of taking down evidence: someone who had 'heard' something was as crucial as someone who was a witness.

Billy the Bull had no English, which is indicated by Constable Darcy saying he was sure whether Billy understood him, yet the constables report him speaking in the colony-wide pidgin apparent in Aboriginal confessions. '*Baal*' in this case is used when Constable Darcy asked Billy if he had speared the victim. Billy said *baal*, he had just hit him above the ear with a tomahawk. '*Baal*' elsewhere was used to mean 'I am telling the truth', and it appears at the beginning of supposed confessions to the Native Police. When the bag of bones was shown to Billy the constables reported Billy as saying that yes, that was the man. Billy may have admitted to nothing and he may have had no conversations with constables.

The constables said they asked Billy what he had done with the body. He said he had put it in a log, so the wild dogs would not get it. Billy took them to the place where the body had been placed, but it was not there. Two Aboriginal people, McDuff and Toowakky, were brought from Reynolds to dive for the body and each dive and its outcome were listed. Finally, they emerged with a rib bone and other bones were found. That bones were all that was found is indicative of how long before the discussion of killing with Mr Ross the event had taken place. Joseph Lowcock, publican, came forward to say a man named Scotchy stayed at his house in September 1850; he was travelling down the Darling River for work. Fourteen days after Scotchy left, a man 'named Richardson, I believe he is in Adelaide', told Lowcock that Scotchy was travelling with Billy the Bull, and he had every reason to believe he had been killed by the Blacks.[108]

The case has elements of concoction. The account represents Aboriginal people as the instigators of the case; Jacky went to Mr Ross, Happy Dingo giving the same information to Constable Eaton. Even if it is a concoction, it gives Aboriginal people the same relationship to law expressed in other cases at Balranald. They were represented as instigators. The positioning of Aboriginal people at Balranald differs from Yass; there was most certainly an Aboriginal subject.

---

108 Billy the Bull, 2 May 1851, Balranald Bench Book.

Billy was committed and escaped from the constable who was taking him to the Goulburn Assizes in June 1851. In August that year, the *Bathurst Free Press* gave a glowing account of the bravery of publican William Graham, who singlehandedly went to an Aboriginal camp near McCullin's run on the lower Murray where he had heard that Billy was staying. 'Gallant' Mr Graham managed to persuade Billy in Billy's own language to accompany him and tied him with a dog chain and returned him 40 miles (65 kilometres) to the lockup at Balranald. He had 'bravely' passed several camps on the way. Such hyperbole was common in newspaper reports of pursuit of Aboriginal people. This hyperbole is apparent also in the magistrate Edmond Morey's memory of Billy for which the language of outlawry was used: Billy was responsible for many deaths, which he affected by staking white men to the 'bottom of the river'. In this account also, Billy was given up by people of his 'own tribe' who were afraid of him.[109] Billy escaped from the watchhouse again in October 1851 and he did not appear before the assizes.[110] A man named Billy the Bull received blankets at Yass in 1858, but it is not clear whether it was the same man.[111] In the newspaper reports and in Morey's memories, one can see how history is produced by non-Aboriginal people with use of the tropes of fear and outlawry. Billy was not pursued across the country in the manner of Sippy at Warialda or Scabby Harry at Cooma, with the press eagerly reporting all sightings and utilising the language of the frontier.[112] This language did not appear at all in the records of the Balranald bench. Rather, Aboriginal people were described as having interest in utilising law.

In the case against Billy of Paika in 1854 for murderous assault of Margaret Hart, the senior constable James Johnson stated that 'he knew nothing of the character of the blackfellow, I have seen him in Balranald before'. Though the case should have resulted in committal, it was kept at bench level— something also found at Warialda and Armidale. The idea of Aboriginal people having a 'character' is not the language of the frontier and the case has other aspects that distinguish it from coastal perceptions of Aboriginal people. Billy had been cutting wood for Margaret Hart, she came into her house in Balranald and he attempted to choke her. Billy intervened in her testimony to say that 'I have been living at Yanga but belong to Paika'.

---

109 Morey, 'Reminiscences of a Pioneer in New South Wales'.
110 *Sydney Morning Herald*, 24 October 1851.
111 *Yass Courier*, 29 May 1858.
112 Scabby Harry: *Sydney Morning Herald*, 2 October 1858; *Moreton Bay Courier*, 13 April 1859. Sippey: *Moreton Bay Courier*, 17 December 1853; *The Banner*, 20 December 1853.

This was duly copied out by the clerk despite it having no immediate relevance to the evidence given. An hour after the assault, James Johnson, Constable Rumfield and Margaret Hart's husband, James, proceeded to the Aboriginal camp where the prisoner was pointed out as being the man who committed the assault. James Johnson said he 'told the prisoner of the charge against him and Billy said he knew nothing of it'. Billy was sentenced by the bench to three months' hard labour at Deniliquin gaol.[113] The formalities of the law were followed in this case where they were only mimicked in Billy the Bull's case. None of the language of the frontier appears among any of the deponents. If one were to ask the people of the town where Aboriginal people fitted in the legal system, they would not resort to words such as 'savage' or 'mischief'.

The deposition and signature taken from Bullen Bangy in 1852 by the bench indicate that Aboriginal information was regarded formally. Two of the four cases before the assizes derived from Aboriginal information. This does not mean that there was no violence against Aboriginal people during the 1850s. In 1854 constable Dennis Hannan shot Old Jacky in the back. Hannan, according to the *Goulburn Herald*, had 'fallen in with him' while travelling, yet the same report states he went to the Aboriginal camp at Wakool specifically to arrest Old Jacky. Hannan kept him locked in the Wakool Inn. In the morning, Old Jacky escaped, Hannan called 'stand', but Old Jacky did not stop. There was no inquest or hearing into this shooting and the *Goulburn Herald* stated that Old Jacky was wanted for the murder of young Mr Beveridge 'a few years ago'.

That shooting of Aboriginal people was wrong was apparent in Balranald in 1855 when a hutkeeper shot an Aboriginal man, Serjeant, to whom he had been giving rations. Samuel Judd, employed at Booyingo, Mc Evoys' run, said he 'came to Balranald on Monday 10 February to deliver myself up to the Police in consequence of being compelled to shoot a blackfellow in my own defence'. He had been in the habit of feeding Serjeant and his family 'to keep peace with him'. An argument resulted from Serjeant wanting wood that Judd had gathered. Judd said no and Serjeant wanted to fight. Judd felt cornered in his hut next morning when Serjeant confronted him with a cutlass and a double-barrelled gun. He shot at Serjeant, who walked away. Later he saw the body rolled up in something like a log and being carried away by the Blacks on their shoulders. Judd was discharged 'to appear again

---

113 Billy, Aboriginal of Paika, 15 February 1854, Balranald Bench Book.

if called upon'.[114] This was neither inquest nor a pretrial decision; there was no bail. Yet Judd, like Jones on the South Coast, had come to the bench to give himself up.

Creating the records

One of the earliest acts of the bench at Balranald was to obtain a copy of Callaghan's *Acts of Council*.[115] The relevant Acts of Council were set out in the bench book when they were pertinent to a case. As well, all that was said in court was copied by the clerks, however irrelevant it may have been. Defendants before the bench were able to ask questions and make statements in their defence, even in minor cases. The requirements of the *Justices Act* were dutifully followed. The bench book, however, cannot be regarded as complete. After 1858, the results of cases were not recorded and numbers decline. George Edwards asked for a transfer east in February 1859 and had an exchange organised with 'Mr Sinclair CPS at Goods Inn, Nanango', but it does not appear his wish was granted. In April the magistrate Joseph Phelps asked for leave of absence for Edwards due to the precarious state of his health.[116]

The bench book is further complicated by the steady appearance of notes regarding the management of money set out in formal terms. Edwards' financial transactions on behalf of the bench were then noted closely in the bench book. George Edwards had John McDonald, chief constable, sign the following entry in the bench book: 'Received from Mr George Edwards Clerk of Petty Sessions £2.10 sterling being my proportion of the Moiety of the fine imposed on Charles Thatcher of Gundagai for Hawking without a licence.'[117]

The formal use of the word 'moiety' suggests Edwards wished to show his knowledge of the law, and that formality is apparent in both the setting out of the bench book and perhaps the magistrate's relationship to the centralised authorities of the attorney-general and the auditor-general. They assert themselves. In *Taylor*, they wrote that the reason they sent the case to the Inspector-General of Police in the form of copied depositions

---

114 Samuel Judd, 17 December 1855, Balranald Bench Book.
115 Magistrates to Colonial Secretary, 18 April 1850, Balranald Bench Letter Book, State Archives Collection, SR 4/5503.
116 George Edwards to Colonial Secretary, 10 February 1859; Joseph Phelps to Colonial Secretary, 9 April 1859: Balranald Bench Letter Book.
117 Balranald Bench Book, 19 December 1857.

was because they 'at the time believing the case to be one for no to act in judicially that ministerially the forms referred to in the Act of Council Vic 43 S7 were not used'.[118]

The person who would be using the forms 'ministerially' was George Edwards. The terminology refers to a no case finding, but the decision should have been the attorney-general's.

Something peculiar to the Balranald bench was the underlining of key evidence in depositions in pen, before they were sent to the attorneys-general. Evidence was later underlined again in pencil by the attorney-general, who was the first person to read depositions on their arrival in Sydney. Who exactly underlined these points at Balranald is unclear; it may have been Murray or Edwards or one of the magistrates, but the same underlining appears in the bench book copy of the case against Elizabeth Robinson, made out before the depositions left Balranald.[119] The Balranald bench was acting as though it knew the law as well as the attorney-general.

Balranald magistrates were Joseph Phelps, John Lecky Phelps, Stephen Cole (the Commissioner of Crown Lands), George Morey, Edmond Morey, George Macdonald, Frederick Walker (for a brief period before he began his command of the Native Police), John Scott, George Hobler, George Murray, Edward Plunkett, Augustus Morris, John Kelly and Henry Shiells—the last two being police magistrates. All the gentlemen listed had travelled overland to take up runs in the lucrative period of the establishment of South Australia in the 1840s when food and stock were transported to Adelaide. Edmond Morey's remembered history gives the story of the early settlement around Balranald. Like elsewhere, it was a place of brothers and relatives marking runs and later negotiating with the government in Sydney as to the validity of these claims. Balranald resembled the rest of New South Wales. These gentlemen would move further afield, taking up runs in Queensland and west up the Lachlan River. They dined, hunted and socialised as well as taking up positions as magistrates. Joseph Phelps was a Quaker, as was apparent when he appeared to give evidence against a servant. He was influential in the early 1850s and it may have been him who produced the openness of the bench and its adherence to the *Justices Act*.

---

118 *R v Taylor*.
119 *R v Anne Robinson* 1850, 12, SR 9/6360; *R v Walsh*.

LAW IN THE NEW DEMOCRACY

The most active chief constable was Dennis Hannan, who, in 1855, began to arrest people he regarded as 'suspicious'. Daniel Smith in July of that year was arrested for 'travelling under suspicious circumstances with firearms and suspected of breaking into a hut'. He was found at an Aboriginal camp where he had been staying for two days. Despite the depositions from the man whose hut had been robbed, there was no property found on him. He was sentenced to 14 days in Balranald lockup 'as a vagrant'.[120] Hannan arrested two other men on suspicion of breaking into a hut. There was property found and sworn to by a Chinese man, Chin Choo. The bench confined the men as rogues and vagabonds.[121] Hannan took William Hendry into custody, 'who he had reason to suspect of intending to commit an assault at the Balranald Inn on a Mrs Mozely'. Hannon took £2 from Hendry. The bench required that this be returned but that Hendry be watched by the constabulary as he was 'a dangerous character'.[122] In the same month, Hannon arrested not only a man he suspected of theft but also Thomas Lowcock and John Ralph, who worked at the Balranald Inn where the money had been stolen.[123] While arrests for drunkenness increased after Simon McDonald became chief constable, there was no indication that the intensive policing of Hannan remained.

Notable at Balranald are cases, 21 of 83, in which constables were charged with neglect, drunkenness or incompetence. Four constables resigned during the period. This may suggest diligence on the part of the chief constables who brought the charges, but it could also indicate discontent and an absence of authority. Allowing prisoners to escape occurred in cases related to the assizes. Billy the Bull, William Taylor, Edward McMahon and Francis Howard were all to be taken to Goulburn for the assizes, yet they escaped when lesser offenders did not. James Carter, the lockup keeper, was suspended. He claimed he did not receive a bribe to let McMahon and Howard go and his wages were returned to him by the Commissioner of Crown Lands and magistrate Stephen Cole.[124]

If the cases before the bench resembled those of Molong, Orange or Yass, Balranald would be another example of a diligent magistracy and constabulary faced with a litigious local population. But chief constables and George Edwards himself were brought up on charges of illegally selling

---

120 Daniel Smith, 20 August 1855, Balranald Bench Book.
121 John Gordon, George Felton, 20 August 1855, Balranald Bench Book.
122 William Hendry, 5 November 1855, Balranald Bench Book.
123 William Dixon, 5 November 1855, Balranald Bench Book.
124 Application of James Carter, 14 June 1855, Balranald Bench Book.

alcohol and the bench seems largely in thrall to local publicans William Graham, James Lowcock and Jane Lowcock—all related and adept at concocting cases.

Publicans and law

Thirty-four entangled cases before the bench show the power of local publicans. In September 1850 Richard Jones came before the bench to say he had heard Constable Thurston say in the kitchen of a public house in Balranald that:

> Lowcock's drays were over the river and Lowcock was selling grog and that he Thurston had received instructions from Mr Scott and Mr Hobler and the magistrates of the district not to interfere with Lowcock and that if he did do so it would only be for his own advantage.[125]

This was an enormous accusation that included all the Balranald magistrates and the constables in corrupt activity around the sale of alcohol from a dray. George Macdonald, the only magistrate sitting, dismissed Thurston from the police for 'speaking improperly of the magistrates in the kitchen of the Balranald Inn'.[126] There was no action concerning the dray, the other constables or the involvement of the gentlemen and magistrates John Scott and George Hobler. The reader is blocked from further inquiry and the Balranald bench itself becomes bound up with the highly profitable trade in spirits and wine.

John Marks, servant to Joseph Lowcock, appeared to say he had received spirits and wine from Lowcock with the understanding he was to pay for them. Lowcock pleaded not guilty. Lowcock had a defence witness, his servant William Hodgson. He was perfectly satisfied, he said, that Marks had received no spirits or wine. The case was dismissed by the magistrates. Marks claimed he received rum on another occasion. Under questioning by Lowcock, he said that he lived at O'Dell's public house and:

> had no understanding with Mr O'Dell that I was to be fed all that time, and well paid if I got you fined. I never told you I was to get £10 from Mr O'Dell if I prosecuted you.[127]

---

125 Constable Thurston, 7 September 1850, Balranald Bench Book.
126 ibid.
127 Joseph Lowcock, 18 November 1850, Balranald Bench Book.

Richard Jones supported Marks' account. Leighton Robinson appeared to say that he had frequently remonstrated with O'Dell for keeping Marks about the place and O'Dell told him that:

> if he did not keep Marks about the place and give him credit he would not file information against Lowcock and the business of the Public House in which I am living would be ruined. Mr O'Dell told me that if he was in my place would allow Marks to go without paying the account provided he would prosecute you [Lowcock].[128]

One can see the court in action in this account where the defendant dominated the space in his questioning and the witness spoke directly to him. The court requested Robinson say when this conversation took place; Robinson said it was after Marks made his complaint. Questioned by magistrate Joseph Phelps, he said:

> I once asked you to receive an information against Lowcock for sly grog selling I then stated to you that I might as well shut up the house if Lowcock was allowed to sell grog in the manner he had been doing.[129]

Lowcock was fined £30 for this offence. On 23 November, Jane Lowcock brought a charge against Marks of stealing trousers 'six months ago' belonging to her husband, Joseph. She said she 'would have pressed the charge against Marks even though [if] he had not appeared against my husband as a witness'. On Marks' questioning, she did agree she washed for him and he claimed he could have obtained the trousers by mistake.[130] He was discharged.

The bench presides over wild accusation and counterclaim. There was no stolen property mentioned in a burglary case that was also marked up as a deposition but not completed. What was important was what people heard about spirits being sold and the disparate and conflicting accounts were left to play out by the magistrates who may or may not have been involved in or tolerant of the trade Lowcock was carrying out. This shifts the purview of the court into feud but because it is all written out so diligently by the clerk, it has the appearance of legitimacy, just as at Carcoar, where such machinations were carefully obscured. We can see some of the dynamic around publicans that is obscured in bench entries in other areas such

---

128 ibid.
129 ibid.
130 John Marks, 23 November 1850, Balranald Bench Book.

5. SOUTH-WEST

as Armidale and Warialda, where constables were at the beck and call of publicans and law centred on public houses. We obtain an insight because of the propensity for detail on the part of the clerk.

A new chief constable, Dennis Hannan, appeared in the bench book. In August 1852, Hannan served Joseph Lowcock a summons for abusing the clerk of the peace Patrick John Murray. Hannan said, '[H]e told me he wanted Mr Christie [the magistrate] to decide, he would be damned if he settled for anyone else.' The magistrates on the case were Joseph Phelps and John Christie. Lowcock was fined £2 for his abuse of the clerk. The case set out the relationship between publican William Graham and Lowcock. The clerk Murray wanted to settle his accounts with Graham. He told Graham to come up to his office. Graham produced the accounts and Murray disputed the amount. Graham went to get Lowcock and they returned with 'Lowcock's books'. Lowcock spoke so improperly he was asked to leave the office. Murray said he had no account with Lowcock but with Mr Graham. Lowcock refused to leave, accused Murray of trying to swindle him and said Murray should lay his hand on his 'if he dared'. When he did leave, he further abused Murray through the window, calling him a swindling dog.[131] The formal approach with the books indicates that Graham's accounts were managed by Lowcock. Graham was further able to insult Murray by claiming he had not heard Lowcock calling him 'a low livered swindling dog'. Lowcock and Graham felt themselves in such a position of power that they were able to request a particular magistrate and abuse the clerk of the peace.

In May 1858 the new chief constable replacing Hannan charged him with a breach of the *Publicans Act*. It is another example of a meaningless entry in the bench book. Chief constable Simon McDonald had apprehended two men who were drunk. When he got into court, his case against Hannan was non-existent. Yes, he arrested the men, 'but he did not see anyone supply them'. The two men failed to appear in court and Joseph Phelps dismissed the case.[132] After the case was dismissed, George Edwards brought a case against Hannan for abusive language. Hannan had said to him:

---

131 Joseph Lowcock, 2 August 1852, Balranald Bench Book.
132 *Simon McDonald v Dennis Hannan*, 3 May 1858, Balranald Bench Book.

So you have taken out a summons against me. I was a white livered coward, he said with great emphasis he knew me of old, he left the Chief Constable's quarters and in the street continued to speak violent language which I do not recollect, not wishing to notice it I made no reply.[133]

We are left with two impressions. First, of a valiant police force holding off self-interested publicans or, second, those same constables running quasi-public houses from the lockup. Both are plausible explanations of the appearance of these cases. Where the law is sited at Balranald is entirely within the power struggles around the selling of wine or spirits. The presence of the settlement on a major trading route from Adelaide was perhaps the reason for the high quality of the alcohol mentioned. We would have none of this information if it were not for the clerks Murray and Edwards. They allow us to see the machinations of settlements where the publican has a central presence and the law buzzes around the public house.

Assize cases

When we turn to the few higher court cases, the lack of attention to any evidence beyond 'hearing' something is crucial. In the case against Anne Robinson for the murder of James Thomson, the single witness did not see the shooting. The squatter Alexander McCallum of 'Minindi Creek' was woken in September 1849 by the sound of a shot. He crossed the creek to the 'Gonea' (gunyah) where his three servants slept. On the way he met Anne Robinson walking 'to and fro'. He did not speak to her but went to the gunyah and found James Thomson lying in bed, groaning. The other servant, David Conway, told him Anne Robinson had shot Thomson and McCallum said that 'to the best of my recollection', Thomson said he had been shot by Anne Robinson. McCallum left the station in search of medical assistance. On his return, he 'heard' the prisoner had died two hours after he'd left. There was no magistrate for 160 miles (260 kilometres) and there were no medical practitioners. McCallum made a close study of the carbine he found in the hut and his information was underlined by the clerk or magistrate. He said that Anne Robinson had been acting strangely, seeming under mental derangement. The body was buried. McCallum explained that his station was 300 miles (480 kilometres) from the court and not within the boundaries of any district. His evidence was given in April 1850 and the delay was not explained. There was no other witness and David

---

133 *Edwards v Hannan*, 3 May 1858, Balranald Bench Book.

Conway had long left service; it was thought he was in California. In the court, Anne Robinson had nothing to say in her defence and in his letter to Attorney-General Plunkett, John McDonald, magistrate, wrote that 'there is little doubt that the prisoner was labouring under mental derangement at the time she shot Thomson who had only been on the station a few days previous'.[134] For Plunkett, the statement of a dying man would have been central as the law requires, but this was qualified by McCallum's 'to the best of my recollection'. The complete absence of the witness Conway was ignored. Anne Robinson was to be tried in August 1850 at the Goulburn Assizes.[135] She was discharged by proclamation at the assizes.[136]

In *Taylor*, what Pompey overheard about 'big one money' was deemed crucial to the case, hence the need to incorporate his evidence of the plan to cut the pocket of Edward Stephens at Jane Lowcock's inn in 1856. The magistrate Joseph Phelps sent the case to Attorney-General Manning. There was no evidence that Taylor hid the money in the tree where Pompey found it, nor that the footprints were his. Manning wrote on the cover of the case that 'perhaps the Chief Constable will be able to prove that Taylor lived near the spot where the purse was found' and 'he may be sufficiently acquainted with the professional language of thieves to be able to explain the meaning of "cutting and making a pair of trousers" spoken of by the witness McKay'. Manning's perspective of the deposition as a document of prosecution is apparent here and his willingness to assist in suggesting ways to find acceptable evidence illustrates a tolerance of inadequate documents.[137]

The case against Patrick Walsh for the murder of William Graham in 1857 also contained evidence of speech. Chief Constable Hannan said he was going to the public house and met Robert Kirby. 'He said Graham was murdered by Patrick Walsh, run down, run down.' John Wilson, who was also stabbed by Walsh, gave a long deposition about his crawling out of the bar and asking the cook to help stop the bleeding. He saw nothing else.[138] The depositions show the same culture apparent in the bench book— including what was heard or overheard. The right to question witnesses, the offer of bail and the recall of witnesses show that the *Justices Act* was clearly followed. Yet, this haziness of what constituted evidence of an offence also characterised the bench.

---

134 *R v Anne Robinson*.
135 *Sydney Morning Herald*, 5 August 1850.
136 *Sydney Morning Herald*, 14 August 1850.
137 *R v Taylor*.
138 *R v Walsh*.

In 1859 John Kelly sat on the bench at Balranald as police magistrate for the first time. He administered a severe reprimand to the clerk of the bench, the chief constable and the lockup keeper for 'not keeping the documents belonging to the court in a fit and proper state for reference'. He suspended the chief constable and the lockup keeper was fined 10 shillings for wearing his hat in court, 'not being a military hat'.[139] Records are imperfect but their inadequacy, their additions and their incorporations do show a particular culture of law at Balranald. This was one where what was heard or overheard was as valid as any direct evidence of an event, where Aboriginal people were given equal status as witnesses, where everything was written out, however irrelevant, and where this kind of law was more valid than the opinions of the attorneys-general.

Balranald shows us the intricacies of the relationship between publican and constable—difficult to ascertain from records elsewhere. Publicans wanted to dominate the courts, utilising them for their own purposes. Publicans also dominated the north-western benches, where constables largely appeared at the behest of publicans and indeed seemed to be working for them. Balranald allows us to see the cooption of law by the publican and constable.

Right of reply

Balranald Local Aboriginal Land Council has a copy of this chapter and found the information useful.

---

139 *Sydney Morning Herald*, 18 January 1859.

6

North

Macleay River

The Macleay River is Dunghutti Country, and there are histories of the region from a Dunghutti perspective.[1] Barry Morris wrote of the period of contact history on the Macleay in terms of Michael Taussig's concept of terror where information was falsely constructed in newspaper and squatter records of the past.[2] Such falsification is nowhere more apparent than in a report of a raid on an Aboriginal camp 300 miles (480 kilometres) from Sydney in 1860, at the end of our period, when most violence in New South Wales has been thought by Australian historians to be well over.

In early 1860 Lieutenant Poulding or Poulden, a veteran of the Crimea, led his Native Police to an attack on Aboriginal camps on the mountain above Fifth Day Creek near Kempsey. He had recently arrived from the Dawson River, 580 miles (935 kilometres) north of the Macleay.[3] Richard Bedford Poulden had arrived in New South Wales with letters of introduction in 1858. Governor William Denison told him he did not think there was a great deal of work for a military man, but Poulden asked to be assigned to the Native Police, so was appointed as a second lieutenant. The commander of the Native Police wrote to the colonial secretary that the appointment of officers was his prerogative and that Poulden was deficient in the 'peculiar

---

1 Kempsey Local Aboriginal Land Council, Facebook page, www.facebook.com/kempseylocal aboriginallandcouncil/posts/some-history-of-the-dunghutti-nationtraditional-countrythe-macleay-valley-forms-/1321043801426542/. See also parts of Clayton Dixon, *Surviving New England*.
2 Barry Morris, *Domesticating Resistance: The Dhan-Gadi Aborigines and the Australian State* (Oxford: Berg, 1989), 10.
3 *Sydney Morning Herald*, 15 August 1859.

character' required for the Native Police. From reports, Poulden's behaviour 'had not been such as to command the respect of those with whom he became acquainted'. The Executive Council discussed the issue and decided that Poulden should continue until there was evidence against him.[4]

In 1860 at Kempsey, Poulding (this spelling is used by the *Sydney Morning Herald*) had received information of an 'outrage' at 'P.D. Creek' run and arrived there to find Mrs McMaher barricaded in the house with a stand of firearms. He made sure she was safe and proceeded in pursuit of the Aboriginal people who had committed the 'outrage'. They found at Fifth Day Creek 'a downward track of a large number of New England Blacks, evidently joining them'. Poulding's party consisted of six men. One, Paddy, an Aboriginal man, had been in service on the Dawson River, another was 'trooper Quilt', a white man. The other Native Police were not named. At Fifth Day Creek they found three camps, one at the top of the mountain, one in the middle and one at the bottom. Three of the troopers were sent to the top of the mountain to drive the Aboriginal people down. 'A shot was heard from above and a black came down close to Lieutenant Poulding and was preparing to spear him when he was shot.' This was:

> [the] signal for a general attack from above and below, many shots were fired, one black passed Lieutenant Poulding with his arm shattered and King Boura was killed when in the act of shooting a trooper with a double barrel gun.

Night was setting in and the small force 'went to one of the Blacks' camps put out all the fires, and waited'. At midnight heavy rain 'cleared off' and they heard 'in the ravine below the loading of guns, and from above the gins calling on the Blacks to come up':

> [The] following morning at daylight … the party of Blacks moved up but being light they were seen from above and Lieutenant Poulding ordered his men to fire, one man was found dead and a child [was found] not four years old, not wounded, but which the dying man had fallen over.

Lieutenant Poulding then destroyed all the Aboriginal people's dogs and weapons, which were very numerous, and 'left this part, knowing the Blacks were off'.[5]

---

4   Leonard E. Skinner, *Police of the Pastoral Frontier: Native Police, 1849–59* (Brisbane: University of Queensland Press, 1975), 262, 339.
5   *Sydney Morning Herald*, 9 May 1860.

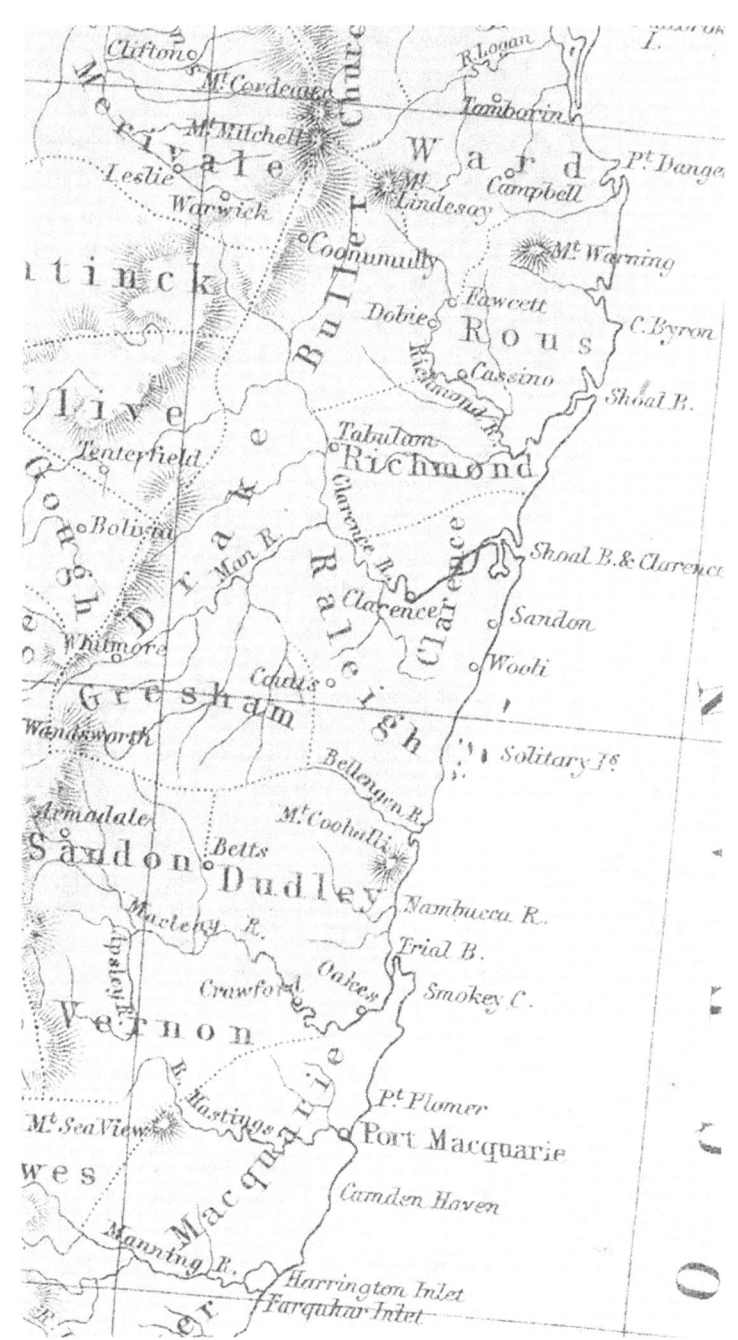

Map 6.1: Northern New South Wales
Source: W. Hughes, London G. Phillip and Son, circa 1858, State Library of New South Wales, MLZ/M1 806/1858/1.

Poulding's detail suggests another story in which women and children were present at all three camps and were in the thick of battle. The 'New England Blacks' disappear out of the story and none of the troopers was shot even though they were opposed by armed men. The child was taken and given to Mr Warne. This elaborate account is careful to seem military in its description and the veteran of the Crimea is lauded at the end of the article. Though three Aboriginal men, including King Boura, were killed, there was no inquiry into the deaths and no legal context for Poulding's actions. As with all such raids at night or in the early hours of the morning, there was no body count, so it is impossible to tell how many Aboriginal people were killed.

This quasi-military state existed alongside a legal system on the Macleay that incorporated Aboriginal people, unlike other places in New South Wales. This is as late in the history of the colony as 1860 and there is some indication that such a military system existed well into this decade on the Macleay, Bellinger and Nambucca rivers.[6] That both systems existed alongside the First Nations political system is made clear by the statement in an 1860 letter to the *Maitland Mercury* by the squatter John Ducat that 'their corroborees and other meetings are mere pretexts and covers for robbery'.[7]

The Macleay squatters were an avid pressure group for the deployment of the Native Police and active participants in government inquiries. John Ducat was clear what he thought of the legal system in his letter of 1860:

> White people are afraid to meddle with aborigines because there is such a sympathy in a certain quarter and with a Sydney jury, for the 'poor blacks' that they feel satisfied they would not obtain a fair trial. They recollect the Plunkettian hecatomb to the names of the aborigines, slaughtered by white men in revenge for the unredressed murders of their brethren by the sable pets of the great luminary, whose friends seem so proud of his share in this memorable massacre that they will, doubtless, record it on his tomb.[8]

Ducat was referring to the Myall Creek massacre in which Attorney-General Plunkett played a significant role in assuring the trial of the murderers. The trial was represented here as having particular cultural force. Macleay squatters were able to obtain the services of a Native Police force. In other

---

6 *Sydney Morning Herald*, 16 January 1861.
7 *Sydney Morning Herald*, 3 May 1860.
8 *Maitland Mercury and Hunter River Advertiser*, 3 May 1860.

places squatter magistrates conducted raids on camps on their own runs that did not appear in the courts and no body counts were given.[9] The Macleay had a curious relationship to the legality of killing Aboriginal people that is not evident elsewhere. It spoke of law and legality where other places did not, as though it were trying to force relations with Aboriginal people into the legal domain—to make subjects out of them and to make the state legally aggressive to Aboriginal people. In 1857 a letter to the *Armidale Express* claimed that:

> the laws relative to Aborigines are the product of an Exeter Hall saint [and] also require some alterations. We on the Macleay will never send another to Sydney for trial in any case except for murder, however flagrant the offence and clear the evidence.[10]

This is a rejection of legal process, but also an association with that process, which required 'alteration'.

Region

The Macleay Valley was described in 1853:

> Take then 'gentle reader' and lay before you a map on which some tolerably sized river is delineated ... Let them suppose the stream winding its torturous way between mountains and through plains with numerous rivulets adding to its volume from the mountain glens and vales, on either side are lagoons and marshes as it approaches its disembouguement into the sea. Now ... take a camel's hair brush and some Indian ink of a lighter shade ... and shade on side of each tributary, together with the main so as to present an irregular border varying from ¼ to ¾ of a mile in width. To this let him add patches here and there, like so many small lakes ... [T]his will be a representation of the available land of the Macleay River, the uncoloured portion of this paper would represent the hill and dale of surrounding forest ... Suffice to say that it is the abrupt side of the great sea coast range facing the ocean, upon ascending which the table land of New England is gained.[11]

---

9   For example, Joshua Bray Diary, 6 September 1866, Bray Family Papers, Mitchell Library, MSS 1929.
10 *Armidale Express*, 11 April 1857.
11 *Maitland Mercury*, 7 December 1853.

The population of the Macleay fluctuated. The town of Kempsey had abandoned and collapsing houses in the 1850s. The boom years were 1840 and 1841 when 200 sawyers were employed by companies to extract cedar and float the logs downriver to waiting ships.[12] A correspondent of the *Empire* wrote in 1854:

> The present population of the Macleay are a tenantry whose only object is to get as much out of the land as possible, with as little advantage to the landlord as may be. They have nothing to stimulate them to effect permanent and valuable improvements. Their mode of culture is careless, their habitations of the most humble character and their conditions in life utterly unimproved … [H]ow could it be otherwise knowing as they do they must leave the more valuable result of their labour to another or by renewing their lease pay a higher rent.[13]

By 1859 there were high weeds in Smith Street between Mr Scott's and the Star Inn, West Kempsey. The weeds were so high that a person walking there could not be seen.[14] Arguments for improvement and representation came from the entrepreneurial section of the town and the targets of their criticism were the magistrates, particularly Jonathon Warne. A public meeting of 1854 claimed the people of the town—freeholders—were no longer 'going to be dictated to by magistrates'.[15]

Magistrates and the attorneys-general

The magistrates from the Macleay sought to direct and advise the attorneys-general. Their attitude was that they knew precisely what was needed in a case and the attorney-general needed to be guided. In *Mogo Garra*, a case from 1850, they wrote that 'it is not considered advisable longer to delay the trial' and continued that, 'in the event of the prisoner being acquitted on the charge of murder he might be indicted for stealing the shawl'.[16] In *Kearns*, 1853, they wrote:

---

12 *Sydney Morning Herald*, 20 April 1842.
13 *Empire*, 9 March 1854.
14 *Maitland Mercury*, 26 November 1859.
15 *Empire*, 7 August 1854.
16 Edward Merewether and Jonathon Warne to Attorney-General, 14 September 1850, in *R v Mogo alias Mogo Garra* 1850, 7, SR 9/6357.

> Two of the witnesses examined at the Inquiry were not called at the hearing as their evidence merely corroborates [other witnesses] and the magistrates thought that the country would be put to an unnecessary expense by calling them at the trial … [S]hould you, however, on referring to the proceedings of the inquiry deem it expedient to have their testimony, I request you will be good enough to forward to the Bench with the least possible delay the necessary subpoenas for their attendance … and as they were examined at the inquiry in the presence of the accused their being again examined at the office will I presume be unnecessary. I have to request further that in the event of you declining to prosecute in the case you will at your first convenience inform the bench.[17]

In *Green*, they wrote:

> The features in the case to which we need to call your attention are that the witness Fulton is an unwilling one … and therefore might be regarded in the light of *particeps criminas* [sic] … [A]s the witness Constable Hampson's evidence is of so little consequence … we are of the opinion that his testimony may be dispensed with … [W]e shall be glad of your decision on these points as <u>early as possible</u>.[18]

All these decisions belonged to the attorney-general; they were not to be made by magistrates. The attorneys-general, however, make no comment and this is comparable with their lack of response to the north-western benches' flaunting of the law. The Macleay bench does not figure large in the letters to magistrates from the attorney-general in the 1840s or the 1860s.[19] Plunkett coolly writes in *Mogo Garra*, '[I]nform the Bench that I shall await further communication from them before I can decide on the course to be taken respecting the Prisoner' and 'let the Crown Solicitor heed the subpoena as requested by the Bench'.[20] In *Green*, Constable Hampson did not attend the court in Sydney and the Crown solicitor notes his absence: '[T]his witness is <u>not</u> in attendance', as though the magistrates' decision that his attendance was unnecessary was ignored rather than responded to.[21]

---

17 Edward Merewether to Attorney-General, in *R v Ann Kearns* 1853, 22, SR 9/6374.
18 Jonathon Warne and Charles Kemp to Attorney-General, 20 April 1857, in *R v George Green* 1857, 7, SR 9/6411. Emphasis in original.
19 NSW Crown Law Office Letter Book; Attorney-General Letters.
20 *R v Mogo alias Mogo Garra*.
21 *R v George Green*.

Detail in depositions

Benches could be stung by the attorneys-general and decisions in one case would affect how the bench constructed depositions and took care in presentation. Even though the attorneys-general did not criticise depositions, the Macleay bench was one affected by earlier decisions and sensitive to evidence. Along with the Orange, Molong and Yass benches, Macleay depositions became highly detailed, with a great deal of extraneous information included. In 1850 the Macleay bench was responding to a former rejection of depositions in an 1846 case against an Aboriginal man, Mogo Garra:

> We would here observe that Mogo was in custody in 1846 for being implicated in the murder of four persons (two men, a woman and a child) at the same river and was discharged by your direction from insufficiency of evidence.[22]

There was no evidence in 1846 against Mogo Garra except for his threat to sawyers that they should stay on one part of the river and not venture further afield.[23] The 1850 case was far more detailed, with Mogo Garra and others living closely and working for Daniel Page. The evidence in this case was reiterated in an 1859 case against Doughboy for the same murder. In that case the magistrates felt it necessary to write to the attorney-general that Mogo Garra had been hanged for the same offence.[24]

The people and cases

Macleay cases emerge from the same field as the majority of the cases in Grafton and the South Coast. Complainants lived closely alongside the accused and the use of law incorporated accusations against Aboriginal people. In 1850 Edward Gallagher, a rafter in the cedar trade of the Nambucca River, came before the bench to say he had known Mogo Garra for 10 years. He thought Mogo belonged to the Clarence River. Hearing there was a warrant out against Mogo for the murder of Daniel Page, Gallagher set a trap for Mogo at Bowra. Three Aboriginal men, Nundie, Billy and Peter, 'induced the prisoner to come into my hut when after very considerable resistance by the prisoner I secured him with the aid of the

---

22 *R v Mogo alias Mogo Garra.*
23 Enoch Rudder to Commissioner of Crown Lands, Documents collected by Sir William Dixson, Dixson Library, State Library of New South Wales, ADD 78.
24 *R v Doughboy* 1859, 1, SR 9/6424.

three natives'. Furthermore, Gallagher found a piece of shawl round the prisoner's waist and when he asked where he had got it, Mogo Garra said he had got it from Page's hut at the same time he had got the blankets.[25] This arrest had not been made by a constable but by an ordinary member of the public.

There were two inquiries into the death of the baby of Ann Kearns at Kempsey after the child rolled into the river and drowned. The first was by Jonathon Warne and 'a jury of the inhabitants' of Kempsey. The second was a magisterial inquiry by Warne and Merewether that committed Ann Kearns to the Supreme Court for manslaughter. The jury case was instigated by Warne because, he wrote, given 'considerable excitement existing in the neighbourhood on the present occasion I thought it expedient to summon twelve of the most respectable neighbours as a jury'.[26] The jury's decision was that the death was accidental, but Warne was unsatisfied and held a magisterial inquiry. Even though the magisterial inquiry invalidated the jury decision, Plunkett still asked that the original inquiry be sent to him and wrote on the cover that Ann Kearns should be indicted for manslaughter.[27] For Warne, the reason for the inquiry was 'excitement' in Kempsey. This was the second time a child of Ann Kearns had died; the first, by scalding, Warne had declared an accident but since then he had found out that she was not a married woman as he had thought.[28]

In 1857 George Green was brought by a neighbour, Thomas Thompson, for stealing a calf even after Green apologised to him for mistakenly taking the calf and offered another calf in exchange. He went to the police after the exchange did not occur.[29]

Aboriginal subjects

In 1859 Doughboy was captured by Poulding/Poulden of the Native Police. Poulding said he had been informed that Doughboy was at the Aboriginal camp on the bank of the right-hand side of the river, a mile below Christmas Creek. He proceeded there and found him in company with several other Aboriginal people. Doughboy 'showed fight'. Poulding took him across the river to Yarrabandini and guarded him there all night and then handed

---

25 *R v Mogo alias Mogo Garra.*
26 *R v Kearns.*
27 ibid.
28 ibid.
29 *R v George Green.*

him over to the Kempsey lockup keeper, Mr O. Smith.[30] The arrest took place 10 years after the offence. Doughboy was not informed what he was arrested for, nor was he warned about incriminating himself.

The Mogo Garra and Doughboy cases show the same kind of contradictory evidence in all cases involving poorer members of the communities of the colony. This suggests concoction. The deceased, Daniel Page, was a cedar dealer at the mouth of the Bellinger River. The witnesses to his death were 'a woman who passed as his wife', Jane O'Neil, and John Haley, a man who had been a week employed by Page as a bullock driver. Marriage was important to mention in Kempsey. According to Mogo Garra, the provocation for the attack came from Jane O'Neil threatening to stab Mickey a few days before. This Mogo Garra admitted to Merewether, wrote the magistrates, when he was first brought to the Commissioner of Crown Lands' station. Further, in the hearing, Mogo Garra brought this up again. He claimed Jane O'Neil threatened to stab Mickey:

> You will perceive upon reference to her deposition that she positively denies having done so—we do not however entirely believe her. The prisoner is a very intelligent black and speaks English tolerably well: the questions that elicited O'Neil's denial of the threats of stabbing and bringing out the gun and the attempt to force a way into the hut by the fire-place (which you will find towards the close of her evidence) were suggested by the prisoner although put from the Bench and will at once show you that he understands the position in which he is placed.[31]

The magistrates could use literacy against an Aboriginal person. In the same letter, these magistrates request an interpreter for the trial—another contradiction. Thomas Owen or Barrabee was to be obtained by subpoena. Mogo Garra in his questions and statement had incriminated himself; the attack was 'preconcerted', according to the magistrates in their letter. The reader is left wondering why Mogo Garra did not question the witness directly himself, as accused persons did in other cases, and why an interpreter was needed if he spoke English 'tolerably well'. The 'admission' to the Commissioner of Crown Lands was not included in the depositions, nor was there any statement of the accused. The court was not acting as it should in this case. None of this was questioned by Attorney-General Plunkett.

---

30 *R v Doughboy*.
31 Edward C. Merewether and Jonathon Warne to Attorney-General, 25 July 1850, in *R v Mogo alias Mogo Garra*.

John Haley could name all the attackers: 'Mogo, Doughboy, Ugly, Mickey Charlie.' These Aboriginal men were named in the warrant and were 'belonging to, or frequenting the Bellinger River'.[32] That this political distinction was recognised in the warrant and the terms 'belonging to' used indicate the awareness the magistrates had of the Aboriginal polity. The recognition of Aboriginal understanding of dispute is hinted at also in the letters, in that Jane O'Neil wanted it understood she made no provocation.

According to Haley, Mogo Garra frequently worked about the hut for Page. On the morning of 25 April 1850, he was to take meat up to the sawyers working upriver. Tobacco was given to Mogo Garra, but he turned to Page and said, 'I want you to put me across the river.' Page and Haley walked with Mogo Garra to the boat and when they got there, Haley turned and there were four Aboriginal men on top of the hill, a few yards away. They came down the hill and closed around Haley and Page. Haley suggested giving them the boat and Page said that they seemed to be wanting to get them away from the hut. When Haley tried to walk back to the hut, Ugly threw a spear, which Haley stooped to avoid, then Ugly threw a boomerang. There followed a group attack with spears, sticks and boomerangs. The whole of the prisoners were beating Page when Haley looked back. Page made it back to the hut and tried to close the window, but it was forced open and spears and stones were thrown in. The hut door was open, yet the attackers went around to the chimney and started taking out the slabs. Haley and Page decided to go outside and fight: '[W]e had better die outside.' The attackers ran away and Page and Haley returned to the hut. The attackers came back and began breaking in the 'store door'. Page 'jumped over the partition that divided the two apartments'. Haley heard a scuffle, Page closed the store door and climbed over the partition, 'when he said to me "Jack I am a dead man", I perceived a large wound in his neck'. Haley asked Page who had done it and 'he said it was Ugly with his boomerang'. Haley asked the attackers who were still outside the hut 'what were they so saucy for and told them if they wanted tobacco and flour I would give it to them'. Haley gave them tobacco and flour, saying, '[N]ow go away and make a cake.' Mogo Garra took the flour and tobacco and all the attackers went away.

Haley took Page to the boat 'and the woman and child followed us'. They travelled half a mile and Page said he could go no longer 'and desired I would place him under one of the mangroves'. Haley, the woman and the child

---

32 John Warne to Chief Constable of the McLeay River District, in *R v Mogo alias Mogo Garra*.

proceeded to the head of the river. On arriving at a ship, Haley procured the sailors' help and went back for Page. He had moved and Haley did not find him until the following morning. Haley and the sailors spent the night in Page's hut. They found Page and travelled again, but from weakness, Page could not continue, so they placed him in the mangroves, leaving him there and going for a doctor and to make a report to the police. There was no account of returning with the doctor and Haley next recounts the opening of the grave in the mangroves where he identified Page.

That the attackers would be appeased with the ingredients for cake seems unlikely, given the ferocity of the described attack. Page requesting to be put off the boat twice seems unusual also, given at this time his windpipe had 'been divided', according to the doctor who examined the body.

Jane O'Neil, left out of Haley's account almost entirely, challenged the court's definition of her: she was 'a single woman and widow'. She had given Mogo Garra breakfast and Ugly came and ate with him, meaning he could not have been at the top of the hill. It was she who fastened the window, not Page. When Page came back over the partition in the hut that separated the store from the living quarters, he called to Jane O'Neil, saying, 'They had settled him.' It was she who went to the door of the hut and 'offered to give them flour and other things to go away'. Mogo Garra threw a boomerang at her, which she ducked. She told Haley to throw them out a hundredweight of flour. He did, it stayed outside the hut for some time before the attackers touched it. They began throwing stones again. Doughboy called for tobacco and O'Neil threw it out. They then demanded a damper, which was also thrown out to them. O'Neil was not quite positive whether the natives made their attempt on the chimney before or after they attacked the store. It was O'Neil who told Haley to get the small boat. Page said he was too weak to go on and they laid him down in the bush with blankets. She went down with Haley to the vessel. She found out Page was alive the next night, which was the night he 'could not be found'. The next morning, she went with two sailors to search, not mentioning Haley at all. They found Page 3 miles along the beach—a different place than that described by Haley. Page had a pillow, 'the blankets I left with him were not there'. She asked him for the blankets and he said:

> Mogo had taken them, they wanted to take his trousers but after a little consultation among themselves they had left the trousers with him. Page said the whole five of the natives were there—there were no others with them.

He also said that 'the natives had robbed the hut subsequent to our leaving it and that he had seen a lot of pipes with Doughboy'. O'Neil and the sailors got a door from the hut and carried Page to the place where he died the following morning.

The recounting of theft was supposedly done by a man with a divided windpipe. The second request to be left in the mangroves was, according to this deposition, never made, and rather than being in the mangroves, he was found on the beach. Haley was completely absent from the account of the rescue, as though it were a completely different expedition. Haley was ordered about by Jane O'Neil in her account; she was absent from his. When Jane O'Neil returned to the hut, 'the whole of the property had been stolen, 70 lbs of flour, 3–400 lbs of sugar, wearing apparel belonging to Page, myself and the child'. The flour and sugar were the property of Mr Caffrey of Sydney, as were 'some articles of slop clothing, cotton shirts, 12 in number, and a great variety of property belonging to different persons, some of the sawyers'. Among 'the articles stolen from the place was a dark shawl 15/-, paid for, in my trunk, in good condition, not torn, but quite whole, the piece of shawl now produced is the portion of the one referred to'.

Jane O'Neil explained that the dispute began when the five men had agreed to carry the beef up to the sawyers. They agreed, started with it and returned. The next day:

> Ugly and Charlie had breakfast and ran away I spoke to them about taking the beef as they had promised when Ugly and Doughboy answered in an impudent manner, in consequence of that circumstance I suspected the blacks intended some mischief and I spoke to the prisoner when he said it was not the case remarking 'Bail, cooler, Jane.' There were no fire arms in the hut and the prisoner was well aware of the fact and that Page had been writing to one of the sawyers to send him down some arms. Page had told the prisoner so … the prisoner had been engaged in making boomerangs for two or three days before the attack. I had seen him so employed but did not suspect him of any bad intention.[33]

Jane O'Neil swore that she had not taken a knife to Mickey two or three days before the attack 'when they first brought the beef back, nor did I threaten to bring out the gun'. There was, apparently, a gun to threaten with.

---

33   *R v Mogo alias Mogo Garra.*

The emphasis on theft rather than murder was the interest of the magistrates, who hoped that a theft charge could be preferred if a murder charge could not. No sailors were deposed who could clearly give an account of the rescue mission for Page, and Mogo Garra was not asked for a defence. The fact that Mogo had been found with part of the shawl around his waist was never deposed to. The curious leaving of a dying man in a mangrove swamp, tidal as they are, was supposedly at the request of the dying man himself, but an injury to a windpipe and the copious blood described would suggest Page was far from being able to speak.

It was clear Plunkett himself had suspicions that all was not as claimed. He pencilled the description Haley gave of not being able to see what happened on the other side of the partition in the hut, he underlined the presence of Ugly at breakfast and the passage on the search for Page the next day was marked. He did not reject the case, however. Mogo Garra was tried in Sydney, found guilty by a Sydney jury and sentenced to death. He was hanged. The case remains a pretence at law, containing gestures at legality on the part of Plunkett, who was the most precise of attorneys-general. In the Sydney court the barrister who had offered to watch the case on the prisoner's behalf, Mr Holroyd, argued that there 'was not the slightest proof of the presence of the defendant at the actual murder, though he might have stolen some property'.[34]

The entire case is representative of the contradictions apparent in the descriptions of the shooting of Cabawn Mickey at the Shoalhaven in the same year and there is the same reticence shown by Plunkett, though in this case he clearly saw the contradictions but did not act on them. Despite the criticism of him and the word 'Plunkettian', he is far from being 'a friend to the Aborigines' in this case.

Doughboy's case in 1859 provides only one deposition and this was by John Haley. Haley's evidence differs slightly from his earlier deposition. He went back to the hut on the day of the attack 'to release the dog'. It had been his idea that Page climb over the partition to the store. Doughboy had been in the doorway when Page received the fatal blow—when, in the original deposition, Haley could not see anything. After Page was injured by Ugly's boomerang, Haley asked the attackers 'why for Caulah' and they demanded tea and sugar. Jane O'Neil put flour and tobacco on the steps and Haley said to them, 'Blackfellow now good friends I suppose' and they all went away,

---

34 *Bell's Life*, 12 October 1850.

taking the articles with them. Page did not ask to be let out of the boat but could not keep up with the walking after they had used the boat to cross the river. Haley left him there with blankets 'and a bottle of tea'. When he came back to rescue Page, the wounded man again said he could not keep up with the walking. On return again, 'I found him in his grave'.

In their letter, the magistrates wrote that the evidence of the chief witness, Haley, 'tallies with that given by him' in *Mogo Garra*, who had, they wrote, been convicted and 'hung'. They again requested an interpreter and wanted the attorney-general to contact Mr Caffrey to see whether Jane O'Neil could be found. They assured the attorney-general that the depositions for Mogo could be found 'in your office'.[35] Though the defending barrister, Milford, argued the death was more likely caused by exposure than any blow received, Doughboy was found guilty and sentenced to death. The advice of Justice Milford to the jury was that if one was part of a group which attacked someone, then all in the group were liable, no matter how long after the death occurred.[36] The reliance on the findings of the earlier case meant the trial nine years later was compromised in Plunkett's office. Haley, at least, seems to see that his actions in the earlier case required further explanation, hence the dog, the bottle of tea, the walking rather than the travelling by boat and the conversation with the attackers. Doughboy, too, is positioned to be there at the time of the fatal blow.

Both Mogo's and Doughboy's cases occurred at a time of considerable squatter pressure for the presence of the Native Police and assertions that Aboriginal people were dangerous. These arguments were public and had in the Legislative Council and, later, the assembly. Both cases played into this discourse. Doughboy had been in and out of Kempsey and working on the Macleay for 10 years before Lieutenant Poulding decided to make his mark.

The public

Kempsey had no coroner, requiring a magistrate's own selection of jurors to establish the cause of death. That there had been unexplained deaths on the Macleay was complained of in 1842:

---

35 Jonathon Warne to Attorney-General, 19 August 1859, in *R v Doughboy*.
36 *Empire*, 7 December 1859; Criminal Crown Solicitor Judgement Books, 1859, SR 4/5739.

> Many persons who have died suddenly here, have been buried or put in a hole without a coffin without any kind of inquest being held, the consequence is that some of these people might have been murdered for anything that the public know to the contrary.[37]

Ten years later there was still no coroner and any inquiry was instituted by the magistrates themselves.

The positioning of the Macleay River magistrates as public figures came from letters of complaint written to the press and the authorities. The Macleay columnists and correspondents avidly fought for services in the region, and this included the deploying of the Native Police.[38] One of the major personages in this history of complaint was Enoch Rudder, cedar trader, who lived on a hill in Kempsey. He had complained of a massacre of Aboriginal people on the beach at Nambucca in 1846, which provoked an inquiry by the Commissioner of Crown Lands, who claimed only one Aboriginal man, Myall Dingo, had been shot.[39] There was no further inquiry into this shooting.

Though commissioners of Crown lands were meant to investigate conditions for Aboriginal people and report on them, Massie, who had responsibility for the river on the western side, seems to have copied out Strzelecki's opinion of 'many years ago', which he recommended. It claimed that 'it would be easier to bring the whites down to the level of the blacks than to raise the latter to the ideas and habits of civilisation'.[40] The acting commissioner for 1854, Bligh, wrote that Aboriginal people gave satisfaction to employers and had adopted the dress and habits of the civilised community:

> Merely having at certain times of the year to join the ceremonies of their tribe. On this point they are inexorable and it appears that no degree of education and civilisation will entirely wean them from the habits of their nation.[41]

---

37 *Sydney Morning Herald*, 3 November 1842.
38 *Armidale Express*, 11 April 1857.
39 Enoch Rudder to Commissioner of Crown Lands, 28 June 1846, Documents collected by Sir William Dixson.
40 Robert Massie to Chief Commissioner of Crown Lands, 24 January 1853, Commissioner of Crown Lands Letter Book, State Archives Collection, SR 4/4563.
41 Bligh to Chief Commissioner of Crown Lands, 12 January 1854, Commissioner of Crown Lands Letter Book.

Commissioners of Crown lands worked in managing land disputes and authorisations, the movement of convicts and ticket-of-leave holders, the management of goldfields and oversight of Aboriginal people. This was an intensive workload and, later in 1854, Henry Fellowes wrote he could not report on the Macleay section of his jurisdiction because he 'had not been there for two years'.[42]

The Commissioner of Crown Lands wrote reports that were transmitted to the Secretary of State for the Colonies. Great consternation occurred in that office on a reading of a letter to *The Englishman* in 1854 claiming an outrage had been committed in the New England district by Native Police against peaceful Aboriginal people. Massie wrote that such a thing would not have occurred without his knowledge. On inquiry, he discovered the report concerned not New England but 'Newton Boyd', a station of George Burgess's on the Clarence:

> Upon the Police attempting to arrest some of these blacks they had run away and that whilst doing so two or three had been shot but as far as I was able to learn every exertion had been made to execute the warrants first and the men fired only when they found out that the men to whom they were sent to apprehend would otherwise with probability escape.[43]

That this action seemed perfectly acceptable to Massie gives some idea of his moral position. The information shocked the secretary of state. An order was given in 1855 to be relayed through the commissioners that such a practice as shooting in the back was to stop. The magistrates of the Macleay River wrote to the Crown lands commissioner that he was 'exceeding his instructions' in giving such an order.[44]

The presence of publicity and debate on the Macleay gives us the environment in which magistrates worked. They held their positions in such disputes and the pressure for a Native Police force to be permanently present began in earnest in 1857. Poulding arrived from the Dawson River in Queensland, bringing the mentality of the Dawson 580 miles (935 kilometres) south to the Macleay. His appearance was the result of the strong representations of the squatters and magistrates of the Macleay.

---

42   Fellowes to Chief Commissioner of Crown Lands, 29 December 1854, Commissioner of Crown Lands Letter Book.
43   Massie to Chief Commissioner of Crown Lands, 7 October 1854, Commissioner of Crown Lands Letter Book.
44   Fellowes to Chief Commissioner of Crown Lands, 14 August 1855, Commissioner of Crown Lands Letter Book.

The public position of magistrates meant they gave strong opinions in each case they sent to the attorney-general. In *Green*, 1857, they wrote:

> The attendance of William Murray [at the Supreme Court] at the same time with his father will be productive of most ruinous consequences to Murray and also to Mr Verge, as there would be no person to take care of the dairy cattle. As Murray deposes to the same facts as his son and his evidence is corroborated to a certain extent by Fulton … perhaps you might consider the son's testimony might be dispensed with.[45]

Their request was complied with. No other magistrates write in such detail about the requirements of dairy cattle. They added that 'Thomas Thompson is not a very willing prosecutor'. Nor was Thomas Fulton, whose evidence could give no account of theft. The criminal Crown solicitor—more likely to see fault than the attorney-general—wrote in pencil on the case: 'The evidence of this witness has no bearing, if he is speaking truly it must be of a different occasion.'[46]

The case began with the son of Mr Verge's storekeeper being suspicious of George Green branding a calf. He had been closely watching the calf and noted a new brand. George Green made a statement in his defence that the calf was branded by mistake. The great effort the magistrates on the Macleay gave to the case, despite the unwillingness of the prosecutor, is comparable with their efforts in *Mogo Garra* to establish a theft. The behaviour of cows was much discussed, particularly by constable William Dangar, who had been, he said, an overseer on a cattle station for many years. Green was found not guilty by the Supreme Court jury.[47]

Magistrate Warne's reason for conducting his own inquiry into the death of Ann Kearns' baby was the public excitement caused by the findings of the jury he had called. It was also the result of his realising that Kearns was not actually married as he had thought.

Ann Kearns' baby drowned in very public circumstances, at the wharf on the riverbank down from the public house in which she had been drinking. She was trying to get positions for her daughters with wealthier townspeople. One of these, Mrs Washington, refused to let Ann Kearns into her boat; she was going to the ship *Elizabeth Cohen* and returned an hour later to hear

---

45 Charles Kemp and Jonathon Warne to Attorney-General, 20 April 1857, in *R v George Green*.
46 *R v George Green*.
47 Attorney-General Register of Cases, Sydney, 1853, State Archives Collection, SR 4/5737.

children screaming and crying. Thomas Bradley, storekeeper, jumped into the water to retrieve the baby. He took it to Mrs Bannerman's kitchen where they tried to revive it by putting it in a bath of warm water. Mrs Bannerman said, 'Nancy, you've done it now, drowned your baby', but she deposed the riverbank was steep and anyone lying there could easily fall in the water.[48] The jury of locals had been satisfied the death was an accident, but Warne did not concur and held his own inquiry.

He wrote:

> As the policy of the law discourages any confessions by parties unless voluntary and the woman was present at the Inquiry and did not volunteer any statement I did not think it proper to examine her. She is a notorious Drunkard, and is living with a man named William Cook by whom she has a large family of children whom she treats with kindness though frequently with great negligence during her intoxications.[49]

Warne was explaining here why there was no statement for the defence; he was perhaps unaware that 'involuntary confession' involved torture, but it perhaps tells more of his understanding of law that he implies this is an unfortunate requirement. 'A policy of the law' was a continual irritant to the Macleay magistrates. In this account of the case, Warne again is closely involved in the community and that community is also closely linked. Warne and his fellow magistrates wrestled cases into what they thought law should be, expending great effort, goading reluctant prosecutors and urging long discussion of stolen goods in a murder case. Magistrates have their own version of the law, the right one, with which they seek to influence the attorneys-general. It is because the Macleay is so public, so much in the news, that the law that emerges from these magistrates is formulated around that public, around those requests for greater recognition of the demands of the Macleay River.

The same magistrates directed the Native Police. In 1861, some fears being expressed by the residents of the Nambucca and Bellinger rivers, 'our senior magistrate, Mr Warne, with his usual promptitude adopted the necessary course to obtain protection for the residents … by communicating with Captain Scott … an active and vigilant officer'. Like Poulding's, the actions undertaken by Scott would not be subject to inquiry. Public interest was thus born out of increasing quasi-military violence against Aboriginal people.

48 *R v Kearns*.
49 Jonathon Warne to Attorney-General, 8 April 1853, in *R v Kearns*.

Right of reply

As a Birrbay and Dhanggati woman, the chapter reads well and the work you are doing is important for truth telling.

Gulwanyang Moran
Manager, First Nations Community Access to Archives Collections, Museums of History NSW

Grafton

In 1853 Charles Tindal wrote from his new station, 'Ramornie', near Grafton:

> 21 August 'For the last three weeks I have only slept one night at home having had to make a second expedition after natives a party of whom we were hunting took the cattle during our absence in pursuit of another tribe … [T]he leaders escaped we start again in the morning' 28 August 'we surprised two camps with remains of beef in each, it was Knightley's first service and we were camped out eight nights' 5 November, 'I have had another nine days hunt two of the ringleaders for whom warrants had been issued were shot.[50]

Charles Tindal was a magistrate at Grafton along with his friends the Milnes, the Walkers, Edward Ogilvie, Francis Phillips, Charles Fawcett, Oliver Fry, the Crown lands commissioner, and Edward Ryan. Richard Bligh, the Crown lands commissioner from 1856, acted as police magistrate. In this account, Tindal had been pursuing one tribe and then found that another tribe had stolen cattle in his absence. His language is that of the hunt, rather than that of the police or magistrate. The warrants were useless in this situation; he was going to shoot 'the ringleaders' and did so. Knightley was what was termed a 'black hat': a new arrival in the colony from a wealthy background who would operate as a superintendent for Tindal while learning how a station was run. His first 'service' was a series of punitive raids at night on Aboriginal camps where people were asleep. Deborah Bird Rose has described the use of the language of law in such raids in the Northern Territory and Lisa Ford has written of 'law like lawlessness'

---

50 Charles Tindal to Father, 21 August 1853, Tindal Family Papers.

in New South Wales.⁵¹ Tindal fits their theorisations because he uses the justificatory word 'warrant' in his description, yet in his description there were not two poles, one inside the court and law and the other outside and imitative, because he was a magistrate. Riley Young Winpilin would be able to countenance Tindal's world view incorporating law and lawlessness because he sees all violence against Aboriginal people as European 'law' that is without morality.⁵² Aboriginal people appear as defendants before the court at Grafton, so there can be no neat dichotomy between punitive raid and appearances before the court.

Grafton was established on the banks of the Clarence River and the town grew as a port and service centre for the hinterland with its established runs from the mid-1840s: 'wharves, shops and hotels were built on both sides of the river, and rowing boats provided the connecting link between the two suburbs'.⁵³ The region is Bunjalung, Yaegl and Gumbayngirr Country and these Aboriginal people have their own histories.⁵⁴

The Grafton bench follows the same pattern as the South Coast and western benches: the origin of cases is evenly distributed (see Figure 6.1). Constables were in the service of the local population, acting after they were called for, and Aboriginal people were brought by the poorer inhabitants, as they were on the South Coast. The law at Grafton was accessible. Like the South Coast also, depositions are contradictory, yet they are also far less perfectly presented.

The magistrates asked the attorneys-general for assistance. In *Anderson*, 1857, Richard Bligh, the Crown lands commissioner and police magistrate, wrote to the attorney-general:

> The prisoner has been committed to trial by C.G. Tindal and C.J. Walker, magistrates for this bench but there being no Clerk of Petty Sessions these Gentlemen have from some misunderstanding taken the depositions in the ordinary record book of the Court—the committing magistrates reside some distance from here and I am therefore compelled to furnish you with the enclosed certified copies in lieu of the original depositions.⁵⁵

---

51   Deborah Bird Rose, *Hidden Histories: Black Stories from Victoria River Downs, Humbert River and Wave Hill Stations* (Canberra: Aboriginal Studies Press, 1991), 18; Ford, *Settler Sovereignty*, 151.
52   Bird Rose, *Hidden Histories*, 18.
53   Ronald E. Davies, 'History of Clarence River and of Grafton 1830–1880', *Daily Examiner*, [Grafton], 3 January 1957, nla.gov.au/nla.obj-2387371978/view?partId=nla.obj-2387373852#.
54   Arakwal People of Byron Bay website: arakwal.com.au; Yaegl Traditional Owners Aboriginal Corporation website: nativetitle.org.au/find/pbc/8254.
55   *R v John Anderson* 1857, 5, SR 9/6410.

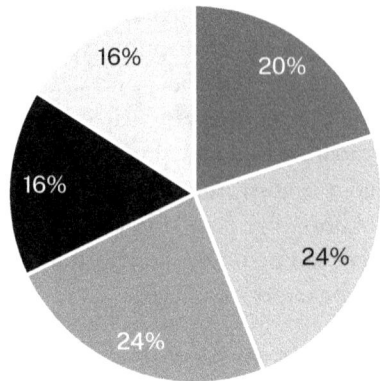

■ Neighbour/same status ■ Publican ■ Employer ■ Constable   Not Known

Figure 6.1: Origin of cases: Grafton[56]

The magistrates were certainly aware of the requirement that cases for the assizes be separate depositions, yet they were tardy and casual in their management of the court. Anderson pleaded guilty in his case and the details of the deposition did not come before the court.[57] Other depositions were copies of the originals, but the attorneys-general received no letter of explanation. In *Noad*, a copying clerk had been used as the number of words is marked at intervals and calculations appear in the side column.[58] The calculations may have been by the Commissioner of Crown Lands' clerk, who lived in a hut on Oliver Fry's run.[59]

In 1853 in *Haywood*, a letter was forwarded to the attorney-general by Oliver Fry and Edward Ryan, stating that 'we are ignorant where the several crimes imputed to Hayward [sic] have been committed and under the circumstances consider it better he should be at once forwarded to Sydney'.[60] Thomas Haywood also pleaded guilty, so the vague generalities of this statement could not be tested in the Sydney Supreme Court.[61]

---

56 Re 'Not known': There are four cases for which the initial prosecutors cannot be established because the depositions are missing. These are *R v Gustavous Smith/Schmidt* for cattle stealing in 1853; newspapers do not give the case in detail. *R v Henry Stapleton and Shady Walsh*, for horse theft, 1853, was discharged for no witnesses, so the case was never heard and not reported consequently. George Yates, 1854, for assault on a girl, cannot be found, possibly because it was heard at quarter sessions. James Aitkins, 1854, wounding with intent, cannot be found.
57 Criminal Crown Solicitor Judgement Books, Sydney, 1857, SR 4/5737.
58 *R v Pumpkin* 1858, 5, SR 9/6415; *R v Billy Noad* 1857, 4, SR 9/6415.
59 *R v James McGee* 1852, 12, SR 9/6369.
60 *R v Thomas Haywood alias John Haywood alias Thomas Anderson alias Thomas Hewitt alias Thomas Whitehouse* 1853, 2, SR 9/6374.
61 Criminal Crown Solicitor Judgement Books, Sydney, 1853, 4/5732.

The clear inadequacies of the Grafton bench, set out in their own letters, were scathingly replied to by the attorneys-general. 'It does not appear from the depositions that there is any such person as William Boyd,' wrote Plunkett in a forgery case in which Boyd's name had been written on a cheque.[62] A pencil note on *Robert Ward alias Bob the Lawyer* reads: '[H]ow does this agree with the Prisoner apparently coming in direction from Armidale to Parrott's the night before?' The depositions were sent back so the questions could be answered.[63] This decision was for Grafton magistrates alone because, as we have seen on the South Coast, contradictory and insufficient information was sent to the attorneys-general but no criticism was made. The magistrates at Grafton invited such criticism in the tone of their letters.

It is not clear that the magistrates understood the meaning of legal terms. In *Noad*, Charles Walker said he 'applied for a warrant from Annie Massie', who was a very young girl who worked on Walker's run. He could not have applied for a warrant against her as she was his key witness.[64]

At first glance, there are no questions for witnesses by the accused at Grafton, but looking closely, one finds that deponents begin to speak to the defendant as 'you' and it is clear they were answering questions from defendants.[65] Depositions at Grafton are difficult to decipher but note was made that 'the prisoner declines to ask questions'. Defendants ask questions of constables but at times incriminate themselves in doing so. James Eggleston got the constable to say that he had said he was sorry for stabbing another constable. John Anderson said he was so drunk he did not know where he got the cheque, thereby admitting to possessing it. In *Noad*, the prosecutor asked questions of witnesses as well as Noad, who was able to get a witness to say there had been an earlier dispute over a rope.[66] A broad group of people came into court, some of whom were clearly there as defence witnesses but their evidence is not headed as such as it is in other benches.[67] The *Justices Act* was followed, but the form of the deposition did not recognise this. The defendant quite often has no statement in their defence but in *Noad*, it was claimed 'the defendant was admonished for his defence', as though later in the period these defences were pressured for. This was outside the *Justices Act* requirements; no-one was to be forced.

---

62 *R v John Motson* 1850, 13, SR 9/6357.
63 *R v Ward alias Bob the Lawyer*.
64 *R v Noad*.
65 *R v James Eggleston* 1858, 6, SR 9/6415.
66 ibid.; *R v Anderson*; *R v Noad*.
67 *R v Noad*; *R v Anderson*; *R v Ward alias Bob the Lawyer*.

Constables

The idea of the 'confession' through a constable was not unique to Grafton; as we have seen, Molong constables obtained confessions as easily. In *Tommy*, the magistrates were concerned they did not have enough evidence. Plunkett wrote: 'I think the confession made by the Prisoner to Chief Constable Abbott was voluntary and if not made under the influence or promise and inducement there is enough evidence to convict the prisoner.'[68] In the case against John Chesham, the magistrates included the information that the admission of guilt was not 'extorted by any threat, promise, interrogation or enquiry'.[69] They had learned from *Tommy*. Any admission of guilt was highly valued by the attorneys-general and Grafton, like Molong, had this habit of confession.

Grafton magistrates did not take pleas like those from the north-west, but two defendants pleaded guilty before the Supreme Court: Thomas Haywood had burned down the main house on Charles Walker's 'Newbold Grange'[70] and John Anderson pleaded guilty in his case involving a forged cheque.[71]

Grafton constables acted when warrants were granted. There was no mention of any warning being given to defendants at the point of arrest and a form of trickery was used. Constable Patrick Kelly saw no problem when he said before the bench that he found Anderson 12 miles (20 kilometres) out of Grafton and 'said nothing about the forgery but pretended I was arresting him for absconding from Sheehan's service'. After 2 miles on the road, Anderson said: '"I am afraid it is worse than you are aware". I said nothing to induce him to make this statement.'[72] Constable Laughlin Curry apprehended Patrick Faugherty in 1854 using a similar pretext. He had received a warrant to apprehend Faugherty for theft of tea from a store. He brought him to Grafton 'under suspicion of being a runaway from Tenterfield'.[73] This is similar to the sleuthing approach of Orange constables except it is well outside the requirements of the *Justices Act*. The Joseph Wilkes case was notorious. Wilkes was accused of the murder of his wife and children. The evidence against him was from constables. He had come home to find his wife and sons brutally murdered. He had behaved

---

68 *R v Tommy* 1850, 1, SR 9/6357.
69 *R v John Chesham* 1850, 1, SR 9/6357.
70 *R v Haywood, alias Haywood alias Anderson alias Hewitt alias Whitehouse*.
71 *R v Anderson*.
72 ibid.
73 *R v Patrick Flaugherty* 1854, 11, SR 9/6381.

unusually when searching for the bodies of his sons, not taking care to leave space for trackers and finding the bodies of his sons himself when everyone had left the scene. In the lockup, he claimed visions of angels had told him his neighbour Lynch had committed the murder. He claimed he had been robbed when there was no property taken. He had been discharged by proclamation. Though the newspapers reported he went to the Legislative Assembly to obtain compensation for lost property, he went to complain of police mistreatment. This drew attention to the case and led to him being committed again for the murder. 'New evidence' was claimed but there appears to be none.[74]

That Grafton constables had pistols and wore uniformed coats is apparent in *Eggleston*. Two constables were in pursuit of absconding servants and stopped at the Traveller's Rest on the Tenterfield road. They were on the verandah drinking 'milk and water' when they saw in the distance a man coming along the road and thought he could help with their search. The man, Eggleston, ran away, and they pursued without their coats and pistols, calling, '[S]top in the Queen's name or I will shoot you.' They caught up with the man and he stabbed one of them. Eggleston said he thought they were robbers. One constable put his knee on Eggleston's neck.[75] The kind of independence exhibited in this case is also apparent at Armidale and it plays with legality and illegality in the same manner. Grafton constables were not stung into proper behaviour by the criticism of the attorney-general.

Aboriginal subjects

At Grafton the same dynamic operates for Aboriginal people as on the South Coast. In *Tommy*, there is the same language we find on the South Coast concerning Aboriginal aggression. Francis Phillips, a key witness, wrote to the attorney-general that he 'hoped that you may be able to dispense with my attendance'. He explained that he would be 'obligated to take my family being in a place with no protection against the blacks'.[76] Phillips was using the language of the frontier in his appeal; there had been no attacks by Aboriginal people in the region for some time and there had never been attacks on the homesteads of squatters like Phillips. The language of the frontier appears also in the depositions. Tommy was 'an old man' who had been accused of murdering John Grey at Deep Creek, 30 miles

---

74 *Bell's Life*, 24 April 1858; *Empire*, 26 November 1856.
75 *R v Eggleston*.
76 *R v Tommy* (1850).

(50 kilometres) from Grafton. Grey was the servant of Mr Small of 'Swan Creek' run. Francis Phillips held the inquest on the body, during which, according to chief constable Sylvanus Abbot, one of the shepherds, George Yates, said that he saw 'old Tommy' walking towards Grey's hut with a tomahawk in his hand. Phillips produced the hat of the deceased, found near the body: it had been cut by a sharp instrument like a tomahawk. The hat, so reminiscent of evidence at Carcoar, and the description by Yates were the only evidence in the case. On the morning of 2 February, Sylvanus Abbott was at 'Busby Park' run owned by James Wilkes 'for the purpose of apprehending some blacks who had committed an outrage there'. No case mentions such an outrage at 'Busby Park'. He saw Tommy there and 'on conversing with him I found he corresponded to the description of Tommy who had murdered Grey'. Tommy also had 'shot wounds in his arm'. Sylvanus Abbott apprehended him. He said Tommy then confessed to the murder of Grey.[77] Tommy had no English and Sylvanus Abbott did not speak Tommy's language, but the confession was highly detailed. Tommy said he wanted flour and tobacco, Grey refused it, so Tommy became 'cobawn myall' and 'tumbled white fellow down'. Such pidgin words appeared on the South Coast also. In his defence, Tommy said before the bench that Grey was murdered not by him but by three other blackfellows, Charcoal, Darby and Bandicoot.[78]

Attorney-General Plunkett did not comment on the contradiction between Tommy's confession and his defence statement nor a series of letters between the bench and George Barney of 'Barney Downs' in the New England region. These letters concerned a man named Edward Griffin, who was to be subpoenaed as interpreter for the Supreme Court in Sydney. The bench mistakenly referred to him as Edward Griffith. George Barney or 'young Barney' had written to the bench initially saying there was no such man as Edward 'Griffith' on his run.[79] Plunkett wrote to the colonial secretary that he thought that such a confusion was 'hardly an excuse' and Barney was obstructing justice. However, the morning after, he added a note. He had shown the letter to George Barney's father, Colonel Barney, who had undertaken to write to his son and assured Plunkett the interpreter would appear.[80]

---

77 ibid.
78 ibid.
79 George H. Barney to Grafton Bench, 3 June 1850, in *R v Tommy* (1850).
80 Attorney-General to Colonial Secretary, 8 July 1850, in *R v Tommy* (1850).

Plunkett here was communicating in the realm of gentlemen. At the same time, he did not seem concerned how an Aboriginal man who could not be understood by an Aboriginal interpreter at Sydney, where Tommy was being held, had managed to give both a defence statement and a confession in English or pidgin at Grafton.

George Barney explained why he wanted Griffin to remain on his run and it was an appeal to the language of the frontier. Barney wrote his second letter to the bench in winter—the 'depths of winter', he said. He was 'surrounded by blacks on all sides'. Commissioner Fry 'is perfectly aware that the Blacks require strict supervision during the rigour of a New England winter, and is no doubt aware that Griffin exercises great authority over them'.[81] Like Phillips, Barney was 'surrounded', and this is despite there being no reports of attacks on homesteads at all in the New England region. Language of the frontier would get results.

But to further complicate matters, Edward Griffin wrote a letter to Attorney-General Plunkett himself. He signed it 'Interpreter'. He gave a far more complex image of his role. He had been subpoenaed four times in 12 months to interpret for the Supreme Court. He was concerned he would lose his situation. However, he had an offer to make. For a 'reasonable salary and a permanent situation', he would use his 'influence and utmost exertion to keep the tribes in amity with the settlement and district in general'. Otherwise, he would be 'compelled to leave the district'.[82] Griffin wanted to make an entirely new government position for himself. He, like most of the workers in this book, had his own agenda and interpretation of his position. He also recognised the Aboriginal polity, as did many gentlemen in the north-west, and was to act as diplomat in the region. Griffin creates an entirely new reading of the contact past, away from dichotomies and into negotiation and discussion. In this way his role is similar to Jemmy Darcy's at Orange: a middleman in a complex political environment.

The magistrates at Grafton included two sets of depositions in *Tommy*. This was also irregular. The second involved the robbery and assault of Elizabeth Bail at Oakey Creek. She was the only deponent; there were no witnesses. On 28 February, she claimed Tommy and several other Blacks assaulted her and robbed her of clothing. Tommy again confessed to Abbott. The combination of two cases resembles the work of magistrates at Molong

---

81 George Barney to Grafton Bench, 13 June 1850, in *R v Tommy* (1850).
82 Edward Griffin to Criminal Crown Solicitor, 1 December 1850, in *R v Tommy* (1850).

and Orange, with their additional information added to assure conviction. Tommy was never tried because there was no interpreter available for the court. He was discharged to make his way back to Grafton.[83]

The attitude of Plunkett in *Tommy*, for which he did not question contradictions, appeared again in *Pumpkin* in 1857. The attorney-general was James Martin; Mary Finlayson brought a case against Pumpkin for assault and attempted rape in which a man who could speak only pidgin was reported as saying 'don't be singing out' and 'you bloody wretch, be quiet or I will cut your throat'. Finlayson's husband refused to swear that Pumpkin was the man whom he saw kneeling next to his wife on his return home. The accused made a statement in court in pidgin: 'Bail me do what Dicky and Darby do', referring to other cases.[84]

In *Ward*, the victim was an Aboriginal man, Peter, and the defendant a white man. This case was instituted by Peter Shea, who described his servant Peter as 'residing with me for the past five years during which time I have found him very honest, obedient and industrious, I have frequently left him in charge of my place'.[85] Similar to the account presented in *McLaughlin* at Wee Waa, there was talk of shots being fired into an Aboriginal camp and a woman killed, but no investigation was made into her death, only the faithful Peter was the subject of the case. He had been murdered on the road and Peter Shea was sure that Robert Ward was the killer. In stark contrast to *Pumpkin* and *Tommy*, this case was gone through meticulously by both the criminal Crown solicitor John Moore Dillon and Attorney-General Manning. Inconsistencies were noted, the case sent back for clarification and it was returned, the inconsistencies answered. The defendant could easily have doubled back, the magistrates claimed.

Both *Pumpkin* and *Tommy* were brought to court by lower-class women and Aboriginal people were thus drawn into the arena of dispute among lower-class people. Cases of this nature come from the runs of squatters and there is the same settlement pattern we see in other areas: a main house, a kitchen some distance from the house and a row of huts quite close together containing families or groups of men. This is the arena of rape and child rape, where we find children as young as two working in the potato fields alongside their father or quite young girls looking after horses.[86]

---

83 Criminal Crown Solicitor Judgement Books, 1850, 4/5732.
84 *R v Pumpkin*.
85 *R v Ward alias Bob the Lawyer*.
86 *R v Chesham*; *R v William Davies* 1852, 12, SR 9/6368; *R v Jeremiah Sullivan* 1853, 21, SR 9/6374.

Five cases were recorded in the Supreme Court as 'discharged no witnesses'. The complainants had not travelled from Grafton for the case. Travel had to be by steamer and there were frequent disruptions. The non-appearance of complainants and witnesses appears before 1855 so is directly related to the difficulties of travel. But there was also time to 'make it up otherwise' and arrange to miss the steamer. This takes us into the extremely murky realm of ordinary people's relationship to the law at Grafton. This appears across the colony and is most apparent at Carcoar, where it dominates the courts.

Grafton non-Aboriginal people

When 'Newbold Grange' was burned down, the servants made no attempt to put the fire out and this kind of attitude is found also in New England cases, the servants' and masters' interests being seen as quite different. There is a different logic governing cases between poorer people that suggests a plethora of different relationships, unable to be precisely captured by the historian. In his response to an accusation from the wife of a cooper and her daughter, Jeremiah Sullivan claimed that the offence he was accused of was 'false'.[87] The way evidence was taken in Grafton in such cases involving people of the same status left room for this accusation to be made. Some cases had only one deposition, no other witnesses and no corroborating medical evidence.[88] Much effort was put into the construction of cases if they involved squatters or their gentlemen superintendents, with several witnesses found even if some of them did not fully corroborate the story, but these cases between poorer people seem simply to be passed on to the Supreme Court in Sydney.

A complex case concerned William Bankhead or Bill the Bullock Driver, who killed John Kenby in Pringles' public house, The Traveller's Rest, on the Grafton–Tenterfield road for calling him a 'bloody sweep'.[89] The first deposition left no doubt that Kenby had been hit by Bankhead. The second deposition, by Michael O'Brien, reads that Kenby was 'abusing Irishmen in general'. But he was not sure whether it was Bankhead who struck Kenby and 'he might have fallen over a stool'. Another deponent, James Tripp, said Mrs Pringle gave the deceased two or three blows at the back of the head

---

87 *R v Jeremiah Sullivan.*
88 *R v Tommy* (1850), added on assault case; *R v Jeremiah Sullivan.*
89 *R v William Bankhead* 1852, 17, SR 9/6369. This word, 'sweep', means one side of a tree branch, the other side is 'crook'. It could also relate to earlier thieves cant, in which sweeping the board meant to take everything. These are the closest possible definitions. Christoph Richter, *Wood Characteristics* (Berlin: Springer Verlag, 2014), 39; Albert Barrere, *A Dictionary of Slang* (Sydney: Read, 2013), 'S'.

and called him a 'drunk old vagabond'; he said he did not see Bankhead strike the deceased. A deposition by Elizabeth Pringle gave an explanation for the assault. Kenby was lying on a sofa or wooden bench and he asked Launt, Bankhead's companion, to drink. Launt said he would be glad to if Kenby would pay the money he owed him. Bankhead said, '[P]ay him what you owe him like a man or else we shall make you.' Kenby said, '[W]hat have you got to do with it you bloody sweep.' Bankhead struck the deceased 'but not violently'. Kenby said he had had a good sleep, he would not lie down anymore and went to the kitchen, Bankhead followed him and struck Kenby again but 'not hard'. Mrs Pringle called for her husband, who told Bankhead that 'you have killed that man'. Bankhead said 'he would not allow his own father to call him a sweep'. Launt got vinegar as he was sure Kenby had 'fainted'. Mrs Pringle said that Kenby had used very abusive language to Launt and that Bankhead and Kenby did not know each other. Launt said that Bankhead struck Kenby 'with his open hand'. The death 'was not from malice but purely accidental'. These depositions suggest an agreed upon narrative concerning the death of Kenby. What jars is James Tripp's evidence that more than one person hit the deceased. It is perhaps not surprising that Bankhead was discharged at the Supreme Court in Sydney because there were no witnesses, but this case demonstrates collusions and contradictions in depositions from Grafton.[90] Grafton depositions were never straightforward accounts of an offence but contained multiple and undisciplined perspectives.

Right of reply

The Gumbaynggirr person contacted thought it was not necessary to reply to the chapter.

---

90 Criminal Crown Solicitor Judgement Books, 1852, 4/5733.

7

Getting into Court

The long journey to court was made in chains if the prisoner had not been bailed. Patrick Toole, the turnkey at Maitland gaol, and three constables were described as escorting one female prisoner and eight male prisoners 'handcuffed on a chain' from Maitland to Sydney in 1850 after their sentencing. The chains were taken on and off during the journey by steamer to Sydney and Toole allowed the prisoners to drink spirits. On their walk from the wharf at Sydney to the gaol, Toole wanted to give the prisoners a drink at a public house 'on account of their good conduct'. Toole had committal papers in his possession that were to be handed to the gaoler in Sydney and he arrived there without one of the prisoners, Francis Purdey or Dubbo.[1] Good conduct was open to interpretation by constables and it helped prisoners to have money on the journey to court.[2]

In our accompanying of prisoners, we hope to be able to access the Supreme Court or the assizes to properly hear their cases, but sources are unreliable and it is difficult to obtain a full picture of how cases proceeded. The newspapers are the obvious choice and these give us the cases inscribed in the legal text produced by Gordon Legge in 1896.[3] However, Janine Rizzetti has argued that Legge picked up *Murrell* rather than *Bonjon* for his volume on case law because he consulted the *Sydney Morning Herald* rather than the Melbourne press.[4] Newspapers did report erratically and according to

---

1   Patrick Toole, Supreme Court Informations, SR T74.
2   *R v Sheridan*, at Yass.
3   Gordon Legge, *A Selection of Supreme Court Cases in New South Wales from 1825 to 1862* (Sydney: Robert Burton Printers, 1896).
4   Janine Rizzetti, 'Judge Willis, Bonjon and the Recognition of Aboriginal Law', *Australian and New Zealand Law and History Journal* 5 (2011): 1–26, classic.austlii.edu.au/au/journals/ANZLawHisteJl/2011/5.html.

the interests of their editors. The *Sydney Morning Herald*, Legge's source for cases, is highly abbreviated, giving the barest detail of legal arguments, defences and the thinking of the jury. The *Goulburn Herald* is by far the best in giving the words of judges in cases and even their gestures are recorded. This may have been because the attorney Daniel Deniehy was editor of the *Goulburn Chronicle* between 1854 and 1857 and he may have provided the approach to reports.[5] The *Maitland Mercury* has reports that centre on the actions and words of the jury and these records give startling insights into the independence of these groups of 12 persons who understood themselves to be at the apex of the court. Other sources that allow the reader into court are reserved cases where the decision of the court is legally questionable according to counsel or the judges themselves. Not all of these survive for the 1850s, but they do give an indication as to how cases were managed. There is newspaper reporting of these decisions of the full bench, but this rarely gives who instigated the inquiry at hand. The judgement books of the criminal Crown solicitor also provide some indication of the initial processes involved in cases.

A concern expressed by prisoners on their way to court or those on bail was how to raise the money to obtain an attorney and, through him, counsel. Thomas Bacon wrote from Darlinghurst Gaol in 1851 that he had £28 of his own money that had been placed with the governor of the gaol after his arrest. He wrote:

> [I had] no other means of procuring counsel to appear for me and I have retained Mr Ryan Brennan as my attorney and am desirous of obtaining Mr Purefoy and Holroyd as my counsel. I therefore will require the £28 ... to be handed over to my attorney to defray my expenses.[6]

At trial Thomas Bacon pleaded guilty and was sentenced to five years on the roads. A guilty plea meant he did not require counsel; it may be assumed his request for his money was denied.[7] Angelina Hughes Hallet had promised attorney John Ryan Brennan that she would sell her furniture to find funds for counsel's fees in March 1850, but she absconded with her furniture, leading to a warrant for her arrest.[8] While counsel was highly desirable,

---

5 Ann-Marie Jordens, *The Stenhouse Circle: Literary Life in Mid-Nineteenth Century Sydney* (Melbourne: Melbourne University Press, 1979), 46.
6 *The Queen v Bacon*, Affidavit, 30 August 1851, Supreme Court Informations, SR T76.
7 *Bell's Life*, 11 October 1851.
8 *People's Advocate*, 9 March 1850.

they were expensive to obtain. In Brisbane in 1857, Andrew Larkin applied in court to Justice Milford to have his attorney represent him and Milford replied that the gentlemen of the bar had come 500 miles (800 kilometres), at considerable personal expense, and he could not with propriety grant such a request.[9] In newspaper accounts counsel only appear in one or two cases in a criminal session and that the accused was undefended was noted. The word 'undefended' appeared in 633 cases in the years between 1850 and 1859 of press reporting of criminal cases: 437 before the Supreme Court and 196 at the assizes. At the assizes 206 cases were defended by a barrister in the same years; at the Supreme Court 1,000 cases were defended.[10]

Those accused of crimes that would result in capital punishment were sometimes granted counsel to 'watch the case'. It would be a mistake to see this as representation in any real sense. No depositions were obtained and counsel simply followed the case in court. Varying degrees of effort accompanied the watching of cases and counsel were asked by the judge whether they would watch at the beginning of the case. There is no record of counsel refusing such a request.

An important distinction exists in cases concerning Aboriginal people. Aboriginal defendants were never treated in the same manner as other defendants and, in the early 1850s, a debate appears in the case papers of *Davy alias Thandy*. The colonial secretary wrote to the attorney-general in July 1855:

> I am directed by His Excellency the Governor General to request that you and the Solicitor General will have the goodness to employ Mr Purefoy or some other competent barrister to defend any Aboriginal natives who may be brought to trial at the Circuits at which either of you may be present … I am to add that his Excellency approves of a fee of five guineas for each case being paid to the Barristers employed on such occasions out of the territorial revenue.[11]

---

9   *Empire*, 16 January 1857.
10 Word search for 'undefended 1850s', *Trove*, [National Library of Australia], 23 December 2024: trove.nla.gov.au.
11 Colonial Secretary to Attorney-General, 8 July 1852, enclosure in *R vs Davy alias Thandy*.

The response to this letter shows the great importance of the personal approach. It was signed by John Moore Dillon, the criminal Crown solicitor:

> Respecting the defence of the Aborigine. A correspondence took place between the Attorney General while the Attorney General was in England and Mr Cheeke was appointed counsel and Mr George Allan attorney for the Aboriginals. Afterward these gentlemen ceased to be employed as the Government declined to furnish the funds. Subsequently however some further communications have been made to the Attorney General on the subject of the precise nature of which I am not aware. I have never seen any instructions neither have I ever been requested to communicate with the counsel of any prisoner Aboriginal or other and I certainly would never have done so. It would be a most indelicate position for a solicitor to be placed in. If the Attorney General directs me to send the depositions against Aboriginals to any Counsel I can do so or even copies, though I cannot see why a prisoner defended at the expense of the Crown should have such an advantage over any prisoner who may be badly off in pecuniary matters and it is certainly not the practice of members of the bar to receive instructions from a prisoner.[12]

This letter asks why Aboriginal people were not treated in the same manner as any other prisoner. Plunkett replied that he was not authorised to employ an attorney for the whole session and that it was important to consider each separate case. The colonial secretary wrote that he approved Mr Purefoy acting for an Aboriginal prisoner at the Maitland Quarter Sessions, but the payment should not exceed £5 5 s.[13] The question as to why Aboriginal people were so represented was not answered. Justice Therry, formerly of the Supreme Court in Sydney, provided one answer in his memoirs in 1863:

> The protection of the lives of this poor inferior race of our fellow men is a strict duty we owe them. To that protection they derive the highest possible claim from the sovereignty which has been assumed over the whole of their possessions ... It would be grievous injustice not to make the black and the white man alike equally amenable to law. All that a humane government can reasonably be expected to do is done to assist the aborigines on such trials. A counsel is provided for them, an interpreter procured and paid for by the Crown and when they have intelligence to suggest the names of witnesses who can testify in their behalf their attendance is provided at the Crown's expence [sic].[14]

---

12 Undated note, in *R v Davy alias Thandy*.
13 Undated enclosure, in *R v Davy alias Thandy*.
14 Roger Therry, *Reminiscences of Thirty Years Residence in NSW and Victoria* (Sydney: RAHS Press, 1974 [1863]), 286–87.

For Therry, Aboriginal people had possessions over which sovereignty had been assumed. With English sovereignty, which Therry sees as property based, came specific rights for Aboriginal people, which included counsel. This was one answer as to why there was this informal recognition of responsibility in return for dispossession. There were no solicitors mentioned in any of the court records concerning Aboriginal people and George Allen made no mention of his appointment as solicitor to the Aborigines. His diaries for 1841 also make no mention of Aboriginal people. This is despite his enormously political role in the Methodist mission and that mission's intense interest in Aboriginal people.[15] Alfred Cheeke's appointment as solicitor for Aborigines was only for a few months in 1841 and after that there was 'no money' to continue the position. The idea of provision of representation by government was, it seems, short-lived. The appointment seems a gesture rather than a proper implementation of a new office.

The way Aboriginal people actually obtained representation was through a delicate and mannered approach to barristers by other legal officials and this is shown in the barrister Callaghan's diary.[16] Barristers appear to have been contacted personally by judges or the attorney-general.[17] Newspapers sometimes report that a barrister 'agreed to watch the case'. This watching could be requested in court by the judge. It was in no way proper representation and was also open to non-Aboriginal defendants for whom the death penalty would apply. Barristers did not obtain a copy of the depositions in such instances and the effort they put in varied. In Mogo Garra's case, there was only one statement given by counsel at the end of the hearing.[18] This does depend, however, on how the reporter approached a case. In 1856 Holroyd cross-examined all witnesses in *Billy Morgan*, according to the *Empire*, but said nothing in the *Sydney Morning Herald*.[19]

---

15 Norman Cowper and Vivienne Parsons, 'Allen, George (1800–1877)', *Australian Dictionary of Biography* (Canberra: National Centre of Biography, The Australian National University, 1966), adb.anu.edu.au/biography/allen-george-1696/text1831; David Andrew Roberts and Margaret Reeson, 'Wesleyan Methodist Missions to Australia and the Pacific', in *Methodism in Australia*, eds Glen O'Brien and Hilary M. Carey (London: Routledge, 2016), 197–210.
16 John M. Bennett, ed., *Callaghan's Diary: The 1840s Sydney Diary of Thomas Callaghan, B.A. of the King's Inns, Dublin, Barrister-at-Law* (Sydney: The Francis Forbes Society, 2005).
17 'Mr Pring at the instigation of the Attorney General volunteered to defend him.' *R v Campbell*, *Sydney Morning Herald*, 5 October 1855. 'Mr Purefoy at the request of his Honour conducted the defence.' *R v Crane*, *Empire*, 28 August 1854.
18 *Bell's Life*, 12 October 1850.
19 *Empire*, 8 April 1856; *Sydney Morning Herald*, 24 March 1856.

We are privy in historical research to far more information than contemporary counsel and attorney. The letters attached to the deposition and the pencil marking are absent from the documents produced for counsel by the copying clerk at the Crown solicitor's office. The documents were obtained from the criminal Crown solicitor by request. Dillon explained in *Sinclair*:

> On the third of February 1851 Mr Hamilton Welsh the solicitor and attorney for the above-named defendant informed me that he had on that day been retained on behalf of the defendant and requested me not to have the case against the defendant called for trial that day because he was not then prepared. He said Welsh expressed a wish to have a copy of the depositions which was found him—he might have forthwith but did not ask for a copy of the information to be filed against the defendant or intimate in any other way directly or indirectly that [the] defendant would require time to plead to the information filed.[20]

Dillon was not about to give anything for which he was not asked. In this case the barrister Purefoy was engaged by the defendant on the first day of the assizes. He requested time to familiarise himself with the case and a copy of the information. This was refused by Chief Justice Stephen in court, who said 'that if the defendant's counsel was ignorant of the form of information for a criminal assault (His Honour) would repeat it to him by heart' and proceeded to do so amidst the suppressed laughter of the court.[21] The jealous guarding of legal documents at the attorney-general's offices and in court is underlined here. Copies of depositions were to be paid for. In 1850 charges were 4 pence per folio of 72 words for the first 12 folios and 3 pence per folio of 72 words for the remaining folios.[22] Charges would form part of the defendant's account.

If money determined the opportunity for representation and defendants like Thomas Bacon were disappointed at not obtaining counsel, there was still an aspect of chance for all defendants. This is to be found in the judgement books of the criminal Crown solicitor. Drawn up before the sessions of the assizes or the Darlinghurst sittings of the Supreme Court, these registers were marked in pencil for the sending of subpoenas for witnesses and marked again if the witnesses arrived in court. If witnesses failed to appear, the amount of security for which they signed recognisances was 'estreated',

---

20   John Moore Dillon to Augustus Carter, *The Queen v James Sinclair*, Supreme Court Informations, SR T76.
21   *Goulburn Herald*, 8 February 1851.
22   *Sydney Morning Herald*, 7 December 1850.

or claimed by the sheriff. In the north-west of New South Wales this was £80 to £100; elsewhere £40 was standard. If witnesses did not appear, the accused was held or released on bail until the next session of the court. If witnesses did not appear again, the accused was discharged. Other means of being discharged were if no interpreter appeared to translate the case into the language of the accused, or the term 'discharged' appeared without explanation. But these were not the only chances the defendant had as the Crown prosecutor, pressed for time, decided at the beginning of the session which case would be heard and which would not.

The attorney-general prosecuted all cases but if he was not available the position was filled by the solicitor-general or a barrister who had obtained a proclamation from the governor that he presented to the court.[23] At Brisbane in November 1855 the barrister Purefoy even officiated as judge by special commission.[24] It is unclear how much time the prosecuting counsel had to familiarise himself with cases. In January 1857, also at Brisbane, the Crown prosecutor, the barrister Pring, stated he was not prepared to go on with cases and the court was adjourned to the next day.[25]

The Crown prosecutor sometimes disagreed with the decisions of the attorney-general and at times the attorney-general who had drawn up the indictments had been replaced with a new attorney-general by the time of the sessions. This made the beginnings of sessions more complex. At sessions it was sometimes decided that a case would not be proceeded with. This was after the defendant's expense of obtaining defence witnesses, obtaining bail and travelling to court. As we have seen, the Bucknell brothers went to great expense, spending £1,000 to prepare for court. They accused Attorney-General Martin of failing to properly consider the case before he proceeded to indictment. In their case the judge recommended acquittal and the jury agreed, but similar kinds of expense would have been contracted by those who arrived at court only to find their case was not to be heard. Twenty cases of the 135 listed in the Maitland Criminal Crown Solicitor's Judgement Book for 1856–60 involved the Crown prosecutor deciding not to continue with a case. This is 15 per cent of all cases from Maitland in those years. At times reasoning is given—that is, there was not sufficient evidence to proceed—but at other times no reason was given, simply that

---

23 *Maitland Mercury*, 11 May 1857, 28 November 1858.
24 *Maitland Mercury*, 28 November 1855.
25 *Empire*, 26 January 1857.

'the Attorney General declines to prosecute'.[26] Defence counsel played no part in these early considerations. Records for the Supreme Court in Sydney are less complete. The Crown Solicitor's volumes for 1854 and 1856 were not sent to the archives. Without them, we find of 546 defendants 55 had their cases not proceeded with (only 2.7 per cent). From 1856, there are 267 defendants and 32 cases not proceeded with, or 12 per cent. The figures apparent at Maitland after the change of government are slightly higher than for the Supreme Court.[27] Both reflect the succession of attorneys-general with their disagreement over cases. Also, from the time of Manning in 1856 there seems to be less interest in reviewing cases in the office, leaving it until the hours before the court.

A further chance for defendants before 1858 is apparent in case numbering. The numbering of cases in the judgement books of the criminal Crown solicitor in Sydney and at assizes is sometimes doubled. In the Maitland register there were two number fours for William Clay in March 1857 for separate cases of horse stealing at Nundle. Clay also appeared in number 12 with William Swan for assault at Singleton. The first two cases were separate indictments for theft of different horses, but before the session of the assizes began, it was decided the two cases of horse theft would be tried together. This may bear some relationship to the haste of the assizes. Patrick O'Donnell, John Hewitt and James Hewitt appeared on two charges of forgery and uttering at Maitland in September 1857; a note on the first case, number three, says: 'Prisoners not to be tried on this charge sentenced on the next.' In September 1857 there were two number threes, two number sixes and five number elevens.[28] This stops abruptly in March 1858. James Martin was attorney-general and had been so since September 1857, so one cannot say it is his doing. This means there is less largesse in decision-making at the very beginning of sessions, each case has a separate number and a sentence for one offence was usually to follow on from the sentence of the first. Each separate entry under a new number meant that a new jury had to be empanelled and neither the sympathy nor the antipathy of the jury would be maintained.[29]

---

26 Criminal Crown Solicitor's Judgement Books, SR 4/5754 – 4/5758.
27 Criminal Crown Solicitor's Judgement Books, SR 4/5732 – 4/5735.
28 Criminal Crown Solicitor's Judgement Books, SR 4/5755.
29 Reported in the *Goulburn Herald*, 30 March 1859.

7. GETTING INTO COURT

The judgement books and the newspapers show the convict status of the defendant faded in importance from the early 1850s. Rigorously completed in 1847, the column listing condition includes only scattered references to 'born in the colony' or 'bond' by 1850. Newspapers do occasionally record reference to status at the point of sentencing by the judge. It is unclear who provided this information. Possibly it was the sheriff, who came to court with his own lists. When Catherine Byrnes was acquitted at Bathurst in 1854, the case continued, 'it appearing that she and her husband were runaways from Van Diemen's Land she was discharged into the hands of police'.[30] Magistrates from the west and south-west clearly noted the status of the accused when they sent depositions in the 1850s; these do not translate upwards to the assizes or the Supreme Court. The convict system existed erratically in some local areas and not others and it was not of major importance in the higher courts.

There are no minutes of the Supreme Court and its assizes surviving, though minutes were taken. Depositions were given high status in the courts, being read out if a defendant pleaded guilty, if a defendant requested it or at the end of the hearing of witnesses.[31] Judges did not obtain a copy of the depositions unless they specifically asked for them. In 1859 Edward Wise requested the Legislative Council that the judge be enabled to read the original depositions in cases. The attorney-general Alfred Lutwyche replied that the depositions were always in court and produced at the request of the judge 'or perhaps counsel for the accused' and Wise withdrew his motion.[32]

Cases were introduced by the Crown prosecutor, witnesses called and questioned by the judge, the jury, the prisoner and the defence counsel if one was employed or asked to watch. The defence or the accused made their defence, followed by the Crown prosecutor. The judge addressed the jury and the jury either retired or did not and gave their verdict. In early 1850s cases, the language of the indictment was still being questioned by defence counsel, despite the *Justices Act* allowing misspelling of names and places and errors in times of offence to be ignored. Table 7.1 gives some of the arguments of the bar during this period, though these are gleaned only from the newspapers and more complex legal points may have been made. Arguments are not always given even though the defence counsel

---

30 *Bathurst Free Press and Mining Journal*, 2 September 1854.
31 Read in a guilty plea, *R v Adolphus Hogemann*, *Sydney Morning Herald*, 8 August 1856. Read at the prisoner's request, *R v Nicholas Hand*, *Goulburn Herald*, 30 March 1859.
32 *Maitland Mercury*, 3 February 1859.

addresses the court. We have only a very partial picture of the skill of the bar. The defences have been chosen to illustrate different approaches. Purefoy and Pring were most likely to bring points of law and case law and it is they who were responsible for many reserved cases.

Table 7.1: Defence counsel argument examples

Barrister	Argument	Result
Purefoy (*Goulburn Herald*, 10 August 1850, *Clarke*)	On the authority of *R v Crowhurst*, there was no case to go to a jury, stated the evidence had been taken behind the back of the prisoner.	Guilty
Purefoy (*Goulburn Herald*, 10 August 1850, *Chapman and Sears*)	The information could not be sustained, the learned gentleman quoted *Archbold* 452, *R v McLoughlin* 8 C and P, *R v Leon Smith* 8 C and P and *Roscoe* 782. Purefoy declined to address the jury.	Sears, not guilty Chapman, guilty
Holroyd (*BFPMJ*, 4 March 1854, *Malony, Cain and Cain*)	No evidence against Malony or the younger Cain, property found 14 months after only guilty of receiving.	All prisoners, guilty
Holroyd (*BFPMJ*, 4 March 1854, *Barton*)	Jury must decide if gun went off accidentally, if so must acquit, no malice should be manslaughter.	Guilty of manslaughter
Holroyd (*BFPMJ*, Bathurst Assizes, 2 September 1854, *Young*)	No evidence to prove malice, all evidence to the contrary.	Guilty of murder.
Holroyd (*BFPMJ*, Bathurst Assizes, 1 September 1855, *Sullivan*)	Prisoner's behaviour not probable; horse could not be identified.	Guilty
Holroyd (*BFPMJ*, Bathurst Assizes, 1 September 1855, *Curran*)	Discredit approver.	Guilty
Pring (*Sydney Morning Herald*, Bathurst Assizes, 5 October 1855, *Campbell*)	Angelina Hughes Hallet, publican, when the note was given to her replaced it with a suspect one.	Not guilty
Pring (*Sydney Morning Herald*, Bathurst Assizes, 8 October 1855, *Nash and Forbes*)	Jury returned no decision. Dickinson asks them what was the majority, Mr Pring says he did not think it was acting fair to ask a jury on return to court what was their majority. Mr Faucett agreed with Mr Pring, it was invariably not done by judges in England.	
Butler (*Sydney Morning Herald*, 8 August 1856, Supreme Court, *Hagemann*)	Extreme youth of prisoner, foreigner mistake contract, good character.	Guilty, recommendation to mercy, previous good character

Barrister	Argument	Result
Pring (*Empire*, Bathurst Assizes, 21 March 1857, *Harvey*)	The evidence is not sufficient to sustain the information, no testimony to prove intent. In support of argument, he cited a case from Russell on crimes.	Guilty, death recorded. Mr Pring desired the point should be reserved; there was no evidence to go to the jury of any intent.
Blake (*Goulburn Herald*, 30 March 1859, Goulburn Assizes, *Norton*)	Prisoner publicly riding horse; brand not clear, prisoner thought it was his own.	Not guilty
Blakeney (*Goulburn Herald*, 30 March 1859, Goulburn Assizes, *Berriman*)	Prisoner entitled to an acquittal because of length of time between losing and finding horse, prisoner thought it stray, should be civil action.	Not guilty
Wild watching the case (*Empire*, reporting on Bathurst Assizes, 27 September 1859, *Davis*)	Murder: the prisoner unable to pay fee, counsel not in a position to give the case the attention it demanded; evidence not conclusive, no-one saw the murder; the property found in prisoner's possession had never been the property of the deceased.	Guilty

Note: *Bathurst Free Press and Mining Journal.

Bennett has already noted the atmosphere of the court and its joking and puns, apparent both in Thomas Callaghan's diary and in the recording of Chief Justice Stephen's joking in the *Bathurst Free Press and Mining Journal* and the *Goulburn Herald*.[33] What is most startling to the modern reader are the antics of the jury in court (see Table 7.2). This is only apparent in the detailed reportage of the *Maitland Mercury*, which reported 550 records of criminal cases for the period 1843–69, giving an average of 10 cases per session and 20 cases in a year. Records before 1843 are patchier and, since the court registers only survive from 1856, it is difficult to accurately quantify cases. The *Maitland Mercury* reports jury interaction with the court in 263 of these cases, which means the reporting is partial; some cases interest the journalist more than others. These partial records concerning jury behaviour, however, are startling to the modern mind.

---

33 John M. Bennett, *A History of the Supreme Court of New South Wales* (Sydney: Law Book Co., 1974), 79; Thomas Callaghan, 12 August 1842, in Bennett, *Callaghan's Diary*, 24; *Bathurst Free Press and Mining Journal*, 23 February 1850; *Goulburn Herald*, 8 February 1851.

Table 7.2: Cases for which jury activity reported in the Maitland press, 1843–1869

Jury interrupts judge at summing up: 23 times in 26 years Years most common: 1846 and 1847, both five times; 1860, four times; last date, 1868
Questions during case: 19 times in 26 years Years most common: 1847, three times; 1849, four times; last date, 1864
Recommendation to mercy: 16 times in 26 years Years most common: 1852, twice; 1862, twice; 1865, twice; 1867, twice; last date, 1869
Finding lesser count: 17 times in 26 years Begins 1853, most common: 1860, four times; 1866, three times; last date, 1867

Juries constantly consulted each other; they interrupted witnesses, they sometimes stopped the judge in his address to them and halted the summing up of the defending counsel, the attorney-general or Crown solicitor to say 'not to bother they'd already made up their minds'. Late in the period they made speeches at the end of a case. While there is not a great deal of evidence for the other assizes and the Supreme Court in Sydney, there is some indication that such behaviour was widespread. In 1852 in *Pennison and Ryan*, at Goulburn Assizes, Justice Dickinson told the jury to find the defendants guilty; they acquitted both prisoners, who were discharged.[34] In 1858 at Goulburn the defence counsel was about to address the jury 'when they said they had made up their minds'.[35] At Maitland no-one commented that the jury was behaving in an unusual manner, indicating such temerity was colony wide.

Ian Barker QC's detailed work—the major work on jury trial—elaborates the laborious struggle for trial by jury in the colony and shows it came from a wide cross-section of society.[36] The jury in colonial debates was a signifier of English right and the imperial administration was slow in considering a penal colony worthy of transferral of such an honour. Barker writes that New South Wales was the only colony that had to fight for the right to trial by jury and this fighting was done in two ways: the recommendations of officials such as governors Philip Gidley King, William Bligh and Lachlan Macquarie and a series of petitions in 1808, 1809 and 1825.[37] Arguments against emancipist jurors appeared in 1836 through another petition signed by those who sought to limit emancipist rights but also to claim these

---

34   *Sydney Morning Herald*, 13 December 1852.
35   *Sydney Morning Herald*, 2 April 1858.
36   Barker, 'Sorely Tried'.
37   ibid., 100–14.

rights for an exclusive group.[38] The debates saturated the press and public meetings were held.[39] Trial by jury was bound up with the whole colony's sense of itself.

The rhetoric around the struggle for jury trial was influential in how juries saw themselves whether or not they had an emancipist connection. This is particularly so at Windsor in the period from 1824 to 1829 where the young natives emphasised their 'freedom' in fights with police, yet at the same time sat on the Windsor Quarter Sessions jury.[40] The idea of the 'native' was a new element in a colonial conception of rights and this was powerfully argued by William Charles Wentworth, as David Neal has shown.[41] The behaviour of the jury in the Windsor Quarter Sessions was not recorded in the press, but it is worthwhile remembering that the population of the Hunter River region and the Liverpool Plains found their origins in this native restive population of Windsor.[42]

The idea of the jury contained mystical components. In 1822 the French observer Maurice Cottu wrote about the transformation of the 12 members of the petty jury on the English northern assizes into a representation of the people by means of the oath. This happened, he said, 'in spite of themselves'.[43] Such a transformation meant truth worked through them and decided upon the guilt or innocence of the prisoner. This superiority of the jury was also reflected in Justice Dickinson's statement to the jury at the Maitland Assizes in 1847: 'Without any disrespect to the bench, the opinion of twelve men chosen from various classes of the community was of greater value than that of any individual moving in a sphere less practically qualifying him to distinguish clearly.'[44]

In the 1850s the press reported on cases as though the jury was the absolute focus of the trial. The prisoner was 'given to the jury'; no-one addressed the court, they 'addressed the jury'. This way of reporting may have been productive as people who served on juries read the newspaper and obtained

---

38   ibid., 111.
39   ibid., 114.
40   Byrne, *Criminal Law and Colonial Subject*, 196–97.
41   David Neal, *The Rule of Law in a Penal Colony: Law and Politics in Early New South Wales* (Cambridge: Cambridge University Press, 2002), 170.
42   Norma Townsend, 'Master and Man in the Myall Creek Massacre', *Push From the Bush* 20 (April 1985): 4–32.
43   Maurice Cottu, *On the Administration of Criminal Justice in England and the Spirit of the English Government* (London: Richard Stevens, 1822), 98–100.
44   *Maitland Mercury*, 17 February 1847.

from it a view of their place in the court.⁴⁵ We know that the jury was speaking together throughout trials because they frequently did not leave the box to decide a verdict.⁴⁶ This was also the custom in England. Cottu saw a kind of purity in the jury not leaving the box to deliberate; truth was apparent instantly, like a blaze of light, he thought.⁴⁷ As Cottu writes and despite modern readings, expressed in Beattie, it was in the nineteenth century deemed a good thing that juries decided very quickly, not a sign of lack of consideration for legal detail.⁴⁸ At Maitland the jury usually reached a decision quickly. At times the jury was locked up for the night. In 1858 Justice Milford was criticised by the *Maitland Mercury* that he should have realised that the jury room in the court was an airless room with no windows. If he had just checked with other justices, he would have found it was customary to have the jury housed at an inn when locked up.⁴⁹ However, overnight decision-making was far less commonly reported than instantaneous decisions in the box.

The judge's address in a trial was usually on points of law that the jury should consider and an explanation of the case. The minutes were read out by him. When the jury told him not to bother in his address, which they did in both 'guilty' and 'not guilty' verdicts, they were effectively saying they knew better and did not need any points of law explained. They were thinking outside law and in the realm of what Cottu termed 'common sense' and Justice Dickinson, 'practicality'. Judges *did* stop speaking at the Maitland Assizes when the jury told them not to bother going on. This was contested once by Justice Therry in 1846, who proceeded anyway. He was interrupted again and told again not to proceed, which he did not.⁵⁰

In the late 1840s and early 1850s, the interruptions by the jury came earlier in cases, before or during the address of defence counsel and once before the solicitor-general's address.⁵¹ This was in 1846 when the jury interrupted

---

45 'Given to the Jury': *Maitland Mercury*, 9 February 1856, 13 September 1856, 11 March 1858, 25 September 1858, 26 November 1859.
46 Sixty-five of 263 cases (24.8 per cent) report the jury not leaving the box. This is also apparent in 'a few minutes to 10 minutes', in 96 of 263 cases (36.6 per cent). *Maitland Mercury*, 1843–69.
47 Cottu, *On the Administration of Criminal Justice in England*, 98.
48 John M. Beattie, *Policing and Punishment in London 1660–1720: Urban Crime and the Limits of Terror* (Oxford: Oxford University Press, 2001), 272.
49 *Maitland Mercury*, 14 March 1857.
50 *R v Christopher Nowlan*, *Maitland Mercury*, 14 March 1846.
51 Interrupt defence: *R v Thomas Green*, *Maitland Mercury*, 17 February 1847; *R v Thomas Egan or Aitkin*, *Maitland Mercury*, 25 September 1847; *R v David McLean*, *Maitland Mercury*, 6 March 1852, 15 March 1845.

a case to say they had made up their minds 'unless there was some other material witness'.⁵² Early interruptions were accepted easily by barristers as well as the justices; there was no argument. In 1846 the Maitland jury stopped a case before the chief justice. A witness had stated that the accused had taken money from the pocket of a man lying on the road 'to prevent others getting it'.⁵³ This was enough to stop the case and the jury's common sense determined he was not guilty. There was no objection to this. In 1854 the Maitland jury returned to the court to announce there was 'no case'.⁵⁴

In a case of horse theft in 1857 the barrister Pring was acting as Crown prosecutor. At a point in the case Justice Milford looked to Pring and exclaimed, 'Is this not a case for an action!', meaning that the case should have been stopped because the witnesses' evidence suggested the innocence of the accused. 'Mr Pring observed that it was in the power of the Jury, if agreed, to stop the case.' The majority of the jury decided the case should go on.⁵⁵ This was complete subservience to the common sense or practicality of the jury and the court was working effectively outside the law. Throughout criminal cases there were not just four voices that mattered in the court—the judge, the attorney-general or Crown solicitor and the defence counsel or, if not represented, the prisoner. The jury at Maitland also asked questions, not through the foreman but singly and without notification. A 'juror' or a 'juryman' asked questions of all witnesses and the prisoner but not of the judge. One juror could recall witnesses to ask a question even well after the case would be considered 'over'—that is, the judge had given his final address. In only one instance was a juror told it was too late to recall a witness; the witness had gone home to another town.⁵⁶ The jury asking questions of witnesses is certainly in line with the volumes of *Blackstone* held in the colony. Together, Blackstone wrote, the justice, jury, defence and prosecution came to 'a knowledge of the truth'.⁵⁷ The jury's questioning in Maitland, however, changed the contours of a case. It opened up the court and the jury was even more in control of proceedings.

---

52 *R v William Hagan*, Maitland Mercury, 21 March 1846.
53 *R v William Smith*, Maitland Mercury, 19 September 1846.
54 *R v Henry Farmer*, Maitland Mercury, 1 March 1854.
55 Maitland Mercury, 14 March 1857.
56 *R v Donald McPhee and John McPhee*, Maitland Mercury, 15 September 1849.
57 Blackstone, 'Trial by Jury', in loang.com/library/referenceblackstonecommentries-law-england/bla-323 [page discontinued].

At Goulburn Assizes in 1858, the jury found James Wood not guilty of stabbing. Chief Justice Stephen questioned their reasoning and the jury said they felt the stabbing was 'justified' because the victim had thrown Wood into a fire. The chief justice replied that

> he should be very sorry for such a doctrine to go forth in public, it was a most dangerous doctrine and if it were admitted life would be unsafe. However, the Jury had acquitted the prisoner and it remained only for him to discharge him.[58]

This is one of the few accounts of a Goulburn jury and it appears that cultural understandings of justice overcame the law. One cannot tell how often such 'common sense logic' appeared in jury decision-making across the colony or how often the judge or the defence counsel were influential.

In *Wilkes*, Judge Therry sent the jury back when they were undecided because he said witnesses had come a long way and great expense had been undertaken by the Crown, as it was a most important case. They returned with 'guilty'.[59] Judges in the 1850s Maitland sessions sent juries back if their decisions made no *legal* sense.[60] This implies juries took little notice of the judge's final address to them. The jury decided in one case before Justice Dickinson in 1851 that the prisoner was guilty because he did indeed utter an order but 'without intent'. Dickinson informed them this was an impossible verdict. The crime needed intention. They were sent back to make another decision and returned with 'not guilty'.[61] In the September 1861 session, the jury returned to say 'there is a strong suspicion of guilt but not sufficient to give a verdict. We give the prisoner the benefit of the doubt and return the verdict not proven.' The chief justice said such a verdict could not be given; if they gave the prisoner the benefit of the doubt, they found him not guilty. The jury retired and returned 'not guilty'.[62]

Ian Barker QC writes that juries were interested in amelioration of sentences. Juries at the Maitland Assizes did ask for mercy for the defendant, sometimes for unusual reasons. In 1858 the jury recommended a prisoner to mercy 'on account of there being only one witness'. The chief justice said that ground

---

58 *R v James Wood*, Sydney Morning Herald, 2 October 1858.
59 *Sydney Morning Herald*, 23 April 1858.
60 *Maitland Mercury*, 14 September 1858, 'guilty of receiving, his honour said the prisoner was not charged with receiving and the Jury retired again, Not Guilty', 17 March 1859, 13 September 1860.
61 *Maitland Mercury*, 10 March 1851.
62 *Maitland Mercury*, 17 September 1861.

was inadmissible.[63] In 1861 in a case of rape the jury recommended the defendant to mercy 'because he was drunk'. The chief justice said he could not concur in such a recommendation and sentenced the prisoner to death.[64] It will be forever impossible to tell why a jury decided as it did in a particular case, but defence and prosecution have both considered themselves winning the argument through a guilty or not guilty verdict. The Maitland jury suggests a separate dynamic came into play and this complicates how the law works in the colony; reasoning behind verdicts is difficult to decipher. The *Adelaide Observer* provides some insight in its 1857 account of the jury after the end of the session giving a speech to spectators that claimed Justice Boothby had misunderstood them. A subsequent meeting of the citizens of Adelaide passed resolutions concerning what they termed the arbitrary assumption of power by the judge and a petition was raised to have him dismissed from his office.[65] This incident was reported in the *Maitland Mercury*, so it informed some of the local knowledge of what a jury was capable of. John McLaren writes of Justice Boothby that he had disrespected the jury in 1855 in *Popham* when he had put an ambiguous question to the jury previous to a rape case, resulting in Boothby declaring the victim a perjurer and the accused as having an unstained character. This resulted in a public meeting and calls for Boothby's resignation. Boothby then began redefining the relative functions of judge and jury at trial—wishing the jury to follow his directions. This was slated by the press as an attack on 'the rights of freeborn Englishmen' and McLaren details the long conflict between Boothby's idea of the power of a judge and popular opinion.[66]

An explanation for jury behaviour might be found in the constitution of the juries and Niamh Howlin has used such an approach in Irish history.[67] Initial lists at Bathurst in 1851 had a majority of 'esquires'—those of status who had significant landholdings—but the list was sent back to be revised because it included justices of the peace who were not to be jurors. The second list was dominated by storekeepers and tradesmen. The jurors list at Sydney contains a similar group, though 'yeoman' was a vague term

---

63 *Maitland Mercury*, 9 March 1858.
64 *Maitland Mercury*, 10 September 1861.
65 *Maitland Mercury*, 10 March 1857.
66 John McLaren, *Dewigged, Bothered and Bewildered: British Colonial Judges on Trial, 1800–1900* (Toronto: University of Toronto Press, 2011).
67 Niamh Howlin, '"The Terror of Their Lives": Irish Jurors' Experiences', *Law and History Review* 29, no. 2 (2011): 703–61.

(Table 7.3).⁶⁸ For each session a list of names from which jurors were selected was created by the sheriff. The Maitland jury was drawn from the merchant and squatting classes, with publicans and tradesmen included. The merchant and tradesmen group, or 'grocerdom' as Manning Clark termed it,⁶⁹ was largely responsible for the formation of public institutions in country towns. Squatters also ran stores and manufactories, were interested in town property acquisition and money lending and speculation as much as any merchant. Squatter actions often defied the central government and the Crown and modelled such rejection of authority that was to be the mainstay of the development of democracy—'bounce' or disrespect and 'gammon' or dissembling characterised the squatter relation to government according to a letter to the *Maitland Mercury* in 1843.⁷⁰ One cannot describe the jury as 'gentlemen jurors' because the publicans and builders who sat alongside squatters would not have been designated as such. In its makeup and increasingly throughout the period, the jury resembled London juries—'tradesmen', as Linebaugh terms them.⁷¹

Jury independence had implications for Aboriginal people. Even though Justice Burton stated that Aboriginal people were to be regarded by the assizes 'as if white men' in 1841, a contrary decision occurred in 1856.⁷² This was the case of the Aboriginal man Billy Cubby, as he appeared in the sheriff's records; Cubby is a moity name in the north-west and north coast of New South Wales into Queensland. It is a skin name adopted as a surname.⁷³ According to the case, Billy had been the only identifiable man out of a large group. Defence counsel Faucett said of colonists:

---

68 The status of jurors at Maitland can also be determined by the newspaper listings of those who did not attend. List of non-attending jurors 1843: Otho Baldwin, had a pasturage licence; David Brown, Paterson, miller; Charles Boydell esq. JP, 'Gresford'; Frederick Dodwell esq., Paterson; James Cox, Maitland, innkeeper; T. Hector esq., Paterson; M. Hutchinson esq., Raymond Terrace; W.D. Kelman esq., Hunter River, grazier; Mr King, Raymond Terrace, grazier; Mr S. Kemp, Hunter River Railway Company. Jurors 1856 (non-attendance fines): Peter Canavan, Morpeth, builder; Abel Cobcroft, grazier; William Chapman, sawyer; William Wentworth Bucknell, grazier; John Dowling Brown, pastoralist, Paterson; John George Betty, pastoralist, Paterson. Ian Barker QC notes the preponderance of innkeepers on the jury lists. Barker, 'Sorely Tried'.
69 Manning Clark, *A History of Australia* (Melbourne: Melbourne University Press, 1973), 250–51.
70 *Maitland Mercury*, 29 April 1843.
71 Peter Linebaugh, *The London Hanged: Crime and Civil Society in the Eighteenth Century* (London: Allen Lane, 1991).
72 *R v Merrido alias Mullen and Nougawi*, *Sydney Monitor*, 17 May 1841.
73 Martin Thomas, *The Many Worlds of R.H. Matthews: In Search of An Australian Anthropologist* (Sydney: Allen & Unwin, 2011).

that they had taken possession of the lands of these natives and whilst pretending to shelter them, they had not protected them. In this case there was only one witness but it was plain there must have been some quarrel which the Jury had not heard of and that in all probability this vengeance had been inflicted in compliance with the laws of the tribe. In all probability, even if acquitted he would have to submit to the laws of his tribe and be tried over again.[74]

The jury found the prisoner not guilty and thus contributed to the erratic history of sovereignty, perhaps without even listening to the defence argument. This verdict recognises Aboriginal political organisation. Such erratic behaviour mirrors precisely the confusions apparent in the press as to Aboriginal sovereignty.[75]

Each justice seems different in the way they managed the court. Therry and Dickinson seem most patient in court while Milford and Stephen seem more irritated, Stephen most likely to joke.[76] Yet, the activity of the jury in the courtroom was never questioned by any justice. Where the justices were highly disgusted was when jurors sought to influence beyond a recommendation in court for mercy. In 1854 at Bathurst, Chief Justice Stephen received a petition from jurors praying for mercy in *Young*. He 'denounced the proceeding and appended in the strongest language and threatened to inflict a penalty of £500'.[77] Such wrath was also incurred when jurors wrote a letter after a case reporting that a decision was not unanimous and there had been intimidation of some kind. There were two incidences of this in the period. The first case was in 1853 and concerned the theft of a cash box. After judgement, four of the jurymen sent a letter to the chief justice:

> Stating they did not really agree to the verdict but were overruled by the majority. His Honour said he presumed the object was to lessen the sentence passed on Bennett, but as that had been passed long since it would not have had that effect. His Honour made some stringent observations on the grave neglect of duty the Jurymen confessed themselves guilty of in allowing their foreman to state publicly that they had agreed and in assenting to it by their silence … and he said he had not yet determined whether it was not his duty to take further proceedings in the matter.[78]

---

74 *R v Billy Cubby*, *Maitland Mercury*, 15 March 1856.
75 An editorial uses the phrase 'if we have no right to this territory'. 'The Aborigines', [Editorial], *Maitland Mercury*, 27 May 1843; Douglas and Finnane, *Indigenous Crime and Settler Law*, 50.
76 *Goulburn Herald*, 8 February 1851.
77 *Bathurst Free Press and Mining Journal*, 2 September 1854.
78 *Maitland Mercury*, 17 August 1853.

Stephen here suggests spurious motives for the note sent to him by four jurors, indicating a kind of distrust. He also blamed the four jurymen who approached him for their silence at the end of the trial.

Another incident of jury disagreement after the assize ended concerned Aboriginal men Jemmy and Roger in 1858. One juror had threatened the others with 'a kicking' if they did not find the prisoners guilty. Jemmy was acquitted but Roger was found guilty and sentenced to death. Three jurors forwarded affidavits to the court stating the intimidation. This event occurred after the *Adelaide Observer* wrote of a jury giving a speech to spectators claiming Justice Boothby had misunderstood them.[79] After the jury's admission of intimidation at Maitland in deciding *Roger and Jemmy*, the entire NSW Bar and 250 members of the public signed a petition in favour of Roger. The *Sydney Morning Herald* had more to say, however, and this concerned the interaction of the jury with Justice Dickinson:

> In answer to his Honour's question as to whether the Jury thought that the prisoners admitted their guilt in the presence of a dying man, the Jury, after some hesitation, said they believed that Roger, by his silence admitted his guilt, and they did not believe Jemmy's denial ... His Honour said Do you consider gentlemen that the prisoners admitted their guilt? The Foreman: We consider that the one said nothing, the other said no.[80]

The *Herald* raged against the intelligence of a jury 'who found men guilty without a tittle of legal evidence against them but their silence or denial of guilt, especially when they were not asked whether they were guilty or not'. The paper accused Dickinson of perversity of judgement because he did not give the jury proper guidance in terms of the law. The *Herald* made the point that it would be sorry to fancy that a Black man could not get a fair trial in the colony and that considerations appealed to 'our honour and humanity'.[81] On 15 September the case had been reserved by Dickinson himself because he feared he had wrongly directed the jury. He told them that when Chennier had been asked who was responsible for his injuries Jemmy denied Chennier's statement and Roger said nothing; this did not mean that Roger admitted guilt. The jury's verdict according to Dickinson was that both men were guilty because Roger said nothing, and they did not believe Jemmy's denial. Dickinson recommended to the Executive Council

---

79 *Maitland Mercury*, 10 March 1857.
80 *Sydney Morning Herald*, 11 October 1858.
81 *Sydney Morning Herald*, 11 October 1858.

that Jemmy be liberated.[82] In the reserved case, Dickinson said that Jemmy had been liberated by His Excellency and asked if the conviction against Roger should be entertained after the reasons the jury gave for the guilty verdict on both men. The special case was heard on 16 October and the conviction was quashed by Stephen and Therry.[83] In this case there is a rare example of jury thinking, without exactly following the reasoning of the judge and returning with a garbled interpretation of what had been said to them.

Table 7.3: Professions of jurors from surviving lists

Original list, Bathurst Assizes, 1851	
Farmer and grazier	15
Licensed victualler	5
Esquire	22
Blacksmith	1
Miller	1
Tailor and draper	1
Wheelwright and blacksmith	1
Tanner and currier	1
Bathurst Assizes, revised list, 1851	
Licensed victualler	5
Farmer and grazier	14
Storekeeper	12
Storekeeper and miller	1
Carpenter and builder	1
Esquire	6
Blacksmith and wheelwright	1
Boot and shoemaker	1
Baker	1
Cooper	1
Auctioneer	1
Wheelwright	1
Butcher	1
Mason	1
Shoemaker	1
Builder	1
Tailor	1

---

82 *Sydney Morning Herald*, 29 September 1858.
83 Roger and Jemmy Special Case, Supreme Court Informations, SR T78.

Sydney list, February 1852	
Gentleman	1
Farmer	1
Publican	15
Yeoman	3
Esquire	1
Livery stable keeper	1
Grocer	2
Saddler	1
Dealer	2
Butcher	3
Painter and glazier	1
Cabinet-maker	1
Stationer	1
Shoemaker	1
Boot and shoemaker	2
Cooper	2
Pianoforte maker	1
Shipbuilder	1
Bootmaker	1
Coach builder	1
Upholsterer	1
Bonnet warehouseman	1
Builder	1
Merchant	2
Baker	1
Sydney, December 1852	
Publican	8
Builder	4
Blacksmith	1
Yeoman	1
Boot and shoemaker	1
Accountant	2
Boatbuilder	1
Tailor and draper	1
Cabinet-maker	1
Esquire	1
General dealer	1

Painter and glazier	1
Print seller	1
Butcher	2
Grocer	2
Merchant	5
Writing clerk	1
Baker	1
Agent	1
Gentleman	1
Crockery merchandiser	1
Oil and colourman	1
Jeweller	3
Bootmaker	1
Sydney, second list, December 1852	
Gardener	1
Shoemaker	1
Publican	13
Agent	1
Timber dealer	1
Soap and candlemaker	1
Yeoman	7
Builder	1
General dealer	1
Grocer	5
Tailor and draper	2
Draper	1
Ship chandler	1
Hatter	1
Shipowner	1
Boatbuilder	1
Engineer	1
Shopkeeper	1
Bookseller	1
Linen draper	2
Cooper	1
Spirit merchant	1

Note: These are in the order listed by the sheriff.

Indications of the jury not listening to the judge and interrupting defence counsel and the attorney-general suggest that juries operated inside an idea of 'common sense'. Judicial acquiescence made the jury more powerful and newspaper accounts of jury behaviour ensured its continuance. Jury behaviour also reflects the contradictory reporting of violence to and by Aboriginal people in the newspapers and in this way the jury can be said to reflect the mind of 'the people' as it was supposed to do. Strands of influence include the history of obtaining jury trial in the colony, hard fought for by all sectors of the colony, elements of mysticism involving transformation inherent in the history of juries and the composition of the jury in New South Wales—deriving from recalcitrant squatter history and the new political force of 'grocerdom'.

Table 7.4 shows the results of cases discussed in this book. Defendants were more likely to be found guilty in the west and south-west of New South Wales. Given the discussion of jury behaviour, it is impossible to say exactly why the guilty verdict was more common at Goulburn and Bathurst. Attempting to explain it through the background of jurors would neglect the erratic nature of the jury shown at Maitland and briefly mentioned at other places. The messiness of the courts is most apparent at Maitland, where the Crown prosecutor did not proceed with cases, accused persons were more likely to escape and witnesses not to turn up in court. No other assize provides us with the judgement books. The west and the south-west, with their harsher police systems, combined with a court system in which a guilty verdict was more common. This would strengthen the power of the law even in its most informal sense, that involving false swearing. Threats had teeth. An idea of law drew people more tightly together. Only we comprehend how malleable law could be in terms of the diligence or idleness of magistrates, clerks and constables, how law could be rummaged in through notions of 'evidence', 'confession' or 'crime'. This ownership of law was intricately linked in different places and different ways to notions of the people and democracy.

Table 7.4: Results of cases

	Assize/Supreme Court and bench									
	Goulburn, Yass bench	Goulburn, Balranald	Sydney, South Coast	Sydney, Grafton	Sydney, Macleay River	Bathurst, Orange	Bathurst, Carcoar	Bathurst, Molong	Maitland, North-west
Guilty	39/61 63%	2/4 50%	13/37 35%	9/25 36%	3/4 75%	21/31 67%	26/54 48%	14/23 60%	35/85 41%
Not guilty	11/61 18%	–	14/37 37%	3/25 12%	1/4 25%	5/31 16%	17/34 31%	1/23 4%	22/85 26%
Acquitted	1/61 2%	–	–	1/25 4%	–	–	2 4%	1 4%	2/85 2%
Discharged, prosecutor not appearing	1/61 2%	–	–	–	–	–	–	–	–
Crown prosecutor declines proceeding	–	–	–	–	–	–	–	1/23 4%	6/85 7%
Discharged	1/61 2%	2/4 50%	–	1/25 4%	–	–	1/54 2%	–	–
Discharged by proclamation	–	–	1/37 2.7%	–	–	–	1/54 4%	–	–
Discharged, no interpreter	–	–	–	2/25 8%	–	–	–	–	–
Trial postponed	–	–	1/37 2.7%	–	–	–	–	–	–
Discharged, no witnesses	–	–	–	5/25 20%	–	–	–	–	3/85 4%

LAW IN THE NEW DEMOCRACY

	Assize/Supreme Court and bench								
	Goulburn, Yass bench	Goulburn, Balranald	Sydney, South Coast	Sydney, Grafton	Sydney, Macleay River	Bathurst, Orange	Bathurst, Carcoar	Bathurst, Molong	Maitland, North-west
Discharged, jury could not agree	–	–	–	–	–	1/31 3%	2/54 4%	–	1/85 1%
Escape	–	–	–	1/25 4%	–	–	–	–	–
To quarter sessions	–	–	–	–	–	–	1/54 2%	–	–
Prisoner does not appear	–	–	–	–	–	–	–	–	1/85 1%
Insufficient case	–	–	–	–	–	–	–	–	3 4%
Postponed	–	–	–	–	–	–	–	1/23 4%	–

Note: This does not include cases where the result cannot be found.

Conclusion

Law 'lands' in different ways in different places in the 1850s. As if before a searchlight, some faces are illuminated and others are not. 'The people' appeared on the South Coast and not in the north-west, where popular democracy was so present at Rocky River goldfields. The sheer malleability of English law, its capacity to shape-shift apparent here, has also been argued in the work of Heather Douglas and Mark Finnane, Lisa Ford, Lauren Benton and Richard Ross, Niels Brimnes and Santanu Sengupta.[1] There are, in this shape-shifting in New South Wales in the 1850s, several dynamics at play that unite all regions. The first concerns the rhetoric of politics. The attorneys-general, the judges and the Crown solicitors represented the underhand and deceitful arm of the Crown—suspicious, waiting for an attempt to put all in gaol. This was how these legal officials were represented in a Legislative Assembly nervously attempting to establish itself, to guard against Crown incursions. Such rhetoric encouraged disrespect. Law was understood differently in New South Wales in the whirl of the new democracy's distancing itself from the Crown.

Deceitful is not the way law itself regards its representatives, and the attorneys-general maintained their self-importance. But interventions by them were mannered, shaped by the culture of gentlemen. Connections manipulated law and influenced the attorneys-general.

The aesthetics of paper and ink, the curve of handwriting and the neat placing and folding of papers also shaped how law was understood. Power over the body of the accused rested partly in the way the deposition was presented to the attorneys-general. At Carcoar, with its beautifully presented and doctored depositions, there was a belief that 'evidence' was crucial. This enabled locals to enforce their own idea of 'justice', which was, in fact, feud. In the South

---

1 Brimnes, 'Beyond Colonial Law'; Hodges, 'Between Litigation and Arbitration'; Sengupta, *Trade, Politics and the English Mayor's Court*; Benton and Ross, 'Empires and Legal Pluralism'.

Coast depositions, similar beauty was to be found. Everything was in the right place, all the signatures accounted for. A beautiful deposition with contradictory or no real evidence at all could get a person into the Supreme Court or assize, to face its judge and jury. Where there was most criticism, of the western benches and at the south-western town of Yass, considerable work went into the production of depositions, and they were what was asked for in legal texts. Constables were stung into improving their policing methods, warnings were given and evidence carefully thought about. The west and south-west would be subject to the most intense road policing—the need to show identity and the ownership of horses were central. Criticism of the deposition resulted in overly diligent magistrates who scrambled for further information and unintentionally added to and altered documents. All this derived from the idea of perfecting the deposition. Aesthetics shaped power, and the sleuthing constable, the months in gaol and the long walk to the assize were influenced by this idea of aesthetics.

Magistrates overstepped the bounds of the law, they waited for what they called evidence, which may have just been a hat left somewhere on the road. Clerks wrote down what people 'heard' or they edited on the side of the deposition, adding new and contradictory information. All these actions resulted from a reading of *Blackstone* that was entirely original. The attorneys-general parsed these depositions and sent cases to the Supreme Court or assizes full of contradictions. There waited the jury, shaped by its history in the colony and by mystical ideas of the self-importance of its role.

Legal historians would usually begin their study with legal change and its implementation but in depositions we have access to secrets, to letters between officials, to added information and to pencil marking that no-one else saw. The *Justices Act* was implemented in a less than uniform way in New South Wales. This was because of all the other factors so far discussed: the low political status of legal officials, the mannered way in which gentlemen related to each other and the aesthetics of the deposition. The rights inherent in the *Justices Act* were most present where magistrates and constables had been subject to the disapproval of the attorneys-general and the criminal Crown solicitor. Yet, diligence and 'duty' on the part of these magistrates often contradicted any rights the defendant may have had. Contrary to expectations, the west of the colony quickly adopted all the requirements of the Act where other regions did not. Distance from Sydney had no bearing on how law worked. Contrary to the belief of those who introduced the Act, police magistrates were no different to their gentlemanly companions, the JPs of the colony. An interest in the discourses of science apparent in Barton at Molong and Blake at Yass—both JPs—seemed to also result in closer attention to the requirements of legal texts and thus the new interest in agricultural science may be seen to impact the way law worked. There were moves towards the modernity of policing to be found in the south-west, where constables referred to themselves as 'police forces'. But this modernity would be erratic, just as the convict system waxed and waned.

The people themselves were a motor for law; whether they described themselves as 'the people' or invested themselves with an authority that remained unnamed, they went to the magistrate, called on a constable, asked questions in court and had their own ideas of justice. This 'people' included Aboriginal people. The people had most power in terms of the law at Carcoar, where the need for 'evidence' allowed them to wheel and deal. This was for them justice—something that allowed them to 'pull'. In the west and south-west, detail was given in evidence. In their astute questioning at Yass in response to magisterial insistence, an effective request for detail, the people helped to modernise law and align it more closely with the *Justices Act*.

The unruly jurors of Maitland in their actions and makeup derived from the people—the disaffected squatter with his loose view of the state and the publicans and shopkeepers whose houses were at the centre of the new democracy. Their rowdy behaviour evoked a sureness that they were at the apex of the court. It was the independence they expressed that characterised democratic man. These erratic jurors give us our 'crime', the bodies punished. Jurors were male and drawn from publicans and 'grocerdom'. 'The people' were both male and female and there was another kind of power linked to democracy to be found in publicans as banks and political centres. A whole corpus of power in the north-west and apparent at Balranald centred on the publican. Publicans were also likely to be women and they could also deal with and delve into the construction of local power relations. The term 'Mrs' was never far from any case in the interior of New South Wales. How women were perceived in depositions varied widely. At Yass, as part of the emphasis on textbook law, women had less recognition and influence. In other places, they could be as active as men in bribery and false swearing. As victims, stories of their drinking and their involvement with men not their husbands were brought into court.

Any location where the language of the public and the people was used intensively as a kind of local identity, as on the South Coast and the Macleay, was also highly dangerous to Aboriginal people. Democracy carried with it the language of the frontier, the words 'Blacks' and 'whites', and they drew the Native Police out of their links to squatters and into wider policing. This language was shaped by the press and it had traction in Sydney. It shaped how the metropolis related to an Aboriginal polity that was recognised throughout the interior.

For the Aboriginal polity, linked by trade routes and ceremony, this way of doing law had its uses. As Marie Fels showed in her study of the Native Police in Port Phillip, the institution could be utilised.[2] However, a form of recognition of Aboriginal politics created a contorted system for Aboriginal defendants in which some cases were deemed the business of Aboriginal people. Sentimental attachment drew Aboriginal people into the courts, as did close living with lower-class non-Aboriginal people. What is notable is the sheer effort by non-Aboriginal officials in the metropolis, not necessarily in the regions, to use law in a way the legal texts did not intend: to imprison or hang Aboriginal defendants or to excuse non-Aboriginal violence. That legal officials of the 1850s saw Aboriginal people as political opponents is apparent not only in the theatrics of the Macleay River justices but also in the contortions of the courtroom evident in *Jones*, *Morgan*, *Mogo Garra* and *Doughboy*. That First Nations people were thought so important suggests they, or an idea of their legal presence refracted through Britain, were considered a more formidable political force than has previously been credited. The mentality of the frontier existed at the heart of the courts. At the same time, we must note the efforts of the NSW Bar, the magistrates of the north-west, west and Balranald and members of the new public to emphasise, alongside First Nations/Aboriginal people, Aboriginal rights as subjects and to recognise the Aboriginal polity.

We return to the clerk with his pen and foolscap paper diligently or lazily writing down the words of witnesses. These words were parsed haphazardly by the attorneys-general depending on where they came from or how well presented they were. They give us the pattern on a shirt, the spears on a dray, the look of a hat, the half-filled pint pot and the nails in a shoe. Assizes or the Supreme Court do not sift such information neatly for us, rather they complicate it further because we know the jury is reasoning, but its logic we cannot always comprehend.

---

2   Fels, *Good Men and True*.

Bibliography

Museums of History NSW

State Archives Collection

Armidale Police Record Book, SR 4/5488.

Attorney-General Letters, SR 4/6659.

Attorney-General Register of Cases, Sydney, 1853, SR 4/5737.

Balranald Bench Book, SR 4/5505.

Balranald Bench Letter Book, SR 4/5503.

Colonial Secretary Letters to Judicial Establishment, SR 4/3382, 4/3858.

Commissioner of Crown Lands Letter Book, SR 4/4563.

Criminal Crown Solicitor Judgement Books, Supreme Court, SR 4/5731 – 4/5758.

Eden Bench Book, SR 4/6501.

Kiama Bench Book, SR 4/5575, part 4/5576-77.

Police Superintendent of Western Districts, Copies of Letters Sent, SR 4/10757.

Shoalhaven Bench Book, SR 4/6501.

Supreme Court Depositions, SR 9/6357 – 9/6425.

Supreme Court Informations, SR T43, T73–T78.

Warialda Bench Book, SR 4/5679.

Wee Waa Letter Book, SR 4/7547.

Yass Bench Books, SR 4/5703.

University of New England Archives

George Mitchell Harper, Diary 1850–51, 5721.

State Library of New South Wales

Bray Family Papers, Mitchell Library, MSS 1929.

Criminal Crown Solicitor's Letter Book, CY 2753.

Documents collected by Sir William Dixson, Dixson Library, ADD 78.

Morey, Edmond. 'Reminiscences of a Pioneer in New South Wales.' Extracted from *Sydney Mail*, 30 October 1907 to 29 January 1908, Mitchell Library, DS MSQ326.

New South Wales Crown Law Office Letter Book, CY 2753.

New South Wales Legislative Council, *Votes and Proceedings*, Q328.9106/6.

Papers of William Montagu Manning, Mitchell Library, MSS 942/3.

Tindal Family Papers, Mitchell Library, A2068.

Newspapers

Advocate and Advertiser for the Clarence, Richmond and New England District
Argus
Armidale Express and New England Advertiser
Australian Home Companion and Band of Hope Journal
Banner
Bathurst Free Press and Mining Journal
Bell's Life in Sydney and Sporting Reviewer
Brisbane Herald
Cornwall Chronicle
Daily Examiner
Empire
Freeman's Journal
Geelong Advertiser

Goulburn Herald and County of Argyle Advertiser
Illawarra Mercury
Maitland Mercury and Hunter River Advertiser
Moreton Bay Courier
Mount Alexander Mail
New South Wales Government Gazette
Northern Times
People's Advocate and New South Wales Vindicator
Sydney Monitor
Sydney Morning Herald
Yass Tribune

Books: Contemporary

Byrne, J.C. 1848. *Twelve Years' Wandering in the British Colonies from 1835 to 1847*. 2 vols. London: Richard Bentley.

Chitty, Joseph, and Thomas Chitty. 1837. *Richard Burn's Justice of the Peace and Parish Officer. In Six Volumes*. London: Sweet, Stevens & Sons, and A. Maxwell.

Cottu, Maurice. 1822. *On the Administration of Criminal Justice in England and the Spirit of the English Government*. London: Richard Stevens.

Stewart, James. 1849. *The Rights of Persons being the First Book of Blackstone's Commentaries Incorporating the Alterations Down to the Present Time*. London: Spettigue and Farrance.

Suttor, Edwin C. 1847. *Plunkett's Australian Magistrate: A Guide to the Duties of a Justice of the Peace with Numerous Forms*. Sydney: W.A. Coleman.

Therry, Roger. 1974 [1863]. *Reminiscences of Thirty Years Residence in NSW and Victoria*. Sydney: RAHS Press.

Welsby, W.N. 1866. *Sir John Jervis, Office and Duties of Coroners with Form and Precedents*. London: H. Sweet, W. Maxwell Stevens and Son.

Books: Present

Allen, Judith. 1990. *Sex and Secrets: Crimes Involving Australian Women Since 1850*. Melbourne: Oxford University Press.

Ash, Anna, John Giacon, and Amanda Lissarrague, eds. 2003. *Gamilaraay/Yuwaalaraay/Yuwaalayaay Dictionary*. Alice Springs: IAD Press.

Atkinson, Alan. 2016. *The Europeans in Australia. Volume 2*. Sydney: UNSW Press.

Barnd, Natchee Blu. 2017. *Native Space: Geographic Strategies to Unsettle Settler Colonialism*. Corvallis: Oregon State University Press. doi.org/10.1353/book 56433.

Barrere, Albert. 2013. *A Dictionary of Slang*. Sydney: Read.

Beattie, John M. 2001. *Policing and Punishment in London 1660–1720: Urban Crime and the Limits of Terror*. Oxford: Oxford University Press. doi.org/10.1093/oso/9780198208679.001.0001.

Bennett, John M. 1974. *A History of the Supreme Court of New South Wales*. Sydney: Law Book Co.

Bennett, John M. 1984. *A History of Solicitors in New South Wales*. Sydney: Legal Books.

Bennett, John M. 2005. *Callaghan's Diary: The 1840s Sydney Diary of Thomas Callaghan, B.A. of the King's Inns, Dublin, Barrister-at-Law*. Sydney: The Francis Forbes Society.

Bird Rose, Deborah. 1991. *Hidden Histories: Black Stories from Victoria River Downs, Humbert River and Wave Hill Stations*. Canberra: Aboriginal Studies Press.

Bongiorno, Frank. 2022. *Dreamers and Schemers: A Political History of Australia*. Melbourne: La Trobe University Press.

Bostock, Shauna. 2023. *Reaching Through Time: Finding My Family's Stories*. Sydney: Allen & Unwin.

Brooks, Lisa. 2008. *The Common Pot: The Recovery of Native Space in the Northeast*. Minneapolis: University of Minnesota Press.

Byrne, Paula J. 1993. *Criminal Law and Colonial Subject*. Cambridge: Cambridge University Press. doi.org/10.1017/CBO9780511586101.

Byrne, Paula Jane. 2012. *Judge Advocate Ellis Bent: Letters and Diaries 1809–1811*. Sydney: Desert Pea Press.

Cahir, Fred. 2012. *Black Gold: Aboriginal People on the Goldfields of Victoria*. Canberra: ANU Press. doi.org/10.22459/BG.09.2012.

Cane, Peter, Lisa Ford, and Mark McMillan, eds. 2022. *The Cambridge Legal History of Australia*. Cambridge: Cambridge University Press. doi.org/10.1017/9781108633949.

Chritchett, Jan. 1990. *A Distant Field of Murder*. Melbourne: Melbourne University Press.

Clark, Manning. 1973. *A History of Australia*. Melbourne: Melbourne University Press.

Clayton Dixon, Callum. 2019. *Surviving New England: A History of Aboriginal Resistance and Resilience through the First Forty Years of the Colonial Apocalypse*. Armidale: Newarea Aboriginal Corporation, formerly known as the Anaiwan Language Revival Program.

Cochrane, Peter. 2006. *Colonial Ambition: Foundations of Australian Democracy*. Melbourne: Melbourne University Press.

Connors, Libby. 2015. *Warrior: A Legendary Leader's Dramatic Life and Violent Death on the Colonial Frontier*. Sydney: Allen & Unwin.

Crotty, Martin. 2001. *Making the Australian Male: Middle-Class Masculinity 1870–1920*. Melbourne: Melbourne University Press.

Curthoys, Ann, and Jessie Mitchell. 2018. *Taking Liberty: Indigenous Rights and Settler Self-Government in Colonial Australia, 1830–1890*. Cambridge: Cambridge University Press. doi.org/10.1017/9781316027035.

Darian-Smith, Eve. 2007. *Ethnography and Law*. London: Routledge.

Davison, Graeme, and Marc Brodie. 2005. *Struggle Country: The Rural Ideal in Twentieth Century Australia*. Melbourne: Monash University Press.

Dillon, Paul. 2017. *Frederick Walker*. Sydney: Self-published.

Douglas, Heather, and Mark Finnane. 2012. *Indigenous Crime and Settler Law: White Sovereignty After Empire*. Basingstoke: Palgrave Macmillan. doi.org/10.1057/9781137284983.

Dussart, Francoise. 2000. *The Politics of Ritual in an Aboriginal Settlement: Kinship, Gender, and the Currency of Knowledge*. Washington: Smithsonian Institution Press.

Fassin, Didier, ed. 2017. *Writing the World of Policing: The Difference Ethnography Makes.* Chicago: University of Chicago Press. doi.org/10.7208/chicago/9780226497785.001.0001.

Favret-Saada, Jeanne. 1980. *Witchcraft in the Bocage.* Cambridge: Cambridge University Press.

Fels, Marie. 1988. *Good Men and True.* Melbourne: Melbourne University Press.

Ferry, John. 1999. *Colonial Armidale.* Brisbane: University of Queensland Press.

Finnane, Mark, ed. 1987. *Policing in Australia: Historical Perspectives.* Sydney: UNSW Press.

Ford, Lisa. 2011. *Settler Sovereignty: Jurisdiction and Indigenous People in America and Australia, 1788–1836.* Cambridge: Harvard University Press. doi.org/10.2307/j.ctv1smjszh.

Ford, Lisa. 2021. *The King's Peace: Law and Order in the British Empire.* Cambridge: Harvard University Press. doi.org/10.4159/9780674269521.

Fox, Paul. 1994. *Sweet Damper and Gossip.* Benalla: Benalla Art Gallery.

Golder, Hilary. 1991. *High and Responsible Office: A History of the New South Wales Magistracy.* Sydney: Sydney University Press.

Goodall, Heather. 1996. *Invasion to Embassy: Land in Aboriginal Politics in New South Wales, 1770–1972.* Sydney: Sydney University Press.

Hanson, Russell L. 1985. *The Democratic Imagination in America.* Princeton: Princeton University Press.

Hirst, John B. 1983. *Convict Society and its Enemies: A History of Early New South Wales.* Sydney: Allen & Unwin.

Hirst, John. 2008. *Freedom on the Fatal Shore: Australia's First Colony.* Melbourne: Black Inc.

Houghton, Walter E. 1957. *The Victorian Frame of Mind, 1830–1870.* New Haven: Yale University Press.

Hunt, Lynn. 1988. *Politics, Culture and Class in the French Revolution.* Berkeley: University of California Press.

Irving, Terry. 2006. *The Southern Tree of Liberty.* Sydney: The Federation Press.

Jordens, Ann-Marie. 1979. *The Stenhouse Circle: Literary Life in Mid-Nineteenth Century Sydney.* Melbourne: Melbourne University Press.

Kercher, Bruce. 1995. *An Unruly Child: A History of Law in Australia*. London: Routledge.

Laidlaw, Zoë. 2005. *Colonial Connections, 1815–45: Patronage, the Information Revolution and Colonial Government*. Manchester: Manchester University Press.

Legge, Gordon. 1896. *A Selection of Supreme Court Cases in New South Wales from 1825 to 1862*. Sydney: Robert Burton Printers.

Lester, Alan, and Fae Dussart. 2014. *Colonization and the Origins of Humanitarian Governance*. Cambridge: Cambridge University Press. doi.org/10.1017/CBO 9781139022026.

Linebaugh, Peter. 1991. *The London Hanged: Crime and Civil Society in the Eighteenth Century*. London: Allen Lane.

Lydon, Jane, and Lyndall Ryan, eds. 2018. *Remembering the Myall Creek Massacre*. Sydney: NewSouth Publishing.

Maynard, John. 2007. *Fight for Liberty and Freedom: The Origins of Australian Aboriginal Activism*. Canberra: Aboriginal Studies Press.

McGrath, Ann. 2015. *Illicit Love: Interracial Sex and Marriage in the United States and Australia*. Lincoln: University of Nebraska Press. doi.org/10.2307/j.ctt1d 98bzf.

McKenna, Mark. 2002. *Looking for Blackfellows Point: An Australian History of Place*. Sydney: UNSW Press.

McLaren, John. 2011. *Dewigged, Bothered and Bewildered: British Colonial Judges on Trial, 1800–1900*. Toronto: University of Toronto Press. doi.org/10.3138/ 9781442699779.

Molony, John. 1973. *John Hubert Plunkett in New South Wales 1832–1869*. Canberra: Australian National University Press.

Moreton-Robinson, Aileen. 2021. *Talkin' Up to the White Woman: Aboriginal Women and Feminism*. Minneapolis: University of Minnesota Press.

Morgan, Gwenda, and Peter Rushton. 1998. *Rogues, Thieves and the Rule of Law: The Problem of Law Enforcement in North-East England 1718–1800*. London: UCL Press.

Morris, Barry. 1989. *Domesticating Resistance: The Dhan-Gadi Aborigines and the Australian State*. Oxford: Berg.

Neal, David. 2002. *The Rule of Law in a Penal Colony: Law and Politics in Early New South Wales*. Cambridge: Cambridge University Press.

Nettelbeck, Amanda. 2019. *Indigenous Rights and Colonial Subjecthood: Protection and Reform in the Nineteenth-Century British Empire*. Cambridg: Cambridge University Press. doi.org/10.1017/9781108559225.

Nicholas, Stephen, ed. 1989. *Convict Workers: Reinterpreting Australia's Past*. Melbourne: Cambridge University Press. doi.org/10.1017/CBO9781139084840.

O'Gorman, Frank. 1989. *Voters, Patrons and Parties: The Unreformed Electoral System of Hanoverian England, 1734–1832*. Oxford: Clarendon Press.

Owen, Chris. 2016. *Every Mother's Son is Guilty: Policing on the Kimberley Frontier*. Perth: UWA Press.

Ozouf, Mona. 1988. *Festivals and the French Revolution*. Translated by Alan Sheridan. Cambridge: Harvard University Press.

Pope, Alan. 2011. *One Law for All? Aboriginal People and the Criminal Law in Early South Australia*. Canberra: Aboriginal Studies Press.

Porter, Susie S. 2018. *From Angel to Office Worker: Middle Class Identity and Female Consciousness in Mexico, 1890–1950*. Lincoln: University of Nebraska Press. doi.org/10.2307/j.ctvgd1v7.

Pratap Deo, Aditya. 2021. *Kings, Spirits and Memory in Central India: Enchanting the State*. Boca Raton: CRC Press. doi.org/10.4324/9781003219224.

Read, Peter. 1988. *A Hundred Years War: Wiradjuri People and the State*. Canberra: Australian National University Press.

Reynolds, Henry. 1987. *Frontier: Aborigines, Settlers and Land*. Sydney: Allen & Unwin.

Reynolds, Henry. 2006. *Aboriginal Sovereignty: Reflections on Race, State and Nation*. Sydney: Allen & Unwin.

Richter, Christoph. 2014. *Wood Characteristics*. Berlin: Springer Verlag.

Roberts, Stephen. 1964. *The Squatting Age in Australia*. Melbourne: Melbourne University Press.

Roginski, Alexandra. 2015. *The Hanged Man and the Body Thief: Finding Lives in a Museum Mystery*. Melbourne: Monash University Press.

Rosen, Lawrence. 2018. *Islam and the Rule of Justice: Image and Reality in Muslim Law and Culture*. Chicago: University of Chicago Press. doi.org/10.7208/chicago/9780226511740.001.0001.

Rowse, Tim. 2017. *Indigenous and Other Australians Since 1901*. Sydney: UNSW Press.

Scheffer, Thomas. 2010. *Adversarial Case Making: An Ethnography of English Crown Court Procedure*. Leiden: Brill. doi.org/10.1163/ej.9789004187269.i-284.

Schofield-Georgeson, Eugene. 2018. *By What Authority? Criminal Law in Colonial New South Wales 1788–1861*. Melbourne: Australian Scholarly Press.

Shaw, Alan G.L. 1966. *Convicts and the Colonies: A Study of Penal Transportation from Great Britain and Ireland to Australia and Other Parts of the British Empire*. Melbourne: Melbourne University Press.

Skinner, Leonard E. 1975. *Police of the Pastoral Frontier: Native Police, 1849–59*. Brisbane: University of Queensland Press.

Starr, June, and Mark Goodale, eds. 2002. *Practicing Ethnography in Law: New Dialogues, Enduring Methods*. New York: Springer Nature. doi.org/10.1007/978-1-137-06573-5.

Sturma, Michael. 1983. *Vice in a Vicious Society: Crime and Convicts in Mid-Nineteenth-Century New South Wales*. Brisbane: University of Queensland Press.

Thomas, Martin. 2011. *The Many Worlds of R.H. Matthews: In Search of An Australian Anthropologist*. Sydney: Allen & Unwin.

Thompson, Max M.H. 2006. *The Seeds of Democracy: Early Elections in Colonial New South Wales*. Sydney: The Federation Press.

Trabsky, Marc. 2020. *Law and the Dead: Technology, Relations and Institutions*. New York: Routledge. doi.org/10.4324/9781351240413.

Ward, Russell. 1966. *The Australian Legend*. Oxford: Oxford University Press.

Wilentz, Sean. 1986. *Chants Democratic: New York City and the Rise of the American Working Class, 1788–1850*. Oxford: Oxford University Press.

Woods, G.D. 2002. *A History of Criminal Law in New South Wales. Volume 1: The Colonial Period, 1788–1900*. Sydney: The Federation Press.

Articles and book chapters

Allen, Matthew. 2015. 'Policing a Free Society: Drunkenness and Liberty in Colonial New South Wales.' *History Australia* 12, no. 2: 144–65. doi.org/10.1080/14490854.2015.11668574.

Australian Law Reform Commission (ALRC). 2010. *Recognition of Aboriginal Customary Laws*. ALRC Report 31, 18 August. Melbourne: Australian Law Reform Commission. www.alrc.gov.au/publication/recognition-of-aboriginal-customary-laws-alrc-report-31/4-aboriginal-customary-laws-and-anglo-australian-law-after-1788/australian-law-as-applied-to-aborigines/.

Barker, Ian QC. 2002. 'Sorely Tried: Democracy and Trial by Jury in New South Wales.' Francis Forbes Lecture. forbessociety.org.au/wp-content/uploads/2013/03/trial_jury.pdf.

Bellanta, Melissa. 2008. 'Feminism, Mateship and Brotherhood in 1890s Adelaide.' *History Australia* 5, no. 1: 1–14. doi.org/10.2104/ha080007.

Bennett, John M. 1961. 'The Establishment of Jury Trial in New South Wales.' *Sydney Law Review* 4: 463–85.

Benton, Lauren, and Richard Ross. 2013. 'Empires and Legal Pluralism: Jurisdiction, Sovereignty and Political Imagination in the Early Modern World.' In *Legal Pluralism and Empires, 1500–1850*, edited by Lauren Benton and Richard Ross, 1–18. New York: NYU Press. doi.org/10.18574/nyu/9780814771167.003.0001.

Bongiorno, Frank, and Andrew Messner. 2006. 'New England.' In *People and Politics in Regional New South Wales, 1856–1950*, edited by Jim Hagan, 150–89. Sydney: The Federation Press.

Braithwaite, John. 1992. 'Reducing the Crime Problem: A Not So Dismal Criminology.' *Australian and New Zealand Journal of Criminology* 25, no. 1: 1–10. doi.org/10.1177/000486589202500101.

Braithwaite, John. 2001. 'Crime in a Convict Republic.' *The Modern Law Review* 64, no. 1: 11–50. doi.org/10.1111/1468-2230.00307.

Brimnes, Neils. 2003. 'Beyond Colonial Law: Indigenous Litigation and the Contestation of Property in the Mayor's Court in Late Eighteenth-Century Madras.' *Modern Asian Studies* 37, no. 3: 513–50. doi.org/10.1017/S0026749X03003019.

Butler, Judith. 2002. 'Bodies and Power Revisited.' *Radical Philosophy* 114: 13–19.

Byrne, Paula Jane. 2018. 'The New South Wales Bar and Aboriginal People: Making Aboriginal Subjects c. 1830–1866.' *History Australia* 15: 413–29. doi.org/10.1080/14490854.2018.1485501.

Byrne, Paula Jane. 2021. 'The Language of Space and Ownership in Rural New South Wales.' *Rural History* 32, no. 2: 167–86. doi.org/10.1017/S0956793321000169.

Byrne, Paula Jane. 2022. 'An Archival Find.' *Criminal Law Journal* 46, no. 2: 110–12.

Byrne, Paula Jane. 2023. 'Australian Squatter Space 1850–1880.' *Britain and the World* 16, no. 1: 58–85. doi.org/10.3366/brw.2023.0400.

Carey, Jane, and Ben Silverstein. 2020. 'Thinking With and Beyond Settler Colonial Studies.' *Post-Colonial Studies* 23, no. 1: 1–20. doi.org/10.1080/13688790.2020.1719569.

Castle, Tim D. 2004. 'The Practical Administration of Justice: The Adaptation of English Law to Colonial Customs and Circumstances.' *Journal of Australian Colonial History* 5: 44–72.

Castles, Alex C. 1963. 'The Reception and Status of English Law in Australia.' *Adelaide Law Review* 2, no. 1: 1–31.

Collier, Jane F. 2002. 'Analysing Witchcraft Beliefs.' In *Practicing Ethnography in Law: New Dialogues, Enduring Methods*, edited by June Starr and Mark Goodale, 72–86. New York: Springer Nature. doi.org/10.1007/978-1-137-06573-5_5.

Cowper, Norman, and Vivienne Parsons. 1966. 'Allen, George (1800–1877).' *Australian Dictionary of Biography*. Canberra: National Centre of Biography, The Australian National University. adb.anu.edu.au/biography/allen-george-1696/text1831.

Darian-Smith, Eve. 2004. 'Ethnographies of Law.' In *The Blackwell Companion to Law and Society*, edited by Austin Sarat, 545–68. Hoboken: Blackwell.

Davies, Ronald E. 1957. 'History of Clarence River and of Grafton 1830–1880.' *Daily Examiner*, [Grafton], 3 January. nla.gov.au/nla.obj-2387371978/view?partId=nla.obj-2387373852#.

Dorsett, Shaunnagh. 2014. 'Burton and the Draft Act for the Protection and Amelioration of the Aborigines 1838 (NSW).' In *Legal Histories of the British Empire: Laws, Engagements and Legacies*, edited by Shaunaggh Dorsett and John McLaren, 171–86. New York: Routledge. doi.org/10.2139/ssrn.3037764.

Fassin, Didier. 2017. 'Boredom.' In *Writing the World of Policing: The Difference Ethnography Make*s, edited by Didier Fassin, 269–92. Chicago: University of Chicago Press. doi.org/10.7208/chicago/9780226497785.003.0013.

Featherstone, Lisa. 2008. 'Sex and the Australian Legend: Masculinity and the White Man's Body.' *Journal of Australian Colonial History* 10, no. 2: 73–90.

Ford, Lisa, and David Andrew Roberts. 2013. 'Expansion 1820–1850.' In *The Cambridge History of Australia*, edited by Alison Bashford and Stuart Macintyre, 121–48. Cambridge: Cambridge University Press. doi.org/10.1017/CHO 9781107445758.008.

Friedman, Lawrence M. 2002. 'A Few Thoughts on Ethnography, History and Law.' In *Practicing Ethnography in Law: New Dialogues, Enduring Methods*, edited by June Starr and Mark Goodale, 185–89. New York: Springer Nature. doi.org/ 10.1007/978-1-137-06573-5_11.

Furth, Charlotte. 2007. 'Thinking With Cases.' In *Thinking With Cases: Specialist Knowledge in Chinese Cultural History*, edited by Charlotte Furth, Judith T. Zeitlin, and Ping-chen Hsiung, 1–30. Honolulu: University of Hawai'i Press. doi.org/10.1515/9780824865184-003.

George, Angela, and Pat Raymond. n.d. 'Oakland's Oak Trees.' Heritage Report. Pambula. hiddenheritage.com.au/heritage-object/?object_id=82 [page discontinued].

Ghosh, Durba. 2012. 'Another Set of Imperial Turns?' *The American Historical Review* 117, no. 3: 772–93. doi.org/10.1086/ahr.117.3.772.

Gilchrist, Catie. 2018. '"Mystery Always Begets Suspicion": Defending the Open and Public Nature of the Coronial Inquest.' *The Female Factory Online*. Sydney: Parramatta Female Factory. femalefactoryonline.org/essays/mystery-always-begets-suspicion/.

Griffiths, Anne. 2022. 'Law as an Enduring Concept: Space, Time and Power.' In *The Oxford Handbook of Law and Anthropology*, edited by Marie-Claire Foblets, Mark Goodale, Maria Sapignoli, and Olaf Zenker, 300–17. Oxford: Oxford University Press.

Highland, Gary. 1994. 'A Tangle of Paradoxes: Race, Justice and Criminal Law in North Queensland 1882–1894.' In *A Nation of Rogues? Crime, Law and Punishment in Colonial Australia*, edited by David Philips and Susanne Davies, 123–40. Melbourne: Melbourne University Press.

Hirsch, Eric. 2022. 'Introduction: Working Through Other People's Descriptions.' In *Property, Substance and Effect: Anthropological Essays on Persons and Things*, by Marilyn Strathern, ix–xxxiv. London: HAU Books.

Hodges, Leonard. 2018. 'Between Litigation and Arbitration: Administering Legal Pluralism in Eighteenth Century Bombay.' *Itineiro* 43, no. 3: 490–515. doi.org/ 10.1017/S0165115318000633.

Hogg, Russell, and Hilary Golder. 1987. 'Policing Sydney.' In *Policing in Australia: Historical Perspectives*, edited by Mark Finnane, 59–73. Sydney: UNSW Press.

Howlin, Niamh. 2011. '"The Terror of Their Lives": Irish Jurors' Experiences.' *Law and History Review* 29, no. 2: 703–61. doi.org/10.1017/S0738248011000319.

Kaladelfos, Andy. 2012. 'The Politics of Punishment: Rape and the Death Penalty in Colonial Australia.' *History Australia* 9, no. 1: 155–75. doi.org/10.1080/14490854.2012.11668407.

Keesing, Nancy. 1972. 'Hardy, John Richard (1807–1858).' *Australian Dictionary of Biography*. Canberra: National Centre of Biography, The Australian National University. adb.anu.edu.au/biography/hardy-john-richard-3715/text5831.

Kēhaulani Kauanui, J. 2016. '"A Structure, Not an Event": Settler Colonialism and Enduring Indigeneity.' *Lateral* 5, no. 1. doi.org/10.25158/L5.1.7.

King, Herbert Henry. 1959. 'The Urban Hierarchy of the Southern Tableland of New South Wales.' PhD diss., The Australian National University.

Lake, Marilyn. 2003. 'On Being a White Man in Australia.' In *Cultural History in Australia*, edited by Hsu-Ming Teo and Richard White. Sydney: UNSW Press.

Lowndes, John. 2000. 'The Australian Magistracy from Justices of the Peace to Judges and Beyond.' *Australian Law Journal* 74, no. 8: 509–32.

Lydon, Jane, and Lyndall Ryan. 2018. 'Introduction.' In *Remembering the Myall Creek Massacre*, edited by Jane Lydon and Lyndall Ryan. Sydney: NewSouth Publishing.

Macintyre, Stuart, and Sean Scalmer. 2013. 'Colonial States and Civil Society, 1860–90.' In *The Cambridge History of Australia*, edited by Alison Bashford and Stuart Macintyre, 189–217. Cambridge: Cambridge University Press. doi.org/10.1017/CHO9781107445758.011.

Merry, Sally Engle. 2002. 'Ethnography in the Archives.' In *Practicing Ethnography in Law: New Dialogues, Enduring Methods*, edited by June Starr and Mark Goodale, 128–42. New York: Springer Nature.

Mills, Kerry. 2012. 'Lawmakers, Select Committees and the Birth of Democracy in New South Wales, 1843–1855.' *Journal of Australian Colonial History* 14: 131–54.

Moreton-Robinson, Aileen. 2020. 'Incommensurable Sovereignties: Indigenous Ontology Matters.' In *Routledge Handbook of Critical Indigenous Studies*, edited by Brendan Hokowhitu, Aileen Moreton-Robinson, Linda Tuhawi Smith, Chris Andersen, and Steve Larkin. London: Routledge. doi.org/10.4324/9780429440229-23.

Parkinson, Naomi Gabrielle. 2019. 'Impersonating a Voter: Constructions of Race, and Conceptions of Subjecthood in the Franchise of Colonial New South Wales, c. 1850–1865.' *The Journal of Imperial and Commonwealth History* 47, no. 4: 652–75. doi.org/10.1080/03086534.2019.1596204.

Perry, Thomas M. 1966. 'Alexander Berry (1781–1873).' *Australian Dictionary of Biography*. Canberra: National Centre of Biography, The Australian National University. adb.anu.edu.au/biography/berry-alexander-1773/text1987.

Riles, Annalise. 2007. 'Real Time: Unwinding Technocratic and Anthropological Knowledge.' In *Ethnography and Law*, edited by Eve Darian-Smith, 169–82. London: Routledge.

Rizzetti, Janine. 2011. 'Judge Willis, Bonjon and the Recognition of Aboriginal Law.' *Australian and New Zealand Law and History Journal* 5: 1–26. classic.austlii.edu.au/au/journals/ANZLawHisteJl/2011/5.html.

Roberts, David Andrew, and Margaret Reeson. 2016. 'Wesleyan Methodist Missions to Australia and the Pacific.' In *Methodism in Australia*, edited by Glen O'Brien and Hilary M. Carey, 197–210. London: Routledge.

Roy, Alpana. 'Post-Colonial Theory and Law: A Critical Introduction.' *Adelaide Law Review* 29: 315–37.

Russell, Lynette. 2007. '"Dirty Domestics and Worse Cooks": Frontiers, Southern Australia, 1800–1850.' *Frontiers: A Journal of Women Studies* 28, nos 1–2: 18–46. doi.org/10.1353/fro.2007.0035.

Sengupta, Santanu. n.d. *Trade, Politics and the English Mayor's Court: Law and Trading Practices in the 18th Century Bay of Bengal*. The History Project Research Report. Cambridge: Center for History and Economics, Harvard University. www.histproj.org/completed/Sengupta.pdf.

Strathern, Marilyn. 2007. 'Criminal Justice and Cultural Justice: The Limits of Liberalism and the Pragmatics of Difference in the New South Africa.' In *Ethnography and Law*, edited by Eve Darian-Smith, 397–412. London: Routledge.

Suttor, T.L. 1967. 'John Hubert Plunkett (1802–1869).' *Australian Dictionary of Biography*. Canberra: National Centre of Biography, The Australian National University. adb.anu.edu.au/biography/plunkett-john-hubert-2556/text3483.

Townsend, Norma. 1985. 'Master and Man in the Myall Creek Massacre.' *Push From the Bush* 20 (April): 4–32.

Varga, Csaba. 2010. 'The Theory of Law: Legal Ethnography or the Theoretical Fruits of Inquiries into Folkways.' *Sociologia del Diritto* [*Sociology of Law*] 1: 81–100. doi.org/10.3280/SD2010-001004.

Wright, Nancy, and Andrew Richard Buck. 2004. 'The Transformation of Colonial Property: A Study of the Law of Dower in New South Wales, 1836 to 1863.' *University of Tasmania Law Review* 23, no. 1: 97–127.

Websites

Arakwal People of Byron Bay. 2011. arakwal.com.au.

Australasian Legal Information Institute. Hosted by University of Technology Sydney Faculty of Law. www.austlii.edu.au/.

Australian Dictionary of Biography. National Centre of Biography, The Australian National University. adb.anu.edu.au/.

Buru Ngunawal Aboriginal Corporation. www.buru-ngunawal.com/426484390.

Colonial Frontier Massacres, Australia, 1788 to 1930. c21ch.newcastle.edu.au/colonialmassacres/map.php.

'Dhaalan: Pronunciation.' 2018. *Garay Guwaala: Talk the Language*. Armidale, NSW: Catholic Schools Office.

Eden Local Aboriginal Land Council. 2025. alc.org.au/land_council/eden/.

Gumbaynggirr Jagun. www.gumbaynggirrjagun.org/.

Jajoo Warrngara: The Culture Classroom. 2022. Brisbane: SharingStories Foundation. jajoowarrngara.org/.

Kempsey Local Aboriginal Land Council. Facebook page. www.facebook.com/kempseylocalaboriginallandcouncil/posts/some-history-of-the-dunghutti-nation traditional-countrythe-macleay-valley-forms-/1321043801426542/.

loang.com/library/referenceblackstonecommentries-law-england/bla-323 [page discontinued].

Obituaries Australia. 1924. 'Barton, Robert Darvall (1842–1924).' *Obituaries Australia*. National Centre of Biography, The Australian National University. oa.anu.edu.au/obituary/barton-robert-darvall-73/text1562.

Orange City Council. 2012. *Orange Aboriginal Heritage Report*. February. Prepared for Orange City Council by NTS Corp. orange.nsw.gov.au/wp-content/uploads/2018/07/Orange-Aboriginal-Heritage-Report.pdf.

Orange Regional Museum. 2018. *A Short History of Orange*. orange.nsw.gov.au/wp-content/uploads/2018/08/Short-History-of-Orange.pdf.

Parliament of New South Wales. www.parliament.nsw.gov.au/Pages/home.aspx.

Wagonga Local Aboriginal Land Council. 2019. www.wlalc.com.au/our-culture-and-heritage/.

walc.com.au/our-culture-and-heritage/ [page discontinued].

Yaegl Traditional Owners Aboriginal Corporation. nativetitle.org.au/find/pbc/8254.

Yuin & Monaro: Eden Community. yuin-monaro.storylines.com.au.

www.ingramcontent.com/pod-product-compliance
Lightning Source LLC
Chambersburg PA
CBHW070308230426
43664CB00015B/2673